# T-Bone Whacks and Caviar Snacks

## Cooking with Two Texans in Siberia and the Russian Far East

by
Sharon Hudgins

Recipes by Sharon Hudgins
and Tom Hudgins

Number 5 in the Great American Cooking Series

University of North Texas Press
Denton, Texas

10  9  8  7  6  5  4  3  2  1

Permissions:
University of North Texas Press
1155 Union Circle #311336
Denton, TX  76203-5017

The paper used in this book meets the minimum requirements of the American National Standard for Permanence of Paper for Printed Library Materials, z39.48.1984. Binding materials have been chosen for durability.

**Library of Congress Cataloging-in-Publication Data**

Hudgins, Sharon, author. | Hudgins, Tom, author.
T-bone whacks and caviar snacks : cooking with two Texans in Siberia and the Russian Far East / by Sharon Hudgins ; recipes by Sharon Hudgins and Tom Hudgins.
pages cm. — Great American cooking series ; no. 5.
Denton, Texas : University of North Texas Press, [2018] | Number 5 in the great American cooking series
Includes bibliographical references and index.
ISBN 978-1-57441-714-2 (cloth : alk. paper) | ISBN 978-1-57441-722-7 (ebook)
1. Cooking—Russia (Federation)—Siberia. 2. Cooking—Russia (Federation)—Russian Far East. 3. Cooking, Russian. 4. Food—Russia (Federation)—Siberia. 5. Food—Russia (Federation)—Russian Far East. 6. Hudgins, Sharon—Travel—Russia (Federation)—Siberia. 7. Hudgins, Tom—Travel—Russia (Federation)—Siberia. 8. Hudgins, Sharon—Travel—Russia (Federation)—Russian Far East. 9. Hudgins, Tom—Travel—Russia (Federation)—Russian Far East. 10. Siberia (Russia)—Description and travel. 11. Russian Far East (Russia)—Description and travel. 12. LCGFT: Cookbooks. I. Title.

TX723.4 .H84 2018
641.5947—dc23
2017053894

Some of the stories in this book are adapted from *The Other Side of Russia: A Slice of Life in Siberia and the Russian Far East* (Texas A & M University Press, 2003), with permission of the publisher. A few were published in a different form in *Saveur* magazine and *Proceedings of the Oxford Symposium on Food and Cookery* (Prospect Books, 1997, 2012, 2013, 2018).

Excerpt from Valentin Rasputin's *Siberia, Siberia* (translated and with an Introduction by Margaret Winchell and Gerald Mikkelson, Northwestern University Press, 1996, page 322) reproduced by permission of the publisher. Excerpt from *Sixteen Years in Siberia: Memoirs of Rachel and Israel Rachlin* (University of Alabama Press, 1988) reproduced by permission of the Rachlin estate.

Cover photo © Jeff Merrill and UNT Libraries.
The electronic edition of this book was made possible by the support of the Vick Family Foundation.
Typeset by vPrompt eServices.

*To the many good cooks in Siberia and the Russian Far East who shared their stories, recipes, and delicious dishes with us at the dinner table and around the samovar—and who taught us so much about the foods of Asian Russia.*

# Contents

Acknowledgments     **viii**

Introduction: The Asian Side of Russia     **xi**

Kitchen Notes     **xxiii**

**Chapter 1: The White House Cook**     **1**

Welcome to Vladivostok     1

The White House Cook     4

Of Cabbages and Carrots     9

Around the Samovar     11

At Alla's Table     13

The Two Galinas     16

Recipes     23

**Chapter 2: The Stove-from-Hell**     **47**

The High-Rise Village     47

Cooking by Candlelight     53

The Modern Russian Kitchen     58

Recipes     61

**Chapter 3: Shop 'Til You Drop**     **85**

Russia's New Market Economy     85

T-Bone Whacks     92

Caviar Snacks     94

From the Dairy     96

Harvest of the Seasons     98

Processed, Preserved, and Packaged     103

Pantry Perennials     106

From the Baker's Oven                                    109

A Wider World of Tastes                                  111

Recipes                                                 114

**Color Gallery**

**Chapter 4: Hosts and Toasts**                         **135**

Party Time                                              135

An Alsatian Meal in Asia                                137

Birthday Bashes                                         140

A Siberian Wedding Feast                                145

Any Excuse for a Party                                  147

Tex-Mex in Vladivostok                                  149

Recipes                                                 153

**Chapter 5: Winter Feasts**                            **183**

The Holiday Season                                      183

Christmas in Vladivostok                                186

Holiday Shopping Rush                                   190

Gala Dinners                                            193

New Year's Eve                                          197

Happy New Year!                                         201

Russian Orthodox Christmas                              203

"Old New Year"                                          205

Recipes                                                 208

**Chapter 6: Siberian Spring**                          **245**

Welcoming Springtime                                    245

"Butter Week" Festival in Irkutsk                       247

The Season of Lent                                      251

A Spanish Meal in Siberia                               256

A Siberian Easter Feast                                 260

Recipes                                                 265

**Chapter 7: Dinner On (and Off) the Diner**                    **295**

Trans-Siberian Commuter Train                                   295

Luxury Line                                                     299

Dacha Days                                                      302

Back of Beyond                                                  307

Raw Liver and More                                             315

Recipes                                                        321

**Bibliography**                                               **345**

**Recipe Index**                                               **349**

**Subject Index**                                              **363**

# Acknowledgments

Writing a culinary memoir of this kind is like creating a complicated dish with ingredients sourced from many places, mixed together in myriad ways, spiced with a handful of history and a pinch of myth, sautéed over the heat of imagination, then slow-cooked in the warmth of memory. Finally the dish is plated with care by the publisher—and served to you, the reader, to taste for yourself.

The ingredients for this book came from many sources, primary and secondary, historical and contemporary. I am especially indebted to the many accomplished cooks in Siberia and the Russian Far East for the personal food stories, family recipes, shopping secrets, and delicious dishes they shared with my husband and me during all the time we lived, worked, and traveled on the Asian side of Russia. In Vladivostok we learned much about the cooking of Russia's Far East from Alla Brovko, Larisa Kazakova, Galina Korotkina, Galina Tarasova, Svetlana Katayeva, Yelena Ivaschenko, our neighbor Natasha, and the guests from far and near who brought their favorite home-cooked dishes to our holiday potluck dinners there. We also appreciated the administrators at Far Eastern State University (today's Far Eastern Federal University) who treated us to the cuisine of Vladivostok's best restaurants at several official dinners when we worked there in the 1990s.

In Irkutsk we discovered the delights of Siberian home cooking at the tables of several Russian colleagues, friends, neighbors, students, and their families, including Nataliya Mikhalkovskaya and Gennadi Konstantinov, Boris and Marina, Valentina and Grigori. We were also invited to visit the only professional culinary school in Irkutsk, where the students prepared a special luncheon for us. And in the small Siberian town of Ust'-Ordynskii we were introduced to traditional Buryat-Mongolian cooking through the hospitality of Elizaveta Alekseyeva, Sofya Garankina, and the extended Tabikhanov family. My heartfelt thanks to all of those fine cooks who provided so much rich material for this book.

I am also grateful to Zegrahm Expeditions and Orion Expeditions (now Lindblad Expeditions-National Geographic) for taking me to remote areas of the Russian Far East, including the Bering Sea, the Kamchatka Peninsula, the Sea of Okhotsk, the Kuril Islands, and Sakhalin Island, where I had the opportunity to see—and to taste—many of the wild plants and animals that live in that part of northeastern Asia.

Although I rode thousands of miles on standard Trans-Siberian trains when I lived in Russia, special thanks goes to National Geographic Expeditions for the opportunity to travel all the way across Russia several times, from Vladivostok to Moscow, on the *Golden Eagle Trans-Siberian Express*. I also thank Tim Littler, founder of Golden Eagle Luxury Trains, for answering my many questions about the train's history and its behind-the-scenes operations; Marina Linke, Operations Manager, for information about the food-service management; Tatyana Kolesnikova, Tour Manager; and all the food-service staff aboard the *Golden Eagle*, especially master chef Ilkhomudin Kamolov who let me watch him at work in the train's galley and who shared several of the *Golden Eagle*'s popular recipes for this book.

In Texas, Sue Nelson Sprague was the first taster on whom I inflicted the results of my initial foray into Russian cooking, when we were roommates at the University of Texas many years ago. Sue later revealed that my experiments with Russian recipes had finally convinced her that cabbage was actually worth eating. Our friends Connie and Jerry Labadie deserve special thanks for being longtime taste-testers of the European and Tex-Mex recipes in this book when they were our neighbors in Germany, years before we moved to Russia. Later they let us invade their well-equipped kitchen in America, where Connie helped with the Russian recipe testing and Jerry provided critical tasting. Thanks, too, to our Texas neighbors, Paula and Pat Sigler, for their opinions of the breads and desserts we shared with them while testing and re-testing the recipes that finally made it into this book.

I am especially grateful to Catherine Cheremeteff Jones and Dave DeWitt who read the entire manuscript and provided insightful comments based on their extensive knowledge of many cuisines, from Russian to Tex-Mex. Darra Goldstein, Glenn Mack, Asele Surina, and Vladimir Donskoy also offered valuable suggestions about selected parts of the manuscript and answered my often arcane questions about Russian history, food history, tableware, edible plants, and fish species. And I owe a big, home-cooked Russian meal, with plenty of champagne and vodka, to all the people who read the final version of the manuscript and offered their endorsements of this book.

Ron Chrisman, Director of University of North Texas Press, saw the merits of this unusual cookbook several years ago and encouraged me to keep working on the project despite inadvertent delays along the way. Managing

Editor Karen DeVinney did an excellent job of editing the manuscript and shepherding it through the publishing process. Thanks also to Jeffrey Merrill for the cover photograph and to Joshua Sylve of UNT Library's External Relations Department.

If you come across any errors in this book, however, just chalk them up to the aftereffects of all the vodka-drinking bouts that I endured in Siberia and the Russian Far East.

Finally, my heartfelt thanks goes to the most valuable contributor to this book, my husband, Tom, an excellent cook whose approach to food shopping, meal preparation, and even kitchen cleaning made our lives in Asian Russia so much easier. He viewed food shortages as a challenge, water and electricity outages as minor obstacles to overcome, and the preparation of daily meals as an adventure that could always be enjoyed, whatever the circumstances. (He also loves to eat.) He developed many of the recipes in this book and cooked them for us over the years, long before I ever thought of writing about our culinary experiences in Russia. And after I embarked on this project, he cheerfully endured my many, sometimes obsessive, recipe tests in our Texas kitchen as I tried to reproduce the exact taste, texture, and look of a dish based on a recipe recounted to me by a cook in Siberia years before. For all those reasons, he deserves more than just gratitude here. Much of the credit for this book belongs to him, for his creativity, perseverance, and continual support. *Bol'shoye spasibo*, Tom. My enduring love and appreciation for all the joy you have brought into my life.

# Introduction

## The Asian Side of Russia

When I signed up for a job in Siberia in 1993, I thought I was headed for a culinary backwater at best, a gastronomic wasteland at worst. Surely the food in that far-away Asian side of Russia couldn't compete with the cuisines of Western Europe where I was living at the time. Dining in a country still suffering from food shortages was low on my list of reasons for going there.

I was in for a surprise.

For the past decade, my husband Tom and I had been teaching for an American university program in southern Bavaria. Before that, we'd lived in several other German cities, a crofter's cottage in the remote Scottish Highlands, and a mountain village in Spain, as well as on the Greek island of Crete and at U. S. military bases in Japan and Korea. Two Texans addicted to travel since childhood, we had followed our itchy feet to more than 50 countries around the world, from the tundra of Norway to the jungles of Indonesia, from the mountains of Mexico to the deserts of Egypt.

But neither of us had ever imagined that someday we'd live in Siberia. Until the collapse of the Soviet Union in 1991, most of that huge part of Russia had been off-limits to foreigners. Passengers riding across Russia on the Trans-Siberian Railroad saw only a narrow strip of the countryside through their train windows, and foreign tourists were allowed to visit only specially designated "open" cities along the route. Other major cities in Asian Russia—such as Vladivostok and Ulan-Ude—were "closed" to all but a few select foreigners, who had to get special permission from the Soviet authorities to travel there and who were almost always accompanied by official government escorts, combination tour guides and watchdogs.

Some of those Soviet travel restrictions were eased when Mikhail Gorbachev came to power in 1985, and many of the remaining barriers were lifted after the Soviet Union fell apart six years later. With the formation of the new Russian Federation in late 1991 and the end of the Cold War, it soon became possible for foreigners like Tom and me to live, work, and travel in many parts

# The Big Question

When I told my family and friends in Texas that I was moving to Siberia, they invariably asked:

"What are you going to do there?"

"Teach at two Russian universities," I replied.

"There are *universities* in Siberia?" they asked incredulously.

"Yes, several major universities," I said.

"Where are they?" was always the next question.

"In the big cities," I replied. "Vladivostok, Irkutsk, and Novosibirsk all have populations over half a million."

"There are *cities* in Siberia?" they gasped, as if I'd just told them there were health spas on the moon.

A pause. And then the last, inevitable question:

"Do they have *meat* in Siberia?"

of the country previously closed to outsiders—including much of the Asian side of Russia, a region where only a few Americans had ever lived before.

It was an offer we couldn't refuse: an opportunity to teach in a new Russian-American education program established by the University of Maryland at Far Eastern State University in the city of Vladivostok, Russia's primary port on the Pacific coast, and Irkutsk State University in Irkutsk, another major metropolis, 2,500 miles deep inside Siberia, near fabled Lake Baikal. We knew it was a once-in-a-lifetime chance to watch history in the making, as Russia went through major economic, social, and political changes after the disintegration of the Soviet Union only 18 months before.

It was also a chance for me to learn more about the foods of Asian Russia. Many years earlier, when I was majoring in Soviet and East European studies at the University of Texas in Austin, I had developed an abiding interest in Russian cuisine. And over the following years I'd collected dozens of Russian cookbooks published in Russian and English. But most of those books focused on the cooking of the European side of Russia, or on the cuisines of the Soviet republics in the Caucasus and Central Asia—not on the foods eaten by people living on the Asian side of Russia, a vast area covering eight time zones between the Ural Mountains and the Pacific Ocean. Before moving to Siberia in 1993, I knew little about the kinds of food products actually available there, or the ways that Russians in Vladivostok and Irkutsk used those ingredients in their home

*Sharon Hudgins in a Siberian forest near Lake Baikal, 1994.*

kitchens. And never in my wildest dreams had I envisioned cooking in three kitchens of my own in Siberia.

Not knowing what to expect, Tom and I carried to Russia our own basic set of kitchen utensils, including American measuring cups and spoons, three sharp knives, two vegetable peelers, a sturdy can opener, a good corkscrew, a pepper grinder, and a whisk. We hid bags of dried hot peppers, two bottles of Tabasco sauce, and several jars of spices in our luggage, hoping our culinary contraband wouldn't be confiscated by the customs agents at the Russian airport. And I boxed up all the cookbooks I thought I'd need in Siberia: a 1964 edition of Irma Rombauer's *Joy of Cooking*, the same well-worn cookbook that I'd carried with me around the globe for 20 years; a Russian-language culinary dictionary that I'd purchased in Prague; and my favorite Russian cookbooks published in English—Darra Goldstein's *A la Russe*, Anne Volokh's *The Art of Russian Cuisine*, Anya von Bremzen and John Welchman's *Please to the Table*, Lesley Chamberlain's *The Food and Cooking of Russia*, and Joyce Toomre's *Classic Russian Cooking*, her recent translation of Elena Molokhovets's *A Gift to Young Housewives* (first published in 1861), Russia's equivalent of Fannie Farmer's *Boston Cooking-School Cookbook* (1896) in America.

I also went to Russia with my own culinary knowledge and skills, including the ability to "cook from scratch," which proved essential for eating well in that part of the world. While teaching in Europe in the 1980s, I'd started a second career as a food writer—first, as the food columnist for *The Stars and Stripes*, the U. S. military newspaper, in Germany, later as the author of an award-winning cookbook about the regional cuisines of Spain. I'd also worked as a freelance journalist, writing food and travel stories for magazines and newspapers on both sides of the Atlantic. So whatever awaited me in Siberia, I figured that my own culinary horizons would be limited only by the ingredients available in the local markets there.

Ignorance is bliss: I was soon to discover that finding food was only part of the challenge of cooking in Russia.

The most important culinary asset I took to Russia was Tom. A savvy shopper and excellent cook, Tom was much more than a mere collaborator in the kitchen. Many of the recipes in this book are for dishes he prepared for us there, often under conditions that would have driven other cooks out of the kitchen in a screaming fit of frustration: scarce ingredients, defective stoves, erratic electricity, polluted water that had to be boiled and filtered before use. Yet he persevered in the face of all those obstacles, cooking memorable meals for us on a daily basis and surprising our guests with his sumptuous spreads at dinner parties. That's why this book is really by both of us—and why Tom gets the credit for many of the recipes included here.

We lived on the Asian side of Russia from the summer of 1993 until the end of 1994—first in Vladivostok for one college term, next in Irkutsk for a semester, then back to Vladivostok for another term. During that time, I kept a detailed record of daily life in a place that many people in the West still perceived as nothing but a land of snowy steppes, frozen tundra, dark forests, and grim gulags. After we returned to the United States, I recounted our

Russian adventures in a travel memoir, *The Other Side of Russia: A Slice of Life in Siberia and the Russian Far East,** where I tried to dispel some of the misconceptions about that part of the world. That book includes chapters on Russian foods, festivals, and markets, with culinary stories woven into the narrative in other chapters, too. But Tom and I also came back from Russia with much more information about local foods than I could include in a travel book. And later, several additional trips to the Asian side of Russia gave me a chance to see many of the changes occurring there during this new century. That's why I decided to write this cookbook—a culinary memoir of cooking and eating our way around Asian Russia, a gastronomic landscape little known beyond its borders.

*T-Bone Whacks and Caviar Snacks* is a collection of our own personal stories about food in Siberia and the Russian Far East, larded with some of the history of Asian Russian cuisine and spiced with 140 recipes for dishes we ate in Vladivostok, Irkutsk, and beyond. It includes stories of our culinary experiences in Russian homes and at Russian restaurants, on boats and on picnics, at Russian dachas near the Chinese border, among the Buryat-Mongolians of southern Siberia, on expeditions to Russia's far north, and along thousands of miles of the Trans-Siberian Railroad route. And some of our finest culinary memories are of the many holidays we celebrated in Russia, where food was often the focus of the festivities.

You might find this hard to believe, but *we ate very well in Siberia*. Partly that was because of Tom's ability to ferret out a wide variety of ingredients at old-fashioned Russian grocery stores, tiny kiosks, and the open-air markets where bloody meats and dirty vegetables were sold off the backs of trucks parked on icy patches of ground during the Siberian winter. Partly it was because of our good fortune in meeting several excellent Russian cooks who gladly shared their recipes with us. And in part it was because Tom and I were always open to new culinary experiences, from cooking fish soup on the beach of a Russian island in the Sea of Japan, to foraging for wild berries in northern Siberia, to feasting with a group of native Buryats near the Mongolian border, who ritually slaughtered a sheep for us in their backyard, then served the head and stomach to us as the honored guests.

---

* Published by Texas A & M University Press, 2003. Some of the stories in this cookbook are reprinted or adapted from *The Other Side of Russia*, with permission of the publisher; many of the others appear for the first time in print.

You might also be surprised to see several recipes for French, Spanish, Italian, German, and Tex-Mex dishes in this cookbook. These are recipes from our own repertoire, which we took to Russia and cooked for ourselves and our guests at our apartments in Vladivostok and Irkutsk. (Why serve *borshch* to our Russian friends when we could make Spanish *gazpacho* instead?) We've included these recipes because they were often our daily fare at home in Russia, and they show how we were able to cook those foreign dishes in Siberia using locally available ingredients along with the spices we'd carried to Russia in our luggage.

When we first went to Russia we were surprised to meet very good Russian cooks who shopped at the same markets we did, and purchased the same products we did, but who had never thought to combine those ingredients in different ways to make dishes from beyond the borders of the former Soviet Union. Only when they expressed delight at our Alsatian *Bäckeoffe* or Spanish sangria, or wanted the recipes for our American carrot cake or chocolate brownies—all made with ingredients bought at local Russian stores—did it occur to us why those dishes were unknown to them.

During the Soviet era, with its intermittent food shortages and limited variety on the grocery shelves, most Russians also did not have easy access to a large selection of cookbooks about countries outside the Soviet bloc. And cooking magazines published in the Soviet Union couldn't compare with our lavishly illustrated, well-printed culinary journals like *Gourmet*, *Bon Appétit*, and *Food & Wine*. Moreover, only a small number of Soviet citizens had been allowed to travel extensively beyond the Soviet Union, its Eastern European allies, and other socialist countries such as Cuba, North Korea, and Vietnam. That's why many people in the Soviet Union had no real taste experience of a wider world. Although Moscow had a few ethnic restaurants serving foods from the Soviet republics of the Caucasus and Central Asia, such restaurants were rare or nonexistent in Siberia and the Soviet Far East. And there were certainly no French or Greek or Mexican restaurants in Asian Russia before the demise of the Soviet Union.

All of that was just beginning to change when we moved to Vladivostok in 1993, when the country was still in the early stage of transition from a state-controlled economy to a free-market one. Every month we found more and more imported food products for sale at the local stores. By the time we arrived in Irkutsk in January 1994, one Italian pizza parlor and another restaurant serving Italian-style dishes had opened in that city of 650,000 people. Both Vladivostok and Irkutsk had a couple of East Asian restaurants, too, although the food was mediocre at all of them.

In the 1990s, after the collapse of the Soviet Union, Russians with enough money began traveling all over the world, to countries that would have been difficult for them to visit only a few years before. At the same time, the influx of new food products from Western Europe, East Asia, Australia, and North America also began to whet the Russians' appetites for more "exotic" fare at home. In 1994 the editor of *Anna*, a popular women's journal in the Russian Far East, asked me to write an article explaining to her readers how to use American convenience foods such as cake mixes, peanut butter, canned soups, and bottled spaghetti sauce, which were just beginning to show up on the shelves of a few stores in major cities like Khabarovsk and Vladivostok.

On the other hand, Tom and I learned much about the cuisines of the former Soviet Union from our Russian friends who were good cooks themselves. And we discovered that the Asian part of Russia has a rich history of culinary influences from a wide range of people and places. We also learned that in such a huge geographical space there is no single Siberian cuisine—just as there is no single French cuisine in France, or Chinese cuisine in China, or American cuisine in the United States.

Asian Russia is a land where a variety of culinary traditions have intersected, overlapped, intermingled, and sometimes fused—over time, in different locations, and for a number of reasons, geographical, historical, political, and cultural:

- The foods and foodways of the indigenous hunter-gatherer Siberian peoples living there for thousands of years before the Europeans arrived.
- New ingredients and cooking techniques introduced after the Mongol invasions beginning in the thirteenth century, which opened up trade on the old "silk routes," ultimately bringing tea, pasta, fermented cabbage and other pickled vegetables, soured milk products, and spices such as black pepper, cinnamon, cardamom, ginger, and saffron into Russia.
- Buckwheat, rice, almonds, spices, and citrus fruits (fresh and dried) brought to Siberia by medieval merchants and migrants from Byzantium, the Caucasus, and Central Asia.
- Foods introduced from the Western Hemisphere (notably potatoes, tomatoes, capsicum peppers, and sunflower seeds) after the first Spanish and Portuguese voyages to the "New World" in the fifteenth and sixteenth centuries.
- The hearty peasant fare of Eastern Europe and the European part of Russia, brought from those regions by settlers, soldiers, prisoners, and exiles

after the "opening up" of Siberia by Russians who explored, conquered, and colonized Northern Asia between the late sixteenth and early twentieth centuries.

- The French, German, Dutch, and Baltic dishes imported into Russian cuisine from the time of Peter the Great in the 1700s until the Bolshevik Revolution in 1917.
- The culinary preferences of people from China, Korea, and Central Asia living in several parts of Siberia and the Russian Far East today.
- The fasting and feasting traditions of the Russian Orthodox Church.
- And after the collapse of the Soviet Union in the early 1990s, the imported food products that have flowed into Asian Russia from all over the world (although recent economic sanctions against Russia by many Western countries have caused Russia to retaliate by restricting imports of many foods from those countries, at least temporarily, which has in turn prompted some restaurant chefs to revive traditional Russian dishes made with ingredients sourced only in Russia).

Throughout the centuries, climate and geography have also influenced the culinary practices of this part of the world, determining which foods could be foraged and crops could be grown, what wild animals could be hunted and domestic ones raised, and how those foods could be cooked or preserved.

Today, as a result of Europeans' settling in Siberia over several centuries, 95% of the citizens of Asian Russia are of European ancestry; only 5% are descended from the native peoples living there when the Europeans arrived more than 400 years ago. And the great majority of Siberia's population inhabits the relatively more temperate south of the country, most of them living along or near the Trans-Siberian Railroad route, in the area between 50° N and 55° N latitude, the same latitudes as England, the southern third of Canada, and the region extending from central Germany to southern Sweden.

In the 1990s, most of the people we knew in Irkutsk and Vladivostok still clung to the culinary traditions of their families who had come to Siberia or the Russian Far East one, two, or three generations ago from the European side of Russia, or from Poland, Ukraine, Belorussia, Moldavia, or the Baltic states. The more adventuresome of our friends had also collected recipes from their travels in other parts of the Soviet bloc, which they adapted to the local ingredients available back home in the Russian lands east of the Ural Mountains, the geographical boundary between the European and Asian sides of Russia. They readily shared many of their own ethnic and family recipes with us, along with the recipes they'd gathered from other sources, too. That's why you'll also find recipes from other parts of the former Soviet Union in this cookbook, albeit some of them with a Northeast Asian twist.

After we moved back to Texas in 1995, nearly 12 years passed before I saw Siberia again. Then, in the summer of 2006, *Saveur* magazine sent me to Russia to write a feature article about the foods of Vladivostok. That same summer National Geographic Expeditions asked me to be their lecturer on a Trans-Siberian Railroad tour, traveling nearly 6,000 miles across Russia from Vladivostok to Moscow, with a side trip down into Mongolia.

That return to Russia in 2006 was the first of several more cross-country journeys I made as a lecturer for National Geographic on the legendary Trans-Siberian line. Other jobs on cruise ships have carried me around the Black Sea to the Russian resort of Sochi, and around the Baltic Sea to St. Petersburg, Peter the Great's "Window on the West," on the European side of Russia. Work on expedition ships has taken me along the remote Russian Far East coast, into the Bering Sea, around the Kamchatka Peninsula, and down the volcanic Kuril Island chain to Sakhalin Island in the Sea of Okhotsk. On all those trips, I was impressed by how much—and how rapidly—Russia was changing in the twenty-first century. Just before the global recession in 2008, I could even see progress in urban development from one transcontinental railway journey through Russia in May to the same train trip across Russia only a few months later.

One of the biggest surprises was the change in the culinary landscape. Vladivostok now sported several new supermarkets and glitzy shopping malls stocked with imported luxury goods that I never could have imagined in Russia of the early 1990s. The jumbled open-air markets where we used to shop had morphed into well-organized bazaars. The grungy little stores had been replaced by bright new specialty shops and colorful modern delis. Even the street vendors had better quality products and a more cheerful attitude to match.

In cities along the Trans-Siberian Railroad route, eateries of all sorts had sprung up like mushrooms after a summer rain: European-style coffeehouses and pastry shops, Japanese sushi bars, Middle Eastern *shish-kebab* and *shawarma* stands, bistros and brewpubs, fast-food franchises, and restaurants featuring the foods of Italy, France, Spain, Brazil, Mexico, India, China, Vietnam, and Korea. Bookstores that in the past stocked only a few poorly printed cookbooks now devoted entire sections to beautifully illustrated books on cooking techniques, cocktails, and foreign cuisines (including American Betty Crocker and

British Gordon Ramsay cookbooks translated into Russian). And even little street kiosks sold a whole range of food magazines, from cheap cook-booklets with "simple, easy" recipes for Mexican and Chinese dishes to glossy, full-color culinary magazines—the Russian equivalent of America's *Gourmet* and *Saveur*—packed with trendy travel stories, seductive photographs, and tempting recipes from around the world.

This book is a memoir of my culinary adventures in Russia—from buying muddy potatoes off the backs of trucks in sub-zero temperatures in Siberia, to shopping for fresh seafood at the port in Vladivostok, to the many dinners that I've eaten on (and off) the diner during more than 40,000 miles of travel on the Trans-Siberian Railroad. It's also a practical cookbook of those adventures, with recipes for dishes both traditional and modern, Russian and foreign, that Tom and I have eaten on the Asian side of Russia. Some of the recipes are for the "comfort foods" that sustained us through two Russian winters in the early 1990s. Others are for the festive dishes that we and our friends prepared for special occasions such as birthdays, Christmas, New Year, and Easter. And some are for the memorable meals cooked by the talented chefs aboard the *Golden Eagle Trans-Siberian Express* train in more recent times.

All of these dishes have been prepared in Russian kitchens—and all the recipes tested again, back home in Texas, with American appliances, cookware, and locally available ingredients. But they haven't been "adapted" or "Americanized" into an ersatz version on this side of the globe. If you follow the recipe instructions and use the ingredients required (you can find most of them at your local grocery store), you'll end up with dishes that look and taste just like the ones we enjoyed in Russia.

As a professional food writer, I'm a stickler for using accurate measurements in the kitchen. But Tom cooks like a Russian grandmother, relying on his hand as a measuring device, eyeballing liquids to determine their volume, and letting his senses of sight, smell, touch, and taste guide him from the pot on the stove to the plate he puts on the table. As we tested all the recipes for this cookbook, Tom joked about having a bruised wrist from the many times I grabbed it before he tossed "a handful of this" or "a pinch of that" into the pot without measuring it first. Whatever your own approach to cooking, we recommend that you follow the recipe the first time, so you'll know how we prepared it—then tweak it to your own taste after that. After all, no recipe is carved in stone: it's just a roadmap to a culinary adventure of your own.

Finally, we hope this book will dispel some of the myths about Siberia as a gastronomic backwater. We also hope it will give you a better appreciation of the challenges faced by home cooks in that part of the world and the possibilities for eating well by making the most of whatever ingredients are available, wherever you live. And we certainly hope these recipes will entice you into your own kitchen to try something new, like spicy fiddle-head ferns, frozen cranberry cream, or Siberian salmon dumplings, or to rediscover an American favorite, like cherry cobbler or our own special carrot cake, both of which we often baked, as a taste of home, during those long winter nights in Siberia.

As the Russians say at the start of a meal, *"Priyatnogo appetita!"* (*Bon appetit*! Have a nice meal!)

## Geographic Note

Historically, Siberia has been the general name for all of the Asian side of Russia, between the Ural Mountains and the Pacific Ocean, covering an area of 5.3 million square miles (three-quarters of the land mass of Russia today) and extending over 8 of Russia's 11 time zones. This "Greater Siberia" has three major geographic subdivisions: Western Siberia, Eastern Siberia, and the Russian Far East (the easternmost region, a large land mass of 2.4 million square miles). In today's Russian Federation, Siberia's official political subdivisions are the Ural Federal District, the Siberian Federal District, and the Far Eastern Federal District (including the Sakha/Yakutia Republic). In this book I use the term "Siberia" in its most general sense when referring to all of Asian Russia and also in reference to specific places within today's Siberian Federal District. I use the term "Russian Far East" when referring specifically to places within that federal district.

## Transliteration Note

Transliterating Russian words into English, from the Cyrillic alphabet to the Roman alphabet, sometimes requires a compromise between adhering to a single system or using the most common spelling familiar to English-language readers. For the text and recipes, I have used the Modified Library of Congress System, with the exception of the English spellings of *yo, yu*, and *ya* for Cyrillic letters that are pronounced that way, and *ye* for the letter "e" at the beginning of a word or after a vowel. For ease of readability, I have omitted the Russian soft sign (') in people's names and used the most common spellings of Russian proper names in English. However, Russian citations in the bibliography are transliterated entirely according to the Modified Library of Congress System, so that citations can be searched in library catalogs.

# Kitchen Notes

## Ingredients

Most Russian dishes can be made with ingredients easily found in American supermarkets—meats, grains, root vegetables, fruits, berries, dairy products. Look for a few specialty items at Russian, East European, German, or Jewish delicatessens in the United States, or at grocery stores like Whole Foods. I've also suggested good substitutes for those ingredients, in case you don't live near a well-stocked deli.

- **Unsalted butter** – Most Russians use unsalted butter, because other ingredients in their dishes often include salty foods such as cured salmon, salted caviar, pickled vegetables, etc. All the recipes in this book were made in Russia—and tested again in America—using unsalted butter.
- **Sunflower oil** – Sunflower oil is essential for the taste of certain Russian dishes. Look for Russian or East European brands at delicatessens and specialty food stores; otherwise, use 100% sunflower oil sold at American supermarkets. Cloudy (less filtered) sunflower oil has the strongest, most authentic Russian flavor.
- **Milk** – Full-fat milk works best in these recipes. (In a Siberian winter, high-calorie dairy fat provides welcome warmth and energy!)
- **Sour cream** – Russian sour cream is full-fat (and high fat, 40% or more), with no preservatives. In Siberia, sour cream is ivory-colored and so thick that a spoon will stand up straight in it. In the U.S., use a full-fat, pure sour cream such as Daisy brand, or any other brand of thick sour cream that contains no additives. "Light" sour cream, or sour cream with stabilizers and other additives, does not work as well when combined with the ingredients in many Russian recipes.
- **Fresh white cheese** – Known as *tvorog*, this soft white cheese is a popular ingredient in Russian cooking. An acceptable American equivalent is farmer's cheese, a slightly different, bland-tasting, fresh white curd cheese, but you need to add a little sour cream to it for that real Russian tang. You can also use a combination of whole-milk ricotta and cream cheese

as a substitute for *tvorog* in many recipes. (American cottage cheese is not a good substitute because of its slack texture and different taste.)

- **Flour** – Use standard American all-purpose bleached white flour, which is the type most similar to the white flour available in Russia.
- **Eggs** – Use Grade-A Large eggs.
- **Mayonnaise** – Russian mayonnaise is full-fat, thick, and flavorful. In the U.S., use a premium brand like Hellmann's full-fat, Real Mayonnaise. "Light" mayonnaise or salad dressing spread will not produce an authentic Russian flavor.
- **Russian mustard** – Most Russian mustard is hot-spicy. Do not use bland American ballpark mustard, which has a different taste altogether. Colman's Original English Mustard is the best substitute, although it has a bit more bite than Russian mustard.
- **Garlic** – Garlic comes in many sizes and strengths, from small to elephantine, from mild to knock-out. (Surprise: Some of the largest are the wimpiest.) For the recipes in this book, use garlic cloves that are about an inch long and a half-inch wide. Don't shy away from garlic! When garlic is well cooked in a dish, it adds an umami-like depth of flavor without tainting your breath. (Raw garlic is the culprit in "dragon's breath.")
- **Beef / Chicken / Fish / Vegetable Stock** – Low-sodium stock is preferred so you can better regulate the amount of salt in the dish yourself. Homemade stock is the best, but there are also good organic, low-sodium versions sold in many nationwide grocery stores.
- **Salmon caviar (lightly salted salmon roe)** – In Siberia and the Russian Far East, salmon caviar is king: delicious, abundant, and not as expensive as sturgeon caviar, the prized gray or black sturgeon eggs that can cost hundreds of dollars per ounce. For the recipes in this book, use the best-quality bright-orange salmon caviar you can find. I prefer the salted salmon roe I've found in Russian delis in the U. S., ladled out of a plastic tub and weighed on a scale (just like in markets in the Russian Far East). Many Japanese, Korean, and Chinese supermarkets near East Asian communities in the U. S. also sell good quality salmon roe by the ounce in their fish departments (although the roe is often cured with a mixture of salt, soy sauce, rice wine, and sugar, and has a slightly different taste from the caviar sold in Russia, which is cured only with salt). Otherwise, use salmon caviar packaged in glass jars, not in cans (which tends to be sticky and gunky in texture). If salmon caviar is not available,

substitute other fish roe available in the U.S., but avoid inexpensive, highly salted roe whose strong taste can overpower other flavors in the dish.

## Kitchen Equipment

Fresh white curd cheese (tvorog) for sale at a market in Siberia, 2007.

- In the chapter about our "Stove-from-Hell," you'll read about the minimal kitchen equipment we had in Russia in the mid-1990s. Today many urban Russians have kitchens as well equipped as those in most American homes, with food processors, electric mixers, blenders, bread machines, and more.

- After originally making all these recipes in our Russian kitchens, we re-tested them in the U.S. using standard American metal baking pans and glass baking dishes, stainless-steel and enameled cast-iron cooking pots, non-stick and enameled cast-iron skillets, a no-frills food processor, and a basic hand mixer (not a stand mixer, unless specified in the recipe).

- Baking: Although our Russian ovens were electric (whenever they worked), all of these recipes were re-tested in America in gas ovens. If you have a convection oven, you'll need to turn off the fan or make the necessary adjustments in oven temperature and baking time. Bake on the *middle rack of the oven* unless the recipe says otherwise.

## Tips

- Wear disposable plastic gloves to prevent "pink paws" when peeling, cutting, and shredding red beets. Use plastic instead of wooden cutting boards and utensils, because that beet juice can leave long-lasting stains on wood.
- Use a metal or wire egg slicer to cut fresh mushrooms quickly.

## Important

Before you begin cooking, have all the ingredients in the recipe measured, washed, drained, peeled, chopped, sliced, diced, and placed near your work surface or stove. Be sure you have the right size bowls and pans, plus any special utensils needed for that recipe.

## Bottom Line

Using ingredients from your local supermarket and the cookware in your own kitchen, you can make all these recipes at home. And if you follow the recipes closely, they'll look and taste just like the dishes we ate in Russia. In other words, you can cook and eat—very well—just like two Texans in Siberia.

# Chapter 1
# The White House Cook

## Welcome to Vladivostok

When Tom and I arrived in Vladivostok in the summer of 1993, one of the first Russians we met was Alla Brovko, a neighbor who lived with her husband, Pyotr, and their two sons in our apartment building, a prefabricated concrete high-rise on the edge of the city. Pyotr was a geography professor at Far Eastern State University, where Tom and I also worked. Alla taught English at an elementary school in our neighborhood and spent much of her spare time trying to help the new American faculty in our university program cope with the challenges of daily life in the Russian Far East.

Shortly after we moved into our apartment, we were delighted when Alla and Pyotr invited us to their home one evening. "Come for pies at eight o'clock," said Alla. Thinking that she planned to serve pie-and-coffee for dessert at that hour, we ate a full dinner at home beforehand, then walked up the five flights of stairs to the Brovkos' place in another wing of our building. As soon as we stepped over the threshold into their small foyer, Alla greeted us warmly, calling us her "dear guests," before asking us to take off our shoes and change into *tapochki*—floppy, comfortable, house slippers provided by the host—an old Asian custom that the Russians have adopted.

Inside Alla's apartment, the scene was typical of many meals we would eat in Russian homes during our time there. Hosts, guests, and children sat elbow-to-elbow on mismatched chairs and little backless stools around a drop-leaf dining table temporarily set up in the middle of the living room, almost filling the small space. (Most Russian apartments didn't have a separate dining room.) Crowded onto the table were plates and glasses of various sizes and patterns—whatever the family had been able to acquire during decades of Soviet scarcity. Platters of home-cooked foods vied for space with bottles of Russian vodka, Georgian brandy, Russian champagne, and imported fruit-juice drinks. Convivial conversation in a mish-mash of Russian and English covered topics from the personal to the political, while one of the Brovko boys

*The main square in Vladivostok, with its landmark monument to the "Fighters for Soviet Power in the Far East—1917–1922."*

performed pieces by Chopin on an upright piano in a corner of the room and Proshka-the-kitten played at our feet.

Pride of place on Alla's table that first evening went to her homemade pies—thick, rectangular, and family size, with top and bottom crusts of yeasty dough enclosing fillings of meat, potatoes, cabbage, mushrooms, and plums. Having expected only a slice or two of sweet pastry with a cup of coffee or tea, we were confronted with our second meal of the night, an entire dinner of main-dish pies. And we quickly learned that when Russians say "pie," they mean much more than just dessert.

# A Plentitude of Pies

Russian cuisine boasts a plentitude of pies—savory and sweet, topless and covered, baked and fried, simple and extravagant. Large ones are called *pirogi* (from *pir*, the Russian word for "feast"), whereas smaller, individual, pocket-size pies are known by the diminutive term *pirozhki*. Russian pies can be round, rectangular, oval, square, or semi-circular, with a double or single crust made of yeast dough or various kinds of pastry, sometimes adorned with dough decorations on top. Fillings include almost anything found in the Russian pantry, from meat, poultry, fish, and game, to vegetables, grains, mushrooms, and hard-boiled eggs, to sweetened curd cheese and fresh or preserved fruits and berries. Pyotr winked and Alla blushed as he told us that in Russia a woman who could make good pies was considered especially desirable as a wife. And I soon discovered that many Russian women pride themselves, rightly so, on their ability to make melt-in-your-mouth *pirogi* and *pirozhki*.

Russians eat small savory pies as appetizers, accompaniments to soups, between-meal snacks, and popular street foods. Sweet pies, large or small, are served with tea at any time of the day. More substantive savory pies turn up as separate courses at lunch or dinner, especially when guests have been invited, since Russians consider pies to be symbols of hospitality. Pies are also baked for special occasions, such as weddings, birthdays, and "name days" (the particular day on the church calendar associated with the Christian saint for whom a person is named). Alla's face lighted up when she recalled her own birthday celebrations as a child. "I always had a big, beautiful homemade pie, filled with jam, fruit, berries, or preserved pumpkin, and decorated with pastry flowers, birds, and fruits on top. The special pie sat in the middle of the table throughout the meal, but we were not allowed to eat it until afterwards, when the pie was finally served with tea."

From that first evening of pies in Vladivostok, when Alla discovered our particular interest in Russian food, she took Tom and me under her wing, sharing family recipes, shopping tips, and culinary stories with us. The Brovkos also invited us to family celebrations, to simple suppers, and to sumptuous feasts for Russian holidays. And through long hours of talking around their dinner table, they taught us more than we had ever hoped to learn about daily life in Russia, past and present.

Alla herself was an excellent cook. Talented and inventive in the kitchen, she had a natural ability to ferret out a wide variety of foodstuffs in a country where shopping was a daily challenge, and to combine those ingredients in ways that made every dish seem grander than the sum of its separate parts. She was always open to new culinary ideas, expanding her range of traditional family recipes to include any new dishes that captured her imagination. Like many good cooks, she could visualize a recipe and predict its taste even before she made it. She was also a wealth of information about folk remedies concocted in the kitchen from flowers, grasses, herbs, berries, lichens, bark, and tree sap. And to top it all off, she was a can-do person whose energy and enthusiasm infected everyone around her. Whenever I mentioned something that I would like to see or do or taste in Russia, Alla would immediately say, "Well, why not? Let's do it!"

## The White House Cook

Alla was a living link to Russia's culinary past, to the cuisine of Russia before the Bolshevik Revolution of 1917. Born in 1948 in Yakutsk, in northeastern Siberia, she had also lived as a child for a year in a village near Irkutsk, more than a thousand miles to the south of her home town. At the age of eight she moved with her family to Sakhalin Island in the Soviet Far East. And for many years of her childhood, Alla—like most other Russian children in a society where both parents worked outside the home—was raised by her grandmother Polina, the woman who first taught her how to cook.

Alla always spoke about her "Granny" with great tenderness and affection, often phrasing her comments in the present tense, as if Polina were still in the next room instead of 18 years in the grave. And after I got to know Alla better, she told me the story of her grandmother's life—the tale of a woman I came to think of as "The White House Cook."

*Nineteenth-century traditional wooden house in Irkutsk, Siberia, 1994.*

The oldest of several children in her family, Polina had been born in the mid-1890s in a village near the Siberian city of Krasnoyarsk. When she was still in her young teens, her father died and her mother remarried. But her new step-father didn't want so many mouths to feed, so he arranged to marry off Polina to an older widower in the village, a cobbler with three children of his own. Polina resented being forced into marriage at such an early age, to a man she hated and with all those step-children to take care of, too. Only a month after the wedding, she sneaked out of the house one night and ran away to the home of a relative who lived in another village a few miles down the road.

Polina eventually made her way to Irkutsk, the capital of Eastern Siberia, where she found employment in the household of the governor-general of that vast region of Russia. For six years she worked in the basement kitchen of the palatial residence that housed the last three governors-general before the revolutions of 1917. Known as the Bely Dom (The White House), it was a three-story, colonnaded, white stone mansion built by a wealthy merchant in the early nineteenth century. The historic Bely Dom is still a landmark in the city today, where it now houses the scientific library of Irkutsk State University. In 1994, whenever I attended university conferences and official ceremonies held in the elegant setting of the Bely Dom's restored tsarist-era rooms, I tried to imagine the meals that Polina had once prepared for the last upper-class families who resided there before the Bolshevik Revolution changed all of their lives.

Polina began working at the Bely Dom when Nicholas II was the tsar of Russia. Initially she was only a "market girl," sent out to purchase fresh food supplies for the kitchen every day. But Polina, who had already learned how to cook from her own peasant grandmother back in the village, continued to hone her culinary skills in the governors' affluent household in Irkutsk. In addition to fetching food from the markets, she began assisting the cook, a kindly, middle-aged woman with an excessive fondness for drink. Over time, as the cook faded further and further into alcoholic oblivion, Polina took over more and more of her duties in the kitchen. Finally the cook left altogether, and Polina took her place, after five years of informal apprenticeship in the basement of the Bely Dom.

Polina's position as the official White House cook lasted only one year, before her culinary career was cut short by the revolutions that shook Russia in 1917. In October 1917, the Bely Dom was occupied by Siberian revolutionaries, and during the fierce fighting between those Red Bolshevik supporters and the White tsarist forces, the interior of the building was severely damaged and the exterior pocked with bullet holes. A year later, the White House was turned over to the newly established Irkutsk State University, which still owns it today.

During the civil war in Russia following the Bolshevik Revolution, Polina married a communist revolutionary, a man whose health had already been broken from the years he'd spent in prison under the tsarist regime. They were married for only two years before he died, leaving behind Polina and their young son. Sometime later, Polina married again, her third husband, a Tatar with whom she had other children, including the daughter who gave birth to Alla in Siberia three years after the end of World War II.

In the 1950s, when Polina began teaching her young granddaughter Alla how to cook, she was passing along culinary knowledge that reached back to the mid-1800s, to her own grandmother's time—recipes and techniques transmitted from generation to generation over an entire century, through wars, revolutions, and purges—from a Siberian village to a governor-general's mansion to post-World War II urban apartments in the Soviet Far East. And indeed, many of the dishes that Alla prepared for us seemed to come from the pages of classic nineteenth-century Russian novels, not a tiny kitchen in a post-Soviet high-rise apartment building on the eastern edge of Russia.

Alla spiced many of our culinary conversations with statements that began "As Granny used to say …" before recounting Polina's domestic advice, cooking tips, and household superstitions. Like many Russians, Granny Polina thought it was especially dangerous to leave a knife sitting out on the table overnight. She told young Alla that when crumbs were left on the table after a meal, she should never brush them off onto the floor with her hand, but instead use a rag to sweep them into some kind of receptacle; otherwise, her future husband would go bald. (The lesson stuck: Alla turned out to be a meticulous housekeeper, and her husband Pyotr had a full head of hair.) Granny also never allowed Alla to sweep the floor at night, or to toss the floor sweepings out into the yard; they had to be burned in the stove instead. In fact, Granny Polina believed that *nothing* should be thrown out of the house after sunset—water, bones, vegetable peels, anything at all—or you might lose everything you owned. Likewise, she would never wash her floor late at night, for fear of washing away all her money. And Granny never let anyone move the furniture or clean the house on the same day that a guest or family member set off on a trip, to ensure that the person's journey would be easier along the way.

Alla became especially enthusiastic whenever she described the dishes her grandmother had cooked at home, including elegant desserts that you'd expect to see on a governor's table in Irkutsk a hundred years ago. But during the three decades following the Bolshevik Revolution, Alla's grandmother did not always have access to the kinds of ingredients that she'd once turned into elaborate dishes in the kitchen of the Bely Dom.

## A Chip off the Old Glass

Alla said that if a cup or plate breaks, then good luck is coming your way. But if a piece of porcelain or glass only chips, you must immediately throw it away because it's bad luck to keep it around. Alla once chipped the bases of five precious champagne glasses during a household move, but she couldn't bring herself to throw them out. Her mother found them, though, and tossed them in the trash without telling her. Such superstitions remain strong in Siberia.

# Siberian Stroganina

A winter dish that Alla made in the Russian Far East was salmon salad—frozen raw salmon shaved with a sharp knife into paper-thin pieces, then mixed with chopped onion, a little oil and vinegar, and some salt and pepper, and left to sit for a few minutes before being served as an appetizer. "Men like it with vodka," she advised.

Her salmon salad was similar to *stroganina*, a raw-fish dish popular with people all across Siberia. Whole frozen fish are sliced into very thin ribbons, then dipped into salt and black pepper or hot paprika, and popped into your mouth immediately, followed by a shot of ice-cold vodka. In northern Siberia, the favored fish is often *muksun*, a silver-skinned whitefish high in fat, with a delicate, salmon-like flavor. I also knew many people around Lake Baikal who considered *stroganina* made from Baikal *omul'*, a type of whitefish found only in that lake, to be a quintessential Siberian dish, a triumph of simplicity over superfluity.

The Siberian writer, Valentin Rasputin, described it well: "When people say that something melts in your mouth, they are trying to convey a sensation of bliss. That's just what happens here: the icy coating vanishes as soon as you put a piece into your mouth and the fish thaws out, melts with a butteriness that penetrates your whole body, is absorbed without being swallowed, and spreads gently and insistently throughout your entire system. Someone who has never heard of *stroganina* instantly finds it agreeable without any coercion (the fish is raw, after all) or pretense."
—Valentin Rasputin, *Siberia, Siberia* (1996)

Except for the privileged few, life has never been easy for people living in Siberia. And conditions were even worse during wartime. Alla told me that during the Great Patriotic War—the Russians' term for World War II—"many people lived on potatoes and grass." This "grass" was actually several types of greens, both wild and cultivated, including the greens known in English as goosefoot, which belong to the same family as spinach and chard. "That's what saved us,"

Granny Polina always said to Alla, as she recalled making a kind of pancake from grated unpeeled potatoes, chopped goosefoot greens, and salt. If she was lucky and had an egg that day, she added it to the mixture, too. After shaping the ugly mass into patties, she cooked them on a hot griddle—not in a skillet, because she had no oil for frying. The patties came off the griddle colored an unappetizing dark brown or black. "Many times that was the only food for my children during the war," remembered Granny.

Alla noted that potatoes, goosefoot greens, *cheremsha* (wild garlic), and *brusniki* (lingonberries) saved many people in Siberia from starvation during the Great Patriotic War. "People in the north of Russia have always preserved a lot of these berries for winter, without sugar, because sugar was often scarce or unavailable," she told me. "The berries are full of vitamin C, and tea made from the leaves of this plant is good for the kidneys." She went on to describe how villagers in the north still pick *brusniki* in September, put them into wooden barrels, fill the barrels with cold water, and leave them on the veranda or in a cold room of the house to freeze solid. Then during the winter they chop out whatever amount they need—to make *sok* (berry juice), to use as a filling for baked pies, and to make frozen berry cream, a simple sweet consisting of berries, sugar, and cream, a winter treat that was one of Alla's favorites when she was a child.

## Of Cabbages and Carrots

One evening in mid-October, before the first frost, Alla and Pyotr came over to our apartment to show us how to make *kislaya kapusta*—Russian soured cabbage, a sort of crunchy, mild-tasting sauerkraut with a delicate flavor far removed from the assertive taste of most commercially pickled products. Earlier in the week, following Alla's instructions, we'd purchased five large white cabbages, several carrots, a small amount of anise seeds, and a kilogram of salt. Alla arrived with her own long knife for shredding the cabbage. "Granny had a special long knife that she used only for making *kislaya kapusta*," said Alla, "and she became very angry if anyone tried to use that knife for anything else." We got the message.

After tearing off and discarding the tough outer leaves of the cabbages, Alla cut the unwashed heads into quarters. Wielding her knife like a pro, she proceeded to shred three cabbages in the time it took me to slice only one, while Tom finely shredded five carrots on his own. When the table was covered with a mountain of cut-up cabbage, we mixed it by hand with the carrots, adding a soup spoon each of anise seeds, sugar, and freshly ground black pepper, along with a cup of salt. Then we crushed the ingredients together by handfuls, pressing them between our palms to "bruise" the cabbage a bit.

Alla showed us how to pack the mixture into a 10-liter enameled metal bucket, alternating it with layers of large cabbage chunks that she'd held in reserve. Alla mentioned that some people season their *kislaya kapusta* with cranberries, lingonberries, bay leaves, allspice, caraway seeds, or dill. And once at a farmers' market we saw *kislaya kapusta* flavored with chunks of apples and green tomatoes. Alla sometimes put thin layers of raw salmon between the layers of shredded cabbage in her own sauerkraut bucket, a variation I was never brave enough to try myself.

## A Taste of Tatary

Every year, the average Russian consumes seven times as much cabbage as the average American, much of it in the form of sauerkraut. Cabbage has long been a staple food of people living in northern climes, but it was supposedly the Mongol-Tatars of Central Asia who, several centuries ago, brought to European Russia the Chinese method of preserving cabbage and other vegetables by "dry pickling" with salt alone, a technique different from the Europeans' practice of "wet pickling" vegetables in a vinegar brine. Sauerkraut and other dry-pickled vegetables soon became an important part of people's diets in northern Europe, especially during wintertime, as a valuable source of vitamin C, calcium, and other minerals.

Russians make two kinds of pickled cabbage: *kvashenaya kapusta*, true sauerkraut, which is fermented in wooden barrels or stoneware crocks for up to two months, and *kislaya kapusta*, soured cabbage, which is fermented for only a few days and is crisper and less sharp-tasting than longer-fermented cabbage. Ironically, settlers from European Russia later carried this technique eastward again, to Siberia, where they also encountered original Asian dry-pickled vegetable products such as Korean *kimchi*.

Finally she put a small plate on top of the cabbage and set a heavy weight on top of it, to press the cabbage down while it fermented. We kept the bucket on our kitchen floor, away from the radiator, for three days. Then we removed the weight and plate on top and poked holes in the mixture to release the gases that had formed during fermentation. Later that day we transferred the pickled cabbage to 3-liter jars, which we set outdoors in the corner of our balcony away from the sun. And a week later, the sauerkraut was ready to eat. One evening's work and a few days of tending the bubbling brew had produced enough *kislaya kapusta* to last us for the next three months.

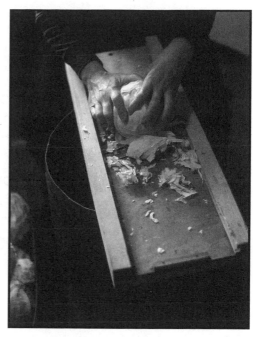

*Shredding cabbage for sauerkraut in a village in the Russian Far East, 1994.*

## Around the Samovar

Alla was one of those women whose high spirits and spontaneity seldom seemed to wane. At a moment's notice she would stop by our apartment or send one of her sons to invite me to her place for tea. (None of us had a telephone, so all invitations—whether to an impromptu brunch or a formal dinner party— were always delivered in person or in writing.) And since Russians never drink tea without eating sweet or savory tidbits along with it, Alla always prepared something different for me to taste—maybe a recipe of her own or one of Granny's, or a recipe given to her by a friend, or a new dish that she'd thought up herself that very day.

At those afternoon teas I also learned how the Russian concept of time can stretch as long as a task takes to accomplish, as long as a conversation needs to last, in a leisurely manner and often with frequent interruptions. I would be sitting in Alla's living room, sipping tea and talking with her about food, about politics, about daily life in Russia, when someone else would drop by, and then maybe two or three others—a teacher from her school, a young boy she was tutoring in English, a friend of her sons', a parent of her pupil's. As the circle of people

# Treasure from the East

Tea first came to Russia from China in the 1600s, along the overland trade routes through Siberia. Originally an imported luxury affordable only by the rich, black tea eventually became the best-loved non-alcoholic drink in Russia, its aroma and taste savored by everyone from the upper classes to the masses. The ritual of tea drinking became a national pastime, a symbol of community and hospitality, with men and women alike gathered around the steaming samovar at any hour of the day to enjoy the amber brew.

Fueled by burning charcoal or pine cones (and by electricity today), the shiny metal samovar itself only heats the water for brewing very strong tea in a separate little pot, which sits atop the samovar to keep warm. (The Russian word *samovar* means "self-boiler.") A small amount of the concentrated, mahogany-colored tea is poured into china cups (for women) or clear glasses set in metal holders (for men), then diluted to the desired strength by more hot water from the spigot on the samovar. Some Russians even sip their tea from their saucers, into which they've poured the piping hot liquid to cool it down. And most Russians like their tea sweet—with a spoonful of fruit or berry preserves eaten between sips, or some jam or sugar stirred into the tea itself. Others hold a lump of sugar in their mouths and suck the hot tea through it.

in the room grew while darkness descended outside, I knew that Tom would soon have supper ready at home and be worried about my safety in returning alone through the unlighted labyrinth of our high-rise building. But I also knew there was no polite way to end the conversations around the samovar in Alla's living room until all the topics had been talked out. And just when it seemed that a convenient parting point was about to be reached, when I could make my excuses and leave, then someone else would knock on Alla's door—a friend, a neighbor, a student's grandmother—at which time it would have been very ill-mannered for me to skip out, right after another person, and a new conversation, had just arrived.

# In Praise of Russian Women

"The way Russian women were able to arrange their homes under such primitive conditions and their ingenuity in cooking and preparing exciting dishes with their limited means made a deep impression on me. They were especially good at making pirozhki, which they filled with meat, fish, preserved berries—or cabbage when they had difficulty getting anything better. One of our neighbors, a wise elderly woman … was an artist at cooking, and she gave me a lot of good advice and recipes, some of which I still use." —Rachel Rachlin, *Sixteen Years in Siberia* (1988)

# At Alla's Table

Alla and Pyotr also invited us to several festive dinner parties at their apartment, lavish meals that displayed Alla's cooking talents to the finest. She had to begin preparing for such parties two weeks in advance—finding the necessary ingredients at food stores and farmers' markets scattered throughout the city, assembling any make-ahead dishes, and finally cooking the last-minute dishes to be served hot. Some of the tastiest foods on Alla's table came from her own garden at the Brovkos' little dacha many miles north of Vladivostok: tomatoes, cucumbers, carrots, potatoes, onions, garlic, strawberries, blackberries, gooseberries, cherries, apples, apricots, and plums. Alla served these fresh, in season, and preserved any surplus as pickles and jams to be savored during the long winter that lay ahead.

On a snowy night in January 1994, Alla prepared a special farewell dinner for Tom and me, just before we boarded a Trans-Siberian train for the 2,500-mile journey to our next teaching assignment in Irkutsk. For that going-away dinner, Alla covered the dining table with a bounty of home-made *zakuski*, the hot and cold appetizers that start every Russian feast. She also surprised me with one of my favorite dishes from the Russian Far East, *paporotniki*, fiddlehead ferns sautéed with paprika, pork, onions, and garlic. Her main course was roasted chicken, which Alla had basted, in a moment of inspiration, with some mayonnaise that we'd brought

# Home Grown, Home Preserved

Urban Russians grow a wide variety of fruits, vegetables, and flowers in their little private dacha gardens outside the cities, as do rural Russians in the larger gardens behind their wooden houses in the villages. During the 1980s, these private garden plots constituted 3% of the agricultural land of the Soviet Union but produced more than 25% of the country's crops.

Much of this food is preserved in glass jars at home, because Russians consider home-preserved foods superior to commercially canned goods, both gastronomically and culturally. Even those people who don't grow their own foods still purchase seasonal fresh produce at the markets in summer and early autumn to preserve at home for the long winter ahead.

In almost every Russian house or apartment, jars of fruit and berry jams, pungent sauerkraut, marinated mushrooms, preserved tomatoes, and pickled cucumbers are stored on top of wardrobe closets, under sofas and beds, on balconies and window ledges, and stacked on the kitchen floor. Visit a Russian and she'll usually send you home with a jar of her homemade raspberry preserves or pickled mushrooms or plum jam. I say "she" because in Russia, kitchen work is women's work. Men may help tend the private gardens and harvest the crops, but women are the ones who clean, shred, peel, chop, and preserve the bounty of the earth.

to her in a box of kitchen supplies we were leaving behind. And dinner ended with a stack of large, lacy *blinchiki* (Russian-style crêpes), as dainty as crocheted doilies, served with Alla's homemade cherry jam and local citrus-scented honey, accompanied by delicate china cups of chicory-flavored coffee—a warm send-off before we headed for the frozen interior of Siberia.

After working in Irkutsk for a semester, we returned to Vladivostok in August of 1994, to teach at the university there again during the autumn. Five months later, at the end of December, Alla prepared a second farewell dinner for us on

# Fond Farewell

In December 1993, on the last day of classes at our university in Vladivostok, Tom's students surprised him with a bottle of Russian champagne and a big bouquet of beautiful flowers. And my students presented me with a lovely gift: one volume of a facsimile edition of the 1909 version of Elena Molokhovets's classic Russian cookbook, *Podarok molodym khozyaikam (A Gift to Young Housewives)*, containing the second half of the 3,400 recipes she had published up to that time. Inside the front cover, my students had inscribed, in English, "… Let this book keep good & fond memories of EDCP 108-B [the course I'd taught there] & our motherland Russia." Three weeks later, as Tom and I were boarding a Trans-Siberian train for the long journey to Irkutsk, Alla handed me her own going-away gift: a facsimile edition of an 1893 version of Molokhovets's cookbook, with the first 1,700 of her recipes—quite enough to keep me cooking Russian dishes for the rest of my life.

the night before we departed by plane back to the United States. Once again, the meal began with a copious *zakuski* spread that would have made Granny Polina proud: hard-boiled eggs garnished with salmon caviar; slices of sausage and ham; beet-and-potato salad; home-preserved cucumbers and mushrooms; pickled yellow tomatoes from Alla's dacha garden; herring in mustard sauce; sliced apples with horseradish sauce; and plenty of vodka to wash it all down. The main course was homemade Siberian *pel'meni*, little meat-filled boiled dumplings served with a choice of butter, sour cream, hot-spicy Russian mustard, and Asian chile sauce. Sitting around the table with Alla, Pyotr, and their two sons, Tom and I raised our glasses to them in a final toast, complimenting Alla on her excellent cooking and thanking the Brovko family for their friendship, their hospitality, and all the fine meals they'd shared with us in their home. But that evening Alla seemed unusually subdued, as if her naturally ebullient spirits had suddenly deserted her. She sat for a long moment without speaking, then, looking up at us with a mixture of pride and weariness on her face, Alla replied, "I wanted you to see that even in the midst of everything that is happening in Russia, people can still live a normal life."

# The Two Galinas

Fast-forward to 2006, when we returned to Vladivostok for the first time in nearly 12 years. That summer *Saveur* magazine in New York sent me on assignment to Vladivostok to write an article about home-cooked foods in the Russian Far East. Tom came along to help, and few days later, Jim Oseland— soon to become the new editor-in-chief of *Saveur*—arrived in Vladivostok to take photographs for the story.

I had hoped to feature Alla in the *Saveur* story because she was such an outstanding cook. But not long before we left for Russia, Alla sent word that she had to be out of town because of a death in her family. I'd already heard that other Russian cooks we'd known in Vladivostok in the 1990s were either away on vacation or had moved to another country. So, on short notice, I contacted friends on both sides of the Pacific, asking if they could recommend any other home cooks in Vladivostok who could help with the magazine assignment.

That's how we met the two Galinas. Both were Russian women who'd lived most of their lives in Vladivostok and were known among their families and friends as excellent cooks. A medical doctor by profession, Galina Korotkina was a stylish, sturdy, 60-year-old with twinkling eyes and a ready smile. Our other contact was Galina Tarasova, an ebullient woman in her late 50s, with an impish grin, who worked as an English professor and translator. Both women had a quick sense of humor but were also serious, and very knowledgeable, about food. And both agreed to plan separate dinner parties for us where we could taste a variety of home-cooked dinners typical of the Russian Far East in the twenty-first century.

We soon began referring to them among ourselves as "Galina One" and "Galina Two"—the order in which we'd met them—to keep them straight in our discussions about the story for *Saveur*. We also worked with each of them for several days in advance, as they planned the menus, shopped for food, and made all the other arrangements for their festive meals. And we asked them to invite as many guests as they wanted, in addition to the *Saveur* team of Jim, Tom, and me, so we could experience two different home-cooked Vladivostok feasts with a variety of Russian diners.

At noon on a Sunday, we arrived at the sixth-floor apartment of Galina Korotkina ("Galina One") to watch as she and a friend (yet another Galina!) prepared a multi-course meal for the guests who'd be arriving later in the day. The women worked well together in the kitchen, chopping, slicing,

*Smoked and salted fish for sale by a street vendor in Vladivostok, 2006.*

and mixing the ingredients for a mammoth menu that featured 23 different kinds of *zakuski*, those hot and cold appetizers that are the glory of every Russian feast, followed by chicken-and-vegetable *borshch*, a roasted-chicken entrée, and a custardy napoleon torte garnished with fresh berries for dessert.

As the afternoon progressed, Galina set up a drop-leaf dinner table in the middle of her living room. Soon the table was crowded with a colorful array of artfully plated *zakuski*: several cold salads composed of various combinations of potatoes, beets, cabbage, white beans, and fresh greens; *paporotniki* (Korean-style fiddlehead ferns like Alla used to make for us); stuffed eggplant rolls; cold calamari salad; steamed mackerel with layers of onions, carrots, mayonnaise, and cheese; sea scallops sautéed in butter and garnished with boiled jumbo shrimp; baked fresh herring seasoned with crushed red peppers; *bliny* (little Russian pancakes) wrapped around red-orange beads of salmon caviar; open-face sandwiches topped with pickled herring and smoked sprats (small, silvery, oily fish, similar to sardines), both garnished with fresh dill; bright-green *wakame* seaweed salad, a Russian Far East favorite; homemade salted cucumbers and home-cured salmon; hot and cold sausages; and slices of cheese.

# Russian Zakuski (Appetizers)

The highlight of every Russian feast is the abundant array of appetizers—sometimes two dozen or more—at the beginning of the meal. Known as *zakuski* ("little bites"), these hot and cold hors d'oeuvres are supposed to set the stage for the soup, main course, and dessert that follow. But they often steal the show. Who could resist such tempting treats as caviar, smoked salmon, pickled herring, marinated mushrooms, crab legs with mayonnaise, elaborately decorated pâtés, cold vegetable salads, colorful aspics, and little pastries filled with cabbage, meat, or fish, all washed down with shots of ice-cold vodka or sips of chilled sparkling wine? First-time visitors to Russia often mistake the *zakuski* spread for the entire dinner, filling up on these succulent savories before discovering that a full meal is yet to come.

Some food historians trace the origin of *zakuski* back to the ninth century, when Rurik, a Scandinavian Viking who ruled over the Slavic people of Novgorod, presumably carried the custom of smorgasbord-style eating to Russia. Others credit Tsar Peter the Great (1672–1725) with introducing *zakuski* to Russia in the eighteenth century, as one of many innovations, from military to culinary, that the progressive-thinking Peter brought back from his travels in western Europe. Two common components of today's *zakuski* tables—hard cheeses such as Gouda and Cheddar, and *buterbrody*, small squares of buttered bread topped with fish, meat, or cheese—can certainly be attributed to the peripatetic tsar. But not everyone agrees with the trickle-down theory of *zakuski* from the court to the commoners. Some historians contend that the impulse to honor guests by loading down the table with tidbits of everything in the larder has always been characteristic of Russian hospitality, regardless of social class or historical period.

In the nineteenth century, when the Russian gentry entertained guests at their city homes or country estates, they served the pre-dinner *zakuski* on a separate table in one corner of the dining room or even in a little anteroom reserved for this use. Diners stood around the *zakuski* table where they knocked back shots of vodka interspersed with little bites of artfully arranged appetizers designed not only to please the eye and the palate but also to mitigate the effects of alcohol on the stomach. After several rounds of toasting and tasting, the convivial company then moved to the formal dining table where they sat down for the rest of the repast.

In the Soviet era, such lavish dining was usually confined to a small minority of well-connected elites. But at times when many foods were scarce, rationed, or very costly, even humble households laid on an extensive *zakuski* spread for special occasions such as weddings and New Year's Eve. Vestiges of the *zakuski* tradition could even be found in workplace canteens, student cafeterias, and railroad dining cars where a single cold appetizer was often served at the beginning of an otherwise prosaic, proletarian meal.

In today's post-Soviet Russia, *zakuski* remain an integral part of many meals, from state banquets to business lunches to private celebrations at home. Some restaurants serve a large selection of *zakuski* on a separate table, like an American salad bar. Home cooks cover the entire surface of their small dining tables with platters and bowls of potato and beet salads, boiled shrimp, baked herring, pickled cucumbers, sliced sausages, fresh tomatoes, cold ham and chicken, mushrooms in sour cream sauce, beef in aspic, stuffed hard-boiled eggs, grated horseradish, hot-spicy mustard, and bottles of booze—the list of edible options is almost endless. Guests sit crowded around the table, elbow to elbow, taking a bite of this or a nibble of that, followed by a sip or a shot of alcohol, before beginning the cycle again ... and again ... and again. Whatever the venue is, variety, abundance, and conviviality are always the cornerstones of the *zakuski* concept.

After stuffing ourselves with those *zakuski*, we all needed a break before tackling the soup, main dish, and dessert. Typically at these dinner parties in Russian homes, any remaining portions of *zakuski* were left on the table when the other courses were served; the platters were just pushed aside to make room for more food. Likewise, we rearranged our chairs around the table as more of Korotkina's friends dropped by during the meal, squeezing into the small space and happily helping themselves to anything left over on the table. And we all laughed in delight when Galina suddenly burst into the room carrying the main course, her "Captain's Chicken." The roasted bird was sitting upright on a platter, like a captain standing at attention, topped by a boiled-egg "head" with a face and officer's cap made of vegetable pieces, three cherry-tomatoes toothpicked to its chest for "coat buttons," and a lettuce-leaf "cape" draped over its shoulders.

Her work in the kitchen finished, Galina finally had time to sit down and enjoy the meal. She unwound with a shot of vodka, offering a toast to Tom and me as her honored guests. Following her lead, we knocked back the ice-cold alcohol in one gulp. But when she immediately proffered another toast, then another, I became wary. I'd endured too many of these drinking bouts with Russians before. As Galina poured another round of vodka, filling my glass to the rim, I thought I saw how to survive the situation. Since the vodka was served in little metal goblets instead of clear glasses, I planned to take only a sip and pretend to drink the rest, with no one the wiser. But Galina caught me out. Looking me in the eye, she downed her own shot of vodka in one go, then turned her goblet upside down to show that it was empty. Knowing that I mustn't lose face, I followed suit. Woman to woman, that contest continued for more than an hour, interspersed with flutes of *shampanskoye* (Russian sparkling white wine). The other guests sat on the sidelines, prudently sipping their own drinks while watching this friendly Russian-American rivalry that ended only when the last bottle had been drained.

The next morning I felt like vodka was flowing through my veins instead of blood. But I had no time to nurse my hangover because Tom and I were joining Galina Tarasova ("Galina Two") on a grocery shopping expedition that day. She had arranged for two of her nieces, Svetlana Katayeva and Yelena Ivaschenko, to host a Vladivostok family feast for us, showcasing many of the region's typical dishes. And we'd volunteered to help with the cooking.

"We eat a lot of fish and vegetables," Galina Two said, "and of course we use many Asian flavors, like soy sauces, since we're so close, geographically and culturally, to Asian countries." (Indeed, I'd already noticed that many of the cold vegetable salads in Vladivostok's glitzy new delis were identified as "Asian" or "Chinese.") And since no festive repast in Vladivostok would be complete without a variety of seafood dishes, we all headed to the fish stores at the harbor, where Galina and her nieces loaded their shopping bags with whole squid, plump sea scallops, jars of salmon caviar, and big rosy Kamchatka crab legs, the Russian equivalent of Alaskan king crab.

We soon settled into the controlled chaos of cooking for 14 people in Katayeva's large, airy apartment in a 1980s-era high-rise, with a modernized kitchen at one end of the open-plan living room. Galina's two nieces worked together quietly and efficiently, like a pair of professional chefs, anticipating each other's need for this ingredient or that utensil, while Tom and I found space on a small table to make the carrot and potato salads we were contributing to the party, too.

I'd eaten lightly all day because I knew what to expect at a Russian meal like that, where hospitality was measured by how little of the tablecloth was still visible after all the food was put on the table. By my count, two dozen hot and cold dishes emerged from the kitchen, including crab and calamari salads enrobed with mayonnaise (a popular ingredient in Russian cooking); shredded beet salad with walnuts and prunes; a second beet salad known as *vinegret*, made with potatoes, carrots, and peas tossed with vinegar-and-oil dressing; baked cod with onions, served with sliced pan-fried new potatoes seasoned with garlic and dill; baked salmon, sautéed scallops, and stuffed squid; marinated herring; cucumber-and-tomato salad; and small bowls of chopped scallion tops and hard-boiled eggs for garnishes, along with tongue-tingling soy-sauce dips spiked with wasabi, fresh garlic, and dried hot red peppers.

There was so much food on the table that several of the guests decided to treat the meal as a buffet and eat standing up. We dined at a leisurely pace, taking a taste of this, a bite of that, as the aunts, uncles, and cousins in that close-knit clan milled around the room offering traditional Russian toasts of vodka, white wine, and *shampanskoye*, swapping personal stories about previous family get-togethers, and laughing at the antics of Galina's young grandson, Yakov, as he devoured piece after piece of thick-sliced baguette, lightly fried in butter and slathered with salmon roe. Several hours later, our marathon meal came to an end with the simplest of summer desserts, a refreshing mixture of chopped apples, pears, bananas, oranges, and kiwis tossed with plain, creamy yogurt—the perfect palate-cleansing finale to that Vladivostok family feast.

# Cucumbers of the Sea

"Trepang Bay" is the Chinese name for the bay on which Vladivostok is located. The waters that wash the city's shores are home to *trepang*, strange-looking edible creatures also known as sea slugs or sea cucumbers because of their shape. The Chinese consider them a delicacy, as do many Russians in the Far East where sea cucumbers are harvested individually by divers and command a high price in fish stores and restaurants. Galina Tarasova's husband, Mikhail—a professional diver and underwater welder at the port of Vladivostok—liked to cook *trepang* at home. He stewed sliced sea cucumbers with onions, carrots, tomatoes, bay leaves, parsley, and dill, or simmered them in soy sauce with celery leaves and other green herbs.

But these bottom-feeding sea creatures were not always so popular with the Europeans who settled on Russia's Pacific coast. A Russian guidebook published in 1900 lists the principal exports from Vladivostok as "sea cabbage [actually *laminaria*, a kind of kelp], zhen-shen [ginseng], mushrooms found on oak stumps, lichens growing on corn [wheat], trepang, etc., forwarded to China and quite useless to the Russian population." Today, dried wild-caught sea cucumbers sell for up to $180 a pound in our local Asian markets in Texas.

Nearly half a century ago, in their Introduction to *Russian Cooking* (1969), Helen and George Papashvily observed, "Rich, robust, and plenteous, [Slavic cooking] is designed to nourish the spirit as well as the flesh. The heaped dish, the crowded table, the pressing hospitality that strangers have sometimes taken as a sign of ostentation—or worse, mere voracity—is actually an assertion of life, an answer to the ancient specter of hunger forever lurking outside the door." Despite the changes that have occurred in Russia in the years since that was written, that elemental assertion of life is still a silent guest at the table whenever family, friends, and strangers gather to celebrate with food.

# Assorted Open-Face Sandwiches
## (*Buterbrody*)

*Looking like miniature works of art, these small open-face sandwiches known as* buterbrody *(literally, buttered bread) are popular on every Russian* zakuski *table. We enjoyed sampling a variety of colorful* buterbrody *at restaurants, dinner parties, and banquets in many parts of Asian Russia. Use your own imagination to construct other versions of these little open-face sandwiches, too.*

- Small squares of thinly sliced whole-wheat bread, or round slices of baguette (⅓-inch thick), spread with unsalted butter and topped with a generous dollop of salmon caviar. (For a richer flavor, lightly pan-fry the baguette rounds on both sides in butter first, and let them cool before topping with caviar.)

- Small squares of rye bread spread with sour cream (mixed with a little horseradish for more kick), topped with thin slices of cold-smoked salmon or canned sprats or sardines (drained), and garnished with half a thin lemon slice and a sprig of fresh dill.

- Round slices of baguette (about ½-inch thick), spread with butter, topped with canned sprats or sardines (drained) and garnished with thin slices of dill pickle.

- Small squares of dark rye or pumpernickel bread spread with hot-spicy Russian mustard, topped with thin slices of hard sausage (preferably paprika-flavored sausage, such as Hungarian), and garnished with sour dill pickles (thinly sliced crosswise), pieces of thinly sliced white onion, and small strips of pickled mild red peppers.

- Small squares of dark rye or pumpernickel bread spread with horseradish-spiked sour cream, topped with a thin slice of cold roast beef, and garnished with thinly sliced sour dill pickle.

- Small squares of buttered rye bread topped with a thin slice of cucumber, a dab of mustard, and a piece of pickled herring or canned sprats (drained).

- Small squares of brown bread spread with mayonnaise, topped with a thin slice of cucumber and a piece of lightly pickled herring, garnished with fresh dill.

- Small squares of dark rye bread topped with **Russian Garlic Cheese** (recipe, page 321), garnished with half a cherry tomato and a sprig of flat-leaf parsley.

▶ **NOTE:** At home, we make these appetizers with French-style baguettes and Rubschlager-brand cocktail breads (2½ inches square)—Pumpernickel, Cocktail Rye, Honey Whole Grain—usually available at large supermarkets and delicatessens. You can also use thin slices of *firm* dark bread, quartered or cut into triangles. *Unsalted* butter is essential because many of the toppings are already salty. Unsalted herbed butters are good spreads for bread, too, as are mayonnaise and sour cream. Use only best-quality caviar. Colman's Original English Mustard is a good substitute for Russian hot-spicy mustard.

# Russian Beet, Potato, and Sauerkraut Salad
## (*Vinegret*)

*Russians love beets, eating them year round in soups, salads, pickles, and savory pies. Our Russian friends often served this popular beet salad as one of several* zakuski *crowded onto the table at the start of a meal. Every cook seemed to have her own special recipe. Some included green peas, chopped dill pickles, cubes of peeled apple, or a handful of golden raisins. Good cooks also recommended roasting the beets instead of boiling them, which makes for a richer flavor.*

## Salad

1 cup coarsely chopped walnuts
2 to 3 large beets, unpeeled
Vegetable oil
2 medium boiling potatoes, peeled
2 medium carrots, peeled
1 cup cooked red or white beans (optional)
1 cup chopped onion
2 cups mild sauerkraut, rinsed under cold water and drained well

## Dressing

¼ cup red wine vinegar
1 teaspoon dry mustard
1 teaspoon salt
1 teaspoon ground black pepper
½ teaspoon sugar
¼ cup sunflower oil

- Toast the walnuts in a single layer on a baking sheet in a preheated 350°F. oven for 6 to 8 minutes. Set aside until shortly before serving.

- Increase the oven heat to 400°F. Wash and dry the unpeeled beets and rub them lightly with vegetable oil. Bake the beets on a baking sheet lined with foil, for about 1 hour or until tender when pierced with a fork. When the beets are still warm, but cool enough to handle, peel and cut them into ½-inch cubes (or smaller).

- Meanwhile, cook the potatoes in lightly salted boiling water for 10 minutes. Add the carrots and cook about 10 minutes longer, depending on the size of the vegetables, until they are tender but not mushy. Drain in a colander, let cool, and cut into ½-inch cubes (or smaller).

- Combine the beets, potatoes, carrots, (optional) beans, onions, and sauerkraut in a large bowl. Toss gently, taking care not to crush the vegetables.

- Make the dressing by whisking together the vinegar, dry mustard, salt, pepper, and sugar in a small bowl. Slowly add the sunflower oil, whisking until all the oil has been incorporated into the dressing. Pour over the vegetables and toss together gently.

- Cover and refrigerate until 30 minutes before serving time. Add the toasted walnuts to the salad and toss to combine well. Let the salad sit at room temperature for 20 to 30 minutes before serving.

- Makes 6 to 8 servings.

# Sauerkraut-and-Bacon Salad

*Salads made with sauerkraut are popular winter dishes in Russia. I like to make this one a day in advance and refrigerate it overnight, to let the flavors meld. If you don't have home-made sauerkraut, use bottled instead (it's generally better than canned). For an even more substantial salad or cold side dish, add some cooked ham cut into small cubes.*

**¾ cup coarsely chopped walnuts**
**4 to 6 strips of bacon, finely chopped**
**½ cup sunflower oil (or walnut oil)**
**2 tablespoons apple cider vinegar**
**½ teaspoon freshly ground black pepper**
**½ to 1 teaspoon sugar**
**2 pounds mild sauerkraut, rinsed under cold water and drained well**
**2 medium-size sweet red apples, cored, peeled, and diced into ½-inch cubes**

- Toast the walnuts on a baking sheet in a preheated 350°F. oven for 6 to 8 minutes. Let cool before using. Fry the bacon pieces in a skillet over medium-high heat until crisp, then drain on paper towels.

- Whisk together the oil, vinegar, black pepper, and ½ to 1 teaspoon sugar (depending on how sweet you like your salads), until the sugar is dissolved and the mixture begins to thicken.

- Combine the sauerkraut and apples in a large bowl, tossing to mix well. Pour the dressing over the salad and toss well again. Add the walnuts and toss once more. Just before serving, crumble the bacon pieces over the top of each serving.

- Makes 6 to 8 servings.

# Spicy Butternut Squash Salad

*Alla's recipe for this colorful, sweet-spicy autumn appetizer uses two seasonal ingredients popular in the Russian Far East, butternut squash and hot red peppers. Alla also liked to use shredded butternut squash for making pancakes and fritters.*

**One 2½-pound butternut squash**
**½-pound boneless pork chop, cut into ½-inch cubes (about 1 cup of pork cubes)**
**6 tablespoons sunflower oil (divided use)**
**1 tablespoon apple cider vinegar**
**½ teaspoon salt**
**3 to 4 fresh hot red peppers (cayennes, arbols, or Thai), cut crosswise into very thin rings**

- Preheat the oven to 400°F. Cut the squash in half vertically, scoop out the strings and seeds, and place the squash cut side up on a baking sheet. Brush the cut sides with 1 tablespoon of sunflower oil.

- Bake for 45 to 50 minutes, or just until the squash is tender but not mushy. Cool completely, then peel and cut into ½-inch cubes (about 4 cups of cooked squash cubes).

- Sauté the pork cubes in 2 tablespoons of hot sunflower oil in a skillet over medium-high heat until the pork is lightly browned on all sides and no longer pink in the middle. Drain on paper towels and cool completely.

- Whisk together the vinegar, salt, and remaining 3 tablespoons of sunflower oil until the mixture is cloudy and thick. Gently toss the squash, pork, and peppers together in a large bowl, then pour in the dressing, and toss again. Cover and refrigerate for several hours or overnight. Let the salad sit at room temperature for 10 to 15 minutes before serving.

- Makes 4 to 6 servings.

# White Radish Salad

*In the Russian Far East, this salad is made with large white daikon radishes. On the European side of Russia, it's made with the large bulbous white radishes that grow there. Either way, it's a good creamy-crunchy side dish to serve with pork or ham.*

**2 large daikon radishes, peeled and shredded**
**1 teaspoon salt**
**1 teaspoon sugar**
**2 large hard-boiled eggs, peeled and chopped**
**1 apple, peeled, cored, and shredded**
**6 tablespoons pure sour cream**

- Put the shredded daikon in a large glass bowl. Sprinkle in the salt and sugar, and toss the ingredients to mix well. Let the daikon sit at room temperature for 30 minutes.

- Transfer the daikon to a large sieve, and press firmly on the shredded pieces to squeeze out as much moisture as possible. (Discard the liquid.)

- Return the daikon to the bowl, toss with a fork to separate the pieces, and add the boiled eggs and shredded apple, tossing again to mix. Stir in the sour cream, mixing gently but thoroughly. Serve immediately or refrigerate up to 1 day.

- Makes 6 to 8 servings.

**Fiddlehead ferns at a farmers' market in Vladivostok, 2006.**

# Fiddlehead Ferns with Pork and Paprika

*One of my favorite foods in the Russian Far East was Alla's* paporotniki *(ferns) cooked with pork and paprika, a hot-spicy dish that originated in nearby Korea. If fiddlehead ferns aren't available, you can substitute an equal weight of asparagus. Some Russians add a shredded carrot or a teaspoon of tomato paste to this dish for extra color and flavor.*

**1 pound fresh or frozen fiddlehead ferns***
**3 tablespoons sunflower oil (divided use)**
**¾-pound boneless pork loin chops, cut into ⅓-inch cubes**
**2 medium onions, chopped medium-fine**
**3 to 4 large garlic cloves, minced**
**1 tablespoon mild (sweet) paprika**
**1 tablespoon medium-hot or very hot paprika**
**½ cup chicken stock**
**¼ teaspoon salt (or more to taste)**

***Or 1 pound fresh green asparagus stalks (see substitution at end of recipe).**

- Wash fresh fiddlehead ferns thoroughly, removing any dirt and papery brown particles clinging to them. Trim 1 inch off the stem ends of fresh ferns. Blanch the ferns in boiling salted water for 2 minutes, or steam them over rapidly boiling water for 3 to 5 minutes. Drain the ferns in a colander, quickly plunge them into a bowl of very cold water, then drain again in the colander. Cut the ferns into 3- to 4-inch lengths. (Since frozen fiddleheads have already been blanched, just thaw them at room temperate before using.)

- Heat 1 tablespoon of sunflower oil in a large (12-inch) skillet, and sauté the pork over medium-high heat until lightly browned. Set the pork aside in a bowl.

- Heat the remaining 2 tablespoons of oil in the skillet and sauté the onions over medium-high heat until soft and golden, but not browned. Add the garlic and sauté for 1 minute more. Reduce the heat to low, sprinkle in all the paprika, and cook, stirring constantly, for 1 minute. Add the pork, stirring until all the pieces are coated with paprika.

- Pour in the chicken stock, mix well, and increase the heat to medium. Add the cooked fiddlehead ferns and salt, tossing gently until all the ingredients are combined.

- Cover the skillet and cook over medium heat for 8 to 10 minutes until the pork and ferns are heated throughout. Taste and add more salt if you want.

- Serve hot or at room temperature as an appetizer, or hot as a main dish accompanied by white rice.

- Makes 6 servings as an appetizer or 4 servings as a main dish.

▶ **Asparagus substitute:** Wash the asparagus and trim off the tough stem ends. Blanch the asparagus in boiling salted water for 3 to 4 minutes, or steam it over boiling water for 6 to 8 minutes, depending on its thickness. Drain the asparagus, plunge it into a bowl of very cold water, and drain in a colander. Cut the asparagus into 3- to 4-inch lengths. (Since frozen asparagus has already been blanched, just thaw it at room temperate before using.)

## Fiddling with Ferns

Fiddleheads are the unfurling fronds of bright green ferns that grow wild in Siberia and the Russian Far East. A favorite food of foragers, the young shoots of these ferns are picked in the summer and cooked fresh, or preserved by drying or salting for use later in the year.

Fiddlehead ferns also grow wild in some parts of Canada, the United States, and northern Europe, where they're sold fresh in farmers' markets and specialty stores in the spring. A few stores also stock brined or frozen fiddleheads year round.

Fresh fiddlehead ferns must be cleaned and their stem ends trimmed off, then blanched, boiled, or steamed before being used in most recipes. Both the dried ferns (which are dull brown in color) and salted ferns (olive green, preserved in jars) must be soaked in several changes of cold water for 24 hours before cooking. Frozen fiddleheads are the most convenient to use. But fresh, frozen, or bottled, they're all pricey. When cooked, they taste somewhat like young green asparagus, which is an acceptable substitute if fiddlehead ferns aren't available.

# Russian Small Savory Pies

## (*Pirozhki*)

*My little* pirozhki *are made with a simple pastry dough that can be either baked or fried. When making any bread or pastry, remember to follow Tom's advice: "Listen to your hands. They'll tell you when the dough is mixed or kneaded just right."*

### Filling

**Make the filling in advance so it can cool before using. (See the following recipes for three different fillings: meat, sauerkraut, potato-bacon.)**

### Dough

**3 cups all-purpose flour**
**2 teaspoons sugar**
**1 teaspoon salt**
**¼ pound (1 stick) cold unsalted butter**
**1 large egg, well beaten**
**½ to ⅔ cup cold milk**

### Glaze

**1 large egg beaten lightly with 1 tablespoon milk**

- Whisk together the flour, sugar, and salt in a large bowl. Cut the cold butter into small pieces over the flour mixture. Use a pastry cutter to blend the flour and butter together until the mixture resembles coarse breadcrumbs and no big lumps of butter remain.

- Stir in the beaten egg. Add the cold milk, 1 or 2 tablespoons at a time, mixing with the spoon, then with your hands, lightly kneading the ingredients together in the bowl to form a soft, smooth dough. Add only enough milk to make a smooth dough that is neither crumbly nor wet (usually 8 to 9 tablespoons is enough).

- Cover the bowl with a kitchen towel and let the dough sit at room temperature for 30 minutes. Preheat the oven to 400°F.

- Divide the dough in half, keeping one half covered with the towel. Roll out the other half on a lightly floured surface, to a thickness of $\frac{1}{8}$ inch. Use a 4-inch round cookie cutter to cut the dough into circles, setting them aside on a lightly floured surface. Roll and cut the remaining half of dough, re-rolling and cutting any scraps, to make a total of 16 to 18 circles of pastry dough.

- Working with 1 circle of dough at a time, roll the dough slightly thinner, then place 1 heaping tablespoon of filling in the center of the circle. Use your finger to moisten the edge of the circle lightly with water, then fold the dough in half, over the filling, to form a half-moon shape. Press the edges together with the tines of a fork, to seal them tightly. Repeat with the remaining dough circles.

▶ **To bake *pirozhki*:**

- Preheat the oven to 400°F. Place half of the filled pastries on a large ungreased baking sheet. Brush the egg-milk glaze lightly over the tops. Bake on the middle rack of the oven for 15 to 18 minutes, or until the tops are lightly browned. Glaze and bake the remaining half of the pastries. Serve hot.

- Makes 16 to 18 *pirozhki*.

▶ **Freezing/reheating options:**

- Baked, non-frozen *pirozhki* can be reheated on a baking sheet for 5 minutes in a preheated 400°F. oven.

- Baked *pirozhki* can also be frozen and reheated (directly from the freezer) in a preheated 350°F. oven for 10 to 15 minutes.

▶ **To fry *pirozhki*:**

- Do not glaze the pastries with the egg wash. Deep-fry the pastries in hot oil (375°F.) for about 4 to 5 minutes, until they are a rich medium-brown color. Drain on paper towels and serve hot.

- Makes 16 to 18 *pirozhki*.

▶ **Freezing/frying/reheating options:**

- Freeze the uncooked pastries and later fry the frozen pies in hot oil (375°F.) for 5 minutes or until browned.

- Fry the pastries, let them cool to room temperature, refrigerate for a day or two, and reheat on a baking sheet in a preheated 350°F. oven for 5 minutes.

- Fry the pastries, freeze, and reheat them directly from the freezer, on a baking sheet in a preheated 350°F. oven for 15 minutes.

# Doughnuts of the Last Tsar

The little pies called *pirozhki* (singular *pirozhok*) are made with either a yeast dough or a pastry dough, stuffed with whatever suits the cook's fancy—meat, fish, mushrooms, potatoes, sauerkraut, cabbage, sorrel, rice, hard-boiled eggs with green onion tops, fresh curd cheese, pumpkin, fruit or berry preserves, you name it—then either baked or fried. We often bought this popular street food from vendors near the harbor in Vladivostok. Tom dubbed the fried yeast-dough versions "doughnuts of the last tsar" because they were sometimes greasier than we liked. We also made them at home to eat like Russians do, as a snack food or an accompaniment to soups.

# Condiments

A selection of condiments can also be found crowded onto the Russian dinner table, many of them used as garnishes for the *zakuski* appetizers: pots of hot-spicy Russian mustard and home-preserved horseradish, a small cruet of white or black vinegar, and, in the Russian Far East, a bottle of soy sauce. Salt and pepper are often served in a three-part set, where paprika (mild, medium, or hot) is the other spice on the table. And if black pepper isn't available, hot paprika is often the substitute.

# Pirozhki Fillings

## (Meat, Sauerkraut, Potato-Bacon)

*Each of these filling recipes makes enough for 16 to 18* pirozhki. *Make the filling first, so it will be cool when you're ready to assemble the* pirozhki *before baking or frying. (If there's a bit of filling left over, freeze it to toss into your next soup or stew.)*

### Meat Filling

**1 pound ground beef or pork**
**2 tablespoons sunflower oil**
**½ cup finely chopped onion**
**2 large garlic cloves, minced**
**½ teaspoon freshly ground black pepper**
**¼ teaspoon salt**
**¼ teaspoon ground allspice**
**2 tablespoons mayonnaise**

- Cook the ground meat in a skillet over medium-high heat, breaking up the meat into small pieces, until it is completely browned. Transfer the meat and all the juices to a bowl.

- Heat the oil in the skillet, and sauté the onion until golden. Add the garlic and sauté 2 minutes longer. Stir the onion mixture and all the oil from the skillet into the meat in the bowl. Stir in the pepper, salt, and allspice, mixing well. Cool thoroughly, then stir in the mayonnaise, mixing well.

- Makes 2 cups.

### Sauerkraut Filling

**2 cups sauerkraut (about 1 pound), rinsed and well drained before measuring**
**¼ cup finely chopped onions**
**¼ cup peeled and finely shredded carrots**
**½ cup white wine**
**½ teaspoon white wine vinegar (optional)**
**½ teaspoon caraway seeds**
**¼ teaspoon freshly ground black pepper**

- Rinse the sauerkraut under cold water and drain it well, squeezing out as much moisture as you can before measuring out 2 cups of it.

- Combine all the ingredients in a saucepan and cook over medium heat, stirring frequently, for 15 to 20 minutes, until the onions are soft. Transfer the mixture to a shallow bowl to cool completely before using.

- Makes 2 cups.

## Potato-Bacon Filling

**2 cups firm waxy potatoes, peeled and cut into ¼-inch cubes before measuring**
**1 strip thick-slice bacon, cut into ¼-inch squares**
**¼ cup finely chopped onions**
**2 teaspoons white vinegar**
**¼ teaspoon salt**
**¼ teaspoon freshly ground black pepper**

- Steam the potato cubes (or boil them gently), just until tender but not falling apart. Drain thoroughly.

- Cook the bacon in a small skillet over medium-high heat until it just begins to brown. Add the bacon to the potatoes in the bowl, leaving the bacon fat in the skillet. Sauté the onions in the bacon fat until golden. Turn off the heat and stir in the vinegar, scraping any browned bits of bacon off the bottom of the skillet. Stir in the salt and pepper.

- Add the onion mixture to the potatoes, stirring gently until all the ingredients are well combined. Cool before using.

- Makes 2 cups.

# Chicken-and-Vegetable Borshch

*Galina Korotkina liked to make this light, healthy version of* borshch *during the sultry hot summers in Vladivostok. Even though it contains water, she called it her "No-Water Borshch" because the vegetables first sweat in their own juices before being cooked with the other ingredients.*

4 cups (packed) shredded green cabbage
2 medium beets, peeled and coarsely shredded
1 large carrot, peeled and coarsely shredded
2 teaspoons salt (divided use)
1 cup water
2 boneless, skinless chicken breast halves, cut into ½-inch-square pieces
3 medium red potatoes, peeled and cut Into ½-Inch cubes
1 tablespoon tomato paste
1 bay leaf
5 cups water (or chicken stock for an even richer flavor)
2 tablespoons olive oil
1 medium onion, chopped
12 grape tomatoes, halved
2 large garlic cloves, minced
2 tablespoons finely chopped fresh dill
15-ounce can Great Northern beans (or other white beans), rinsed and
   drained

Garnish

**Chopped fresh dill**

- Combine the cabbage, beets, carrot, 1 teaspoon salt, and 1 cup of water in a large soup pot. Bring the mixture to a boil, reduce the heat, cover, and simmer for 30 minutes, stirring the vegetables two or three times while they cook.

- Stir in the chicken, potatoes, tomato paste, bay leaf, and 5 cups of water or chicken stock. Bring the mixture to a boil, reduce the heat, partially cover the pot, and simmer for 20 minutes.

- Meanwhile, heat the olive oil in a medium skillet and sauté the onion over medium-high heat until soft. Stir in the grape tomato halves and garlic and sauté for 3 minutes more.

- Add the sautéed ingredients, 2 tablespoons chopped dill, and 1 teaspoon salt to the soup. Simmer, partially covered, for 10 minutes more, then stir in the white beans and simmer for another 10 to 15 minutes. Taste and add more salt if desired.

- Serve hot, ladled into soup bowls and garnished with a generous sprinkling of fresh dill.

- Makes 6 to 8 servings.

# Stuffed Squid

*This recipe from Galina Tarasova's nieces, Svetlana and Yelena, shows the influence of nearby China and Korea on the cooking of Russians in Vladivostok. It uses pre-cleaned squid tubes for convenience, which you can find at many Asian food markets in the United States. If you purchase squid tubes that have the tentacles in the package, too, you can parboil the tentacles for 2 minutes, then finely chop them to use in place of the crab in this recipe.*

1 tablespoon sunflower oil
1 cup finely chopped green onions (white bottoms and green tops)
1 cup peeled and finely shredded carrots
2 cups cooked short- or medium-grain rice, cooled
1 cup cooked crab meat
1 large garlic clove, squeezed through a garlic press
¾ teaspoon salt
6 medium-large squid tubes, each about 7 inches long (1¾ pounds total, without tentacles)
½ cup mayonnaise

Garnish

Spicy Soy Sauces (recipes follow)

- Sauté the onion in hot sunflower oil, in a skillet over medium-high heat, until soft. Remove from the heat, stir in the carrots, and let the mixture cool slightly. Using a fork, mix together well the onions, carrots, rice, crab, garlic, and salt in a bowl.

- Preheat the oven to 400°F. Rinse the squid tubes well with cold water and drain in a colander. Pat them dry, inside and out, with paper towels.

- Spoon the stuffing into each squid tube, but don't pack it in tightly. Close the openings with toothpicks.

- Place the squid in a single layer in a lightly oiled 13 × 9-inch glass baking dish. Spread the mayonnaise evenly over the top of the squid. Bake, uncovered, at 400°F. for 25 minutes.

- Transfer the squid to a large plate and let them sit at room temperature for 10 to 15 minutes. Then slice each squid into quarters, crosswise on a slight diagonal. Serve with Spicy Soy Sauces to spoon over the squid at the table.

- Makes 6 servings as a main dish or 12 servings as an appetizer.

▶ **Spicy Soy Sauces (two versions)**

- Whisk together ½ cup Chinese light soy sauce, 2 large garlic cloves (squeezed through a garlic press), and 1 teaspoon hot red pepper flakes. Let sit at room temperature for 30 minutes before using. Serve in a small bowl at the table.

- Whisk together ½ cup Chinese light soy sauce, 2 large garlic cloves (squeezed through a garlic press), and 2 teaspoons wasabi or freshly grated horseradish. Let sit at room temperature for 30 minutes before using. Serve in a small bowl at the table.

## Sakhalin Summer Snack

One of Granny Polina's favorite summer snacks on Sakhalin Island was a freshly picked cucumber, straight off the vine and still tasting of the sun, dipped into honey and eaten raw. Try it with the freshest, greenest, unwaxed, small cucumbers you can find.

# "Salmon in a Coat"

*"Herring in a Coat" or "Herring under a Blanket" is a classic Russian cold appetizer composed of layers of salted herring, sliced potatoes, and sliced beets, covered with a coating of mayonnaise or sour cream (recipe, page 155). This very different Vladivostok recipe for "Salmon in a Coat" is a hot main dish of salmon seasoned with soy sauce and baked under a mantle of garlic-flavored mayonnaise.*

**2 cups full-fat mayonnaise**
**2 tablespoons all-purpose flour**
**4 large garlic cloves, squeezed through a garlic press**
**One 2-pound fresh salmon fillet, skin and any remaining bones removed**
**Soy sauce**

## Garnish

**Fresh lemon wedges**
**Chopped fresh cilantro**

▶ **NOTE:** Start preparing this dish at least 1-½ hours before you plan to serve it.

- Whisk together the mayonnaise and flour until the mixture is smooth, then whisk in the garlic. Cover and refrigerate for 30 minutes.

- Meanwhile, wash the salmon, pat it dry with paper towels, and set it flat, with the former skin side down, in a lightly oiled non-aluminum baking pan just large enough to hold the salmon. Brush the entire top surface of the salmon with soy sauce, and refrigerate until the mayonnaise finishes chilling.

- Spread the cold mayonnaise mixture evenly over the top and sides of the salmon (like frosting a cake). Refrigerate the fish, uncovered, for 30 minutes more. Preheat the oven to 400°F.

- Bake, uncovered, at 400°F. for 20 to 25 minutes, depending on the thickness of the fish.

- Serve hot, garnished with lemon wedges and a sprinkling of cilantro, and accompanied by white rice.

- Makes 6 servings.

▶ **VARIATION:** Omit the flour and soy sauce. Whisk into the mayonnaise 6 tablespoons of mild paprika (smoked or not), 1 tablespoon dried lemon pepper, and 1 tablespoon dried hot red pepper flakes (optional), along with the garlic. Refrigerate 30 minutes before spreading on the salmon.

# The Captain's Chicken

*This sizeable casserole-for-a-crowd is Galina Korotkina's recipe for her chicken version of "The Captain's Meat," made with boneless chicken breasts baked between layers of root vegetables. For special occasions Galina also roasted a whole chicken stuffed with onions and raisins, then comically styled it as a "sea captain," to serve alongside the casserole.*

1 teaspoon salt
¾ teaspoon finely ground black pepper
½ teaspoon dried thyme
½ teaspoon dried ground sage
½ teaspoon dried marjoram
½ teaspoon freshly ground nutmeg
¼ teaspoon ground cayenne pepper
2 bay leaves, finely crushed
3 pounds firm boiling potatoes, peeled and thinly sliced crosswise into rounds (or cut with the 4 mm blade of a food processor or mandoline)
4 large carrots, peeled and sliced diagonally into ¼-inch-thick ovals
⅓ cup dark raisins
⅓ cup golden raisins
3 pounds boneless, skinless chicken breast halves, each cut lengthwise into 4 pieces, then crosswise in half
2 large white onions, sliced in half vertically, then crosswise into ¼-inch-thick pieces
3 large garlic cloves, minced
1 cup chicken stock
2 cups coarsely shredded hard yellow cheese (such as Jarlsberg)
1 cup full-fat mayonnaise

*Galina Korotkina preparing "The Captain's Chicken" in her modern kitchen in Vladivostok, 2006.*

- Preheat the oven to 400°F. Oil a 15 × 10-inch (or 14 × 11-inch) deep-sided baking pan, lasagna pan, or roasting pan. (The pan size is important for correct baking.)

- Mix together the salt, black pepper, thyme, sage, marjoram, nutmeg, cayenne pepper, and bay leaves in a small bowl.

- Arrange the potato slices in an even layer in the baking pan. Add a layer of carrot slices and scatter the raisins over the carrots. Place the chicken pieces in a single layer on top. Sprinkle the spice mixture evenly over the chicken and vegetables. Add a layer of onions and sprinkle with the garlic. Carefully pour the chicken stock around the edges of the pan. Top with an even layer of shredded cheese. Use a squirt bottle to squiggle the mayonnaise over the cheese layer.

- Cover the casserole tightly with foil. Bake at 400°F. for 30 minutes, then remove the foil and bake 15 minutes more. Let the casserole sit at room temperature for 10 minutes before serving.

- Serve hot as a main dish accompanied by a tomato, bell pepper, and onion salad dressed with white vinegar and sunflower oil.

- Makes 8 to 12 servings.

## The Captain's Meat

"The Captain's Meat" is a Vladivostok specialty, made by restaurants and home cooks alike. Both Alla and Galina Korotkina said that when mariners returned home to the port city on the Pacific—after months of eating fish, fish, and more fish at sea—they had a craving for rich, hearty dishes made with meat: pork, beef, chicken, anything but fish. And they came home with plenty of money to spend on more expensive meat dishes, too. So local cooks concocted "The Captain's Meat," a shallow baked casserole often made of tender medallions of beef or pork layered with thinly sliced potatoes and onions (sometimes carrots and tomatoes, too), usually with shredded cheese or mayonnaise on top. (See Alla's recipe for **The Captain's Meat**, page 224).

# Russian Salmon Pie

## (*Kulebyaka*)

*This classic Russian fish pie has several layers of savory filling enclosed between two crusts decorated with pretty pastry-dough cut-outs. Yes, it takes time to make—but it's well worth the effort. You can even prepare all the ingredients a day in advance, then assemble and bake the pie the next day. In Europe we made* kulebyaka (coulibiac) *the French way, with puff pastry. In Siberia, for convenience, we made it with fresh yeast dough (testo) bought at local markets. But I still like the plain pastry-dough version that I learned to make a decade before we moved to Russia. Whatever kind of dough you use,* kulebyaka *makes an impressive presentation for a dinner party.*

## Pastry dough

**4 cups all-purpose flour**
**1 teaspoon salt**
**½ pound (2 sticks) cold unsalted butter**
**⅓ cup chilled solid vegetable shortening**
**½ cup ice water**
**2 tablespoons cold vodka**

## Filling

**1 pound boneless, skinless salmon fillets, cut into 3-inch squares**
**¾ cup water**
**¾ cup dry white wine**
**½ teaspoon salt**
**10 tablespoons unsalted butter (divided use), plus butter for the baking sheet**
**¾ cup raw medium-grain rice**
**3 tablespoons finely chopped fresh dill**
**3 tablespoons finely chopped fresh parsley**
**½ teaspoon freshly ground black pepper**
**1 pound fresh white mushrooms (champignons), thinly sliced**
**1 large onion, finely chopped**
**3 tablespoons dry breadcrumbs**
**2 tablespoons fresh lemon juice**
**4 large hard-boiled eggs**

42

## Glaze

**1 large egg beaten with 1 tablespoon milk or cream**

▶ **TIP:** Use an egg slicer to cut the mushrooms and eggs.

▶ **Pastry dough:** Whisk the flour and salt together in a large bowl. Cut the cold butter and vegetable shortening into small pieces over the flour. Use a pastry blender to combine the flour, butter, and shortening until the mixture resembles coarse breadcrumbs and no large lumps remain. Pour the ice water and vodka over the flour mixture. Working quickly, use your fingers to combine the dry and wet ingredients. The pastry dough should feel like modeling clay. If it seems too dry, add a little more ice water, 1 or 2 drops at a time, working it into the dough with your fingers until the mixture can be gathered up into a ball.

- Divide the dough into 2 portions, one slightly larger than the other. Shape each portion into a flat rectangle 1-inch thick. Wrap the 2 portions separately in plastic wrap and refrigerate at least 3 hours or until needed.

▶ **Filling:** Put the salmon pieces in a single layer in a large (12-inch) skillet. Add the water, wine, and salt. Bring the liquid to a simmer over medium heat. Turn the salmon over and partially cover the skillet. Reduce the heat to low. Poach the fish for 5 to 7 minutes, depending on its thickness. Use a slotted spoon to transfer the fish to a bowl to cool. Pour the poaching liquid into a glass measuring cup, measuring out 1-½ cups of liquid. If there is not enough, add more white wine.

- Melt 2 tablespoons of butter over medium heat in a heavy-bottom saucepan. Add the raw rice and cook in the hot butter, stirring constantly, for 3 minutes. Pour in the 1-½ cups of poaching liquid and bring to a boil over high heat. Reduce the heat to low, cover the pan tightly, and cook for 20 minutes. Set aside to cool, then stir in the dill, parsley, and black pepper.

- While the rice is cooking, heat 3 tablespoons of butter in the large skillet over medium-high heat. When it begins to bubble, sauté the sliced mushrooms until they are tender and very little liquid is left in the skillet. Transfer the mushrooms to a bowl to cool.

- Melt 3 tablespoons of butter in the same skillet over medium-high heat. When it begins to bubble, add the onion and sauté until soft and golden, about 5 to 7 minutes. Combine with the mushrooms.

▶ **NOTE:** At this point, all the ingredients can be used right away or refrigerated, separately, until needed.

▶ **To assemble the *kulebyaka*:** Remove the chilled pastry dough from the refrigerator and let it sit, still wrapped, at room temperature for 30 minutes. (If you've refrigerated all the cooked ingredients overnight, remove them from the refrigerator, too.) Lightly butter a large baking sheet.

- Roll out the smaller portion of dough on a lightly floured surface, to form a rectangle measuring 8 × 16 inches, ⅛-inch thick. Trim off the rough edges with a knife and save the dough scraps for decorating the *kulebyaka*. Roll up the dough over your rolling pin and unroll it onto the baking sheet. Sprinkle the breadcrumbs evenly over the dough, leaving a border of 1 inch uncovered around the edges. Whisk together the lemon juice and 2 tablespoons of melted butter.

- Spread half the rice in an even layer over the breadcrumbs, leaving uncovered that 1-inch margin along the edges of the dough. Drizzle some of the lemon-butter mixture over the rice. Add an even layer of half the mushrooms and onions on top of the rice. Drizzle with some of the lemon butter. Place the salmon in an even layer on top of the mushroom mixture, and drizzle with the remainder of the lemon butter. (If some of the fish pieces are very thick, slice them in half horizontally.) As you add each layer, press the ingredients together with your hands to form a compact, rectangular loaf. Slice the hard-boiled eggs crosswise with an egg slicer and place a layer of eggs on top of the fish. Now reverse the order, adding a layer of the remaining mushrooms and onions, then a layer of rice, patting the ingredients together into a loaf shape as you work. Brush the exposed rim of dough with the egg-milk glaze.

- Roll out the larger dough portion to a rectangle measuring 10 × 18 inches, ⅛-inch thick. Trim the edges with a knife and save the dough scraps. Roll up the dough over your rolling pin and unroll it over the filling. Press the top and bottom edges of the dough together well on each side of the *kulebyaka*. Seal the pie by crimping the dough all the way around with the tines of a fork or a pastry crimper, or by pleating the edges together with your fingers.

- Cut a 1-inch-diameter hole in the center of the top crust (like the blowhole of a whale) to let the steam escape as the pie bakes. Roll out the dough scraps and cut them into decorative shapes of your choice (flowers, leaves, mushrooms, fish, etc.). Moisten the backsides with water and arrange the decorations on the top crust, pressing them gently to adhere. Refrigerate the unbaked *kulebyaka* for 20 minutes while you pre-heat the oven to 400°F.

- Brush the entire surface of the top crust with the egg-milk glaze. Bake at 400°F. on the middle rack of the oven for 50 to 60 minutes, until the pastry is golden-brown. Let the *kulebyaka* cool on the pan for a few minutes, then carefully transfer it to a large serving platter. Use a serrated knife to cut it crosswise into 2-inch thick slices.

- Serve warm, accompanied by a green salad and dry white wine or ice-cold lemon vodka.

- Makes 8 large servings.

▶ **NOTE:** This recipe makes a rectangular *kulebyaka*, but you can also cut the dough into a large oval or even a fish shape (and decorate it with pastry-dough "scales").

▶ **WASTE NOT:** Freeze any leftover dough scraps for making little individual savory pies (*pirozhki*).

# Kulebyaka: King of Pies

Although I'd read about *kulebyaka* in Russian novels and cookbooks, the first time I tasted it was in France in the early 1980s. At a fancy delicatessen in Paris, Tom and I bought takeout slices of this savory salmon pie (*coulibiac* in French) and a little tub of Russian potato salad for a springtime picnic in the Tuileries Garden. From the tsar's table to a Parisian park bench, that recipe had traveled a long way. One bite—and we knew why.

The first time we made *kulebyaka* at home was a couple of years later, in Munich, for a dinner party. Two of the guests, Sasha and Svetlana, were defectors from the Soviet Union who'd lived in Germany for several years. Knowing our interest in Russian food, they brought us a wonderful hostess gift that evening—a 1955 edition of *Kniga o vkusnoi i zdorovoi pishche (Book of Tasty and Healthy Food)*, Russia's twentieth-century equivalent of America's classic *Joy of Cooking*.

"What a beautiful *kulebyaka*!" exclaimed Svetlana when I brought my salmon pie to the table that evening. I'd made it in the shape of a large fish, covered with "fish scales" cut out of pastry dough. After I'd sliced the pie and served all the guests, I asked Svetlana—with trepidation, I admit—if my *kulebyaka* actually looked and tasted like an authentic Russian one. "I wouldn't know," she laughed, "We never ate anything this elegant in Moscow!"

# Siberian Frozen Cranberry Cream

*Alla's Siberian grandmother made this winter dessert by combining wild berries with thick sweet cream or sour cream, tvorog (fresh curd cheese), and sugar pulverized with a mortar and pestle. She then dropped dollops of it onto a baking sheet, and set it out on the verandah to freeze. I've updated the recipe by adding a bit of lemon juice and vanilla and serving it in bowls as an elegant frozen dessert garnished with pine nuts, another favorite Siberian wild food.* **Siberian Pine Nut Meringues** *(recipe, page 293) are a nice accompaniment, too.*

**2 cups fresh or frozen unsweetened cranberries (about 8 ounces in weight)**
**1 pound whole milk ricotta cheese (or farmer's cheese, or Russian *tvorog* cheese)**
**3 cups confectioners' sugar**
**1 tablespoon fresh lemon juice**
**1 teaspoon pure vanilla extract**
**2 cups heavy whipping cream, well chilled**

## Garnish

**1 cup toasted pine nuts, coarsely chopped**

- Stem and wash the cranberries; drain well in a colander. Grind the cranberries with the coarse blade of a meat grinder, or coarsely chop them in a food processor.

- Press the soft fresh cheese through a fine sieve into a large bowl. Stir in the confectioners' sugar, then beat the mixture by hand with a wooden spoon until no lumps remain. Stir in the cranberries, lemon juice, and vanilla. Cover the bowl and refrigerate for 30 minutes.

- Using an electric mixer, beat the whipping cream in another large bowl until very stiff. Fold the whipped cream into the cranberry mixture.

- Spoon the cranberry cream into individual dessert bowls or stemmed parfait glasses. Cover with plastic wrap and freeze until needed.

- Toast the pine nuts in a single layer on a baking sheet in a preheated 325°F. oven for about 8 minutes. Watch carefully so they don't burn! Cool completely before chopping.

- To serve, let the frozen cranberry cream sit, uncovered, at room temperature for 10 to 15 minutes, then garnish with toasted pine nuts sprinkled over the top.

- Makes approximately 8 cups (8 to 12 servings).

▶ **"FROZEN COOKIES":** You can also drop the cranberry cream mixture by heaping tablespoons onto 2 large baking sheets lined with waxed paper, spacing the dollops about 1 inch apart. Freeze until very firm. Makes approximately 50 "frozen cookies." Children love them!

# New Siberian Cuisine

In 2013 Tom and I were invited to organize a Siberian dinner for 85 members of a gastronomic society in England. The 6-course menu featured 15 different dishes, including a variety of *zakuski*, wild mushroom soup, *pel'meni* (stuffed Siberian dumplings) with venison and wild berries, and Siberian Frozen Cranberry Cream, all made from our recipes. Instead of serving the cranberry cream in parfait glasses (as the recipe suggests), the professional chef who cooked the meal modernized the dessert by plating it in the style of "New Nordic Cuisine," with a berries-in-the-forest theme. He froze the cranberry cream in a large metal pan, about 1-inch deep, then cut the frozen dessert into long rectangular bars, which he arranged seemingly haphazardly on each serving plate, like fallen logs in a forest, with edible leaves and berries sprinkled over them. The presentation was colorfully contemporary—and showed how a creative chef can successfully update an old-fashioned recipe.

# Chapter 2
# The Stove-from-Hell

## The High-Rise Village

In the mid-1990s we lived in three different apartments in Russia, one in Irkutsk and two in Vladivostok. All of them were located in huge, recently constructed high-rise buildings, housing thousands of people, on the outskirts of those cities. I came to think of these drab, ugly agglomerations of buildings as "high-rise villages": block after block of nearly identical towers made of gray prefabricated concrete, each 9 or 10 stories tall, encircled by barren fields of dirt that were frozen in winter, muddy in spring, dusty in summer. Around the buildings, rusty metal shipping containers served as makeshift garages, workshops, and storage sheds. Packs of hungry stray dogs scavenged the garbage that littered the landscape. Gangs of rowdy children built bonfires out of old tires and played inside the corroding skeletons of cars that had been stripped clean. No grass. No trees. No flowers. Not a pretty place.

The buildings themselves, their exterior surroundings, and their interior stairwells rivaled the worst American tenement housing for squalor and decay. The elevators seldom worked, so we had to lug our heavy shopping bags full of groceries and household supplies up the crudely finished, unlighted concrete stairs to our apartments on the upper floors. We always carried a flashlight to guide us over the obstacles often lying on the steps: dog feces, human vomit, rotting rubbish, broken bottles, smeared blood. Yet once we'd opened all the sturdy locks on the two steel-fronted doors to our apartment, we stepped into small but comfortable quarters similar in size and furnishings to apartments we'd rented in West German towns during the 1970s.

All three of our Russian apartments had an entry hall, small kitchen, living room, bedroom, bathroom only large enough for a tub and a sink, and a separate tiny closet for the toilet. The apartments in Vladivostok also had a second bedroom that we used as a home office (and a place to dry clothes on the radiator). A little balcony outside each apartment provided extra storage space (refrigerated

48

*Our high-rise village on the edge of Vladivostok, 1993.*

by nature, at least seven months of the year), where we kept big jars of preserved tomatoes, cucumbers, and sauerkraut, along with stacks of cabbages, winter squash, and root vegetables.

Our apartments ranged in floor space from 500 square feet in Irkutsk to 700 square feet in Vladivostok. Despite their small size, these Russian quarters were large by local standards, almost an embarrassment of space compared to the crowded conditions under which most Russians lived. But our brand-new Russian apartments suffered from the same shoddy construction characteristic of most buildings in that country: doors dropped off their hinges, drawers fell out of cabinets, linoleum buckled on the uneven concrete floor, and winter winds howled through double-glazed windows that were never properly sealed.

All three of our Russian kitchens were similar in size and basic appointments: approximately 12 feet long and 6 feet wide, with a porcelain sink attached to one wall, a few cheaply made pressboard-and-plastic-veneer cabinets, blue-green tile wainscoting in Vladivostok, painted plaster walls in Irkutsk. Underneath a small plastic-topped table were four low, square stools with hard seats and no backs. A separate dining room—with its own dining table and matching comfortable chairs—were luxuries that we could only dream about in Russia.

Both of our kitchens in Vladivostok were much better equipped than the one in Irkutsk, which had only a stove, a small refrigerator, a couple of cooking pans, and minimal tableware. In Vladivostok, we had a full-size Korean refrigerator, a Russian microwave oven, and a French combination food-processor-and-blender—all courtesy of the university where we taught, which provided these furnished apartments for the American faculty working there. The kitchen cabinets were stocked with a Russian-made porcelain dinner service and tea set for six, a gaudily painted electric samovar that reeked of lacquer whenever it heated up, an enameled kettle and two saucepans from China, a Teflon frying pan from Algeria, a set of Russian stainless-steel flatware, a couple of covered porcelain casseroles from Czechoslovakia, six Donald Duck drinking glasses, and two big Bart Simpson bath towels.

Each kitchen also had a Russian-made, three-burner electric stove. All of these stoves were defective in their own idiosyncratic ways. Tom dubbed our first one in Vladivostok "The Stove-from-Hell"—a name that aptly described the stoves in our later Russian apartments, too. None of the heating elements on the top functioned correctly, and sometimes they didn't work at all. The oven temperature knob had no control over the actual heat inside the oven: cookies burned on the bottom and remained raw on the top; a cake that normally required an hour to bake, burned black in 12 minutes; homemade pizzas sometimes browned too quickly at 50°C. (122°F.), other times cooked too slowly at 200°C. (392°F.). Worse yet, if all the heating elements on the top were turned on at the same time, the stove blew a fuse and knocked out the electricity in half the apartment.

We coped as best we could with the unpredictable heating elements, although they remained a constant source of frustration. And we gauged the oven temperature simply by sticking a hand inside, a technique we'd learned

## The Domovoi

Many Russians still harbor an ancient folk belief in the *domovoi*, a "house spirit" who lives underneath or behind the stove in their homes. In *Daily Life in Russia under the Last Tsar* (1962), Henri Troyat described the *domovoi* as "old and disheveled, with a hairy body and tail. He protected the family, shared in its daily life, amused himself in provoking a sleeper's snores, tangling a flirtatious woman's hair, hiding the master's boots, maddening the hen, and breaking the leg of a bench; but on the other hand he often healed the sick and appeased domestic quarrels." According to Troyat, other house spirits also "hid in the chimney, under the soil or amongst the beams," but the *domovoi* was their leader. So Tom and I blamed the *domovoi* whenever some unexplained mishap occurred in the apartment: when the electric fuses blew out or the tap water turned purple or the bread dough wouldn't rise, or when Tom accidentally tumped a bowl of eleven slimy egg whites into his empty shoes in the hallway, just before our guests arrived for a big dinner party.

many years before in the Scottish Highlands, where we did all of our baking in the fireplace oven of an old stone cottage. After months of putting up with the unreliable electric stoves in Vladivostok and Irkutsk, Tom concluded that he'd trade a "modern" Russian stove for an old-fashioned, wood-burning, open-hearth fireplace any day.

Even though our Russian apartments were supposed to be fully furnished, they lacked many basic appliances that most people take for granted in the West (automatic dishwasher, coffee maker, clothes dryer, telephone). But it was the unavailability of smaller things that we noticed most. When we first arrived in Vladivostok, none of the stores sold plastic wrap, waxed paper, aluminum foil, paper towels, or plastic bags. Instead, we used old student papers (homework assignments and exams) for paper towels in the kitchen. We saved all the thin aluminum foil from inside the wrappers of imported German chocolate bars, which we carefully washed, dried, smoothed flat, and pieced together to make larger sheets of foil for wrapping leftover foods. We washed, dried, and re-used for months every one of our own precious plastic bags that we'd brought from the United States, even the ones in which we carried home bloody cuts of unwrapped meat, dirty potatoes, and leaky liquids from the Russian markets several times each week. We rinsed and re-used every plastic bottle and glass jar that came filled with food from the stores. And we kept every piece of twine or wire tied around the paper lids of home-preserved jams from the farmers' markets, because twine and wire were in such short supply.

Simple cookware that had been sold in the West for decades wasn't available in Vladivostok and Irkutsk during most of the time we lived there: basic tin or aluminum cookie sheets, cake molds and pie pans, mortars and pestles, colanders and cheese graters, soufflé dishes and serrated knives—most of them standard kitchen items pictured in my Russian cookbooks from the Soviet era, but not to be found on the shelves of Vladivostok and Irkutsk in the mid-1990s. When I asked Russian cooks about this, they all said that you could buy those things "before"—a vague sometime in the past, where they remembered life in the Soviet Union being better than in the present—but that such items were now no longer in the stores. So we had to make do with whatever we could find.

Our only mixing bowls were two shallow, cheap, enameled-metal wash basins imported from China, which also did double duty as roasting pans. I could never find a bowl deep enough to beat more than two egg whites at a time—and none of my Russian friends owned one, either. We eventually did acquire two 20-centimeter (8-inch) round, gunmetal gray, non-stick cake pans from Algeria (the only cake pans we ever saw), which we called our

# Clutter-Free Kitchen

American cooks love kitchen gadgets. Our kitchen cupboards and drawers are stuffed with tools and machines designed to "take the work out of cooking." Some gadgets are indeed labor-savers, used over and over again for quickly slicing eggs or coring apples or zesting lemons. Others are used only once or twice, then languish in the backs of drawers or the dark corners of cabinets, never to be called upon for their services again.

Looking back with nostalgia, perhaps, to an earlier time, our Russian friends in the early 1990s assured us that many kinds of cooking utensils had been sold in Russia during the Soviet era. But their own kitchens didn't reflect such plenty. They were much more basic than most American kitchens, stocked with far fewer culinary tools. All the Russian kitchens had a big, heavy, hand-cranked, metal meat grinder, like the ones I remembered from my childhood in Texas—a useful tool indeed, but long ago supplanted by more modern devices in America. With fewer consumer goods available in Soviet times, Russians had improvised, as their ancestors had always done, with whatever was on hand. Following their grand-mothers' practice, Russians used goose feathers (still sold in urban stores in the early '90s) for brushing melted butter or egg washes onto pastries. Some cooks had a wooden whisk honed from a small tree branch with smaller, short branches sticking out from it on one end. And a friend told me about an excellent cook in Vladivostok who beat her egg whites to fluffy peaks for meringues, using only a plate and a fork. I was impressed. Who needs a whisk or electric mixer when you can do *that*?

"Teflon tanks" because they were made of exceptionally heavy steel, tough enough to withstand the hellfire of any Russian oven.

We used metal buckets for wastebaskets. We washed our dishes with a big bar of ugly, foul-smelling, dark brown soap, the only kind we could buy. I rolled out pastry dough with a champagne bottle because I could never find a simple wooden rolling pin. I cut out cookies and dumplings with a glass tumbler because cookie cutters weren't sold in the stores. (My Russian baking books from the tsarist and Soviet eras had pictures of many kinds of metal cookie cutters, although one drawing included a glass tumbler and a stemmed wine glass among the choices—the same utensils all my Russian friends used, too.) I baked cookies and pizzas on a shallow tray that came with the stove. One of my American colleagues turned her metal dish-drainer into a roasting rack for meats in the oven. Another improvised a filter-coffee maker from a tea strainer lined with tough Russian toilet paper. And another constructed a more elaborate coffee-making device out of a plastic detergent dispenser and HandiWipes (both of which she'd brought from the United States), the whole apparatus supported by an inverted kitchen stool.

# Measure for Measure

None of the cooks we knew in Russia used calibrated measuring cups or measuring spoons in their kitchens, although most of them had a small metal scale, calibrated in grams and kilograms, for weighing dry ingredients like sugar and flour, especially for the more precise measurements needed for baking. The standard "measuring cup" in Russian kitchens was simply a *stakan*—a heavy faceted-glass tumbler, commonly used at the table for drinking milk and fruit juices—which, filled to the brim, held a volume of approximately 250 milliliters or just slightly more than one American 8-ounce cup. For spoon measurements, Russian cooks used the different kinds of spoons (*lozhki*) that were part of their table flatware. A small *kofeinaya lozhka* (coffee spoon) was equivalent to an American half-teaspoon measure. A *chainaya lozhka* (tea spoon) held nearly the same quantity as an American teaspoon. A *desertnaya lozhka* (dessert spoon) was similar to an American tablespoon, with the same volume. And a Russian *stolovaya lozhka* (table spoon, often used as a soup spoon) was a bit larger, holding nearly four American teaspoons in volume, instead of three as for a tablespoon in the United States. But most Russian cooks merely measured their ingredients like their mothers and grandmothers did: a pinch of this, a handful of that, half a teacup of one liquid, a full wine glass of another.

# Cooking by Candlelight

The biggest impediment to cooking in Vladivostok and Irkutsk was not our Stoves-from-Hell or the scarcity of cookware, but the lack of dependable utilities in our apartments. Electric power, hot and cold water, and steam heat for the radiators were all provided by the municipal governments and dispensed from a few huge plants located in various sections of each city. Residential customers had no control over these centralized, basic utilities. All we could do was turn on the light switch, the water faucet, or the radiator and hope that any or all of them functioned as they were supposed to.

Electricity was fairly dependable in Irkutsk, but it was a major problem in Vladivostok. The city lacked sufficient coal and oil to fuel its electric power plants, so the municipal authorities rationed fuel supplies by cutting off electricity to various parts of the city at different times of the day and night, in such a seemingly random manner that we never knew for certain when, or for how long, the electricity would be on or off.

The first power outages in Vladivostok occurred in October and got progressively worse as winter came on. We usually returned home from work around 6:00 p.m., after the sky was already black and icy winds had driven the temperature below freezing. But often only 5 or 10 minutes after we arrived at our apartment, the electricity went off—which meant that we had to prepare and eat our evening meal by the light of a single candle. (And candles were scarce in a city of 700,000 people where power outages were a daily occurrence.) Moreover, when the electricity was cut off, the steam heat in our radiators went off, too. If power outages lasted more than a day, we had to wear thermal underwear indoors to combat the cold—and also eat more cold food just to keep warm.

Our first candlelight dinner in October 1993 was typical of many cold meals we'd eat under similar circumstances during much of the time we lived in Vladivostok: smoked salmon with sour cream, cucumber-and-tomato salad, slices of sausage and cheese, whole-wheat bread liberally spread with butter, a bottle of Hungarian wine chilled on our frigid balcony, and chocolates from the local "Preztizh" candy factory for dessert. The menus for these impromptu candlelight dinners varied only according to the season and the availability of certain foods—fresh or pickled vegetables, depending on the time of year, smoked or canned fish, depending on the stocks in the stores.

# Dining in the Dark

On a Saturday in mid-October, Tom and I returned home from shopping at Vladivostok's farmers' markets, looking forward to making pizza with all the fresh ingredients we'd bought, probably the last fresh produce we'd find before winter set in. We fired up the Stove-from-Hell. Tom sliced the tomatoes, eggplants, hot green peppers, and onions, while I minced the garlic, shredded the cheese, and patted out the pizza dough. We opened a can of black olives and a bottle of red wine. But just as we started to assemble the pizza, the electricity went off.

We lighted two candles, looked at each other, and said, "Okay, what can we do now?" From past experience, we knew the electricity could be cut off for only 15 minutes or up to 36 hours. But we'd lived in Russia too long to be upset by such inconveniences. Although our hearts had been set on that fresh pizza for dinner, we shifted our heads to what was now possible: a cold Russian meal made from whatever we could scrounge from the pantry and fridge.

Working by candlelight, we sliced fresh bread, slathered it with creamy butter, and topped it with plenty of salmon caviar. While I put together a large portion of cold crabmeat with garlic mayonnaise, Tom made a cucumber, tomato, and onion salad seasoned with dried herbs; a bowl of canned salmon combined with green onion tops and sour cream; and another bowl of chopped hard-boiled eggs mixed with Russian hot-spicy mustard. We poured out glasses of chilled Russian vodka and opened a bottle of Moldovan white wine.

Only a few minutes after the electricity had gone off, we were dining by candlelight on a delicious meal of Russian cold *zakuski*. But wouldn't you know it: an hour later, after we'd finished the last bite of caviar and the last glass of wine, the lights came on again. We looked at each other, laughed, and stacked all the dirty dishes in the sink. There was no way we could clean up the kitchen that evening, because when the electricity came on, all the water was cut off—an all-too-common occurrence in our Russian high-rise village.

Running water, hot or cold, was always a problem, too. The water that flowed through our taps in both Vladivostok and Irkutsk ranged in color from clear to amber to orange to purple to black, with accompanying aromas of petroleum, sewer gas, ham, rotten eggs, or fish. Often the water also left an oily, slimy sludge in the bathtub and kitchen sink. While we were in Russia, cholera bacteria were found in the water supply in Vladivostok, and high levels of industrial and organic pollutants were measured in the tap water of both Vladivostok and Irkutsk.

Tom and I took no chances. From our first day in Russia, we purified all the water we used for drinking, cooking, and tooth brushing, pumping the water by hand through a portable filtration device we'd brought from the United States. Often we boiled the water

*Entrance to our apartment building in the high-rise village, Vladivostok, 1993.*

first, a nightly ritual in Vladivostok whenever we had electricity. The next morning, Tom got up early, fixed breakfast, and pumped through the filter all the boiled water for use that day, storing it in eight big plastic fruit-juice bottles and a 10-liter plastic container that we kept in reserve as an emergency supply for whenever the water was cut off. Every day of our stay in Russia, Tom repeated this tedious task, often working by candlelight on dark winter mornings. So we never suffered from digestive problems or other waterborne illnesses, as did some of our American colleagues who learned too late that purifying the tap water was just another daily chore in the high-rise village.

But polluted water was better than none at all. Russians living in cities were accustomed to having their hot water cut off for one or two months during the summer (ostensibly for the pipes to be repaired), but sometimes even in the winter we went for weeks without any hot water—and no way to heat cold water on the stove when the electricity was cut off as well. At other times the cold water was cut off, and only scalding hot water flowed from the taps, which created problems of its own. Most difficult of all, however was when the entire water supply was cut off, sometimes for only an hour, other times for two or three days in a row. Living as we did at various times on the fifth,

56

## Saved by a Silver Spoon?

I knew many highly educated Russians who insisted that you can purify tap water simply by leaving a silver spoon in the water container overnight. We even stayed with a retired chemist in Moscow who believed this, and who laughed at us for buying bottled water to drink at her apartment. I thought the silver spoon method was just an unscientific folk belief, but later a chemistry professor in America told me that silver in certain forms does have germicidal properties. "I can see where folklore could transfer this property to a solid silver spoon," he said, "but I doubt that enough would dissolve in a pitcher of water overnight to be effective."

sixth, and eighth floors of high-rise buildings, it was not easy to haul water by hand, from outdoor communal taps a few blocks away, up all those flights of stairs to our apartments. So we kept large buckets of water in reserve, in our kitchen, bathroom, and hall, for such basic necessities as toilet flushing and hand washing.

Living in Russia's high-rise villages was most challenging when all of the utilities were cut off at the same time. The first time this happened to us was on Thanksgiving Day, 1993—which made us acutely aware of how thankful we were to have candles and water in reserve. Few people in the Western industrialized world know what it's like to live in a multistory apartment building in a major metropolis in the middle of the winter, with no heat, no water, and no electricity, when outdoor temperatures are well below zero. In Vladivostok—where that situation occurred frequently—Tom and I started the day by candlelight, cooking breakfast over a small, single-burner, camping-gas stove that the university had given us when the energy crisis reached its height. Dressed in corduroy jeans and wool sweaters over thermal long underwear, we made tea with water rationed from our emergency supply and toasted pieces of whole-wheat bread skewered on a fork held over the flame. Chunks of cheese and previously hard-boiled eggs completed our morning meal. After leaving the apartment for work at 8:00 a.m. every weekday, we returned at 6:00 p.m. to the same cold, dark abode—and another cold meal eaten by the light of a single, scarce candle.

*Balcony on a high-rise apartment building in Vladivostok, 1993—typically used for storing food, growing plants, and drying clothes.*

One chilly weekend in the autumn of 1994, Tom and I traveled with a Russian friend to her dacha in a village not far from the border with China. Warmth for the small, three-room house was provided by a traditional wood-burning, brick-and-stucco Russian stove that was built into the dacha itself, serving as a cookstove, oven, and heater for the entire place. After two days of helping our friend harvest the last vegetables from her garden, we returned to Vladivostok on an overnight train—in a cold, crowded, dirty, third-class car—arriving just in time to start teaching our classes at the university on Monday morning. Tired, hungry, and much in need of a hot bath, we finally got back to our own high-rise village at six o'clock that evening—only to discover, on that coldest day of October, that our apartment had no electricity, no heat, no hot water. Fondly remembering the warmth of that old-fashioned wood-burning stove in the country, we lit a single candle and set about preparing yet another meal from the

*Brightly lacquered samovar in our Vladivostok kitchen, 1993.*

supplies in our pantry: canned sprats garnished with sour cream and chopped green onion tops; a salad of canned garbanzos seasoned with chopped onion, garlic, and paprika; and a cucumber-and-tomato salad, the last fresh salad of the season, all washed down with a bottle of Bulgarian white wine. At such moments, we actually missed our Stove-from-Hell, which suddenly seemed like a modern, labor-saving device despite the fact that it worked so badly. And by the time we left Russia, Tom had concluded that dinners by candlelight would never seem romantic to him again.

## The Modern Russian Kitchen

Imagine our surprise when we returned to Russia 12 years later. Our hosts in Vladivostok—members of Russia's new, small-but-growing middle class—still lived in apartment buildings much like ours of the mid-1990s, but basic utilities such as water and electricity were much more dependable now. And the kitchens in their recently renovated apartments were more expensively appointed than our own suburban kitchen in Texas. We were amazed to see Russian kitchens fitted out with beautiful glass-fronted wooden cabinets imported from Germany and Scandinavia; European electric ranges with glass tops and digital controls; stainless-steel sinks; pretty tile walls and shiny hardwood floors; high-end Formica countertops that looked like granite and marble; pricey Zepter cookware and utensils; electric rice cookers, hand mixers, and tea kettles; bread machines, blenders, and food processors; microwave ovens, electronic scales, and countertop televisions; and fancy tableware for serving all the foods prepared in those modern Russian kitchens.

*Two Russian friends cooking in a modern kitchen in Vladivostok, 2006.*

However, not everyone enjoyed the relative affluence of Russia's emerging middle class. During that first visit back to Vladivostok, instead of staying at a hotel we rented (sight unseen) a two-room apartment conveniently located near one of the city's major food markets and a public transportation line. But the building's exterior and stairwells turned out to be in worse condition than those of the high-rises where we'd lived more than a decade before. The apartment itself, although fairly clean, was dark and low-ceilinged, and its miniscule kitchen (not so clean) was considerably older than those in our former high-rise villages. Still, in Russia's newly inflated housing market, that tiny, substandard apartment was worth at least $50,000 (in 2006), an almost unbelievable sum, yet typical of Vladivostok's overheated real estate prices.

The apartment's saving grace was its eager-to-please, 30-something, entrepreneurial landlord, Dima, who showed up every morning to cook breakfast for us on his own Stove-from-Hell. When Tom and I were seated at the tiny kitchen table, there was barely room for Dima to move between the greasy stove and the grungy sink. But he was a decent cook, and when he discovered our interest in Russian foods, the breakfasts became more elaborate every day. We never knew what to expect, but the food was always copious and well prepared: fried ham slices topped with melted cheese and chopped green onion tops; fried eggs sprinkled with fresh parsley and dill; fish pâté spread on white bread and garnished with green onions; fresh tomato slices and home-pickled cucumbers; big bowls of fresh haskap berries (like elongated blueberries) from his uncle's dacha garden; jars of strawberry, raspberry, and blueberry preserves made by his mother; fruit-flavored yogurt; commercially made heat-and-eat blintzes stuffed with ground chicken, apricot jam, or cream cheese; a variety of store-bought pastries; and always plenty of bread (white, whole-wheat, dark rye), along with steaming-hot cups of black tea. One morning Dima's mother sent over a special cold soup (*okroshka*) for that hot July day. And every morning Dima put out a plate of thinly sliced sweet lemons topped with grated yellow cheese and sprinkled with sugar, a strange combination that we found surprisingly addictive. Dima's breakfasts proved that you don't need a modern kitchen and fancy appliances to turn out tasty meals—just good ingredients, a basic knowledge of cooking, and a genuine interest in food.

Those were the same conditions under which Tom and I cooked all of our meals in Russia in the 1990s—breakfast and dinner every day during the week, brown-bag lunches for school, and three meals a day on weekends, as well as large dinner parties for colleagues and friends. The dishes we prepared were full of fats, proteins, and carbohydrates, so essential for survival in the Russian climate—soul-warming soups and stews, hearty casseroles, and stick-to-your-ribs pasta dishes with plenty of butter, cheese, and sour cream—all made from personal recipes that we'd brought to Russia and new recipes we developed there. And after many trials and plenty of errors, we finally learned how to bake our favorite cakes, cookies, and breads in our three Stoves-from-Hell: cinnamon rolls, Snickerdoodles, gingersnaps, chocolate brownies, Scottish gingerbread, German *Zwiebelkuchen* (onion tarte). Despite the challenges of cooking in kitchens with minimal appliances and erratic utilities, we ate very well in Russia.

# Salmon Salad

*We often made this salmon salad for cold suppers during electric power outages in Vladivostok. Six species of wild salmon are caught in the waters of the Russian Far East, so salmon was usually available in the markets there (fresh, smoked, canned). Russians make a similar salad that includes cooked rice and chopped blanched onions mixed with canned salmon and mayonnaise, garnished with grated hard-boiled egg. During the Soviet era the proletariat called this combination "Kremlin Salad"—supposedly because salmon was often scarce in the interior of European Russia, a long way from the Atlantic and Pacific coasts, and only the Kremlin elites could afford it. Our Vladivostok version was simpler than the Kremlin's, made with whatever cooked ingredients were already on hand when the electricity was cut off.*

**¾ to 1 pound precooked salmon (canned, smoked, or fresh)***
**½ cup pure sour cream or mayonnaise (or a mixture of both)**
**½ cup chopped green onion tops**
**1 large hard-boiled egg, chopped**
**1 teaspoon lemon juice (or ¼ teaspoon salt)**
**¼ teaspoon finely ground black pepper**

***If using canned salmon, use the best quality you can find.**

- Flake the salmon with a fork. (If using canned salmon, first drain the juice and remove the larger bones.)

- Mix all the ingredients together in a medium bowl. Eat right away or refrigerate until needed. (For a pretty presentation, mound the salad on lettuce leaves and garnish with additional hard-boiled egg, grated, and finely chopped chives or green onion tops.)

- Makes 4 servings as an appetizer.

# Waste Not: Clean-Out-the-Fridge Curry

In graduate school at the University of Michigan I shared an apartment with an American woman who'd previously been married to a man from India. She introduced me to a whole new world of spicy curries, seasoned rices, and colorful condiments from that part of the planet. During the frigid Michigan winter, we often warmed up with substantial servings of her homemade curry, concocted with her own blend of spices and whatever meats and vegetables were on hand. Years later in Russia I used the techniques that she'd taught me to cook an ad hoc dish that Tom called "Clean-Out-the-Fridge Curry."

In our biggest cooking pot, I sautéed a large chopped onion in one-fourth cup of hot sunflower oil. When the onion was soft and translucent, I sprinkled in a heaping tablespoon or two of hot curry powder and cooked the mixture, stirring constantly, for another couple of minutes, to remove any raw taste from the spices. Then I stirred in four or five canned whole tomatoes, crushing them to a pulp with the spoon, followed by any foods in the refrigerator that needed to be eaten soon, before they spoiled: meats, root vegetables, even fruits—all chopped into chunks about the same size. If the mélange seemed too thick, I added a bit of beef or chicken stock. Finally I brought the mixture to a boil, reduced the heat to a simmer, and partially covered the pot.

This aromatic curry cooked as long as it needed to—usually an hour or so, depending on the particular ingredients in the pot. After the first 30 minutes, I tasted the stew and added more spices: another tablespoon or two of curry powder, some cayenne pepper, a pinch of cinnamon, a spoon of powdered ginger, a hint of cumin and cloves—all of them first fried together briefly in a little hot oil in a skillet, to eliminate rawness and bring out their flavor.

I served this spicy curry with boiled white rice and whatever garnishes I could find in Russia: raisins, peanuts, chopped hard-boiled eggs, and sour cream (our substitute for more traditional yogurt). Regardless of the ingredients I'd thrown together, "Clean-Out-the-Fridge Curry" always turned out much tastier than its name implied.

# Into the Pot

"Food seemed not to play a major role in Nozdrev's life: some of it was burned, while other things were undercooked. His cook must have been guided by the inspiration of the moment and have chucked into the cooking pot whatever came to hand: if he happened to catch sight ot pepper, he would pour in pepper; if a piece of cabbage, a jug of milk, some ham, a plateful of peas came to hand, he threw it in pell-mell, deciding that it was all right so long as it was hot and the whole business was surely bound to have some taste or other." —Nikolai Gogol, *Dead Souls* (1842)

# Green Pea and Red Pepper Salad

*This is another cold dish we often made when the electricity was cut off. In Russia we used bottled green peas, which are larger, firmer, and less sweet than American canned peas. Bottled or canned peas are more authentic for Russia, but frozen green peas make an especially pretty salad.*

3 cups cooked green peas (1 pound frozen green peas, or two 15-ounce cans)*
3 large, fleshy, canned or bottled roasted red peppers
⅓ cup mayonnaise
2 to 3 large garlic cloves, squeezed through a garlic press
½ teaspoon lemon juice or white vinegar
½ teaspoon freshly ground black pepper
¼ teaspoon salt

Optional

¼ to ½ cup cooked ham (smoked or not), diced into ¼-inch cubes or julienned before measuring

Garnish

½ roasted large red pepper, cut lengthwise into thin strips

*If using frozen green peas, cook for only 3 minutes in boiling water, so they're not too soft.

- Drain the peas thoroughly in a colander. (Rinse canned peas under cold running water and drain well. Let freshly cooked frozen peas cool to room temperature before using.)

- Pat the red peppers dry with paper towels. Cut them lengthwise into ¼-inch wide strips, then crosswise into ¼-inch squares.

- Whisk together the mayonnaise, garlic, lemon juice or vinegar, pepper, and salt in a medium bowl. Add the green peas and red pepper squares (and optional ham). Toss gently to combine well.

- Cover and refrigerate at least 1 hour (preferably longer) for the flavors to meld. Before serving, toss the salad again. Taste and add a bit more salt if desired. (You'll probably want more salt if you used frozen peas, which are less salty than canned ones.)

- Serve in a pretty cut-glass bowl or Russian lacquer bowl, garnished with red pepper strips on top.

- Makes 4 to 6 servings.

# Russian Cold Summer Soup

## (Okroshka)

Okroshka *is a refreshing cold soup that's a summertime favorite in Russia, where temperatures even in Siberia can rise into the 90s Fahrenheit. The name of this soup comes from the Russian verb meaning "to chop finely." The liquid ingredient is often* kvas, *a slightly fizzy, lightly alcoholic beverage. (If* kvas *isn't available, you can substitute semi-sweet sparkling cider.) Other versions of* okroshka *are made with* kefir, *sauerkraut juice, or pickled cucumber brine, combined with fresh herbs and whatever cooked meats are on hand (fish, chicken, sausage, ham), all cut into very small pieces.*

**3 to 4 medium carrots peeled and diced into ¼-inch cubes**
**2 medium red boiling potatoes, peeled and diced into ¼-inch cubes**
**1 large cucumber, seeded and diced into ¼-inch cubes**
**1 cup finely chopped green onions (white and tender green parts)**
**1 cup finely chopped red radishes**
**1 cup finely chopped tender boiled beef**
**6 cups chilled *kvas***
**1 teaspoon salt**
**2 large hard-boiled eggs, finely chopped**
**2 tablespoons finely chopped fresh dill**

**Garnish**

**Mayonnaise or sour cream**

**\*Available at Russian delis in the United States**

- Bring a medium pot half full of water to a boil. Add the carrots and cook until just tender (not too soft), about 3 to 4 minutes. Use a slotted spoon to transfer the carrots to a colander to drain and cool.

- Add the potatoes to the water in the pot and bring to a boil over high heat. Reduce the heat to medium-low and simmer, uncovered, until just tender, about 5 minutes. Drain and let cool.

- Combine the potatoes, carrots, cucumbers, green onions, and radishes in a large bowl, tossing them together gently to mix well. Cover and refrigerate for 2 hours.

- Just before serving, add the chopped cooked beef, then pour in the chilled *kvas*. Add the salt and stir gently to combine. Gently stir in the finely chopped eggs and fresh dill.

- Ladle the *okroshka* into individual soup bowls. (The heavier ingredients will sink to the bottom and the lighter ones float on top.) Garnish with a dollop of mayonnaise or sour cream. Serve cold, accompanied by slices of rye bread.

- Makes 6 servings.

# Lighter Brew

*Kvas* is a classic Russian beverage with roots far back in history. A fizzy, lightly fermented, slightly alcoholic drink with a sweet-sour taste, *kvas* is a popular summertime refreshment that's also used as the base for some kinds of cold soups. *Kvas* can be made at home or purchased in bottles. In Russia, it's often sold on the streets, dispensed by the glass from spigots on little vehicles that look like miniature tanker trucks.

The most common kind of *kvas* is brewed from rye bread, sugar, and yeast. Some versions are made from, or flavored with, fruits or berries, vegetables (carrots, beets), honey, herbs, spices, or even horseradish. *Kvas* is definitely an acquired taste. Some Americans reckon it to "Russian root beer" or "Russian Dr Pepper." After Tom's first sip of *kvas*, he exclaimed, "No wonder the Russians drink vodka!" But we later developed a liking for this very Russian brew, and we still enjoy drinking a glass of cold *kvas* in the summer.

# Macedonian Salmon-Trout Soup

*We fell in love with this spicy soup when we first ate it at Lake Ohrid in Macedonia, where it was made with a species of pink-fleshed trout that's endemic to the lake. Since we carried chile powders with us to Russia, we were able to make a similar-tasting soup there with canned or fresh salmon, whichever we could find at the markets. Macedonian paprika (ground dried red peppers) produces the most authentic flavor, but New Mexico red chile powder (especially ancho chile powder) is a very good substitute.*

**One 15-ounce can of best-quality pink salmon (or ¾ to 1 pound fresh skinless salmon fillets, cut into 2-inch squares)**
**2 tablespoons butter**
**1 tablespoon vegetable oil**
**3 medium onions, coarsely chopped**
**4 to 5 large garlic cloves, chopped**
**1½ tablespoons New Mexico ancho chile powder (mild)**
**1 tablespoon New Mexico ancho chile powder (hot)**
**2½ to 3 cups fish (or chicken) stock**
**¼ cup cream, at room temperature**

**Garnish**

**Sour cream**
**Chopped fresh parsley or green onion tops**

- Drain canned salmon, reserving the liquid to use in the soup. Remove all bones from canned or fresh salmon.

- Heat the butter and oil together in a medium pot over medium-high heat until bubbling. Add the onions and sauté until soft and golden. Stir in the garlic and sauté 1 minute longer. Reduce the heat to low and sprinkle in the chile powders, stirring constantly until the ingredients are well mixed.

- Pour in the stock (plus the reserved liquid if using canned salmon). Stir well. Bring to a boil over high heat, then lower the heat and simmer for 5 to 10 minutes. Add the salmon and cook for 3 to 5 minutes more if using canned salmon (or 5 to 7 minutes if using fresh salmon), stirring gently, to heat the fish throughout.

- Stir in the cream, then remove from the heat. Ladle into soup bowls and garnish each serving with a large dollop of sour cream and a sprinkling of chopped parsley or green onions on top. Serve hot.

- Makes 4 servings as a first course, or 2 to 3 main-course servings.

# Fish Stew with Garlic-Rye Croutons

*Warm, filling soups and stews were often our main dish for supper during the Russian winter. We concocted them from the root vegetables stored in our pantry and whatever meats happened to be available that day. For this simple fish stew, make the **Garlic-Rye Croutons** in advance, so they'll be ready when the stew finishes simmering.*

**2 tablespoons butter**
**2 teaspoons vegetable oil**
**2 large onions, quartered and cut into ¼-inch thick slices**
**2 large carrots, diced into ¼-inch cubes**
**2 pounds firm boiling potatoes, peeled and cut into 1-inch cubes**
**3 teaspoons salt (divided use)**
**2 quarts (8 cups) full-fat milk, at room temperature**
**2 teaspoons coarsely ground black pepper**
**2 pounds boneless, skinless cod fillets (or other firm white fish fillets), or salmon fillets, or a combination of fish fillets, cut into 2-inch squares**

Garnish

**Garlic-Rye Croutons (recipe follows)**
**Chopped green onion tops or fresh dill**

- Heat the butter and oil together in a skillet and cook the onions and carrots over medium-high heat, stirring frequently, until the onions are soft and translucent but not browned.

- Put the potatoes in a large stockpot, adding enough cold water to cover them by 1 inch. Stir in 1 teaspoon of salt. Bring to a boil over high heat, reduce the heat a bit, and boil, partially covered, until the potatoes are tender (about 20 minutes).

- Pour off the cooking water. Add the onions, carrots, and milk to the potatoes in the pan, along with 2 teaspoons salt and the black pepper. Bring the milk to a gentle boil over medium-high heat, stirring occasionally. Add the fish pieces, reduce the heat to medium, and simmer the stew, partially covered, until the fish is cooked (about 10 minutes). Taste and add more salt and pepper if desired.

- Ladle the stew into large soup bowls and garnish with **Garlic-Rye Croutons** and chopped green onion tops or fresh dill. Serve hot.

- Makes 8 servings.

**Garlic-Rye Croutons**

**3 tablespoons vegetable oil**
**1 large garlic clove, minced**
**¼ teaspoon coarsely ground salt**
**2 thick slices of dark rye bread, trimmed of crusts and cut into ½-inch cubes**

- Mix the oil, garlic, and salt in a large shallow bowl. Preheat the oven to 375°F.

- Toss the bread cubes with the seasoned oil until all the cubes are well coated. Spread them in a single layer in a shallow baking pan, and scrape any remaining garlic pieces out of the bowl onto the bread.

- Bake for 10 to 15 minutes, stirring the bread cubes once or twice, until the croutons are crisp. Transfer them to a bowl to cool.

# Spicy Beef Borshch

*Tom liked to make this spicy* borshch *with the juicy red beets we often found in the farmers' markets in Russia. But his soup was never as richly flavored as he wanted until a Siberian friend taught him to separately sauté the vegetables that are added toward the end (some cooks roast the beets, too, for an even deeper taste). Tom always spiked his spicy* borshch *with the Tabasco sauce and cayenne pepper we carried to Russia.*

**4 cups finely shredded green cabbage**
**3 large red beetroots, peeled and coarsely shredded (or cut into ½-inch cubes)**
**1 large carrot, peeled, and coarsely shredded**
**2 quarts (8 cups) water, beef stock, or chicken stock (divided use)**
**2 teaspoons salt (divided use)**
**4 tablespoons sunflower oil (divided use)**
**1 pound boneless beef (chuck roast), cut into ½-inch cubes**
**3 medium red boiling potatoes, peeled and cut into ½-inch cubes**
**1 tablespoon tomato paste**
**1 bay leaf**
**1 medium onion, diced**
**1 medium green bell pepper, coarsely chopped**
**1 medium red bell pepper, coarsely chopped**

**2 to 3 large garlic cloves, minced**
**2 medium tomatoes, coarsely chopped**
**2 tablespoons red wine vinegar**
**1 teaspoon Tabasco sauce**
**¼ to ½ teaspoon (or more) ground cayenne pepper**

Garnish

**Sour cream**
**Chopped fresh dill**

- Combine the cabbage, beets, carrot, 4 cups of water (or stock), and 1 teaspoon salt in a large stock pot. Bring to a boil over high heat, then reduce the heat, cover, and simmer 30 minutes, stirring occasionally.

- While the vegetables are cooking, heat 2 tablespoons of oil in a large skillet and lightly brown the beef on all sides.

- After the vegetables have simmered for 30 minutes, add the beef and pan juices from the skillet to the stock pot, along with the potatoes, tomato paste, bay leaf, and remaining 4 cups of water or stock. Bring to a boil over high heat, then reduce the heat and simmer, covered, for 45 minutes. (Set a timer.)

- Meanwhile, heat 2 tablespoons of oil in the same skillet and sauté the onion and pepper until the onion starts to soften. Stir in the garlic and sauté 2 minutes longer. Add to the simmering ingredients in the stock pot.

- Without wiping out the skillet, cook the tomatoes over medium-high heat for 3 minutes, then add them to the stock pot along with the vinegar, Tabasco sauce, cayenne pepper, and 1 teaspoon salt. Continue to simmer, covered, until your timer says the 45 minutes are finished. (Cooking time might be longer if you cubed the beets instead of shredding them.)

- Serve hot, each bowl garnished with a large dollop of sour cream and a liberal sprinkling of chopped fresh dill. Eat with a Russian lacquered wooden spoon, if you have one. The classic accompaniments to Russian *borshch* are a slice of bread or a single *pirozhok* (recipe for ***Pirozhki***, page 30) and a glass of chilled vodka.

- Makes 15 cups (10 servings).

# Borshch and Beyond

Popular throughout Eastern Europe and Russia, *borshch* is said to have originated in Ukraine (although not all food historians agree). Starting out as a hearty peasant dish, *borshch* eventually made its way onto the tables of the nobility and later the menus of Soviet restaurants and into the soup vats of Soviet canteens. Today it's still a favorite of home cooks from the eastern Baltic to the northern Black Sea to the Russian Far East—served on holidays and other special occasions, as well as for daily fare.

There are surely as many recipes for *borshch* as cooks who make it. Red beet *borshch* is the most famous, but many other variations exist, too—local, regional, personal. Soups called *borshch* can be red, white, or green in color, meaty or vegetarian, chunky or smooth, thick or thin, slow-cooked or fast-cooked, hot or cold. And the range of ingredients includes all kinds of meats (beef, pork, fish, poultry), root vegetables (beets, potatoes, onions, carrots, parsnips, turnips), cabbage (and sauerkraut), bell peppers, celery, tomatoes, squash, leafy greens, apples, hard-boiled eggs, spices and herbs (especially bay leaves and dill), butter and oil, sugar or honey for sweetness, and lemon juice, pickle brine, *kvas*, or vinegar for sourness. The whole concoction is often garnished with a dollop or drizzle of sour cream and served with slices of bread or a couple of *pirozhki* on the side.

So you name it: almost anything can go into a soup called *borshch*. But any Russian will tell you which specific ingredients must and must not be included in a "real" *borshch*—at least according to whomever you're talking with at the moment.

# Goulash Stew with Mushrooms

*We learned to make this hearty goulash when we lived in Central Europe, where it was a popular dish at German, Czech, and Hungarian beer taverns. We liked the recipe so much that we took it with us to Russia, along with the dried hot peppers, New Mexico chile powders, and Hungarian paprikas also packed in our luggage. In Siberia, we often ate this stew as a soul-warming main dish on cold winter nights.*

¼ cup lard or sunflower oil
2 large onions, chopped
¼ pound bacon, finely chopped
3 tablespoons Hungarian sweet (mild) paprika*
1 tablespoon Hungarian hot paprika*
1½ pounds boneless beef (chuck or shank) or boneless pork shoulder, cut
    into 1-inch cubes
½ pound mushrooms, cleaned and quartered lengthwise
4 large garlic cloves, minced
1 tablespoon tomato paste
1 cup beef stock
1 teaspoon salt
1 teaspoon freshly ground black pepper

Garnish

1 small onion, sliced thinly Into rings
Grated fresh horseradish

*Or a mixture of mild and hot paprikas, to taste

- Melt the lard or heat the sunflower oil in a 4-quart stovetop casserole or stockpot. Sauté the chopped onions and bacon over medium-high heat until the onions are translucent and very soft. Remove the pot from the heat, sprinkle the paprika over the onions and bacon, and stir to combine well. Add the cubed meat and mix well.

- Return the pot to the stove and cook, stirring constantly, over medium heat until the meat is browned on all sides. Stir in the mushrooms and garlic.

- Stir the tomato paste into the beef stock and add it to the pot, along with the salt and pepper, stirring to mix well. Bring the mixture to a boil over high heat, then reduce the heat to very low, cover, and simmer for 45 minutes, stirring occasionally.

- Serve hot, on a plate, garnished with fresh onion rings and a sprinkling of freshly grated horseradish, and accompanied by boiled potatoes or egg noodles and plenty of cold beer.

- Makes 6 servings.

# Spaghetti with Salmon and Sour Cream

*In Vladivostok, when the electricity stayed on long enough to boil a pot of pasta, we liked to make this quick spaghetti dish with whatever smoked or canned salmon was on hand. The best we ever tasted was a wild-caught salmon we bought at a local farmers' market, sold by a fisherman's wife who had hot-smoked the fish herself over a birch-wood fire.*

½ **pound hot-smoked salmon, skin removed**
¾ **pound dried spaghetti**
1 **tablespoon salt (for the pasta water)**
1 **tablespoon unsalted butter**
2 **to 3 large garlic cloves, thinly sliced**
1 **cup sliced green onions (bottoms and tops, thinly sliced crosswise)**
1 **tablespoon lemon juice**
1¼ **cups sour cream, at room temperature**
½ **teaspoon freshly ground black pepper**

- Flake the salmon with a fork and set aside.

- Bring a large pot of water to a boil, add 1 tablespoon salt, and swirl the spaghetti into the pot. Cook uncovered, at a rolling boil and stirring frequently, for the amount of time indicated on the package (usually about 8 minutes), just until the pasta is *al dente* (slightly firm to the bite).

- As soon as the pasta goes into the pot, melt the butter in a large skillet over medium-high heat. When the butter bubbles, cook the garlic for 2 minutes, then stir in the green onions and lemon juice, mixing well.

- Add the sour cream, salmon, and black pepper. Cook over medium-low heat just until the sauce is hot, but don't let it boil. (If it seems too thick, thin it out with a little hot water from the pasta pot.) Turn off the heat. Taste and add more salt and pepper, if desired (but most hot-smoked salmon is pretty salty already).

- When the spaghetti is cooked, drain it immediately in a colander.

- Divide the spaghetti among 4 to 6 shallow soup bowls and spoon the sauce on top.

- Serve hot, with a cucumber-tomato salad on the side and plenty of chilled dry white wine.

- Makes 4 to 6 servings.

▶ **VARIATION:** Toss one or two handfuls of frozen green peas (thawed first) into the skillet when you add the sour cream and salmon. Garnish each serving with 1 tablespoon of toasted pine nuts.

# Braised Green Cabbage with Carrot and Caraway

*Tom often cooked this easy-to-make cabbage dish in Russia, as an accompaniment to roasted beef or chicken. He called it his "hot cole slaw" because of its ingredients.*

⅓ cup sunflower oil (or ¼ cup other vegetable oil and 1 tablespoon rendered duck fat)
One 2-pound green cabbage, cored and cut into 1-inch chunks
1 medium onion, coarsely chopped
½ teaspoon salt
1 large carrot, peeled and shredded
2 large garlic cloves, minced
½ teaspoon freshly ground black pepper
½ teaspoon caraway seeds
2 tablespoons chicken stock
1 tablespoon white or apple cider vinegar

- Heat the oil over medium-high heat in a 12-inch, deep-sided skillet. When the oil is hot, add the cabbage and toss to coat well with the oil. Add the onion and salt, and toss again. Cook over medium-high heat, stirring occasionally, for 5 minutes.

- Add the carrot, garlic, black pepper, and caraway seeds, tossing all the ingredients together to mix well. Stir in the chicken stock and vinegar. Cover and cook over medium heat for 5 to 7 minutes longer. Serve hot.

*Newly harvested cabbages in a village in the Russian Far East, 1994.*

- Makes 4 servings.

▶ **VARIATION:** Just before serving, stir in some crumbled, crisp-fried bacon. For a creamy version of this "hot cole slaw," stir ⅓ cup of sour cream (at room temperature) into the cabbage when it finishes cooking, and continue to heat for 1 or 2 minutes until the sour cream is warm.

▶ **WASTE NOT:** Mash together any leftover braised cabbage and leftover mashed potatoes, then reheat later to make a Russian version of traditional Irish colcannon. Garnish each serving with a generous pat of butter.

# Red, White, and Green

Hundreds of cabbage varieties are cultivated around the world—large, small, round, oblong, pointed, smooth, crinkly, red, white, green. Red cabbage is actually closer to purple in color. Green cabbage ranges in hue from light to dark, whereas white cabbage can be ivory-colored to very pale green.

Russia is the world's third-largest producer of cabbage (after China and India), but has the highest consumption of cabbage per person. In Russia, firm white cabbage, which matures in mid-autumn, is used for making sauerkraut, winter salads, and soups. Green cabbage leaves are favored for **Stuffed Cabbage Rolls** (recipe, page 275). Red cabbage is often braised for a sweet-sour side dish (recipe, page 121). And in the Russian Far East, bok choy and other kinds of Chinese cabbage are used in dishes influenced by Russia's East Asian neighbors, China, Korea, and Japan.

# Mashed Red Potatoes with Horseradish and Sour Cream

*These calorie-rich mashed potatoes were one of our favorite easy-to-make comfort foods in the Russian winter. Don't even think of mashing them with an electric mixer, food processor, or immersion blender! You'll end up with baby food. Always use a hand potato masher or just a fork. We use a heavy metal Russian potato masher with a pretty lacquered handle, which we've owned for years. In Texas we discovered that it's great for making chunky guacamole, too.*

**2 pounds new red potatoes, washed but not peeled, cut into quarters**
**¼ cup vegetable oil**
**1 large onion, finely chopped**
**3 large garlic cloves, minced**
**½ cup sour cream, at room temperature**
**¼ cup grated horseradish***
**1 teaspoon salt**
**1 teaspoon freshly ground black pepper**

***Freshly grated horseradish (my own preference) is much more pungent than most horseradish sold in jars. Use whatever suits your own taste.**

- Cover the potatoes with cold water in a large saucepan. Bring to a boil over high heat and boil, uncovered, until tender (about 20 minutes).

- While the potatoes are boiling, heat the oil in a skillet and cook the onion over medium heat until it begins to brown. Add the garlic and continue cooking until the onion is well browned but not burned.

- Drain the water off the cooked potatoes. Immediately add the browned onions and garlic, sour cream, horseradish, salt, and pepper. Mash by hand with a potato masher until all the ingredients are combined but the potatoes are still a bit chunky.

- Taste for seasoning and add more horseradish and/or sour cream, if desired. Serve hot.

- Makes 4 to 6 servings.

# The Potato Bin

Potatoes were one of the staples we could usually find year round in Russia, even if it sometimes took hours of hunting through town by bus, tram, and on foot whenever spuds were in short supply. We devoured potatoes, hot or cold, in soups, salads, side dishes, and casseroles. And we enjoyed adapting recipes like old-fashioned scalloped potatoes to our Russian kitchen, using what-ever ingredients were on hand.

When making scalloped potatoes, we added a few dots of butter, a scattering of flour, and a sprinkling of salt and pepper to each layer of thinly sliced potatoes in a casserole dish. We often included a middle layer of sour cream mixed with garlic or horseradish, or crab with sautéed onions and sour cream, or layers of smoked salmon, green onions, even green peppers. Then we poured in some milk to moisten the potatoes, spread a generous layer of sour cream on top, and baked the mixture in a hot Oven-from-Hell (at around 400°F.) for 45 minutes to an hour, until the potatoes were tender. On long winter evenings in Siberia, that creamy casserole was always a welcome dish on our table, sometimes as an accompaniment to meats roasted in the oven with it, or often just as a main dish on its own.

# Savory Buckwheat Kasha

*Tom developed this recipe for nutty-flavored buckwheat kasha in Russia, where it was often our first choice as a side dish for roasted meats. For variety, you can replace the walnuts with toasted unsalted peanuts or pecans, or substitute rendered duck fat for some of the oil. In Texas, we sauté a finely chopped jalapeño with the other ingredients and serve this seductive kasha with steaks or shish-kabobs sizzling-hot off the grill.*

▶ **NOTE:** Buckwheat is often sold as "buckwheat groats," the whole seed or the cracked seeds (the latter sometimes labeled coarse-grind, medium-grind, fine-grind). Buckwheat is also finely ground into flour, and the Russians even brew beer from buckwheat. For this recipe, use whole buckwheat seeds, not cracked.

**1¾ cups chicken or beef stock**
**¼ cup sunflower oil**
**1 medium onion, diced into ¼-inch pieces**
**½ medium green bell pepper, diced into ¼-inch pieces**
**½ medium red bell pepper, diced into ¼-inch pieces**
**2 large garlic cloves, thinly sliced crosswise**
**1 cup whole buckwheat groats**
**⅓ cup chopped toasted walnuts***
**½ teaspoon salt**
**½ teaspoon freshly ground black pepper**

***Toasted in a 350°F. oven for 8 minutes**

- Start heating the chicken stock in a small covered saucepan over medium heat so it will be hot when you need it later in the recipe. Rinse the buckwheat in a colander under cold running water and set aside to drain.

- Heat the oil in a separate 2-quart heavy saucepan over medium-high heat. Sauté the onion, peppers, and garlic together until the onion is translucent. Stir in the buckwheat groats to coat them with the oil, and continue stirring constantly until they give off a nutty aroma. Stir in the walnuts.

- Pour the hot stock into the pan, add the salt and pepper, and stir to mix well. Bring the mixture to a boil, then reduce the heat to low, cover tightly, and cook for 30 minutes.

- Fluff the kasha with a fork. If it seems a bit too wet, let it continue to cook, uncovered, over low heat for 5 minutes longer.

- Serve hot, as a side dish for roasted or grilled meats.

- Makes 4 servings.

▶ **VARIATION:** When wild garlic was in season, Tom made his special **Garlic-Lovers' Kasha** with buckwheat groats cooked the same way as his **Savory Buckwheat Kasha**, but omitting the nuts and replacing the bell peppers with 10 small garlic cloves cut in half. After the kasha had cooked for 20 minutes, he stirred in 3 to 4 chopped green onions (tops included) and a small handful of chopped wild garlic bottoms, then continued cooking the kasha, tightly covered, another 10 to 15 minutes. The final garnish for each serving was a generous sprinkling of chopped wild garlic leaves. Kiss your table companion and enjoy!

## Versatile Kasha

"*Shchi da kasha, pishcha nasha*"—"Cabbage soup and porridge, that's our food"—is an old Russian adage, referring to the two dishes that sustained Russian peasants for centuries, sauerkraut soup and grains cooked in water. We, too, ate our fill of kashas, from fine semolina prepared with milk, butter, and sugar, to savory buckwheat groats seasoned with onions, garlic, and duck fat.

In Russia, kasha refers to any grain—barley, oats, millet, wheat berries, semolina, cracked dried corn, even rice—boiled or baked in water, stock, or milk, usually (but not always) to the consistency of porridge. Often kasha is made from buckwheat, which isn't a grain at all but instead the tiny triangular brown seed of a plant belonging to the rhubarb and sorrel family. Buckwheat kasha is eaten as a hot breakfast cereal; served as a starchy, savory side dish; stuffed into meats, poultry, fish, and squash; fried up as fritters, cutlets, and croutons; tossed into salads, soups, and stews; and combined with curd cheese, milk, eggs, sugar, and sour cream, then slow-baked in an earthenware pot to make a sweet, soul-satisfying pudding.

# Fluffy Buckwheat Kasha

*This light, fluffy version of buckwheat kasha is the kind that Russian cooks often serve as a simple side dish.*

**2 cups chicken or beef stock (or just water)**
**2 tablespoons unsalted butter**
**½ teaspoon salt**
**½ teaspoon finely ground black pepper**
**1 cup medium- or coarse-ground buckwheat groats**
**1 large egg, lightly beaten**

- Put the stock, butter, salt, and pepper in a heavy 2-quart saucepan over medium heat to come to a boil.

- Meanwhile stir the buckwheat with the beaten egg in a large skillet until all the grains are wet. Cook over medium heat, stirring constantly, until the buckwheat is dry and toasty smelling (about 8 to 10 minutes).

- Stir the buckwheat into the boiling stock. Bring to a boil over medium-high heat, then reduce the heat to low, cover tightly, and cook for 40 minutes. Fluff the kasha with a fork, cover the pan tightly, and cook 20 minutes longer.

- Fluff the kasha again with a fork. Serve hot, as a side dish.

- Makes 4 to 6 servings.

# Apple-Horseradish Sauce

*This slightly piquant sauce is an excellent accompaniment to grilled meats (including sausages), as well as cold meats (beef, tongue, pork, ham) and smoked fish (salmon, mackerel, sprats). Don't even consider making it "lighter" by using American "lite" sour cream and mayonnaise. Rich, creamy, pure full-fat sour cream and full-fat mayonnaise are essential for the best flavor and texture of this sauce.*

3 tablespoons fresh or bottled horseradish*
½ cup pure sour cream
½ cup mayonnaise
1½ teaspoons cider vinegar
1 Granny Smith apple, peeled, cored, and shredded
¼ teaspoon sugar (optional)

*Put bottled horseradish in a sieve and press out as much liquid as possible before measuring.

- Whisk all the ingredients together in a small glass bowl until well combined. Cover and refrigerate for at least 1 hour before serving.

- Makes about 1½ cups of sauce.

# Gingerbread Squares

*We often made this spicy gingerbread when we lived in a remote part of the Scottish Highlands, long before moving to Russia. In Scotland we baked all our own breads, cakes, and cookies in the fireplace oven of an old stone cottage located on the far northwest coast. We especially liked this recipe because it was easy to make and inexpensive, requiring no butter, milk, or eggs. So it was a good dessert to make in Siberia, too, where we could never count on those ingredients being available in the stores.*

▶ **NOTE:** It is important to use an 8-inch square metal baking pan for this recipe.

**2 cups all-purpose flour**
**¾ cup sugar**
**2 teaspoons baking powder**
**1½ teaspoons ground ginger**
**1 teaspoon ground cinnamon**
**½ teaspoon ground cloves**
**½ teaspoon ground nutmeg**
**¼ teaspoon salt**
**¾ cup very hot tap water**
**½ cup dark honey**
**¼ cup vegetable oil**

- Preheat the oven to 350°F. Butter an 8-inch square metal baking pan.

- Whisk the flour, sugar, baking powder, ginger, cinnamon, cloves, nutmeg, and salt together in a medium bowl, until well combined. Mix the hot water, honey, and oil in a separate bowl, stirring well.

- Make a well in the center of the dry ingredients, pour in the liquid mixture, and stir gently, just until the ingredients are blended and no large lumps remain. Do not over-beat or the gingerbread will be tough.

- Spread the batter evenly in the baking pan. Bake at 350°F. for 25 to 30 minutes, or until a skewer inserted in the center comes out clean. Let the gingerbread cool in the pan, set on a wire rack, then cut into 2-inch squares. Wrap leftovers tightly in foil or plastic wrap for storage.

- Makes: 16 2-inch squares.

▶ **NOTE:** This light-colored, densely textured gingerbread tastes even better the day after baking, when the flavors have had time to develop. After the gingerbread has cooled completely in the pan, cover it tightly with foil, then cut it into squares the next day. For a darker-colored Scottish version, substitute dark brown sugar and molasses for the white sugar and honey.

## Russian Gingerbreads

Russians love their *pryaniki*, gingerbreads and cake-like spice cookies made since medieval times. Often the stiff dough was pressed into an intricately carved wooden mold that embossed attractive designs on the surface, and sometimes the dough was filled with sweet preserves before baking, as it still is today.

Culinary historian Darra Goldstein has pointed out that the early Slavs originally made a simple version of *pryaniki* by combining rye flour with water. But after the mid-tenth century, trade with other parts of the world brought new spices into Russia—including black pepper, cloves, anise, coriander, cardamom, and ginger, as well as citrus fruits—which were used for making more complex and interesting kinds of spice cookies and cakes that were sweetened with honey and, later, sugar. Eventually the cities of Tula, Gorodets, Tver, Novgorod, Pokrov, and Ryazan became well known for their commercial gingerbread production. But Russian home cooks make gingerbreads, too, including their own *pryaniki* cookies that are often served with tea.

# Whipped Raspberry Pudding

*The recipe for this fluffy pastel-colored pudding probably came to Siberia with immigrants and exiles from the Baltic region, where it's a traditional treat beloved by children. In earlier days, this simple farmhouse dish would have taken a long time to beat by hand with a big wooden spoon or a homemade wooden whisk, but today it's much easier with modern electric mixers. Russians often serve this homey comfort food with a spoonful of berry preserves on top. I also like to garnish it with berry liqueur and a frill of whipped cream.*

**3 cups unsweetened raspberry juice***
**1 tablespoon lemon juice**
**½ cup sugar**
**½ cup uncooked farina****

Garnish

**Whipped cream**
**Berry liqueur**

*Or any unsweetened berry juice, such as cranberry, blueberry, strawberry, lingonberry, red currant, or sea-buckthorn, or a fruit juice such as apple or cherry. If the juice is very tart, add a bit more sugar when heating it.
**Or standard commercial Cream of Wheat (not instant or quick cooking).

- Combine the raspberry and lemon juices in a non-aluminum saucepan. Bring to a boil over medium heat, then stir in the sugar, a small amount at a time. When the sugar has dissolved completely, slowly add the farina, stirring constantly. Reduce the heat to low, and let the mixture simmer for 8 minutes, stirring frequently. It will become very thick.

- Transfer the hot mixture to a large metal bowl set on a pot holder. Beat while still hot with a hand-held electric mixer on high speed for 15 minutes (or a few minutes less with the wire whisk attachment on a stand mixer), rotating the bowl constantly and scraping down the sides, until the pudding is fluffy and stiff enough to stand up in peaks.

- Gently spoon the pudding into individual dessert bowls or stemmed glasses. Cover and refrigerate until chilled. Serve cold, with a teaspoon or two of berry liqueur drizzled over it (or berry jam thinned with a bit of sweet liqueur) and a swirl of whipped cream on top.

- Makes approximately 4 cups (6 servings).

▶ **NOTE:** For an even richer version, stir ¼ cup of almond liqueur into the thickened mixture before beating it to fluffy peaks.

# Bountiful Berries

In addition to turning summer's bounty of wild berries into sweet preserves and freezing whole berries to keep throughout the winter, Russians also press the juice from berries and bottle it to drink with meals or to use as a cooking ingredient. An especially popular summertime beverage is made with raw cranberries boiled to bursting, pressed in a cheesecloth to extract the juice, and cooked with water, sugar, and a bit of lemon juice, then cooled. These healthy fruit juices are often favored as non-alcoholic drinks with meals.

*Kompot* is another beverage made with a variety of fresh berries and chopped fresh or dried fruits, cooked with sugar and plenty of water, then cooled to room temperature and served as a refreshing drink with meals both at home and in restaurants. When you finish drinking the liquid, be sure to spoon out the delicious fruit and berries that settled to the bottom of the glass.

# Chapter 3
# Shop 'Til You Drop

## Russia's New Market Economy

Shopping for food in Russia was a time-consuming daily chore, with no guarantee of success. But we took a positive attitude toward this challenge, approaching the quest for food as a kind of treasure hunt, a search to find the best products for sale at a price we were willing to pay—and, many times, just to find anything at all.

In Asian Russia of the mid-1990s, there were no Western-style supermarkets where you could buy most of your groceries under one roof, and no neighborhood quick-stop stores where you could pick up a loaf of bread, a carton of milk, or a six-pack of beer any time of day or night. Instead, we had to travel—on foot and by public transportation—to a number of different stores, open-air markets, and kiosks all over Vladivostok and Irkutsk, in hope of finding the foods and household supplies we needed.

Russian cuisine—and the agricultural products on which it is based—has a long history and tradition of richness and variety, at least in those areas of the country where the climate and economic conditions were favorable. But after the Bolshevik Revolution of 1917, seven decades of Soviet rule produced a nation that, throughout much of the twentieth century, suffered from food shortages, poor quality products, and long lines of people waiting to purchase even the most basic foodstuffs.

Under the Soviets, all the food stores had been state-controlled, but in the Russian Federation of the 1990s many of them were slowly becoming privately owned businesses as the country made the transition to a market economy. The largest of these stores were the *gastronomy*, which carried a range of foods from dairy products to flour to canned goods, although we never knew for certain which products might be available on any particular day. Architecturally, some of these *gastronomy* were gray, concrete, Socialist-Realist blocks, dull, drab, and dirty by Western standards. Others, built before the Bolshevik Revolution, had authentic but poorly maintained Art Nouveau interiors, with mirrored walls, marble counter tops, colorful ceramic tiles, and ornate brass lighting fixtures. A smaller number of stores were called *kulinarii*—the Russian equivalent of delicatessens—which sold a limited selection of prepared foods, such as potato and cabbage salads, along with some canned goods, condiments, and packages of tea. Other stores specialized in a single product—bread, milk, meat, poultry, fish—whereas the little kiosks springing up like mushrooms all over the place sold whatever goods they could acquire, from vodka and snack foods to brassieres and auto parts, all jumbled together inside a tiny enclosed street stall.

With few exceptions, the food stores in Vladivostok and Irkutsk were not pleasant places to shop. Sometimes customers standing in line had to step around a derelict drunk passed out on the floor. Shop cats wandered around behind the counters and curled up on the dusty shelves. Mice and rats scurried across the floors of stores without resident felines. At a bakery in Vladivostok Tom spotted a small cake decorated with what appeared to be raisins but turned out to be flies stuck to the frosting. A friend from Serbia said she lost 15 pounds when she moved from Belgrade to Vladivostok in 1993, because of her nausea at the sights and smells of the local food stores: insects crawling on the unwrapped butter, cheese, and meat, the aroma of rotting produce, the grunge and grime on the counters and floors, the foods unappetizingly displayed in large, shallow, white enameled pans shaped much like old hospital bedpans.

*Vegetable vendor at the central market in Irkutsk, 1994.*

Our own favorite places to shop—especially during the summer and autumn—were the so-called farmers' markets. Like farmers' markets in many parts of the world, these included vendors who'd actually grown the foods they were selling, as well as middlemen retailing other people's products. Outside the major cities, these farmers' markets often looked, sounded, and smelled like the markets depicted in Russian paintings and described in Russian literature several centuries ago.

The permanent farmers' markets in Vladivostok and Irkutsk all had an indoor area, usually in a concrete-slab building like a small warehouse, with designated sections for meat, dairy products, vegetables, and so on, or simply several counters where vendors sold a limited variety of fresh or preserved foods, domestic and imported. Outdoors, vendors displayed their wares in an open-air section of weathered wooden stalls, long wooden trestle tables, and small folding metal tables. Around the edges of some of these markets, a few little kiosks and rough wooden sheds served as shops selling bread, pastries, soft drinks, alcoholic beverages, and a hodgepodge of new imported food products. Moveable markets, on the other hand, were set up temporarily on a public square or patch of ground where we stood in line, often in sub-freezing weather, to buy food off the backs of trucks, sold directly from the trucker to the consumer: one line for beets, another for onions, another for potatoes, the damp earth still clinging to them from the farms.

Vendors at all these markets ranged from Russian farmers with rough, gnarled hands, to raw-boned country women, their heads covered with kerchiefs; from fresh-faced young girls eagerly hawking their wares, to heavily made-up matrons sitting bored behind stacks of imported canned goods; from Chinese and Korean sellers clad in cheap track suits, in the Russian Far East, to colorfully dressed women from the Caucasus and Central Asia, in Irkutsk and other cities of southern Siberia. Skinny cats darted between the stalls in search of scraps, while nervous little birds hopped around on the wooden crates of unwrapped meat, pecking at the frozen blocks of beef, pork, chicken, and fish piled on the ground. And a woman with nothing but a table full of frozen fish heads munched on a fish tail as if it were a potato chip.

## Shopping at Work

In the mid-1990s, many Russians could also purchase food at a company store or canteen at their place of work—office, school, or factory—a practice dating from the Soviet era. In our dean's office at the university in Vladivostok, we bought flour scooped out of a big linen bag, Chinese apples, Russian cheese, bulk sugar, and fresh meat, all weighed out on a hand-held scale by the departmental secretary.

At the farmers' markets we paid the vendors directly for their wares. But at most of the standard stores, even the privatized ones, we had to go through a three-stage purchasing process perpetuated from earlier times. First we stood in the line leading up to the merchandise counter where there was something we wanted to buy—dairy products, dry staples, coffee and tea, whatever—and where a surly shop girl listlessly waited on the customers one at a time. Since all the products sold in that section were displayed on the shelves behind the counter, we had to ask the shop girl for each item we wanted. She scooped the rice or beans or flour out of a wooden barrel or burlap bag and weighed them on a big, old-fashioned, metal scale. She stacked the requested bottles of fruit juice, packages of pasta, and cans of green peas on the counter. She weighed out chocolate candies and frosted gingerbread cookies, breaking in half the last cookie or candy to make the weight come out to exactly 250 or 500 grams. Then she added up the total price on a wooden abacus and handed us a scrap of paper with the price of each item, and the total cost, penciled on it.

At that point, we went to another part of the store and stood in line at the cashier's booth to pay for the products in cash. After the cashier had totaled up the items once more on an abacus (sometimes also double-checking her math with a hand-held electronic calculator), she took our money and handed back the change with a receipt marked "paid." Then we returned to the merchandise counter and stood in line again, to exchange the receipt for the products themselves—which we stuffed into our own shopping bags because the stores provided neither paper nor plastic bags for their customers.

In larger stores, we had to repeat that three-stage process several times, once for each separate section of the store where there was something we wanted to buy. Finally, Tom and I lugged our purchases home on the crowded and dirty public transportation system, or we walked for miles—often in fog, rain, or snow—whenever the buses and trams weren't running because of fuel shortages or power outages. Then we still had to haul all those heavy groceries up several flights of stairs to our apartment in the high-rise village.

Hyperinflation in Russia's new market economy added another dimension to the purchasing process. When we arrived in Russia in the summer of 1993, the currency exchange rate was around 1,000 rubles to a dollar. By the time we left Vladivostok at the end of December 1994, the exchange rate was almost 4,000 rubles to a dollar, after having peaked at 5,000 to the dollar that October. During 1993, Vladivostok was Russia's second most expensive city, with prices for goods sold in that region increasing 900% that year,

# Sticker Shock

From 1990 through 1994, consumer prices in Russia increased 2,020% for all goods and services. Prices for food products rose 2,154%, although only 653% for alcoholic beverages. —Rand Corporation and Moscow's Center for Demography and Human Ecology

and the cost of staple foods almost double the national average. Prices were rising so quickly we couldn't always keep up with them. Once at a food store in Vladivostok, I stood in line to purchase a box of tea, received my payment slip from the girl behind the merchandise counter, then stood in line at the cashier's booth, paid the amount penciled on the slip of paper, and got my receipt. But by the time I returned to the other line to collect my purchase at the counter, the price of tea had increased 100 rubles (4 cents). Since my cashier's receipt was now 100 rubles short, the shop girl refused to give me the tea, and I had to repeat the whole three-stage purchasing process all over again.

By October of 1994, the value of the ruble had declined so much that few sellers even bothered handing back small change to their customers. And with the collapse of the Russian currency later that month, the prices of consumer goods started rising even faster. People began paying for products—and getting any change in return—with stacks of banded bank notes, totaling 10 thousand, 20 thousand, and 50 thousand rubles each. Seldom did anyone use individual notes of 100- or 200-ruble denomination, because those rubles were now almost worthless. Each time before going out to purchase food that fall, Tom and I filled our shopping bags with stacks of thousands of rubles to exchange for whatever products we might find that day. And as inflation worsened, some Americans in Vladivostok began referring to the Russian currency as "the rubble."

During this time of transition in Russia's new market economy, "rolling food shortages" were always a problem, although they were never as severe as the chronic shortages of the Soviet era. In Vladivostok, eggs would disappear from the markets for two weeks at a time, then suddenly become available again at a much higher price. For several weeks the store shelves would be bare of flour, cheese, or salt (which was particularly scarce during "pickling season" in the autumn). Once we went for two months without finding any sugar in

Vladivostok. And store-bought spices were such a rarity in Asian Russia that we were thankful we'd brought two bottles of Tabasco sauce and plenty of our own spices from America: cinnamon, allspice, ginger, cumin, thyme, oregano, Italian seasoning, and black peppercorns; small containers of powdered lemon peel, vanilla, Worcestershire Sauce, and Colman's hot mustard; and several pounds of Texas chili powder and New Mexico powdered chiles, along with dried whole New Mexico chiles, chipotles, habaneros, japones, and pequins.

## Larry Hagman's Gift

In 1993, two months before we moved from Germany to Russia, Tom and I escorted a group of Americans and Britons on a tour from Munich to Moscow and St. Petersburg. Our local guide in Moscow was a 61-year-old Russian woman who spoke English fluently and enjoyed telling us uncensored stories about life in Russia, now that people could speak openly without fear of being arrested.

When she discovered that Tom and I originally came from Texas, she was very excited. "Do you know Larry Hagman?" she asked.

"You mean the star of the TV show, *Dallas*?" I replied. "Sure, we know who he is, but we don't know him personally."

"I was his translator and personal guide when he came to Moscow a few years ago," she went on, "and he was so pleased with my work that he asked if I'd be his translator the next time he came to Russia. He also asked what he could bring me from America. 'Cinnamon!' I immediately said. He looked surprised. 'That's all?' he asked. 'Yes,' I told him, 'I have recipes I want to cook, and they need cinnamon, but it's impossible to find in Moscow.'"

A year or two later, long after she'd forgotten that request, Hagman came back to Moscow and hired her as his translator-guide. And he'd brought two bottles of cinnamon as a gift. "I thought he'd forgotten all about it," she said. "But he remembered! He was such a nice man! And I used that cinnamon so carefully, because I didn't know when I'd ever be able to get cinnamon again."

After searching for months in Vladivostok, I managed to find only paprika, salt, bay leaves, anise seeds, black peppercorns, and a single bottle of highly priced Tabasco sauce. So where did the Russians get their own spices? Friends in the Russian Far East said they bought spices in the markets of Moldova, Bulgaria, or Ukraine whenever they traveled there to visit relatives in the summer. And Russian sailors from Vladivostok brought home to their wives precious spices from China, Vietnam, and India, wherever their ships had made ports of call.

Despite the difficulties of finding certain foods, Tom and I ate well in Russia. In part, that was because we were already experienced cooks. But we also dined well because of our positive attitude toward whatever culinary hand we were dealt in the marketplace. Unlike in the United States, we didn't go to the market with a shopping list of specific items we wanted to buy. That would have been a folly in Russia. Instead, we looked at whatever products were available that particular day and said, "Okay, what can we cook with *these*?" Even when we couldn't find certain things we sorely wanted, we always viewed our shopping bags as half full, not half empty—and we constructed our menus around those ingredients, reveling in the bounties of summer and accepting the scarcities of winter.

Not long after we first moved to Vladivostok—while we were still basking in the warmth of an unexpected Indian summer—I was suddenly overcome by a strong feeling that we should lay in a large stock of provisions for the winter. Perhaps it was some ancestral memory of all the famine fears of my farmer forebears. Despite temperatures that rose into the 80s Fahrenheit during September and early October, I possessed a peasant's pessimism about the mild weather. That late spell of warm weather lasted so long I expected to wake up any

## And the Winner Is ... Dairy Products!

During the time we lived in Siberia and the Russian Far East, each person in the Russian Federation annually consumed an average of 24 pounds of fish and fish products, 64 pounds of fruit, 68 pounds of sugar and confections, 118 pounds of meat and meat products, 150 pounds of vegetables, 274 pounds of potatoes, and 630 pounds of milk and milk products. —*OECD Economic Surveys: The Russian Federation* (1995)

morning and find the puddles from last night's rain turned into sheets of ice, as autumn suddenly froze into winter. And I knew that as the months went by, finding food in Russia was only going to get worse, not better. So Tom and I began filling our little apartment's kitchen, pantry, and balcony with bags of flour, rice, and beans; bottles, jars, and cans of preserved fruits and vegetables; and stocks of hardy root vegetables, all in preparation for our first Russian winter.

## T-Bone Whacks

Shopping for meat in Russia was not for the squeamish. Fresh meat was sold out of the trunks of cars or on tables set up in the farmers' markets—directly from the animal to the customer. The severed, bloody head of the recently slaughtered cow or pig was displayed on the table or the hood of the car, the animal's lifeless eyes seeming to stare in reproach at the customers purchasing pieces of its butchered body. Behind the meat counters or beside the cars sat massive chopping blocks made from tree trunks, where the butchers chopped the carcasses into pieces with an ax. The result was not so much a "cut" of meat as a "whack." Our favorite "whacks" were T-bone "roasts," at least 2 inches thick (with an ax, thinner steaks were out of the question). These prime whacks of beef cost only about a dollar a pound in the autumn of 1993, and when roasted properly they always turned out to be more tender and flavorful than their method of slaughter and sale would ever suggest.

At an open-air market in Ussuriisk, 60 miles north of Vladivostok, I saw a cheap, shiny, red-and-gold brocade tablecloth trimmed with heavy gold fringe, draped over half a pig still waiting to be cut into parts, its fresh blood stains mingling with the ornate designs in the cloth. And at a moveable market in Vladivostok's main square, Tom watched as several Chinese construction workers haggled with a Russian butcher to buy the fresh cow's head sitting on the hood of his truck. Such scenes were typical in Asian Russia, where the marketing of fresh meat was more elemental than the sanitized displays of plastic-packaged pork, beef, and poultry in American grocery stores.

At the outdoor markets in winter, stacked wooden crates also held big blocks of unwrapped frozen meat. Customers couldn't select a certain cut of this frozen fare. You merely told the vendor the amount you wanted to purchase, and he either chopped off a chunk from the icy block with an ax or dropped

# A Russian Meat Market in Winter

"The anatomical dissections of a Russian butcher are extremely simple. Bones and meat having been all rendered equally hard by the frost, it would be difficult to attempt to separate the several joints. The animals are, accordingly, sawn up into a number of slices of an inch or two in thickness, and in the course of this operation a quantity of animal sawdust is scattered on the snow, whence it is eagerly gathered up by poor children, of whom great numbers haunt the market." —Johann Georg Kohl, *Russia* (1842)

the solid mass of meat onto the ground to break it up into smaller pieces, then weighed the frozen debris on an old-fashioned hand-held scale.

Fresh beef was seldom difficult to find in Siberia and the Russian Far East, but pork appeared in the markets less often, and it always commanded a premium price. Smoked pork was even more rare, as were small whole piglets which we were surprised to see once at a farmers' market in Vladivostok. Russian sausages, of which there were only two or three kinds, were the epitome of mystery meat: fatty, gristly, and an unappetizing grayish-pink color. We avoided them most of the time, opting instead for higher quality Hungarian salami, rust-red and redolent of paprika, whenever we were lucky enough to find it.

Locally raised chickens were so stringy and gamy that Tom called them "Russian roadrunners." Our chickens of choice were frozen leg quarters—large, fleshy, and tender—imported from the United States and priced at the ruble equivalent of about a dollar a pound. Tom and I jokingly called these topless chickens "yuppie leftovers," because the majority of chicken parts sold in the United States were white-meat products (chicken breasts, tenders, wings) favored by health-conscious and convenience-oriented customers, whereas much of the darker meat was exported to Russia and China, countries where the fact of having any chicken at all was more important than the latest food fads. We also bought large frozen turkey legs and big tubes of ground turkey, both high-quality poultry products imported from the United States.

# What's in a Name?

Chicken leg quarters imported from the United States have acquired a number of different nicknames in various parts of the Russian Federation. In Vladivostok, these cuts of chicken were called *gorbushki*, supposedly because the Russian-American trade agreement for importing them was signed when Mikhail Gorbachev and George H. W. Bush were both in office. Perhaps this was also a play on words: *gorbushka* also means "end crust," or the heel of a loaf of bread, which is considered the tastiest part of the loaf—just like dark meat is not only the back end, but also the tastiest part, of a chicken.

# Caviar Snacks

Fish and other seafood were much more prevalent in the markets of Vladivostok than in Irkutsk, not surprisingly since Vladivostok was Russia's major Pacific Ocean port. But even that close to the sea, supplies of fresh, frozen, smoked, and canned fish products were often irregular. At various times in Vladivostok, we found fresh salmon, flounder, carp, sprats, scallops, squid, crab, shrimp, crayfish, and salmon caviar—and once I even saw a whole, huge, kaluga sturgeon at a *gastronom* in the center of town. In Irkutsk, we contented ourselves with canned salmon or crab, when we could get it, and dined well whenever we lucked into a load of fresh *omul'*, a white-fleshed fish belonging to the salmon family, taken from the waters of nearby Lake Baikal.

One of my most memorable purchases was a huge, live, Kamchatka crab (the same as Alaskan king crabs in America), which I bought directly from the Russian fishermen on a rusty trawler docked in Vladivostok. When Alla took me down to a fish market at the harbor that frosty November day, neither of us could pass up the big bargain-priced crabs selling for the ruble equivalent of about $6.50 to $10 apiece, depending on their size. We struggled to get the large, spiky, wriggling creatures onto the tram and back home to our apartments, where Tom and I cooked our catch in a way all-too-reminiscent of the famous lobster scene in Woody Allen's film, *Annie Hall.* Then we cracked open the shell with Tom's

Leatherman tool and pulled out the flesh with toothpicks. For the next two days, we gorged on the freshest, most flavorful crab we'd ever eaten, sprinkled with lemon juice or garnished with garlic mayonnaise.

In Texas, "a bowl of red" means a bowl of meaty chili—hot, spicy, and redolent of cumin and chile peppers. In Russia, Tom's idea of "a bowl of red" was a huge helping of salmon caviar, which was so abundant in Vladivostok that we almost took it for granted—if not as a staple, at least as a garnish as common as parsley in the United States. Fresh, glistening, red-orange salmon roe was sold in half-liter and one-liter jars by vendors in the farmers' markets and in bulk at some

*Fresh fish for sale at a farmers' market in Ussuriisk, Russian Far East, 1993.*

of the fish stores, where shop girls ladled the sparkling beads of caviar into jars that customers brought from home. One day when we were shopping with Alla at an outdoor market, she urged Tom to purchase a particular whole salmon stacked among the hundreds of seemingly identical-looking fish filling the back of a truck. "It's a female," she explained, "and it's still full of eggs. Make sure the seller gives you *that* one." Never one to dismiss Alla's advice, Tom brought the salmon home, where we cut it open and processed the red-orange roe ourselves. We ended up with so much fresh caviar that it was difficult to eat all of it before it spoiled. For the next three days, we spread gobs of salmon caviar on buttered bread, spooned it onto halves of hard-boiled eggs, mixed it with scrambled eggs for breakfast, and even carried it to school for lunch.

# From the Dairy

Russian dairy products were of such good quality that we considered them indispensable in our kitchen, even though they were pricey in relation to other foods. Milk was usually sold in old-fashioned, ½-liter and 1-liter returnable bottles made of thick greenish-blue glass, or in flimsy plastic, pyramid-shaped containers that often broke open on the way home from the store. In Irkutsk, however, milk was also marketed in a manner dating from far in the past. Fresh milk, straight from the cow, was poured into 1- or 3-liter buckets and set outside to freeze in the Siberian winter. As the milk froze, a thick wooden dowel or small tree branch was stuck upright in the middle of each pail. When the milk had frozen solid, it was removed from the pails in the form of large, white, truncated cones, like giant Popsicles, which were taken to the market and stacked for sale on tables outdoors in the frigid air. We slipped these cones of milk into our own plastic bags and carried them home using the sticks as handles, and the milk never melted in transit, even on the crowded trolleys and trams. After the milk had thawed overnight in

*Vendors of dairy products (cheese, milk, sour cream, kefir) at the main market in Ussuriisk, Russian Far East, 1993.*

a bucket in our kitchen, I slowly heated it to kill the germs, then strained it through cheesecloth to remove the bits of animal hair and other adulterants floating in it. That farm-fresh milk smelled strongly of the barnyard as it heated on the stove, but the milk itself tasted fine, and we reveled in the rich cream that rose to the top as the milk cooled.

Sweet cream that we didn't process ourselves was hard to find and very expensive. But Russian sour cream, with at least 40% butterfat, was a staple in our kitchen. The best we ever bought was at a farmers' market in Ussuriisk, where rosy-cheeked country women with kerchiefs on their heads ladled out the ivory-colored sour cream from big enameled buckets. That nutty-flavored cream was so thick and buttery that wooden spoons stuck into it stood upright. Another popular milk product was *kefir*, a cultured milk drink that we used as a substitute for buttermilk in our recipes.

Four kinds of butter were sold in Siberia and the Russian Far East: salted, sweet (unsalted), clarified, and chocolate-flavored, although the latter two were available only sporadically. Almost all the butter we found in Russian stores was pale-yellow, creamy, unsalted butter with an excellent flavor, sold in chunks cut to the customers' specifications from a big slab on the counter, then wrapped in whatever scrap paper was on hand. It was usually called "*kres'tyanskoye maslo*" ("country butter," "peasant butter"), but Alla said that term was only a marketing device. "*Real* country butter," she said, "is so creamy and soft that it can be used for making cakes without beating the butter first." She recalled that in the rural Siberian markets of her childhood, this nearly-white butter was shaped by hand into balls and sold in containers made of birch bark.

## Birch-Bark Boxes

Functional and decorative items made of birch bark—boxes, baskets, shoes, drinking vessels—have been handcrafted in Russia for centuries. In the past, birch-bark containers were often used for storing seeds, berries, salt, bread, sour cream, butter, and even milk. Today, Russian artisans continue to fashion handsome folk-art objects out of birch bark, bending, weaving, and braiding the pliable bark into objects, often decorated with lacelike cutwork looking like tooled leather, made of this common material from Russia's forests.

Cheese was a major part of our diet in Russia. We ate slices of aged, firm cheese nearly every day and used it as an ingredient in many dishes, too—unlike Russians who mainly ate hard cheese as a *zakuska* at the beginning of a meal. We found several varieties of Russian cheeses in the local markets: soft (but rather gunky) cream cheese; pale-colored, processed "*kolbasa*" cheese, pressed into tubes like *kolbasa* sausage; semi-hard cheeses like Tilsit and Edam and more aged ones like Cheddar; and once an excellent grating cheese that tasted surprisingly like real Italian Parmigiano-Reggiano. But on any given day, there was usually only one kind of cheese available at any particular store, and sometimes there was only one type of cheese—the same type—sold at every place we shopped throughout the city.

We shared with Russians their love of *tvorog*, a kind of soft, white, fresh curd cheese made from slightly soured milk. Drier and firmer in texture than American cottage cheese, Russian *tvorog* came in several varieties, from fat-free to creamy-rich, and even occasionally a sweetened version. Like the Russians, we used *tvorog* frequently in cooking both sweet and savory dishes, as well as eating it for breakfast and snacks, garnished with a drizzle of sour cream and a sprinkling of sugar.

Dove Bars, Snickers and Mars ice cream bars, and bricks of Australian ice cream were just beginning to be imported into Asian Russia, but we still favored the old-fashioned Russian ice cream sold by street vendors. In winter, unwrapped cones pre-filled with ice cream were sold out of cardboard boxes stacked on the sidewalks with no fear of the frozen treats melting in the frigid air. Vanilla was by far the best—rich, creamy, and not too sweet. Other varieties—coffee, chocolate, banana, and strawberry—were too artificially flavored for our tastes.

Despite eating so many of these fat-laden foods—butter, whole milk, eggs, cheese, mayonnaise, sour cream, ice cream, and red meats, along with plenty of carbohydrates, too—Tom and I both lost 20 pounds in Russia without even trying, and our cholesterol levels remained normal. After we returned to the Texas, the doctor who did our blood tests attributed our svelte figures and overall good health to the "Siberian spa regimen" of rigorous daily exercise in the calorie-burning cold climate: walking for miles with heavy shopping bags in hand and climbing several flights of stairs every day, at work and at home—all by necessity, of course.

## Harvest of the Seasons

As Americans living in Asian Russia in the mid-1990s, we often had cravings for foods that we could only dream about there: artichokes, asparagus, and avocados; broccoli and Brussels sprouts; chestnuts and chirimoyas; molasses and maple syrup; peaches and papayas; saffron and summer squash; fresh tarragon and

# Potatoes: The Second Bread

Russians often refer to potatoes as their "second bread." But this hardy tuber has not always been so popular or widespread. Most sources say that potatoes were first imported into Russia in the early 1700s, during the time of Peter the Great. Others claim that potatoes didn't come to Russia until several decades later, during the reign of Catherine the Great. Despite a government decree in 1797 that potatoes be planted throughout the country, they were not accepted as a food by most of the Russian population until the second half of the nineteenth century.

Russians now grow a variety of potatoes in many parts of the country, on large potato farms and in the small garden plots behind village houses or around little dachas. But when we lived in Siberia and the Russian Far East, urban consumers had a very limited choice of potato types. Most of the potatoes sold in the markets were the small, firm kind that are best for boiling. In 1994, Russians in Vladivostok were thrilled when huge, mealy-textured baking potatoes started being imported from the United States, and they formed long lines to purchase those novel potatoes at the one store in the city that sometimes stocked them.

thyme. But from August through October, the markets of Vladivostok displayed the bounty of the local late-summer harvest, along with the fruits of Russians' foraging in the forest and their "silent hunting" for mushrooms.

At the farmers' markets in the autumn of 1994, I found the biggest quantity and best quality of fresh produce I'd seen in Russia during the past year: red, yellow, and green

*Dried white mushrooms at the central market in Irkutsk, 2007.*

tomatoes; purple and orange eggplants; dark green cucumbers, golden ears of corn, and even a few green beans; big white onions, slender green onion tops,

# Real Russian Tomatoes

While living in Russia I fondly remembered the luscious, bright-red, sun-ripened tomatoes, straight from the vine and still warm to the touch, that we'd happily devoured in huge quantities when we'd lived in Greece and Spain. But Russia taught me to appreciate tomatoes in whatever form I could find them: fresh or pickled, large or small, red, yellow, orange, or green. Russia, thank goodness, had not yet reached the level of development of the Netherlands or Belgium or the United States, where cannonball tomatoes—pulpy, anemic-looking, and tasting of artificial fertilizers—were shot out of their winter hothouses directly into plastic packages for shipping to supermarkets. Russians, too, grew hothouse tomatoes—of necessity, because of their climate—but even those were more flavorful than many tomatoes I'd eaten in the industrialized West.

With the exception of commercial hothouse varieties grown on a large scale to supply urban markets and canning factories, the *real* tomatoes of Russia are grown by individual people, on tiny plots of land. And those Russian tomatoes have *character*. Gardeners start their seedlings in the spring, in pots on the glass-enclosed balconies of city apartments and in little greenhouses in the gardens behind village houses. When warm weather finally arrives, the seedlings are planted with love outdoors, nurtured with care during the short summer, and harvested with hope in late-July to mid-August, depending on the latitude and the local microclimate. In season, they're eaten fresh, in abundance and with vigor. The rest are preserved in brine, often flavored with garlic or dill, to be consumed throughout the long Russian winter.

The Siberians have developed more than 60 varieties of tomatoes that ripen during the short growing season in their northern latitudes. Some of these cold-tolerant varieties even survive the spring frosts that kill other tomato plants. But when we lived in Eastern Siberia in 1994, there never seemed to be enough fresh tomatoes to satisfy the demand for them. And in winter the realities of the new market economy became painfully obvious when fresh tomatoes flown in from the warmer climes of the Caucasus cost 12,000 rubles ($7.50) per kilogram—at a time when the average Russian's wage was around $100 a month.

and thick leeks; bunches of garlic, shallots, and radishes; leafy green sorrel, Swiss chard, bok choy, and three kinds of lettuce; six different types of peppers, from mild to hot; red and green cabbages; pumpkins, potatoes, carrots, turnips, and beets; cilantro, mint, and two types of parsley; and a multitude of wild mushrooms, of so many colors and shapes that I had to ask Alla to identify them for me.

Fresh fruits and berries added their jewel tones to the colors of Vladivostok's open-air markets: oranges, apples, bananas, kiwis, melons, persimmons, pomegranates, and pears; purple wild grapes from the southernmost parts of the Russian Far East; small red *limonnik* berries (*Schisandra chinensis*), big celadon-colored gooseberries, and jade-green *kishmish* (the term for seedless raisins in the rest of Russia, but the name of a rather rectangular-shaped fruit found in the Russian Far East, which tasted like a cross between a kiwi and a guava). Smoke-dried cherries were for sale in the autumn, and fresh lemons suddenly (and briefly) became available in December.

But during our first year in Russia we learned that when the weather turned colder, the supply of fresh produce dropped sharply, leaving most of the stores stocked mainly with those standbys of the Russian winter: root vegetables, grains, and bottled green tomatoes picked shortly before the first frost. And by the end of March, after five long months of freezing temperatures, fresh produce of any sort seemed only a distant dream.

That first year we also saw how hard the Siberian winter could be on perishables. For instance, eggs were sold loose, not in cartons, at the indoor markets; we carefully stacked them one by one in our shopping bags and carried them

## Onions with No Bottoms

Root vegetables and their green leaves were often sold separately in Russian markets, where vendors could make money off both parts of the plant. Some dacha gardeners kept the roots—onions, turnips, beets, rutabagas, garlic, parsley, horseradish—to store in cellars at home throughout the winter, and sold only the perishable fresh greens instead. Green onion tops were a welcome ingredient in our kitchen, especially at times when those "onions with no bottoms" were often the only greens available.

home, struggling to keep them from breaking in the crush of the crowds on the jam-packed buses, trolleys, and trams. But sometimes all the eggs froze solid in transit and cracked along the way. In mid-March of 1994, at the city's central food market in downtown Irkutsk, Tom discovered a small, precious head of Romaine lettuce—the first lettuce we'd seen since arriving in Russia seven months before. It froze on the way to our apartment, then wilted into limp, lifeless, brown-tipped leaves as it thawed. But we ate it anyway. And that single head of lettuce turned out to be the last we would find until the end of June.

As the weather slowly began to warm in Irkutsk that spring, merchants from Central Asia and the Caucasus erected enticing displays of fresh fruits and vegetables; peanuts and walnuts; raisins, sultanas, prunes, and dried

## Saturday Night Salad

One Saturday in October, 1994, we were thrilled to find three kinds of fresh salad greens for sale at a farmers' market in Vladivostok—more greens than we had seen during the entire past year in Russia: curly-leaf lettuce, butterhead lettuce, and some kind of darker greens with spiky, serrated leaves that the vendor described to me as "bitter." Back home in our kitchen, we lovingly washed the mass of bitter greens in filtered water, shook them dry over our bathtub, and tore them into bite-size pieces, filling a big metal washbasin (because we didn't have a mixing bowl large enough).

We added chopped green onion tops and leaves of fresh sorrel from a friend's dacha, tossing the greens with sunflower oil and homemade red wine vinegar. Then we tossed the salad once more with a finely chopped onion, three large garlic cloves, thinly sliced, and a generous handful of dried herbs, along with a good sprinkling of salt and coarsely ground black pepper.

When we tasted the salad, we discovered that the "bitter" greens were actually horseradish leaves, which gave a delightful bite to the crispy mélange. And we were so starved for greens that we devoured that huge salad for our entire Saturday night meal—three big helpings each!—because we knew the Russian winter soon lay ahead, when green salads would be only a distant memory once more.

apricots—although many of those imported products were priced considerably higher than an equivalent amount of fresh meat. Russian vendors sold roasted Siberian pine nuts, dried sunflower seeds, golden-orange sea-buckthorn berries, and the season's first fiddlehead ferns. Old women peddled small bunches of parsley and dill, wild garlic and green onion tops, like wishful little bouquets, often the only fresh greens we saw in the markets for weeks at a time.

## Processed, Preserved, and Packaged

Preserved foods (homemade and commercial) have long been an important part of the Russian diet: jams made of fruits and berries picked in the forest; home-canned vegetables from the farm or the dacha garden; fermented foods such as sauerkraut, *kefir*, and *kvas*; sausages, dried meats, and salted fish; and certain foods frozen outdoors in the harsh winters of the north. In Asian Russia's new market economy of the mid-1990s, however, food stores and farmers' markets in the major cities also began to stock a host of brightly packaged products from all over the world, rapidly displacing the drab displays of Russian goods. But the supply of these highly desirable, sometimes "exotic" foodstuffs was often erratic: Hungarian sausages, Danish and Chinese canned hams, Greek olives and Turkish olive oil, Australian marmalade and German tea cakes, Swiss, Belgian, and Chinese chocolates, American potato chips and Velveeta cheese, Korean crab-and-shrimp-flavored chips, and wines from Italy, Spain, France, and California. Foreign products previously imported from socialist countries during the Soviet era continued to be available, too, especially bottles of fleshy red peppers from Hungary, Bulgaria, Moldova, and China, along with wines and brandies from Hungary, Bulgaria, Georgia, and Armenia.

While we appreciated being able to buy imported edibles that were still new to most Russians, we also sought out locally produced foods of good quality. Russians are well known for their home-preserved fruits, berries, mushrooms, and vegetables. Sometimes they sold their surplus at the farmers' markets, to earn a few extra rubles in Russia's rapidly inflating economy. In summer and fall, we'd often see an old *babushka* sitting behind a small folding table, hoping to sell a couple of jars of raspberry jam or pickled garlic cloves, a single jar of homemade sauerkraut, or a bag of frozen homemade *pel'meni* (Siberian dumplings), ready to drop into a pot of boiling water, the quintessential Siberian "convenience food." More common were 3-liter jars of green or

# Sweet Treats

Russians delight in making their own sweet preserves from several kinds of fruits, berries, melons, and even vegetables.

- *Varen'ye* is the most popular type, made from whole berries and fruits (or large pieces of fruit) cooked together with an equal weight of sugar to produce a preserve in which the glistening fruits and berries are suspended like precious jewels in a thick, translucent sugar syrup tinted by their juice. Raspberries, strawberries, whortleberries, blackberries, blueberries, bilberries, gooseberries, cherries, apricots, peaches, pears, and plums are often made into *varen'ye* in Russia—preferably preserved the same day they're picked from the orchards or foraged from the forests, and sometimes flavored with the addition of leaves from the berry bushes and fruit trees. One of my favorite kinds of *varen'ye* isn't made from fruits or berries at all, but consists of large chunks of orange pumpkin in a dark, heavy sugar syrup redolent of vanilla. *Varen'ye* are often served as an accompaniment to tea (many Russians like to stir these preserves into their tea), and used as garnishes for desserts, pancakes, and crêpes.

- *Dzhem* is more like the Western-style jams that its name comes from—very sweet and made with diced, shredded, or mashed fruits and berries. In Russia, however, *dzhem* is rarely eaten as a spread on bread or toast, but used instead as a topping for pancakes and crêpes and a filling for layer cakes, doughnuts, and small pies.

- *Povidlo* is a kind of "fruit butter," or very thick jam, made from crushed or puréed fruits, with or without the addition of sugar, slowly cooked over low heat for several hours. Apples, plums, and apricots are often preserved as *povidlo* and used as fillings for pies and fruit dumplings.

- *Pastila* is a dense, tough "fruit leather," originally from the Caucasus and Central Asia, made by cooking fruits such as apples, apricots, and quinces with sugar until they disintegrate and form a thick paste, which is then dried in the oven and cut into squares or strips for storage.

red tomatoes, sometimes packed with whole cucumbers, preserved in a salt brine or vinegar marinade and seasoned with long hot red peppers, garlic cloves, mustard or coriander seeds, and a sprig or two of dill. The best we ever bought was a 3-liter jar of red tomatoes and green cucumbers sold by a woman with only a few items displayed on the hood of her car. Home-preserved over a wood fire, her pickled vegetables had a subtle smoky flavor that evoked scenes in nineteenth-century Russian novels where strong-willed women supervised the preservation of summer's bounty at country estates, surrounded by dense forests of birch and pine.

Tom and I both have Texas tongues, trained from an early age to eat the sort of hot-spicy foods that send other diners running from the table, clutching their throats and gasping for a gulp of ice water. So we were pleased to find a few truly spicy foods for sale in Russia, including five kinds of killer *kimchi* peddled by Koreans in the Russian Far East. Another tongue-tingling discovery was homemade *adzhiga*, the Russian version of salsa, containing hot peppers, sweet peppers, tomatoes, and garlic, which we bought from the *babushki* in the farmers' markets. Russian brown mustard, which looked deceptively like

## A Radish to Root For

Prepared horseradish, home-processed or commercially bottled, can be used both as a cooking ingredient and as a condiment to accompany roasted pork, beef, and poultry, as well as smoked meats like ham, sausages, tongue, and fish. Sugar, lemon juice, crushed dill seed, dried basil, or thyme can also be mixed with horseradish. In Russia and Eastern Europe, cooks sometimes color their horseradish pink by adding grated beets or beet juice, or tint it orange with shredded carrots or carrot juice. They combine horseradish with sugar and cranberries, bilberries, or currants to make a hot-sweet condiment, like chutney, served with meats. Russians often add a piece of horseradish root or some horseradish leaves to the jar when making pickled cucumbers and other preserved vegetables. And horseradish vinegar is made by simply macerating pieces of peeled horseradish in a bottle of distilled white or apple cider vinegar.

sweet Bavarian mustard, turned out to rival Colman's English mustard for its head-clearing properties. But hottest of all was home-preserved horseradish root. One enterprising vendor at an open-air market in Vladivostok graphically described his product's pungency by pretending to taste a spoonful of it, then quickly lifting his fur hat straight up from the top of his head—the perfect pantomime of "It's so strong it'll blow your head off!" He was right: Tom bought the single jar of horseradish he was selling, and we laughed at the memory of his gesture every time that horseradish scorched our palates and seared our sinuses.

## Pantry Perennials

We tried to keep our kitchen stocked with flour, sugar, pasta, rice, beans, honey, oil, and vinegar—basic foods that were not always available every time we went out to shop. But those Russian-produced staples were often of a quality that would have been unacceptable to consumers in the West. Russian pasta—elbow macaroni, spaghetti, vermicelli—was an unappetizing gray-brown color and fell apart, or sometimes dissolved completely, while it was boiling. Far superior were the dried pastas made from durum wheat that were beginning to be imported from abroad, even though they were considerably more expensive than Russian brands.

Only once in 16 months did we ever find cornmeal—sold out of a big barrel by a vendor in the vestibule of an office building in Vladivostok. At least that cornmeal was cleaner than other flours and grains we purchased in Russia, which always had to be sifted thoroughly to remove the dirt, rocks, hairs, insect parts, and clumps of unidentifiable matter that infested every bag. Sometimes I became so disgusted that I threw out the entire lot of rice or flour or buckwheat groats—and just hoped the next bag I bought would be a bit less adulterated.

Russian sugar was of such poor quality that it always caused problems in the kitchen. Except for the one time that Tom found a 5-pound bag of extra-fine granulated cane sugar imported from the United States, all the other sugar we purchased in Russia was the type known as *pesok* (sand) because the grayish-colored beet-sugar granules were shaped like big grains of sand. They were so difficult to dissolve that I often had to mix them with the liquid ingredients for a recipe and let them sit for an hour before combining them with the other ingredients. Worse yet, this Russian sugar always had to be sifted before using, to sort out the impurities. And sometimes we unknowingly purchased sugar that was so damp I had to dry it in the oven before I could decide whether it was even usable at all.

Many of these dry staples—flour, sugar, salt, semolina, buckwheat groats, rice, millet, and other grains—were sold in bulk, scooped out of wooden barrels or big burlap bags. At some of the slowly modernizing food stores, however, they were sometimes pre-packaged in plain, clear-plastic bags, each weighing 500 grams or 1 kilogram, with no labels identifying the contents. Russians could recognize these basic foodstuffs, but most Americans—accustomed to clearly labeled products in distinctive, brand-name packaging—could not always distinguish salt from sugar, or flour from cornstarch, which made for some surprising recipe results in the kitchens of the few other Americans living in Siberia back then.

Thirty percent of all the honey produced in the Russian Federation came from Russia's Maritime Territory, of which Vladivostok was the capital. Two specialty shops in the city offered a wide variety of honeys, some flavored naturally by the particular pollen the bees had fed on, others infused with herbal extracts made from birch leaves, honeysuckle, sweet clover, camomile, valerian, and St. John's wort. Excellent honey could be found at the farmers' markets, too—from light yellow to dark amber, the sweet nectar still dripping from the honeycombs. Alla always preferred to buy this "country-style" honey because she knew it was more pure than many commercial types, which were sometimes diluted with sugar-water and other liquids.

Several kinds of cooking fats were available in Siberia, including a solid vegetable shortening (or an animal-vegetable mix) similar to Crisco; *salo*, salt-cured pork fat; rendered goose and duck fat (homemade, not commercially produced); and vegetable oils such as corn, cottonseed, soy, and—more rarely—pine nut and olive oil. But our primary cooking fats were the two most commonly sold in the stores: unsalted butter and dark, strong-tasting, unfiltered sunflower-seed oil. Once we found a precious 1-liter can of Turkish olive oil—the only olive oil we ever saw in Siberia—which we rationed carefully to last throughout the entire spring. And we were thrilled to find plump, whole ducks for sale once in Vladivostok: after roasting our duck with apples and raisins, we saved the rendered fat to use for cooking and flavoring other dishes. Early on, we'd learned not to waste anything in our Russian kitchen.

# Fat of the Land

Historically, Siberians have cooked with whatever fats were locally available from the plants and animals in their particular geographic area. Before the widespread availability of commercially produced cooking oils in modern Siberia, they used animal fats from cattle, sheep, pigs, horses, bears, and marine mammals, as well as fish oil and vegetable oils such as hempseed, flaxseed, poppy seed, and pine nut. After sunflowers were introduced from North America in the early 1800s, sunflower-seed oil has also been made commercially in Russia (including Siberia), and has now become the most widely used vegetable oil there today.

From the early 1890s to 1917, Western Siberia was a major producer of cows' butter, becoming second only to Denmark, worldwide, by the turn of the century. Siberian butter was shipped to the European side of Russia and beyond, reaping large profits for the domestic butter industry. Prior to the use of refrigerated railway cars on the Trans-Siberian line in the late 1890s, butter transported over long distances was mainly clarified butter packed in glass jars. Slowly heated to remove the milk solids and water that cause standard butter to spoil more quickly, clarified butter, which is nearly 100% fat, has a shelf life of 6 to 8 months at room temperature compared to about 10 days for standard butter. Refrigeration made possible the transport of standard butter, in more durable wooden boxes, over thousands of miles by rail and boat from Western Siberia to foreign markets as far away as England.

During our first autumn in Vladivostok, we searched all over the city for vinegar—nothing fancy, just plain distilled white vinegar—but none of the stores stocked it. Finally, Alla found us a single small bottle of vinegar during one of her own shopping trips. But when I unscrewed the top, the fumes smelled like gas escaping from a chemical weapons plant. When I read the small print on the Russian label, I discovered that this vinegar was not 5% acid, like most vinegars sold in the United States, but industrial-strength acetic acid that had to be diluted 20-to-1 with water before it was safe to ingest. Russians already knew that this lethally concentrated vinegar had to be diluted before use in the kitchen, but many foreigners (especially those who couldn't read Russian) did not. When an American friend in Vladivostok made a vinegar-and-oil dressing from this potent stuff, she was shocked to discover what it did to the vegetables she tossed it with, not to mention the acrid aroma that lingered in her kitchen for days. For our own cooking, we made wine vinegar from bottles of the cheap Bulgarian red wine sold in the local markets.

## From the Baker's Oven

Bread is the staff of life for Russians. For them, a meal is not complete without plenty of fresh bread to accompany every dish but dessert. When we lived in both Vladivostok and Irkutsk, the most common type of bread was light-colored, whole wheat, with a moderately dense texture, that was sold in blocky 500-gram loaves, unsliced and unwrapped. Bakery shops sometimes also offered *bulochki*, yeast-raised buns like dinner rolls; *bubliki* and *sushki*, small rings of baked bread dough; and *kalachi*, large rounds of yeasty white bread that we indelicately called "toilet seat bread" because of their shape and size (a truly Western cultural reference in Siberia, where toilet seats were as rare back then as French *croissants*).

## In the Dough

A Russian "convenience food" we discovered in Vladivostok was *testo*—big blobs of fresh, ready-made yeast dough sold by the kilogram at some of the *gastronomy* and by vendors at street stands in front of bakeries or small restaurants. This *testo* could be kept in the refrigerator for two to three days, where the living dough continued to rise—growing like a monster in a science fiction film—always ready, on short notice, for making Italian pizzas, Russian *pirozhki* and *rasstegaï* (small savory pies), and German *Zwiebelkuchen* (onion tart).

*Vendor selling a variety of breads from a truck at an outdoor market in Vladivostok, 2006.*

Occasionally a bakery, or a bread truck parked at the farmers' markets, would offer oblong loaves of crusty white sourdough bread. In Irkutsk, vendors in kiosks and small vans sold large rectangles of soft, yeasty flatbread, each about a foot long, 8 inches wide, and an inch or so thick. Everyone called this bread *"lavash,"* even though it was actually more like Italian *focaccia* and Central Asian *naan* than the very thin, unleavened, Armenian flatbread known as *lavash*. A single bakery in Irkutsk produced a very dense, medium-brown, multi-grain bread with an excellent flavor, which came with a printed sheet of paper listing all of the bread's healthful properties. And once in Vladivostok we found authentic Central Asian *naan*, large rounds of chewy, yeast-leavened flatbread, the dough stamped on top with repeated motifs of a ring encircling a five-pointed star.

But we looked everywhere, in vain, for real Russian "black bread"—those dark, heavy, round loaves of rye bread described so lovingly in Russian novels and short stories. When I asked several of my Russian friends why this traditional black bread was nowhere to be found, they all replied that it had disappeared from the bakeries two to three years earlier, just as the country was beginning to move away from a state-controlled economy. Further inquiries were fruitless. No one seemed to know why black bread was no longer available—nor did anyone really seem to care.

Many bakeries in Asian Russia sold delicious little dome-shaped gingerbread cookies called *pryaniki*, sometimes glazed with white icing. Much less edible were the sugar cookies, dense and floury, with the taste of hog fat and the texture of sawdust. And in a land where Western-style baking powder was almost unknown, most cakes (both commercial and homemade) were leavened with a combination of baking soda and a cultured milk product such as *kefir*, plus plenty of beaten eggs. This technique produced cakes with the tough dry texture of soda breads and a strong eggy taste that usually overpowered any other flavors in the batter, even chocolate. Many of these bakery cakes were also baroquely decorated with gooey, artificially colored "buttercream" icing, tinted in several garish hues, made of sugar and a large proportion of cheap, stale-tasting fats. No wonder we chose to bake most of our own cookies and cakes at home, relying on the Russian commercial bakeries only for our daily bread.

## A Wider World of Tastes

"Someone bring me the smelling salts!" Tom exclaimed as we stepped inside Vladivostok's bustling First River food market in the summer of 2006. When we'd last shopped there, in 1994, it was a large, ugly, indoor market with cold concrete floors and walls, rows of gray counters, and surly vendors, mostly men from the Caucasus, who refused to bargain down their high prices for fresh produce. Back then, we shopped at First River mainly because it had products like almonds and dried apricots that were scarce or not available anywhere else in the city.

When we returned to that market in 2006, we walked through automatic sliding-glass doors into a brightly lit foyer where water gurgled from a huge marble fountain decorated with sculpted seashells, dolphins, and lions' heads, situated directly across from a modern ATM. In place of the rough wooden tables where a hodgepodge of goods used to be sold around the market's periphery, modern well-stocked boutiques offered black and green teas, freshly roasted coffees, European confections, California wines, and a brilliant bazaar of spices. Inside the central market hall, friendly East Asian and Russian women, outfitted in smart blue-and-white uniforms, smiled as they asked how they could help us. We stared in wonder at the abundance of fresh meats, fine cheeses, and ready-made deli salads on display in shiny glass cases. Tall stacks of colorful, unblemished fruits seemed to defy gravity until a shop girl plucked a perfect orange off the top and dropped it into a new plastic bag. In the

*Entrance to the modernized Central Market in Irkutsk, 2008.*

Vladivostok of my not-so-distant memory, bloody pieces of meat and muddy potatoes were thrust directly into my hands as I fumbled to find a place for them in my own well-worn, dingy carry-all.

In another part of the city, a massive modern "hypermarket" rivaled many in the West. Fully stocked with thousands of domestic and imported products—from fine wines to deli takeout to pet foods—it provided one-stop shopping for anyone with the ability to pay Western prices in a country where the average monthly income was only $250 per person. Although some Russians complained about the high prices, one friend told me, "Sometimes when my mother is feeling low, she just comes here and seeing all this cheers her up."

Forays to other food markets in both Vladivostok and Irkutsk continued to amaze me: delicatessens with dozens of different hot and cold dishes, fancy bakeries offering cakes and pastries that rivaled those in Paris and Vienna, glitzy stores selling luxuries like *foie gras* and French champagne, smoky German *Rauchbier* and spicy Spanish sausages—all with prices to match. The big open-air markets where vendors previously sold a few foodstuffs and household supplies haphazardly displayed on old wooden tables, had now been transformed into neat rows of kiosks and small shops each specializing in one type of product: kitchen utensils, smoked meats, jars of honey, fresh vegetables, spices, cleaning supplies. And the number of markets had increased, too, including a new farmers' market set up on the site of a former soccer stadium. "The farmers used to come here to watch football games," a Russian told me, "but now they come here to sell their products." By the mid-2000s, just a decade after we'd lived in Russia, consumer demand, savvy marketing, and Russia's new wealth (although definitely ill-distributed) had turned food shopping into a more pleasant experience and transformed the country's culinary landscape.

# Russian Red Salsa

## (Adzhiga)

*There are as many recipes for* adzhiga *as Russians who make it. Some are dry spice mixtures, others are spice pastes, and some are more like fresh salsas. I bought several versions of homemade* adzhiga *salsas in the open-air markets of Siberia, some of which contained tomatoes, onions, carrots, sugar, coriander seeds, parsley, dill, or cumin in addition to the requisite peppers and garlic. But my favorite recipe is for this simple bright red salsa, given to me by a vendor in Vladivostok.*

¼ **pound large fleshy hot red peppers (such as large ripe red jalapeños), coarsely chopped**
2 **red bell peppers (about ½ pound), seeded, deveined, and coarsely chopped**
8 **large garlic cloves, quartered**
½ **teaspoon salt (or more, to taste)**

- Pulse all the ingredients together in a food processor into a coarse, thick paste. The mixture should not be completely puréed or liquefied. (Russians made theirs in a meat grinder.)

- Keep in a tightly covered glass jar in the refrigerator for 2 to 3 days for the flavors to ripen, before using. Taste and add more salt if desired. Store in the refrigerator up to 1 week.

- Use as a condiment to accompany grilled meats, or stir a tablespoon or two into soups and stews to spike up their flavor.

- Makes 1½ cups.

# Blender Mayonnaise

*Russian mayonnaise was a very good product, but the supply wasn't always dependable. When we couldn't find mayonnaise in the stores, we made our own, often flavoring it with garlic or hot red peppers. We especially liked eating garlic mayonnaise as an accompaniment to fresh Kamchatka crab legs in Vladivostok.*

▶ **NOTE:** Mayonnaise is easy to make in a blender. The flavor will vary depending on the type of oil, vinegar, and mustard you use. If you worry about eating raw eggs in mayonnaise, just substitute pasteurized eggs.

**1 large egg**
**1 large egg yolk (optional)**
**3 tablespoons lemon juice or vinegar**
**1 teaspoon prepared mustard**
**1 teaspoon honey**
**½ teaspoon salt**
**1 cup vegetable oil**
**1 teaspoon cold tap water (if needed)**

- Blend the egg, lemon juice or vinegar, mustard, honey, salt, and ½ cup of oil together on medium-high speed until completely smooth.

- With the blender still running, pour the remaining ½ cup of oil very slowly, in a thin, steady stream, into the center of the egg mixture. Continue blending until all the oil has been thoroughly incorporated. (If the oil separates out, just add 1 teaspoon tap water and blend until smooth.) Store up to 2 weeks in a tightly covered jar in the refrigerator.

- Makes about 1½ cups of mayonnaise.

▶ **Garlic Mayonnaise:** Whisk together 1 cup mayonnaise and 2 to 3 garlic cloves squeezed through a garlic press. Wait for at least an hour to use the mayonnaise, so the flavors can meld.

# Horseradish: Do It Yourself

Freshly grated horseradish is stronger in flavor and pungency than the commercially bottled product. So if you like the taste and don't mind the tears, process your own horseradish at home. Buy a firm, whole horseradish root, scrub off the dirt, and peel the root with a vegetable peeler. Then grate it by hand with a Microplane grater, or shred it in a food processor fitted with the standard cutting blade. Work in a well-ventilated place, and don't wear eye makeup! Mix the grated horseradish with a little vinegar and salt (some people like to add a bit of sugar, too), and store it in a jar in the refrigerator for up to one month. Once you've tasted freshly prepared horseradish, you'll understand why it's truly a radish to root for.

# Hot Tips

- To make *really* devilled eggs (I'd call them *domovoi* eggs, in Russian), add grated horseradish to the egg yolk mixture.

- Mix ¼ cup grated horseradish and 2 teaspoons lemon juice with 1 cup mayonnaise to use as a sandwich spread.

- Combine 1 cup applesauce, ¼ cup grated horseradish, and 1 teaspoon Hungarian paprika to use as an accompaniment to roasted turkey, goose, duck, or pork.

- Mix ¼ cup grated horseradish and 1 teaspoon lemon juice with 1 cup sour cream to use as a garnish for grilled or smoked meats and fish, and also as a filling for baked potatoes, sprinkled with chopped chives.

- Whip ½ cup of heavy cream until stiff, then fold in ¼ cup horseradish and use as a garnish for cold ham or roast beef.

- Mash together 8 ounces of cream cheese (at room temperature), ½ cup grated horseradish (drained of any liquid), ¼ cup finely chopped fresh chives or green onion tops, and 1 to 2 tablespoons of buttermilk as a spread for rye or pumpernickel bread, bagels, and crackers.

# French "Stomped Vegetable Soup"

*Before going to Russia, we'd eaten many versions of this soup at little country restaurants in France, where frugal chefs made it from leftover vegetables, raw or cooked. Tom called this dish "Stomped Vegetable Soup" because all the cooked vegetables are puréed, or "stomped down," in the process. We often made the same kind of soup in Russia, with root vegetables that were easy to find there. (Since some people don't like turnips, just don't tell them you put turnips in this soup. They'll never guess from the taste!)*

▶ **NOTE:** Roasted or sautéed vegetables produce a richer, sweeter-flavored soup than raw vegetables. You can roast or sauté them in advance—or simply skip that part of the recipe and cook all the raw vegetables together in the water or chicken stock until tender. Use canola or olive oil for a French-tasting soup, or sunflower oil for a more Russian flavor.

**Vegetable oil for roasting or sautéing (see following instructions)**
**3 large turnips, peeled and cut into 1-inch chunks**
**2 large onions, peeled and cut into 1-inch chunks**
**6 to 8 large carrots, peeled and cut into 1-inch chunks**
**2 quarts (8 cups) water or unsalted chicken stock**
**6 large potatoes, peeled and cut into 1-inch chunks**
**6 large garlic cloves, minced**
**4 teaspoons salt**
**2 teaspoons freshly ground black pepper**
**1 teaspoon freshly grated nutmeg**
**4 to 6 cups milk (or more, for a thinner soup)**

Garnish

**Snipped fresh chives, green onion tops sliced thinly into rings, or chopped parsley**
**Sour cream (optional)**

- Roast or sauté the turnips, onions, and carrots in advance (see following instructions)—or omit this step to make a quicker soup.

- Bring the water or chicken stock to a boil in a large (6- to 8-quart) stockpot. Add the turnips, onions, and carrots (roasted, sautéed, or raw), along with the raw potatoes, garlic, salt, pepper, and nutmeg. Bring the mixture to a boil over medium-high heat. Reduce the heat to medium, partially cover the pot, and cook for 30 to 40 minutes, stirring occasionally, until the potatoes are tender and falling apart.

118

- Let the mixture cool to lukewarm. Purée it (in batches) in a food processor or blender, or through a hand-cranked food mill, or in the stockpot with an immersion blender.

- Combine the puréed vegetables and the milk in the stockpot. (Add more milk if you prefer a thinner soup.) Cook uncovered over medium-low heat, stirring frequently, until the soup is very hot. Taste and add more salt and pepper, if desired.

- Serve hot, in shallow soup bowls, and garnish with snipped chives, sliced green onion tops, or chopped parsley. (In Russia, we often added a dollop of sour cream, too.)

- Makes approximately 5 quarts (20 cups, or 10 individual 2-cup servings).

▶ **To roast the vegetables** (optional): Preheat the oven to 450°F. Heavily oil two large, shallow baking pans that will both fit on one rack of the oven at the same time. Put the turnip pieces in one pan and roll them around to coat them with oil. Mix the onions and carrots in the other pan and roll them around to coat with oil.

- Roast the vegetables on the middle rack of the oven for 15 minutes, then use a spatula to turn them over in the pans, and continue roasting for 15 more minutes. Take the turnips out of the oven. Turn the carrots and onions over in their pan again and roast for 15 minutes longer. Then proceed with the recipe.

▶ **To sauté the vegetables** (optional): Heat $1/3$ cup of vegetable oil in a large (6- to 8-quart) stockpot. Add the onions and sauté over medium-high heat until they are golden. Add the turnips, carrots, and garlic. Continue sautéing for another 3 minutes. Add the water or chicken stock to the pot, along with the other ingredients, and proceed with the recipe.

## Waste Not: Cheese

When you've cut or grated a piece of hard cheese down to the rind, peel off any wax on the outer side and save the rind to toss into your next pot of meat or vegetable soup as it cooks. The cheese rind will melt in the hot liquid and enrich the flavor.

# Sauerkraut with Mushrooms

*This side dish is a taste of autumn, made with ingredients still available at the markets in Russia when the supply of fresh vegetables was on the wane. But it's so good we like eating it at any time of the year.*

¼ pound smoked bacon or smoked ham, finely chopped
2 tablespoons vegetable oil (goose fat or lard is traditional)
1 large onion, finely chopped
1½ teaspoons mild or medium-hot paprika
2 pounds sauerkraut, rinsed under cold water and drained well
½ cup chopped dried mushrooms (boletus, brown or white champignons)
⅓ cup raisins or chopped prunes
1 medium apple, peel, cored, and diced (optional)
1 cup chicken stock
½ cup medium-dry or sweet white wine
6 whole juniper berries
2 whole cloves
1 bay leaf

- Cook the bacon and oil together in a large heavy saucepan over medium-high heat, stirring frequently, until the bacon begins to brown. Add the onion and continue sautéing until the onion is golden. Reduce the heat to low, sprinkle the paprika over the ingredients in the pan, and cook, stirring constantly, for 30 seconds. Immediately stir in the sauerkraut, dried mushrooms, raisins or prunes, (optional) apple, chicken stock, wine, juniper berries, cloves, and bay leaf. Mix well.

- Bring the mixture to a boil over medium-high heat, reduce the heat to medium-low, cover the pan, and let the seasoned sauerkraut simmer, stirring it occasionally, for 1 hour.

- Serve hot, as an accompaniment to grilled, braised, or roasted meats.

- Makes 6 servings.

# Silent Hunting

Mushroom-picking—known as "silent hunting"—is a national pastime in Russia. From late spring through autumn Russians of all ages head for the forests and fields, hoping to find their favorite fungi growing on a tree stump or hiding under a few fallen leaves. More than 100 kinds of mushrooms grow wild in Russia, and mushrooms are an important ingredient in many dishes.

From July through October the open-air markets are full of mushrooms, in colors ranging from beige, pale yellow, and cappuccino-brown to bright orange and deep purple. Russians eat them fresh, in season, and preserve the remainder by salt-pickling, marinating, or drying. First dried in the oven, on a radiator, or near a wood fire, the mushrooms are then loosely threaded on strings, tied at the top to form a loop, and hung up to finish drying in a well-ventilated place. In late autumn these "necklaces" of mushrooms are a common sight, hanging on the wooden verandas of village houses and inside the glass-enclosed balconies of big-city apartment buildings.

# Braised Red Cabbage

*Sweet-sour braised red cabbage is a beloved side dish from Central and Eastern Europe all the way across Russia to the Far East. It's the first recipe I learned to make from the first Russian cookbook I bought, back in the 1960s. Many years later, Tom and I cooked this dish in our own Russian kitchens whenever we lucked upon a red cabbage in the farmers' markets. Using rendered duck fat or goose fat (instead of butter and oil) gives this pretty purple dish an even richer flavor.*

1 tablespoon unsalted butter
1 tablespoon vegetable oil
1 large onion, chopped medium-fine
1 red cabbage (about 2 pounds), cored, cut into eighths, and finely shredded
1 large apple, cored and chopped medium-fine
¼ cup beef stock
2 tablespoons red wine vinegar (or apple cider vinegar)
1 tablespoon sugar
1 tablespoon caraway seeds
1 teaspoon salt
½ teaspoon finely ground black pepper
3 whole cloves
1 to 2 tablespoons lingonberry preserves (optional)

- Heat the butter and oil together in a large (4-quart) heavy stock pot over medium-high heat, until the fat begins to bubble. Add the onion and cook over medium heat, stirring frequently, until onion is lightly browned (15 to 20 minutes).

- Add the cabbage, apple, beef stock, vinegar, and sugar to the pot, tossing the ingredients together until all the cabbage pieces glisten with oil. Sprinkle in the caraway seeds, salt, pepper, and cloves, and toss the ingredients again to combine well.

- Cover the pot tightly, reduce the heat to medium-low, and simmer for 50 to 60 minutes, stirring frequently. The cabbage will "sweat," releasing plenty of moisture while cooking, but don't let it cook dry. Add 1 more tablespoon of beef stock or red wine vinegar, if needed—but there should be hardly any liquid left when the cabbage is done (tender, but not mushy, when pierced with a fork). For a sweeter version, stir in the lingonberry preserves at the end, heating the cabbage for 1 or 2 minutes longer.

- Serve hot, as an accompaniment to roasted pork, beef, venison, duck, or goose, or grilled sausages.

- Makes 6 to 8 servings.

▶ **NOTE:** This dish tastes even better when made a day in advance, then reheated for serving.

## Keeping Cabbage Bright

When making any dish with red cabbage, it's important to use an acidic ingredient—lemon juice, wine, or vinegar—to keep the cabbage from losing its bright color. For the same reason, cabbage should always be cooked in a non-reactive pan. (Standard aluminum pans will cause cabbage to discolor.) Red cabbage turns an unappetizing blue-gray if it becomes alkaline during cooking—but you can easily restore its original color by adding a teaspoon or two of lemon juice or vinegar to the pot.

# Roasted T-Bone "Whacks"

*Pre-cut and packaged T-bone steaks at your local grocery store are not thick enough for this Russian recipe. Ask your butcher whack off a 2-inch-thick T-bone steak (about 2 pounds) for you. That's enough to feed two average eaters, one ravenous Russian, or a hungry Texan.*

▶ **NOTES:** Start early. Roasting a steak this thick is not like throwing a thinner T-bone on your grill. Straight from the refrigerator, it needs an hour to come to room temperature, another 40 minutes to roast, and 10 more minutes to rest before serving.

- The roasting time in this recipe is for a steak cooked "medium." In Russia we just estimated the oven temperature in our Stove-from-Hell by poking a hand into the oven, then watching and smelling the meat as it cooked, to figure out when it was done. If you want your meat more rare or more well done, adjust the cooking time accordingly.

**1 T-bone steak, 2 inches thick (2 pounds)**
**Coarse salt**
**Coarsely ground black pepper**

**Garnish (optional)**

**1 tablespoon vegetable oil and 1 large garlic clove, minced**

- Take the meat out of the refrigerator 1 hour before roasting. Season both sides well with coarse salt. Put the meat on a plate lined with several paper towels and let it warm up to room temperature.

- Preheat the oven to 425°F. Lightly oil a rimmed baking sheet or pan not much larger than your steak. Wipe the salt off the T-bone and dry the meat well with paper towels. Place the T-bone on the baking pan and roast it on the middle rack of the oven for about 30 to 40 minutes, turning it over after the first 20 minutes of roasting. (If you use a meat thermometer—which we didn't even know existed in Russia back then—it should register about 145°F. to 155°F. for meat cooked "medium.")

- Remove the pan from the oven and put the steak on a cutting board. Sprinkle the top of the meat lightly with coarse salt and coarsely ground black pepper. Cover loosely with aluminum foil and let the steak rest for 10 minutes before serving.

- For a flavorful garnish, gently warm 1 tablespoon vegetable oil and 1 minced garlic clove together over medium-low heat while the steak is resting, until you can smell that lovely aroma of garlic. Spread over the top of the steak just before serving.

- Makes 2 servings.

▶ **NOTE: Mushroom-Sour Cream Sauce** (recipe, page 128) is also delicious with this steak. Omit the suggested oil-and-garlic garnish on the steak, and make the sauce while the steak is roasting.

▶ **WASTE NOT:** Don't throw away that roasted bone! Simmered for several hours in water with some carrot, onion, parsley root, garlic, bay leaves, salt, and pepper, it makes an excellent beef stock for French onion soup—a warming dish we enjoyed on cold winter nights in Siberia.

## Garlicky Green Peas

After we roasted our T-bone whacks—carefully, in the Stoves-from-Hell—we served them with Tom's **Savory Buckwheat Kasha** (recipe, page 77), along with this simple side dish of garlicky peas: In a small saucepan, heat together a 15-ounce can of green peas (with all the liquid), a tablespoon or so of butter, and a clove or two of garlic, thinly sliced. Add salt and black pepper to taste. Serve hot. Save any of the leftover liquid to add to a soup stock—or just drink it for instant gratification, like we usually did while cleaning up the kitchen after the meal.

# Roasted Duck with Apples and Raisins

*We were delighted one day in autumn when Alla told us that duck was suddenly for sale at Dary Taigi (Gifts of the Forest), a small food store in Vladivostok that specialized in wild game. It was also the most attractive food shop in the city, with large, beautiful, hand-painted tile murals depicting the various wild animals of the Russian Far East. We happily brought our duck home from the store, roasted it with apples and raisins, and saved all the good rendered duck fat for use in our kitchen the rest of the year. But that was the only duck we ever found for sale again. And sadly, "Gifts of the Forest" is no longer there, torn down to make room for a more profitable real estate development in the center of the city—another example of the many changes in the market economy in Vladivostok.*

▶ **NOTE:** Roasted duck with apples is a traditional Russian dish for Christmas or New Year. Some cooks stuff the duck with apples and raisins, and also roast potatoes and turnips in the same pan as the duck. Others cook the root vegetables separately and make an apple-raisin sauce for the duck, which we prefer to do.

## Duck

**One 5- to 6-pound duck, at room temperature**
**1 medium onion, peeled**
**1 cup boiling water**
**1 to 2 tablespoons honey**

## Sauce

**2 tablespoons unsalted butter**
**3 large (or 4 medium) sweet apples, cored, peeled, and thinly sliced just before cooking**
**¼ cup chicken stock**
**3 tablespoons brandy or dark rum**
**⅓ cup dark raisins**
**¼ teaspoon ground cinnamon**
**¼ teaspoon salt**
**¼ teaspoon freshly ground black pepper**
**⅓ cup sour cream**

- Preheat the oven to 450°F. Remove the innards and fat from the inside the duck and any pin feathers on the outside.

- Rinse the duck well, inside and out, with cold water. Put the onion into the duck's cavity. Tie the legs together and tuck the wings under the back. Pierce the skin with a fork a few times around the legs and wings, so the fat can drain.

- Place the duck, breast side down, on a rack in a roasting pan. Pour 1 cup of boiling water over it. Put the roasting pan, uncovered, on the middle rack of the oven and turn the temperature down to 350°F. Roast for 20 minutes per pound of duck, basting frequently with the pan juices.

- During the last 40 minutes of roasting, make the sauce (see following instructions).

- For the last 20 minutes of roasting time, turn the duck over so the breast side is up. Prick the breast skin in a few places with a fork. Baste the duck with the honey. Roast for the remaining 20 minutes. Prick the thigh with a fork—the duck is ready when the juices run clear.

- Discard the onion and cut the duck into quarters for serving. Serve hot, accompanied by a generous portion of the sauce on the side. Braised red cabbage and a starch such as roasted potato chunks, boiled potato dumplings, or egg noodles are the classic accompaniment to roasted duck.

- **Apple-Raisin Sauce:** Heat the butter in a large skillet over medium-high heat until it begins to bubble. Stir in the apples to coat them with the fat, then cover and cook, stirring occasionally, until the apples begin to soften (about 5 minutes or so). Stir in the chicken stock, brandy or rum, raisins, cinnamon, salt, and pepper until all the ingredients are well mixed. Reduce the heat to medium, stir in the sour cream, mix well, and continue to cook until the sauce just barely begins to bubble around the edges. Quickly reduce the heat to very low, cover, and keep warm until serving time.

▶ **WASTE NOT:** A roasted duck produces plenty of fat that can be used for cooking and flavoring. Carefully pour the duck fat from the pan through a double layer of cheesecloth into a clean jar. Cap the jar tightly and refrigerate up to 3 months (or freeze in a plastic freezer container up to 1 year). For an even more flavorful version, slowly cook the duck fat with some finely chopped onion and garlic, then strain the rendered fat into a jar. Use an equal amount of duck fat as a substitute for butter or oil in dishes that can handle a stronger-flavored fat.

# Balkan Pork-and-Pepper Stew

## (Mučkalica)

*We discovered this hot-spicy pork-and-pepper stew on our travels in Yugoslavia in the 1970s, where we enjoyed eating it at several places from top hotel restaurants to dingy little truck stops. In Russia, it was an especially good dish to make on cold winter evenings in Siberia. (Its name is pronounced MOOCH-kah-leet-sa.)*

4 tablespoons unsalted butter (divided use)
4 tablespoons vegetable oil (divided use)
2 pounds boneless pork, thinly sliced and cut into long strips ½-inch wide
3 medium onions, sliced thinly (crosswise) and separated into rings
2 tablespoons all-purpose flour
3 tablespoons hot paprika (Hungarian paprika, Spanish pimentón, or New Mexico chile powder)
3 bell peppers (1 each green, red, yellow), seeded and cut lengthwise into strips ¼-inch wide*
2 to 3 hot green peppers (fresh or canned), cut crosswise into small rings
1 cup beef or chicken stock
3 tablespoons tomato paste
2 to 3 large garlic cloves, minced
1 teaspoon salt
1 bay leaf

**\*If peppers are very large, cut in half crosswise before slicing into strips.**

- Heat 2 tablespoons each of butter and oil in a large stew pot over medium-high heat. When the fat is very hot, add the pork and brown it on all sides, stirring constantly. (You might have to brown it in 2 or 3 batches, about 5 minutes for each batch.) Use a slotted spoon to transfer the pork to a bowl.

- Add the remaining 2 tablespoons each of butter and oil to the drippings in the pot, still over medium-high heat. When the fat is hot, reduce the heat to medium and sauté the onions until soft and golden. Sprinkle the flour and paprika over the onions and cook for 2 minutes longer, stirring constantly.

- Turn the heat to low. Stir in the pork and all of the peppers. Add the meat stock, tomato paste, garlic, salt, and bay leaf, stirring to mix well. (The mixture will seem too dry, but don't panic and add more stock. As the peppers cook, they'll release plenty of moisture.) Increase the heat to bring the mixture to a boil. Then reduce the heat to low, stir well, cover the pot, and let the *mučkalitsa* simmer for 1 to 1½ hours, stirring occasionally.

- Serve hot, accompanied by rice or egg noodles.

- Makes 6 servings.

# Mushroom-Sour Cream Sauce

*"Mushrooms love sour cream," said Alla. And they do love each other deeply in this richly flavored sauce that we often served with our roasted "T-bone whacks" in Russia. It's a good sauce for other roasted meats, too—pork, venison, turkey, chicken—and a delicious way to dress up an everyday meatloaf.*

**¾ cup unsalted chicken stock**
**1 tablespoon dried mushroom powder ("Mushroom Dust")**
**2 tablespoons unsalted butter**
**1 large shallot (or ¼ small onion), finely chopped**
**½ pound fresh mushrooms (white or brown champignons), thinly sliced lengthwise**
**2 tablespoons brandy**
**1 teaspoon Worcestershire Sauce**
**½ teaspoon dried thyme**
**½ teaspoon salt**
**½ teaspoon freshly ground black pepper**
**2 teaspoons all-purpose flour**
**½ cup pure sour cream**
**1 rounded tablespoon lingonberry preserves (optional)**

- Combine the chicken stock and mushroom powder in a small bowl. Melt the butter in a medium saucepan over medium-high heat. Add the chopped shallot or onion and sauté until golden. Add the fresh mushrooms, stir well, then pour in the brandy and stir again. Add the chicken stock (with the mushroom powder), Worcestershire sauce, thyme, salt, and pepper.

- Let the mixture come to a boil, then cover the pan, reduce the heat to medium, and cook for about 20 minutes, or until the mushrooms are tender. Remove the lid and reduce the heat to low.

- Whisk the flour and sour cream together in a small bowl until no lumps remain. Add the sour cream to the mushroom mixture, stirring constantly for about 5 minutes, until the sauce is smooth and begins to thicken.

- Serve hot, as an accompaniment to roasted meats or meatloaf.

- Makes approximately 2 cups of sauce (6 average or 8 small servings). Recipe can be doubled if you're serving a large number of hungry people.

▶ **NOTE:** A nice touch is to stir in 1 rounded tablespoon of lingonberry preserves after the sauce has thickened. Cook for 1 minute longer, over low heat, to warm up the preserves.

## Mushroom Dust

Make mushroom powder by pulverizing dried mushrooms in a blender or electric coffee grinder. Let the dust settle thoroughly before you open the top. Store in a tightly covered jar, in a dry place. Use a small amount of this "mushroom dust" to give a deep, rich, umami flavor to sauces, soups, stews, and casseroles.

# German Onion Tart

## (*Zwiebelkuchen*)

*We learned to make this savory onion tart in Germany, where it's a popular snack at autumn wine festivals. In Germany we always mixed and kneaded the dough by hand. In Russia we made it with fresh yeast dough from the local markets. But in Texas we take the easy way out and make the dough in a bread machine, then bake it in a regular oven—as do many modern Russian cooks who now own bread machines, too.*

### Dough

2¼ cups all-purpose flour
¾ cup warm water
1 tablespoon vegetable oil
1 teaspoon salt
1 teaspoon sugar
1 teaspoon dry yeast

### Topping

½ pound (4 to 5 slices) thick-cut bacon, diced into ¼-inch pieces
2 tablespoons unsalted butter
4 medium onions (about 1¾ pounds), quartered lengthwise and thinly sliced
  crosswise (about 6 cups)
2 large eggs
1 cup pure sour cream
½ teaspoon salt
½ teaspoon freshly ground black pepper
2 teaspoons caraway seeds (divided use)

- Put the dough ingredients in your bread machine in the sequence specified in the directions for your brand of machine. Select the "Dough" setting and start the machine.

- While the dough is making, fry the bacon over medium-high heat in a large (12-inch) skillet until the pieces begin to crisp. Remove with a slotted spoon and set aside. Heat the butter in the skillet with the bacon fat, add the onions, and cook over medium heat, stirring frequently, until they are very soft and beginning to brown around the edges (about 30 minutes). Remove the pan from the heat. Lightly oil a 15 × 11-inch jelly roll pan.

- When the dough is ready, turn it onto a lightly floured surface, punch it down, and knead for about 5 minutes. Let the dough rest for 5 minutes. Then pat it by hand into a large rectangle (like making pizza or focaccia), and roll it out to measure slightly larger than the pan. Place the dough in the pan, pressing the dough edges up the sides to make a rim. Set aside for 20 minutes. Preheat the oven to 400°F.

- Meanwhile, lightly beat the eggs in a medium bowl, then whisk in the sour cream, salt, pepper, and 1 teaspoon caraway seeds. Stir in the bacon and onions. After the dough has rested in the pan for 20 minutes, spread the topping evenly over it and sprinkle with the remaining 1 teaspoon of caraway seeds.

- Bake at 400°F. for about 25 minutes, until the crust is golden brown and the topping just begins to brown. Cool in the pan on a wire rack. Cut the onion tart into 12 squares while still warm.

- Serve warm or at room temperature. (Reheat leftovers briefly in a microwave, or wrap them tightly in foil and warm in a preheated 325°F. oven for 15 minutes.)

- Makes 12 servings.

## Waste Not: Soured Milk

Whenever we used up the contents of a jar of sour cream, we poured in 1 cup of milk, covered the jar tightly, shook it thoroughly, and let it sit at room temperature for 8 to 12 hours, to use as a substitute for buttermilk in our Russian kitchens.

# Honey-Almond Bars

*The one time we found cornmeal in Vladivostok, we bought 5 pounds as a hedge against future shortages. And we were right: we never saw cornmeal again in Siberia or the Russian Far East. When we moved to Irkutsk, we even carried the rest of our precious supply with us on the Trans-Siberian train. I often used it to make these sticky-sweet Honey-Almond Bars, one of my favorite recipes from the first Russian cookbook I bought, decades ago. The author said it was a "sweetmeat" (confection) from Kirghizstan, a part of the Soviet Union back then. I later discovered that similar sweets, made with cornmeal or semolina, were popular all across Central Asia, the Middle East, and North Africa.*

▶ **NOTE:** For the best flavor and texture, make these bars a day in advance. It's also very important to use the correct pan size.

**¼ pound (1 stick) unsalted butter, at room temperature**
**3 tablespoons sugar**
**1 large egg, well beaten**
**1 cup finely ground yellow cornmeal (American corn flour)\***
**¼ teaspoon salt**
**⅛ teaspoon cream of tartar**
**1 cup honey**
**1 cup blanched or unblanched almonds, chopped medium-fine before measuring**

**\*The texture of these bars will depend on the type and grind of cornmeal used. If you can't get corn flour, grind regular cornmeal ¼ cup at a time in a food processor. (Note that corn flour in America is not the same as cornstarch.)**

- Preheat the oven to 300°F. Butter the bottom and sides of an *8-inch-square metal* cake pan. Line the bottom of the pan with baking parchment and butter the top of the parchment paper.

- Beat the butter and sugar together with an electric mixer in a medium heatproof bowl, scraping down the sides, until the mixture is light and fluffy. Add the beaten egg and beat until the ingredients are well combined (looks sort of like scrambled eggs). Stir in the cornmeal, salt, and cream of tartar, mixing and mashing with a wooden spoon until all the ingredients are thoroughly blended.

- Bring the honey to a boil in a small saucepan over medium heat, stirring occasionally. As soon as the honey comes to a full boil, pour it over the cornmeal mixture and stir until the batter is completely smooth. Stir in the chopped almonds.

- Pour the batter into the prepared baking pan. Bake for 30 to 35 minutes, just until lightly golden brown on top and a little darker around the edges. (Do not overbake.) Set the pan on a wire rack to cool. The batter will look like it's not fully cooked, but don't worry. It will continue to cook and firm up as it cools.

- After 1 hour, run a sharp knife around the edge of the pan, to loosen the baked batter from it, and cut into 2-inch squares in the pan. Don't be tempted to eat them now! Leave them in the pan overnight, at room temperature, covered with plastic wrap or foil, so the honey can set and the flavors can meld. Then cut the mixture again with a sharp knife, along the original cuts, and use a spatula to carefully transfer the bars to a serving platter. Refrigerate any leftovers (covered with plastic wrap) for up to 3 days.

- Makes 16 very rich, sticky-sweet, absolutely delicious Honey-Almond Bars.

## Hedge against Scarcity

When a Serbian-Bosnian couple, Slavitsa and Igor, moved to Russia in 1993 for Igor's new job, they shipped an entire boxcar of food supplies and household goods (including their cook stove) nearly 7,000 miles by train from Belgrade to Vladivostok because they'd heard horror stories about food shortages in the Russian Far East. Among their treasured possessions were cases of Yugoslav wines, bottles of brandy and sweet pear liqueur, several kilos of cornmeal, cans of commercial baking powder, and bags of Turkish coffee. Slavitsa used some of her precious cache to make a special Serbian cornbread for us, seasoned with chunks of salty *brinza* cheese, much like feta, which she found in the markets only once during their two years in Vladivostok.

*Tom shredding beets in a kitchen in Vladivostok, 2006.*

*Galina Aleksandrovna Korotkina with one of the 23 zakuski (appetizers) she made for the first course of a feast in Vladivostok, Russian Far East, 2006.*

*Elena Yurievna Ivaschenko preparing Stuffed Squid (recipe, page 36) in her modern kitchen in Vladivostok, Russian Far East, 2006.*

*Salesclerk at one of the caviar counters in the Petropavlovsk central market, Kamchatka Peninsula, Russian Far East, 2014.*

*Vegetable vendor with fresh parsley and dill in the Petropavlovsk central market, Kamchatka Peninsula, Russian Far East, 2014.*

*Korean vendor of hot chile powder at an open-air market in Vladivostok, Russian Far East, 1994.*

*Buryat women selling dairy products, including smetana (sour cream) and tvorog (fresh white curd cheese), at the central market in Irkutsk, Siberia, 2007.*

*Bright green, sesame-scented* vakame (wakame) *seaweed salad is a popular delicatessen item in Russia's Far East, in the Maritime Territory where Vladivostok is located.*

*Fresh strawberries, raspberries, red and white currants, blueberries, and gooseberries for sale by a street vendor in Vladivostok, Russian Far East, 2006.*

Hot red peppers at the farmers' market in Ussuriisk, near the Chinese border, Russian Far East, 1993.

Tomatoes, cucumbers, potatoes, and beets—popular ingredients in Russian cooking—at the farmers' market in Ussuriisk, Russian Far East, 1993.

*Silvery smelts, salted and dried with the roe still inside, at a fish counter in the central market in Novosibirsk, Siberia, 2006.*

*Perch, burbot, bream, and two kinds of carp at the central market in Irkutsk, Siberia, 2007.*

*Cultivated garlic and wild pine nuts (still in their cones) offered by a street vendor in Novosibirsk, Siberia, 2006. Both are popular ingredients in the cooking of Asian Russia.*

*A variety of seeds, dried beans, tree barks, dried hawthorn berries, rosehips, and other wild and cultivated foods at an open-air market in Vladivostok, Russian Far East, 2006.*

*Foraged wild foods for sale at open-air markets in Ussuriisk, Russian Far East, 1993, and Irkutsk, Siberia, 1994. Several kinds of wild mushrooms (top), wild garlic (bottom left), and fresh fiddlehead ferns (bottom right).*

*Cold* Okroshka *soup (recipe, page 64), a refreshing dish on a hot summer day, at a dacha picnic in the Russian Far East, 2006.*

Shashlyki *(shish-kabobs; recipe, page 332) grilling over hot coals at a picnic on the shore of Lake Baikal, Siberia, 2007.*

*Colorful* Vinegret *(beet-potato-and-sauerkraut salad; recipe, page 24) is a popular* zakuska *(appetizer) on many Russian tables, including on the dining car of the* Golden Eagle Trans-Siberian Express, *2007.*

*Grilled eggplant garnished with horseradish-spiked cream cheese and fresh lingonberries, on the* Golden Eagle Trans-Siberian Express, *2007.*

Pel'meni, *the "National Dish of Siberia" (recipe, page 226), are dumplings stuffed with meat, fish, vegetables, mushrooms, berries, or other ingredients and traditionally served in a gorshok (ceramic pot).*

*Spicy Mongolian Beef Salad (recipe, page 327), from a meal at the Gorkhi Terelj National Park south of the Mongolian-Siberian border.*

*Traditional ingredients, modern plating: Potato pancake topped with cured salmon and salmon caviar, garnished with a fish-stock foam, Russian Far East, 2012.*

*Siberian Frozen Cranberry Cream (recipe, page 45), plated in modernist style, garnished with pine nuts, fresh mint, and a variety of berries.*

*Salmon Kulebyaka (recipe, page 41), often called the "King of Pies" in Russia.*

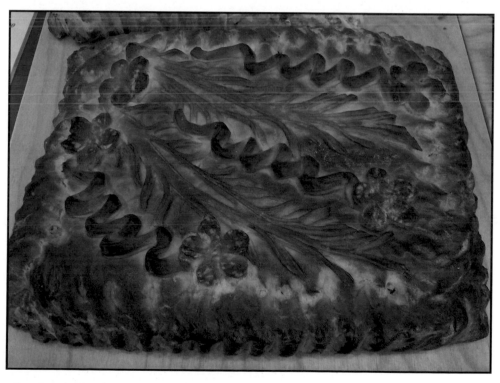

*Fancily decorated, meat-stuffed pirog (pie) at one of the popular Stolle pie shops in Siberia.*

*Potatoes waiting to be peeled in the vestibule of the galley (kitchen)
on a Trans-Siberian train, 2006.*

*Chef Ilkhomudin Kamolov cooking* bliny *(Russian pancakes; recipe, page 280) in the galley of the* Golden Eagle Trans-Siberian Express, *2008.*

*Head waiter serving cold sturgeon in aspic as an appetizer in the dining car of the* Golden Eagle Trans-Siberian Express, *Russian Far East, 2008.*

*Rodion Tabikhanov and members of his family butchering a sheep behind their house in the village of Ust'-Ordynskii, Siberia, 1994.*

*Rodion Tabikhanov's wife and mother filling the sheep's stomach with a mixture of fresh cow's milk, sheep's blood, garlic, and spring onions, before boiling it outdoors in a big iron pot with the rest of the sheep's meat, in Ust'-Ordynskii, Siberia, 1994.*

# Chapter 4
# Hosts and Toasts

## Party Time

Russians love to party. They like to eat and drink and offer toasts and swap gossip and propound philosophy for hours on end around a table set with a bounteous spread of foods and beverages. We soon discovered that our Russian friends preferred to party at home, where a tight budget stretched much further than at a restaurant, the food was certainly better, and everyone could relax and be themselves without having to put on a public face.

In the early post-Soviet period, neither Vladivostok nor Irkutsk was a "dining out" city with good selection of restaurants, despite their both having populations of more than half a million. But Vladivostok had an edge over Irkutsk in the variety and number of restaurants, probably because it was a port that got the first food products off ships that docked there, ships that also brought more contact with a wider world. Vladivostok was where sailors (local and foreign) arrived from far-flung places around the globe, as did government officials and businessmen (nearly always men) from nearby China, North Korea, South Korea, and Japan, who preferred to eat at the few restaurants that featured the cooking of their own countries. But in the early 1990s most of those restaurants in Vladivostok were priced far above what an average Russian could afford.

Our first autumn in Vladivostok, we found fewer than a dozen restaurants in that city of 700,000 people. A handful of them were worth eating at (if you had enough money), but the others were not especially notable. When we returned the following autumn, however, we were pleasantly surprised at the new eateries that were beginning to open there, restaurants striving to offer better food, friendlier service, and nicer décor, even if the prices at most of them were still relatively high.

By the mid-2000s the restaurant scene in Vladivostok had changed dramatically, with dozens, maybe hundreds, of restaurants, large and small, expensive to cheap, serving dishes from six continents. Not surprisingly, several of

*Professional cooks in their kitchen in Siberia, 1994.*

them specialized in seafood and were decorated in a nautical style. Others showcased regional foods from the interior of the Russian Far East, such as wild game, berries, and mushrooms. And some took pride in reviving classic Russian dishes from the nineteenth century, dishes that might have been considered too "bourgeois" during the Soviet period (or their ingredients just too hard to get).

By the mid-2000s Irkutsk had also made a noticeable transition from a city with few public-eating choices 15 years earlier to a place with restaurants catering to a variety of tastes and wallets. But when we lived in Asian Russia in the 1990s, our best culinary experiences were the meals we cooked for dinner parties at our own apartments and those we ate at the homes of Russian friends, American colleagues, and other members of the international community there. We all gave parties to celebrate Russian and American holidays, religious and secular festivals, weddings, birthdays, and sometimes just the serendipity of finding a scarce ingredient in the market that day. In the depth of the Siberian winter, a dinner party with good food and good friends was often the best way to dispel the darkness and bring a bit more light and levity into our lives.

We also learned the rules of Russian party etiquette. As in many other countries, guests should always bring a gift to their hosts—flowers, a box of chocolates, a jar of special homemade preserves, a bottle of wine or liquor, or maybe even something for the house, such as a pretty little vase.

## Bread & Salt

The Russian word for "hospitality"—*khlebosol'stvo*—is derived from the words for bread (*khleb*) and salt (*sol'*). Bread and salt are the two symbols of hospitality that Russians have traditionally offered to their guests upon arrival at the hosts' homes. But in Siberia and the Russian Far East we never saw this custom practiced at private homes, only as an expected ritual at certain public occasions.

(If the gift is edible, the hostess will usually set it on the table with everything else to eat and drink at the meal.) When bringing flowers to the hostess, always bring an odd number, because an even number is considered unlucky—an old Russian superstition. (An even number of flowers is appropriate only if someone has died.) And guests in Russia commonly shake hands with the host and hostess upon arriving and departing—or, if they are good friends, kiss them three times on the cheeks: right, left, right. (In a grand, old-fashioned manner, older men sometimes kiss a woman's hand instead.) But be careful where you stand: Russians believe that shaking hands over the threshold brings bad luck.

## An Alsatian Meal in Asia

In early November of our first year in Russia, Tom and I hosted our first major dinner party there, a multi-course meal for 10 people. In Europe or the United States, we could have organized an event of that size on a couple of days' notice, but such a meal in Vladivostok required three weeks of planning, shopping, cleaning, and cooking—as well as making arrangements to borrow all the additional kitchenware and tableware necessary for preparing and serving the meal. We even had to borrow a dining table for the guests to eat on and chairs for them to sit on.

Tom and I wanted to offer a menu of dishes that our Russian and American guests were unlikely to have tasted before. But we were limited by the dwindling food supplies in the local markets that autumn. After looking at what was still available, we finally decided to make an Alsatian-inspired meal based on some of the dishes we'd often enjoyed on our travels in that part of France.

For the main course we chose to serve *Bäckeoffe*, a hearty dish of marinated pork and beef, layered with potatoes, onions, carrots, and leeks, all slowly braised in white wine. To make enough *Bäckeoffe* for 10 people, I needed two large, heavy, covered casseroles, but none were to be found in the sparsely stocked kitchen-ware sections of Vladivostok's stores. Finally, my neighbors Alla and Natasha came to the rescue. Calling on their network of contacts in our high-rise village, they located two well-used, much-chipped, enameled cast-iron covered casseroles, like heirloom versions of Le Creuset. Since the oven in our Stove-from-Hell was too small to hold both of them at the same time, Alla offered to cook one of the casseroles at her apartment on the day of the party.

Early that afternoon, I trudged up five flights of stairs to Alla's apartment, to load up several big shopping bags with the china, crystal, and flatware she offered to loan us for the party. An hour before dinner, Alla's teenage son and several of his friends showed up at our door, breathless from carrying her dining table and four kitchen stools down those five flights of stairs in Alla's wing of the building, then up five more flights to our apartment in another wing. Without the assistance of so many kind neighbors, it would have been difficult, if not impossible, to give the kind of dinner party in Russia that we just took for granted in the West.

Alla, Natasha, their husbands, and our other guests arrived that chilly November night bearing gifts of Russian champagne and caviar, Bulgarian

## Best of the Bubbly

To my surprise, Russian champagne—the sparkling white wine that Russians call *shampanskoye*—was far better than I had expected. On trips to Eastern Europe in the 1980s, I'd suffered from drinking even one glass of the sickly sweet Soviet champagne that always left me with a miserable headache the next day. But most of the *shampanskoye* we bought in Asian Russia in the 1990s was dry enough for our tastes and often the best deal—at $2 a bottle—compared with all the other alcoholic beverages available there. Champagne was usually our wine of choice even for everyday meals—and we consumed more of it during our time in Russia than the total amount of champagne we'd ever drunk in our lives before.

white wine, German chocolates, and (most exotic of all) a plastic bag of baking powder, a product not available in the stores of Vladivostok, that one of our American guests had carried all the way from Washington, D.C. After welcoming our friends with glasses of Russian champagne, we sat down to a four-course French meal, with different wines for each course—a meal that approximated, as closely as we could in Russia, the kind of dinners that we'd eaten many times at country restaurants in Alsace.

Each guest was served a large plate of mixed cold hors d'oeuvres that Tom had assembled ahead of time in the kitchen: a salad of shredded red cabbage tossed with small cubes of pistachio-studded mortadella sausage; another salad of shredded carrots, diced apples, and golden raisins; green peas marinated in a mustard vinaigrette with plenty of fresh garlic; halves of hard-boiled eggs garnished with garlic mayonnaise; and thin slices of salami and ham—the whole colorful assemblage decorated with slices of the last fresh tomatoes and cucumbers of the season and accompanied by glasses of Russian dry champagne.

When these hors d'oeuvres were finished, we cleared away the plates and brought out the *Bäckeoffe*. I set the two covered casseroles in the center of the table, their lids still hermetically sealed with a ring of dough that had formed a hard crust as the *Bäckeoffe* cooked in the oven. When I cracked open the crusts and lifted the lids, the heady aromas of garlic, onions, and wine wafted around the room, while the guests oohed and aahed over the dramatic presentation. Then I carefully carried the casseroles back to the kitchen to serve up the plates, while Tom poured out glasses of the same white wine that the meat had been marinated and cooked in.

In Alsace this substantial main-dish *Bäckeoffe* would usually be followed by a simple salad of lettuce tossed with a Dijon-mustard dressing. But we hadn't seen a single leaf of lettuce since arriving in Russia three months before. So we moved on to the cheese course, featuring the only two kinds of aged cheeses we could find in Vladivostok. We garnished each plate with a few strips of preserved mild red peppers and pimiento-stuffed green olives, set a basket of white bread on the table, and poured glasses of French red wine.

For dessert I served individual small bowls of fruit compote—a kind of Alsatian *Rumtopf* made from mandarin orange slices, morello cherries, and dark raisins macerated in Russian spiced rum and Azerbaijani sweet red wine similar to ruby Port. Each serving of fruit was surrounded by a pool of custard sauce scented with vanilla and lemon peel. And as a "taste of home" for the

American guests, I'd also baked a batch of Snickerdoodle cookies, a crunchy counterpart to the fruit-and-custard finale.

Everyone around the table seemed to enjoy the meal immensely. But unexpected cultural differences surfaced during the dinner. The Russians commented on the novelty of eating a meal where the individual servings were plated and garnished in the kitchen, then brought to the table in separate, distinct courses. And throughout the meal they looked longingly at the bottles of wine and liquor lined up on our coffee table nearby, which we served separately with the different courses. These customs seemed strange to our Russian friends who, at their own dinner parties, placed most the foods on the table together, on platters from which the guests served themselves, starting with the *zakuski* then moving on to the other dishes. And all the bottles of vodka, brandy, champagne, red and white wines, fruit juices, mineral water, sweet liqueurs, and bitter *digestifs* were often crowded onto their dining table, too, to be drunk—sometimes seemingly indiscriminately—throughout the meal.

After dessert, we offered our guests coffee and small glasses of Georgian brandy or sweet liqueurs, accompanied by a plate of excellent chocolates from the local candy factory. But all the Russians requested hot tea instead, asking also for some fruit or berry preserves to stir into it, for a very Russian ending to our very foreign French meal.

## Birthday Bashes

Three months after arriving in Vladivostok, we were invited to a double birthday dinner hosted by Larisa and Nikolai, a young Siberian couple who'd been born four days apart. They lived in a tiny, low-ceilinged, one-room apartment in a gray, boxy building dating from the Khrushchev era, sharing that small space with their two children and a friend from their hometown.

Larisa must have spent days in her minuscule kitchen alcove preparing that sumptuous spread for eight people. An edible mosaic of hot and cold dishes completely covered the gate-leg table that nearly filled their combination living-dining-sleeping room. Most of the ingredients came from Larisa and Nikolai's own dacha garden: finely shredded ruby-red beets, snow-white radishes, and bright-orange carrots, all lightly napped with sour cream; dark-green pickled cucumbers and jade-green tomatoes;

## Which Day of the Year?

Secular Russians celebrate their birthdays on, or shortly after, the day of the week on which they were born. (It's considered unlucky to celebrate before your birthday.) Many Orthodox Christian Russians also celebrate their "name day"—the day on which the Church honors the particular saint after whom a person is named. Although this custom was dormant during the anti-religious Soviet period, it has been revived by some Russians, with the resurgence of Orthodox religious practices after the collapse of the Soviet Union.

"Herring in a Coat," a pretty red-pink-and-white salad of salted herring fillets layered with sliced boiled potatoes and beets, nestled beneath a mantle of mayonnaise and sour cream; potato salad made with carrots, peas, and cubes of boiled beef; *lecho*, the Slavic rendition of French *ratatouille*; shredded red cabbage shiny with vinaigrette dressing; stewed chicken legs served on a bed of creamy mashed potatoes; and rissoles, crispy croquettes of ground meat and rice browned in hot oil—all accompanied by bottle after bottle of Russian champagne.

After such a feast I barely had room for the chocolate candies and chocolate cake brought by the other guests. But I was seduced by the plate of fresh yellow lemon slices that Larisa served with hot tea after the meal, luscious lemons so naturally sweet that I ate them like candy, peels and all. And I was even more impressed when I learned that Larisa's lemons came from a tree at their dacha more than 200 miles north of Vladivostok, in a region better known for Siberian tigers than for citrus fruits.

The following spring in Irkutsk, two Russian women whom we'd never seen before knocked loudly on our door late one night. The pleasant-looking, well-dressed strangers held up a bottle of expensive vodka and asked if they could come in. When I hesitated, they explained that they just wanted to get away from the noisy party going full blast next door. Neither of them seemed drunk, so I decided to take the risk. They headed straight for our kitchen, plopped the vodka bottle down on the table, and started rummaging in the cabinets for glasses.

# "Little Water of Life"

- Vodka—the diminutive form of *voda* (water)—is the Russians' "little water of life," clear alcohol, 80- to 90-proof (40% to 45% alcohol), distilled from grains, potatoes, sugar beets, and other organic materials.

- *Samogon* is home-distilled moonshine, made all over the country, using whatever ingredients are locally available. When we lived in Russia, *samogon* was legal to make, but illegal to sell.

- *Spirt* (spirit) is the strongest distilled alcohol in Russia, 180- to 200-proof ethanol, which some Russians desperate for alcohol are known to drink. We used it as an all-purpose cleaning agent, paint remover, disinfectant for cuts and scratches, and (diluted 10-to-1 with water) an effective mouthwash.

- Pure vodka is a neutral spirit—odorless, colorless, and taste-less, except for the sting of alcohol on your tongue and in your throat, as it flows downward to warm your stomach and soothe your soul.

- Flavored vodkas are produced by infusing the vodka with natural flavoring agents during the distilling process or by steeping the flavorings in the vodka afterward. Some flavored vodkas have only one taste added; others contain up to 40 different ingredients.

- Vodka flavorings include fresh or dried fruits (raisins, lemons, oranges, peaches, apricots, cherries or just their pits); berries (strawberries, raspberries, cranberries, juniper berries, rowan berries, black currants); herbs (tree bark, birch buds, mountain ash shoots, buffalo grass, roses, apple and pear leaves, mint, garlic, basil, sage, tarragon, angelica root, ginger root); spices (cinnamon, cloves, caraway, coriander, anise, allspice, nutmeg, saffron, vanilla); heather honey, pine nuts, tea leaves, and coffee beans. One of my favorite flavored vodkas is *pertsovka*, pepper-flavored vodka made by infusing small hot dried red peppers in the clear liquor, producing a drink that tastes like alcoholic jalapeño juice. Milder versions of *pertsovka* are flavored with whole black or white peppercorns.

- Buyer beware: Bootleggers also turn out tainted vodkas made with cheaper synthetic spirits or even toxic substances. They also fake the bottle shapes and label designs of popular brands such as Stolichnaya and Moskovskaya, and counterfeit the government excise stamps on them. That's why many Russians prefer imported brands such as Finlandia, Absolut, and Smirnoff.

- Too much: Although vodka seems to be a staple of the Russian diet, alcoholism has long been a major health problem in Russia. Tens of thousands of deaths occur every year in Russia from alcoholism, alcohol poisoning, and alcohol-related accidents. Yet the vodka companies even exploit these same problems to market their product, using brand names such as Terminator (with a picture of Arnold Schwarzenegger on the label) and Black Death (with a white skull on a black background).

- Drink up: Russians drink vodka ice cold and straight, not diluted with water or ice cubes. They also have an "all or nothing" attitude toward vodka. Once a bottle has been opened, it must be drunk to the end, completely consumed by the host and guests—or just knocked back by any group of friends or strangers gathered in a doorway or standing on a street corner.

*Table set with 15 different kinds of zakuski (appetizers) for the first course of a home-cooked Russian feast.*

The four of us spent the better part of an hour sitting around the kitchen table, getting acquainted and finishing off the bottle of vodka. Then a rap on the door interrupted our conversation. "Come back to the party! Come back!" slurred a happily drunken fellow, as he motioned for all of us to follow him down the hallway.

Inside our neighbor's apartment, 17 people were crammed into a small, but well furnished, living room, celebrating the thirty-third birthday of Anna, a neighbor we'd never met before that night. Taking up half the space in the room was a dining table set with the best porcelain dinnerware and stemmed wine glasses I'd ever seen in a Russian apartment, the entire surface of the table covered with the remnants of Anna's birthday feast: Siberian dumplings, slices of sausage and cheese, beet salad, beefy potato salad, homemade sauerkraut, bright green strips of salted wild garlic sauced with sour cream, stuffed cabbage leaves, roasted chicken, and mashed potatoes, along with several half-empty bottles of crystal-clear vodka and psychedelic-colored Dolce Vita sweet liqueurs.

Anna insisted that we join the dinner, as she brought out platters of fresh food from the kitchen and introduced us to the other guests. But conversing with this party of soused Siberians was almost impossible over the sounds of 1960s Beatles' ballads and 1970s heavy-metal rock blaring from a boom box in the claustrophobic room. After several rounds of inebriated toasts, some of the women got up and started to dance, motioning us to join them. By that time, Tom was the only man still able to stand on his feet; all the others were sprawled out on their chairs, in various stages of drunken stupor. Amid this congenial chaos, Anna disappeared into the kitchen to make tea for the guests, while an old *babushka* and I danced the Twist to a scratchy Chubby Checker recording. When the clock struck 2:00 a.m. and Anna hadn't yet reappeared, Tom and I decided it was time to go. We went into the kitchen to say goodbye to Anna, only to find her sitting on the floor, slumped against the wall, passed out cold. So we quietly slipped out of the apartment, carefully closing the door behind us, trying not to wake the other guests who were now snoring loudly, like an asthmatic, out-of-tune calliope, in the stuffy little living room.

## A Siberian Wedding Feast

In April we were invited to the wedding dinner of a woman we'd never met, the sister of Andrei, one of our older students who also happened to live in our apartment building. Andrei lacked the social skills of our other Russian friends. Four days before the wedding, he stopped by our apartment to tell us that his sister was getting married on Thursday—and that he *might* invite us to the dinner afterward, depending on how much food they had.

Late that Thursday afternoon, Tom and I returned home from the central food market with shopping bags full of ingredients for our own meal that evening. Tom was already cooking dinner when Andrei rang the doorbell and asked us when we were coming to the party downstairs. I replied that since we'd never heard from him again, we'd assumed we weren't invited. Andrei looked at us like we were demented, then shrugged and left. "What the heck," I said to Tom. "Neither of us has ever been to a Russian wedding party before. Let's put our dinner on hold and go see what's happening down there."

# To Your Health!

- Russian dinner parties always begin with a toast. Vodka is the drink of choice, served ice-cold in small glasses filled almost to the brim. It's also the drink that traditionally accompanies the first-course *zakuski* at a meal.

- The host (or sometimes a designated toastmaster) always makes the first toast, welcoming the guests and often making a short speech about the occasion that brought everyone together around the dinner table. Then each guest clinks glasses with the person sitting next to him, before knocking back the shot of vodka in one gulp (although it's acceptable for women to sip their vodka instead).

- The second toast follows very soon after the first, and is customarily made by the highest-ranking guest as a tribute to the hosts. (Cossacks say that "a bullet should not pass between the first and second toasts.")

- The third toast—made by the host or one of the guests—is to family and friends absent from the table. Some variations exist, depending on the particular region of Russia, as well as the gender, ethnicity, or profession of the participants. In the port city of Vladivostok, the third toast is always to sailors away at sea. And among the military in general, it is to those who have died in service to the Motherland.

- Exceptions (among many) include birthdays, where the first toast is to the health of the celebrator and the second to the parents; weddings, where the first toast is to the newlyweds and the next to their parents; and wakes, where the first toast is always to the honor of the deceased, and the glasses are never clinked.

- Toasting—with glasses of vodka, wine, or champagne—often continues throughout the meal, with toasts made both by the host and various guests. But many Russians consider vodka, brandy, or other distilled hard liquors, not "lesser" alcoholic beverages, to be the only proper beverage for making a toast.

- The meal concludes with a final toast "for the road"—this time with the brandy that often accompanies or follows dessert, or with any vodka left, since custom dictates that all the vodka opened for the party must be drunk before the guests go home.

- Toasting is such an important social custom in Russia that entire books have been written on the subject and content of toasts, with suggested speeches included. At least one of these includes an entire section on religious toasts!

Seventeen people were squeezed into an apartment much smaller than ours, most of the guests already well-oiled with alcohol. Many of them were crowded around a long narrow table set up in the little living room, including the newlyweds' parents, the groom, and his very pregnant new wife still in her white wedding dress. The table was covered with platters of food prepared by the women on the bride's side of the family: mushrooms they'd picked themselves and pickled together with pearl onions; Russian potato salad; garnet-colored beet-and-sauerkraut salad; slices of excellent smoked salmon; tongue in aspic; canned green peas; roasted chicken; sliced tomatoes and cucumbers seasoned with sour cream and dill; homemade sauerkraut; pickled herring garnished with onions; and a meatloaf with macaroni baked in the center. The guests helped themselves to these dishes at will, washing them down with whatever beverage was nearest to hand—vodka, champagne, brandy, or sweet liqueurs—while some of the others danced to a Patsy Cline tape and the bride's father passed out on the floor.

After three hours of this revelry, Tom and I signaled to each other that it was time to leave, much to the chagrin of the few Siberians who were still sober enough to recognize us. Andrei's mother enticed us to stay a bit longer, offering cups of hot tea laced with her own homemade blueberry *varen'ye*. "Those are the best blueberry preserves I've ever eaten!" I exclaimed. Upon hearing my praise for her accomplishments in the kitchen, Andrei's mother immediately insisted that we take home a very large jar of her preserves. I was embarrassed, because in the fog of the evening's festivities, I'd forgotten that if you compliment a Russian about something he or she owns, that person will usually give it to you as a gift (a custom that no doubt lends itself to subtle abuse). But as we slathered that rich Siberian blueberry *varen'ye* over our morning toast during the following month, never for a moment did I regret telling Andrei's mother what a good cook she was.

## Any Excuse for a Party

Throughout the year, American holidays provided a ready excuse to socialize with our colleagues outside the workplace in Vladivostok and Irkutsk. At Halloween, Thanksgiving, Christmas, Groundhog Day, Valentine's Day, St. Patrick's Day, and Easter, American holiday traditions and regional cooking intersected with Russian ingredients and Stoves-from-Hell to produce some bacchanalian dinner parties that all of us still vividly remember even decades later and continents away.

In February, shortly after we'd moved to Siberia, an official visit by a University of Maryland honcho provided the excuse for hosting our first dinner party at home in Irkutsk. At that time of year winter still held its icy grip on Siberia, with nearby Lake Baikal frozen to a depth of six feet and with several inches of snow covering the ground. As always in Russia, the menu was determined by the ingredients available in the market and the most inventive ways that we could think to combine them into a meal that would be different from what our Russian and American guests were accustomed to eating on their home turf.

That night eight of us gathered around the table for an eclectic dinner of Spanish crab *alioli* and *ensaladilla rusa* (the Spanish version of Russian potato salad), followed by a main course of chicken roasted with plenty of sliced fresh garlic and dried hot peppers inserted under the skin, and our favorite side-dish from the Balkans, *djuveč* rice highly seasoned with paprika, red and green peppers, garlic, and onions. Chilled vodka accompanied the appetizers, Russian-style, with white wine for the main course. And we concluded with a no-fail dessert from my childhood in Texas, cherry cobbler with vanilla custard sauce, followed by coffee and Georgian brandy to finish that round-the-world meal in the heartland of Siberia.

That same month American colleagues from New Orleans invited us to celebrate Mardi Gras at their apartment in Irkutsk, with an appropriately boozy meal featuring all the Bulgarian red and white wine they'd been able to schlepp home from the market, and a menu of small pizza-like appetizers, bowls of chicken gumbo, homemade hot-spicy salsa, and two versions (his and hers) of red-beans-and-rice. I offered to bring dessert, my ever-popular cherry cobbler with custard sauce. Costumes were expected, of course—not an easy feat in Siberia, where party stores and costume shops were not part of the scene. So we approached the challenge with the same attitude we had in the kitchen: What can we do with the raw materials we've got?

Tom, suffering from a cold, took the easy way out, choosing to go as a clown wearing a jumble of mismatched clothes, with circles of bright red lipstick on his cheeks and the tip of his nose. I went as my favorite domestic animal, a black cat, dressed in black slacks and turtleneck sweater, with a "tail" made from a black cloth belt, and with cat's eyes and whiskers drawn on my face with black eyeliner. Another American guest, a former U. S. Navy captain, showed up as a pirate. But winning the prize for best costume that night was our New Orleans host himself, who appeared as Neptune, wearing blue thermal long underwear draped with a toga made from his bedroom curtains, sporting a white beard and bushy eyebrows fashioned from cotton balls gleaned from medicine bottles, and brandishing a rusty trident salvaged from a nearby garbage dump.

## Tex-Mex in Vladivostok

Tom and I hosted several dinner parties, large and small, during our last autumn and winter in Vladivostok. But the most memorable was a Tex-Mex meal we prepared for our Russian neighbors, Alla and Pyotr, our Siberian friends, Larisa and Nikolai, and a Bosnian-Serbian couple, Igor and Slavitsa—all of whom were good cooks themselves. Knowing that our guests were also adventuresome eaters, we felt completely confident about serving them a variety of Tex-Mex and Mexican-inspired dishes that we assumed they'd never tasted before.

Eight of us gathered around the dining table that we'd borrowed once again from Alla and set up in our small living room. Arrayed in the center was a selection of pre-dinner snacks: a large bowl of garbanzo salad with black olives and fresh peppers, two platters of the Russian version of Ritz crackers (our not-too-satisfactory substitute for tortilla chips, which were impossible to get in Vladivostok), and several bowls of dips, including homemade green-tomato-and-chile dip, mild and hot versions of *pico de gallo* (fresh salsa), cheese-and-sour-cream dip seasoned with Texas chili powder, and smoky black bean dip. For drinks, we offered cold German beer or Bulgarian red wine.

Tom, as host, offered the first toast, hoisting his glass of beer and welcoming our friends to that special Tex-Mex dinner showcasing the kinds of foods that we often ate back home. But none of the guests knew how or where to begin. We had to show them how to use the crackers to scoop up the dips, while explaining that these foods were typical of the snacks that Texans would nibble on, with drinks, before the main meal was served. Pyotr and the Yugoslav couple didn't have much trouble with this culinary concept,

## Tom's Nichevo Nachos

*Nichevo* is the Russian word for "nothing." Since tortilla chips weren't available in Vladivostok and Irkutsk in the early 1990s, Tom made "Nichevo Nachos" using Russian crackers similar to American Ritz crackers, each topped with a piece of Russian hard yellow cheese and garnished with slices of Bulgarian pickled red peppers and a dried wild pequin for a capsaicin kick. Whenever our Stoves-from-Hell didn't burn them to a crisp, these "Nichevo Nachos" were a big hit among our homesick American friends in Russia.

but everyone else just dunked a cracker or two, out of courtesy, then stopped. The garbanzo salad seemed slightly more acceptable to them, although the Russians had never seen black olives before and thought the shiny slivers were some kind of dark mushroom.

The guests chatted in the living room while Tom and I dished up the main course in the kitchen, filling each diner's plate with two turkey *mole* enchiladas garnished on top with sour cream, raw onions, and black olives, accompanied by side servings of Texas ranch-style beans and spicy Spanish rice. Tom was especially proud of his *mole*, the rich dark-brown sauce made with dried ingredients that we'd carried from Texas and fresh ingredients found in Vladivostok's markets. To accompany the meal (and sop up the thick *mole*), he also put out a platter of steamy-hot corn tortillas, the last of our precious supply brought from Texas and stored in the freezer.

The guests looked at their plates, then at each other, in complete silence.

"What is it?" Alla finally asked, pointing to the enchiladas.

"I recognize beans," said Slavitsa, the Serbian, who knew them from her own country's cuisine.

"Why is the rice that color?" Pyotr asked hesitantly, as everyone just sat there without even lifting a fork.

Alla ventured the first bite, but only after I'd explained that enchiladas were a kind of Mexican *blinchiki* (thin pancakes), made from corn and filled

# Traveling Tortillas

During our first year in Russia, one of the foods-from-home that Tom and I truly missed was Mexican corn tortillas. When we returned to Texas for a short visit the following summer, we stocked up on several supplies for our next autumn in Russia. Top on our list was tortillas. Just before we flew back to Vladivostok, after we'd packed our luggage for the trip, we went to a local supermarket and bought big plastic bags full of fresh corn tortillas, which we stuffed into every nook and cranny remaining in our suitcases. I was worried that these precious tortillas would be confiscated at the Russian border—but the airport customs officials couldn't have cared less about all those plastic bags full of Mexican flatbread in our luggage. We filled our freezer in Vladivostok with tortillas and carefully rationed them for meals throughout the autumn, using the final two packages for our last Tex-Mex dinner in November.

with turkey cooked in a special sauce. Following Alla's lead, the other guests started picking at the food on their plates, but without much enthusiasm. When Pyotr asked if we had any bread, I explained that tortillas are the flatbread that Mexicans customarily eat with their meals. But when I passed the platter of tortillas around the table, Tom and I were the only ones who took any.

The guests continued to push the food around on their plates, venturing only an occasional bite. The looks on their faces reminded me of a matter-of-fact statement one of my Russian students had written in an essay: "When you are cooking, you can make some mistakes. When you will eat it, you will find them."

Alla said she'd never eaten anything like those enchiladas before, adding that she could taste cinnamon in the sauce. Thinking that such a good cook as Alla would want to know what else was in the *mole*, I proceeded to name the other ingredients. That was my mistake. When I got to "cocoa powder," all the guests put down their forks and stared at their plates.

"You put *chocolate* in the meat sauce?" asked Alla incredulously, as if I'd just admitted adding insects to a salad. After that, no one ate much else except for a few bites of rice or beans, just to be polite.

Dessert was another disappointment. I thought surely the Russians would like my sweet-potato pudding flavored with orange juice, cinnamon, nutmeg, and raisins, each portion garnished with chopped pineapple soaked in spiced rum. But that dish seemed as strange to them as the enchiladas did.

"I've never eaten such a thing for dessert," Alla said wonderingly, as she took a second small bite in a kindly attempt not to offend me.

"These things come from Africa, don't they?" asked Pyotr, referring to the sweet potatoes, as he tried to find something—anything—to say about the peculiar pudding sitting in front of him.

Later that night, after the guests had left, Tom and I speculated about what had gone wrong with the meal. During our entire time in Russia, we'd successfully entertained friends at a variety of dinner parties with menus ranging from French to Spanish to Italian—but that Tex-Mex dinner in Vladivostok had been a real disaster. As we scraped all the uneaten food off the plates and into the trash, we concluded that the meal had seemed strange to our Slavic guests for several reasons: the tastes were too alien even for those adventuresome people's palates; we didn't serve any wheat or rye bread, the staple expected at every meal in Russia (tortillas didn't count); and we didn't serve any vodka. Reflecting on the fact that this was the first time in our lives we'd given a dinner party that was such a flop, all we could do was laugh, chalk it up to experience, and recall a line that Nikolai had uttered during the birthday dinner at his apartment in Vladivostok: "It's always better to have banquets than to have battles."

# Carrot, Apple, and Raisin Salad

*This colorful, easy-to-make salad can be prepared a day in advance and refrigerated until needed. The ginger in the dressing provides a surprising zing.*

**1 pound carrots, peeled and shredded (about 3½ to 4 cups of shredded carrots, lightly packed)**
**1 large apple, peeled, cored, and diced into ¼-inch pieces**
**½ to 1 cup golden raisins**
**⅓ cup canola or sunflower oil**
**2 tablespoons apple cider vinegar**
**1 tablespoon honey**
**1 teaspoon ground ginger**
**½ teaspoon salt**

- Toss the carrots, apple pieces, and raisins together in a large bowl. Whisk together the oil, vinegar, honey, ginger, and salt in a smaller bowl until the mixture becomes emulsified (cloudy and thick). Pour this dressing over the carrot mixture and toss very well to coat all the pieces with dressing. Cover and refrigerate until needed.

- Let the salad sit, uncovered, at room temperature for 15 minutes, then toss it again just before serving.

- Makes 6 to 8 servings.

# Red Cabbage Salad

*We first ate this colorful salad at a Michelin-starred restaurant in Alsace, where it was made with small cubes of* foie gras *and garnished with slivers of black truffle. But in Russia we had to improvise with the ingredients available, substituting pistachio-studded* mortadella *for the* foie gras, *sunflower oil for walnut oil, and only dreams for the truffles. Now we make it more like the Alsatian original, but with less expensive ham instead of* foie gras—*and still no truffles.*

▶ **NOTE:** The cabbage needs to meld with the dressing for several hours before serving. The remaining ingredients are added only a few minutes before serving, to keep their texture firm.

**1 small red cabbage (2 pounds), cored and finely shredded**
**1 medium red onion, finely chopped**
**1 cup cooked ham, diced into ¼-inch cubes before measuring**
**½ cup walnut oil**
**⅓ cup red wine vinegar**
**1 teaspoon freshly ground black pepper**
**1 teaspoon salt**
**1 medium red apple**
**¾ cup coarsely chopped toasted walnuts***
**½ cup crumbled blue cheese**

***Toasted in a 350°F. oven for 10 to 12 minutes**

- Toss the cabbage, onion, and ham together in a large bowl.

- Whisk the oil and vinegar together in another bowl until emulsified (cloudy and thick). Whisk in the pepper, and salt. Let the dressing sit at room temperature for 10 minutes, then whisk again, and pour it over the cabbage. Toss to mix well, until all the pieces are coated with the dressing. Cover and refrigerate at least 2 hours (or even overnight), tossing the salad again 2 or 3 times while refrigerated.

- Thirty minutes before serving, core the apple and chop it medium-fine. Toss the cabbage again to mix it well with the dressing, then add the chopped apple and toasted walnuts and toss again. Add the crumbled blue cheese and toss gently once more. Let the salad sit at room temperature until serving time.

- Makes 10 to 12 servings.

# "Herring Under a Fur Coat"

*Known in Russian as* Selyodka pod shuboi *("Herring under a Fur Coat"), this colorful layered salad is also sometimes called "Herring in a Coat," or "Herring under a Blanket," or just* Shuba *(from the Russian word for fur coat). Whatever its name, this is one of several kinds of beet salads popular across Russia from the Baltic Sea to the Bering Sea. Brought to Siberia by people from the Baltic States, Ukraine, and the European side of Russia, this recipe has many variations, depending on the cook. It's traditionally one of the* zakuski *served for the festive New Year's Eve dinner and for other special occasions such as birthdays.*

▶ **NOTE:** This recipe requires advance preparation. I like to cook the vegetables, boil the eggs, and chop the herring a day or two beforehand, refrigerate them, and then shred the vegetables when I'm ready to assemble the salad. It must then be refrigerated for several hours before serving. (TIP: Lock your cat in another room when you start to chop the herring.)

**2½ pounds red beetroots (weight without stalks and leaves), unpeeled**
**2 pounds firm boiling potatoes, unpeeled**
**2 large carrots, peeled and cut in half crosswise**
**10 to 12 green onions, finely chopped (or 1½ cups finely chopped mild white onion)**
**1 pound preserved herring (net weight after draining)\***
**2 tablespoons chopped fresh dill**
**1 cup mayonnaise**
**1 cup pure sour cream**
**Salt**
**Freshly ground black pepper**
**2 large hard-boiled eggs**

**\*Preserved herring is sold in three basic forms: (1) salted and layered in barrels, producing a brine that pickles the fish (the herring must first be soaked overnight in water, milk, or kefir to remove the saltiness); (2) pickled in vinegar in jars and often seasoned with onions, black peppercorns, dill, mustard seeds, and sometimes sugar; (3) packed in oil (often smoked first). The net weight of herring (after draining off the brine or oil) will depend on how the fish is preserved and packaged. A 26-ounce jar of pickled herring from my local deli contains 1 pound (16 ounces) of fish, after draining.**

● Preheat the oven to 400°F. Wash and dry the unpeeled beets and rub lightly with vegetable oil. Bake on a baking sheet lined with aluminum foil, for 1 hour (more or less, depending on their size), until the beets are tender when pierced with a fork. Let them cool completely.

- Meanwhile, bring a large pot of water to a boil. Add the potatoes, carrots, and 1 teaspoon salt. Cover and cook over medium-high heat until the vegetables are just tender—about 10 to 15 minutes for the carrots, 20 to 40 minutes for the potatoes, depending on their size. Drain well in a colander and let cool completely.

- Peel and coarsely shred the beets and potatoes, putting them into separate bowls. (Use the large holes on a box grater.) Finely shred the carrots into a separate bowl. Chop the onions.

- Drain the herring, rinse well in cold water (for salt- or vinegar-pickled herring) or in hot water (for oil-packed herring). Pat dry with paper towels. Remove any bones and tough skin, then cut the herring into very small cubes. Add the dill and mix well.

- Whisk the mayonnaise and sour cream together in another bowl.

▶ **To assemble the salad [see also NOTE at end of recipe]:**

- Pat the grated potatoes into an 8-inch, straight-sided round on a 10- to 12-inch serving plate with a rim, flattening the top of the potatoes to form an even layer. Sprinkle lightly with black pepper.

- Put the chopped herring on top of the potatoes, forming it into an even layer. Press gently with your hands to compact the ingredients a bit. Spread ¼ cup of the mayonnaise mixture over the herring, then top with all the onions as the next layer. Press gently by hand to hold the ingredients together. Sprinkle lightly with black pepper.

- Mix the carrots with 2 tablespoons of the mayonnaise mixture, then spread the carrots in an even layer over the onions. Sprinkle lightly with salt and pepper.

- Cover the entire salad, top and sides, with an even layer of grated beets, forming the salad by hand into a shallow dome shape and gently pressing the ingredients together. Finally, cover the entire salad with the remaining mayonnaise-sour cream mixture (like frosting a cake).

- Cover the salad by inverting a large mixing bowl over it, not touching the salad. Refrigerate at least 8 hours or overnight. The outer layer will turn pink.

- Just before serving, cut the hard-boiled eggs in half, and separate the whites from the yolks. Finely grate the whites with a box grater, and sprinkle them evenly over the top of the salad. Hold a fine sieve over the salad, and press the yolks through the sieve to make an even layer on top of the whites.

- Cut into wedges for serving as a cold appetizer.

- Makes 10 to 12 servings.

▶ **NOTE:** You can also layer the ingredients in a large (2½- to 3-quart) deep-sided glass baking dish. Use less mayonnaise-sour cream mixture on top. Cut into squares for serving.

▶ **VARIATIONS:** Add a layer of grated apple or chopped dill pickles between the herring and onion layers. Add chopped parsley to the carrots. Boil the beets instead of roasting them (but roasted beets have a richer flavor). Some cooks dice the vegetables into small cubes instead of grating them. Some put more mayonnaise and/or sour cream between the inner layers but none on top, ending with a layer of beets garnished with the grated hard-boiled eggs, or with squiggles of mayonnaise or even a layer of finely shredded cheddar cheese. The choice is up to you!

## Symbolic Salad

Although Russian cooks have probably been making salads like "Herring in a Coat" for centuries, one legend (surely apocryphal) says that the recipe was invented in a Moscow tavern shortly after the Bolshevik Revolution of October 1917. The red beets supposedly symbolized the red flag of the revolutionaries, with the herring representing the workers and the potatoes standing for the peasants, groups that supported the revolution. Or you could make up another legend that the colors symbolize the Reds (Bolsheviks) and the Whites (anti-Bolsheviks) who fought against each other in Russia's Civil War (1918–1922). In that story, the herring represents the leaders of both sides—since an old political proverb says, "Fish rot from the head" (meaning "The rot starts at the top," whichever side you support). But since the herring in this salad has been pickled to preserve it from rotting, maybe it's more symbolic of those hard-drinking Russian leaders known for being pickled in vodka much of the time. Vodka is the classic accompaniment to "Herring in a Coat," so drink up and believe any legend you want.

# Garbanzo Salad

*In Russia we had to make this salad with canned California olives, which have too mild a flavor for our own tastes. In Texas we make it with Greek Kalamata or Italian black olives, and reduce the salt in the recipe accordingly.*

**3 tablespoons vegetable oil**
**1 medium onion, finely chopped**
**2 medium tomatoes, coarsely chopped**
**3 large garlic cloves, finely chopped**
**1 teaspoon red wine vinegar or lemon juice**
**½ teaspoon salt**
**½ teaspoon crushed dried red pepper flakes**
**2 cans (15 ounces each) garbanzos (chick peas)**
**½ cup chopped pitted black olives**

- Heat the oil in a medium skillet over medium-high heat, and sauté the onion until golden. Stir in the tomatoes, garlic, vinegar, salt, and dried pepper flakes. Cook over medium heat, stirring frequently, until the tomatoes are cooked to death and all the liquid has evaporated (about 15 minutes). Remove from the heat and let the mixture cool slightly.

- Combine the tomato mixture and garbanzos in a large bowl, tossing them together to mix well. Add the chopped olives and toss to mix again. Taste and add more salt if needed (depending on the saltiness of your olives).

- Cover and refrigerate until needed, but let the salad come to room temperature before serving.

- Makes 6 to 8 servings.

# Tex-Mex Salsa

*This spicy sauce is often called* pico de gallo *(beak of the rooster) in Spanish, possibly because the hot peppers in it peck at your taste buds. In Mexico it belongs to the category of* salsas frescas *(fresh sauces) or* salsas crudas *(raw salsas), its red-white-green ingredients a reflection of the colors of the Mexican flag. It's best made with lemon or lime juice, but in Russia we had to substitute vinegar. Use it as a dip for tortilla chips and a piquant garnish for grilled meats, enchiladas, and scrambled eggs.*

1 medium tomato, chopped very fine
½ medium onion, chopped very fine
3 serrano or jalapeño peppers, chopped very fine
½ teaspoon salt
2 tablespoons fresh lime juice (or 1½ tablespoons lemon juice)
2 tablespoons cold water
1 to 2 tablespoons minced fresh cilantro

- Combine all the ingredients in a small bowl and let the sauce sit at room temperature for a few minutes before serving, for the flavors to meld.

- Makes approximately 1½ cups.

▶ **NOTE:** It's best to make this sauce no more than a couple of hours in advance, because it will lose some of its crispness after that. Refrigerate until a few minutes before serving. The recipe can be doubled, but don't double the amount of salt.

# Tex-Mex Rice

*Called "Spanish rice" in Texas, this reddish-colored rice is one of the two standard side dishes served at Tex-Mex restaurants, along with "cowboy beans" (recipe, page 162) or "refried beans" (cooked pinto beans mashed together with onions, garlic, and hot lard in a skillet). A long time ago a Mexican grandmother taught Tom how to spice up this rice by "sweating" a whole jalapeño pepper on top of the rice as it cooks.*

1 tablespoon vegetable oil
1 medium onion, finely chopped
2 large garlic cloves, minced
1 cup raw medium- or long-grain rice
2 teaspoons Texas chili powder
1 medium tomato, chopped
¾ teaspoon salt
2 cups water (or chicken stock)
1 jalapeño pepper

- Heat the oil in a heavy 2-quart saucepan. Sauté the onion and garlic over medium-high heat until the onion is very soft. Add the rice and cook over medium-low heat 2 minutes longer, stirring constantly, to coat all the grains with oil. Add the chili powder and stir constantly for 1 minute. Stir in the tomato and cook for 1 minute more.

- Stir in the water (or stock) and salt. With a sharp knife, make several lengthwise slits in the jalapeño, without cutting the pepper apart. Bring the liquid in the pan to a boil over high heat, then reduce the heat to low and place the jalapeño on top of the rice. Cover the pan tightly, and cook for 20 minutes.

- Turn off the heat and let the rice steam, still covered, for 5 minutes. Remove the jalapeño and fluff the rice with a fork. (For a spicier version, finely chop the jalapeño and stir it into the rice just before serving.) Serve hot.

- Makes 4 to 6 servings.

# Chili or Chile?

In Texas, "chili" means a dish of coarsely ground or finely cubed meat (usually beef) cooked in fat and seasoned with finely ground red peppers, cumin, garlic, oregano, salt, and sometimes additional spices. Onions, tomatoes, and other ingredients often find their way into the chili pot, too. Various combinations of the spices used in making chili are also commercially bottled and sold as "chili powder," generically called Texas chili powder. Most Texas chili powders are richly flavored but not highly hot-spicy in taste.

In much of the American Southwest, "chile" or "chile pepper" is the general term for any pungent, spicy capsicum pepper, red, green, or another color, fresh or dried. (In contrast, mild-tasting bell peppers are not considered "chiles.") "Chile powders" are made from any of several varieties of dried chiles (mostly red ones), ground into a powder and not mixed with other spices or other types of chiles. These chile powders range in taste from fairly mild to flaming hot. Some of the most popular are made in New Mexico.

That's why some of our recipes list "Texas chili powder" as an ingredient, while others call for "New Mexico chile powder" (mild, medium, or hot), depending on the desired flavor of the dish. We carried both kinds of powder to Russia, along with Hungarian paprikas, mild and hot, which have their own distinctive taste.

# Spicy Tex-Mex Beans

*In Tex-Mex restaurants these are often called "charro beans" (cowboy beans), after the Spanish word for cowboy. They're cooked in a way that's popular at ranches along the Texas-Mexico border, where the beans are seasoned with bacon and a sofrito, a richly flavored combination of tomatoes, onions, peppers, and spices fried in a skillet. In Vladivostok we made these charro beans with chili powder brought from Texas and whatever kinds of peppers we could find in the farmers' market that day.*

**1 pound dried pinto beans**
**¼ pound bacon, diced**
**1 tablespoon vegetable oil**
**2 medium tomatoes, chopped medium-fine**
**1 large onion, chopped medium-fine**
**1 green bell pepper, diced into ¼-inch pieces**
**4 large jalapeño peppers, finely chopped**
**4 large garlic cloves, minced**
**¼ cup Texas chili powder**
**½ to 1 teaspoon ground cumin**
**1 to 2 tablespoons dried hot red pepper flakes**
**2 teaspoons salt**
**1 teaspoon freshly ground black pepper**

- Sort any rocks out of the beans, then wash the beans in a colander and drain well. Soak the beans overnight in a 6-quart heavy pot filled with enough cold water to cover the beans.

- Drain the beans in a colander and rinse them once more. Return the beans to the pot and add enough cold water to cover them by 1 inch.

- Bring the beans to a boil over high heat, stirring occasionally. Reduce the heat and simmer the beans, uncovered, for 30 minutes, stirring occasionally. Add enough water to keep the beans covered while simmering, and cook until they are just tender but not mushy soft.

- Meanwhile, fry the bacon in a large skillet over medium-high heat until almost crisp. After the beans have cooked for 30 minutes, transfer the bacon to the bean pot, leaving the rendered fat in the skillet. Add the tomatoes, onion, bell pepper, jalapeños, and garlic to the skillet, and cook over medium-high heat, stirring frequently, until the onions are translucent and the mixture is very thick. Stir the chili powder and cumin into the mixture and continue to cook, stirring constantly, for 2 minutes more.

- Stir the tomato *sofrito*, dried red pepper flakes, salt, and black pepper into the beans. Add a little more water, if needed, but don't make the bean mixture too liquid. It should be fairly thick.

- Let the beans continue to simmer gently, uncovered, for 30 minutes longer, stirring frequently and adding a bit more water if necessary. Just before serving, taste and add more salt if you want. Serve hot.

- Makes 8 to 10 servings.

# Turkey Mole Enchiladas

Mole *(pronounced MO-lay, from the Nahautl word* molli, *meaning sauce) is a category of complex Mexican sauces made from several kinds of toasted dried chile peppers slow-cooked with a variety of other ingredients.* Moles *can be savory or sweet, mild or spicy, thick or thin, hot or cold. The* mole *we made as a sauce for turkey enchiladas in Vladivostok was inspired by the classic dark brown, chile-and-chocolate* mole poblano *from Puebla, Mexico. But our sauce was rust-brown in color, made with the only ingredients we had available on the eastern edge of Russia.*

▶ **ADVANCE PREPARATION:** Make the sauce 1 or 2 days before using it, so the flavors can develop.

Sauce

¼ cup Texas chili powder
2 tablespoons New Mexico hot chile powder
2 small dried hot red peppers, finely crushed
½ teaspoon ground cinnamon
½ teaspoon ground coriander
¼ teaspoon ground allspice
¼ teaspoon finely ground black pepper
¼ cup sunflower oil
2 medium onions, finely chopped
6 large garlic cloves, minced
⅓ cup finely chopped peanuts
¼ cup dark raisins
¼ cup toasted sesame seeds
2 medium tomatoes, chopped

2 cups turkey or chicken stock (divided use)
1 corn tortilla, torn into small pieces
2 tablespoons unsweetened cocoa powder
½ teaspoon salt

## Enchiladas

1 to 1¼ pounds boneless cooked turkey meat (stewed, poached, or roasted),
  shredded
½ cup turkey or chicken stock
16 corn tortillas

## Garnishes

Sour cream, at room temperature
3 to 4 green onions (white and tender green parts), thinly sliced on a slight
  diagonal
Toasted sesame seeds

▶ **To make the sauce:**

- Mix together the Texas chili powder, New Mexico chile powder, crushed hot red peppers, cinnamon, coriander, allspice, and black pepper in a small bowl.

- Heat the oil in a large skillet, and sauté the onions over medium-high heat until soft and golden. Add the garlic and sauté for 2 minutes more. Reduce the heat to medium, stir in the peanuts, raisins, and sesame seeds, and cook, stirring constantly, for 2 minutes longer. Add the spice mixture and cook, stirring constantly, for 1 minute more. Finally, stir in the tomatoes and cook for 1 more minute. Turn off the heat and let the mixture cool to lukewarm.

- Purée the mixture in a blender. Add 1 cup of stock and the corn tortilla pieces, and blend until smooth.

- Pour the mixture into a heavy saucepan. Stir in the cocoa powder, salt, and remaining 1 cup of stock. Cook the sauce over medium heat, stirring constantly to prevent scorching, for 15 minutes.

- Let the mole cool to lukewarm, then transfer to a bowl, cover, and refrigerate for at least one day, preferably 2 days, for the flavors to meld.

▶ **To make the enchiladas:**

- Wrap 2 stacks of 8 tortillas each in foil and put them in a cold oven. Turn the oven to 350°F.

- While the oven is heating, put 3 cups the mole sauce in a medium saucepan. Put the remainder of the sauce in a large skillet with ½ cup stock and the pre-cooked turkey pieces, stirring to mix well. Bring both mixtures to a simmer over medium heat, stirring frequently to prevent scorching. Then turn off the heat under both pans, cover the saucepan, and leave the pans on the stove.

- Lightly oil a 15 × 10-inch (or two 11 × 7-inch) shallow glass baking dish. Take the warm tortillas out of the oven, but leave the remainder wrapped in foil as you work. Put 1 tortilla on a plate, scoop out ¼ cup of the turkey mixture from the skillet, and place it in the center of the tortilla, pressing it with your fingers into an oval about 4 inches long. Carefully roll up the tortilla and place it seam side down in the baking pan. Continue with the remaining tortillas.

- Spread the warm sauce from the saucepan evenly over the top of the enchiladas. Cover the baking dish tightly with foil. Bake at 350°F. for 25 to 30 minutes.

- To serve, use a spatula to transfer 2 enchiladas to each plate. Garnish with a dollop of sour cream, then scatter some of the green onion rings on top, followed by a sprinkling of sesame seeds. Serve immediately, accompanied by **Spicy Tex-Mex Beans** (recipe, page 162) and **Tex-Mex Rice** (recipe, page 160).

- Makes 8 servings.

## Thankful for Turkey

The only turkeys we could find in Russia in the mid-1990s were huge, fleshy legs newly imported from the United States. We roasted them with slices of garlic and hot red peppers slipped under the skin, then stripped the meat off the bones and served it in corn-tortilla enchiladas garnished with **Pickled Green Tomato Sauce** or **Mexican Mole Poblano**. In Texas we always make turkey *mole* enchiladas with leftovers from our Thanksgiving bird. And we still laugh when we recall an American colleague working in Irkutsk in 1994, who couldn't find a whole turkey to roast for Thanksgiving that year. So she bought seven of those huge legs at the city's central food market and constructed a complete, full-size, Thanksgiving "turkey" out of the meat from the legs.

# Pickled-Green-Tomato Sauce

*Since we couldn't get Mexican tomatillos in Russia, Tom developed this recipe for "Russian Tomatillo Sauce" using hot green peppers sold by Korean vendors in the Vladivostok markets and Russian green tomatoes pickled in 3-liter jars. (In the United States, you can find pickled green tomatoes at East European and Jewish delis.) We used this celadon-colored sauce as a garnish for chicken or turkey enchiladas, with a dab of sour cream on top. It's also delicious drizzled over grilled pork and chunks of roasted potatoes.*

**⅓ cup canola oil**
**1 medium onion, chopped medium-fine**
**2 small (or 1 large) green bell peppers, diced into ¼-inch pieces**
**7 jalapeños or other small hot green peppers, finely chopped**
**5 large garlic cloves, squeezed through a garlic press**
**2 pounds pickled green tomatoes, drained and coarsely chopped**
**1 tablespoon white vinegar**
**2 tablespoons chopped fresh cilantro**

- Heat the oil in a large skillet over medium-high heat, and sauté the onions, bell peppers, and jalapeños together until the onions are translucent and the peppers are soft. Add the garlic and sauté for 2 minutes more.

- Stir in the green tomatoes. When the mixture comes to a boil, reduce the heat to medium-low, cover the skillet, and cook for 35 to 40 minutes, stirring occasionally, until the tomatoes are soft and most of the liquid has cooked away.

- Stir in the vinegar and cilantro, and cook uncovered, stirring frequently, for 5 minutes more. Let the mixture cool to room temperature, then purée it in a blender or food processor.

- Serve warm—or refrigerate or freeze until needed, then reheat over low heat. (The sauce should be thick, but if you need to thin it out a bit, heat it with a little water or chicken stock.)

- Makes approximately 4 cups.

# Alsatian Meat-and-Potato Casserole

## (Bäckeoffe)

*The name of this classic Alsatian stick-to-your-ribs casserole means "baker's oven." It was traditionally made on laundry days and at harvest time, when the women were busy with chores outside the kitchen. The ingredients were assembled early in the morning in a deep, oval-shaped, Alsatian earthenware casserole, then taken to the local bakery to be slow-cooked in the commercial oven after that day's bread had finished baking. In Alsace, Bäckeoffe is often made with three kinds of meat—pork, beef, and mutton or lamb—marinated and cooked in Alsatian white wine. We like to serve Bäckeoffe for dinner parties because it's easy to make and our guests always enjoy the dramatic presentation when we break open the bread-dough seal on the casserole and release the heady aromas of meat and marinade.*

▶ **NOTE:** This recipe requires advance preparation. Save time by using a food processor to finely chop all the vegetables and to slice the potatoes into thin rounds.

### Meats and marinade

1½ pounds boneless chuck roast, cut into 1½-inch cubes*
1½ pounds boneless pork shoulder, cut into 1½-inch cubes*
1 medium onion, finely chopped
1 leek (white and light green parts only), finely chopped
1 to 2 cups finely diced peeled carrots (optional)
3 large garlic cloves, finely chopped
2 bay leaves
1 tablespoon juniper berries (optional)
1 tablespoon salt
2 teaspoons dried thyme
1 teaspoon freshly ground black pepper
1 bottle (3 cups) Alsatian dry white wine (Riesling, Sylvaner, or Gewürztraminer)

*Or 1 pound each of boneless beef, pork, and lamb

### Casserole

Butter (unsalted) or rendered goose fat
3 pounds firm boiling potatoes
3 large onions, finely chopped
3 leeks (white and light green parts only), finely chopped
Salt

**Freshly ground black pepper**
**1 whole nutmeg, grated**
**1½ cups Alsatian dry white wine**

Dough seal for casserole

**1 cup flour**
**1 tablespoon vegetable oil**
**4 to 8 tablespoons water**

Garnish

**Snipped fresh chives or chopped parsley**

▶ **ADVANCE PREPARATION:** Mix the meats and marinade ingredients together in a large glass bowl. Cover and refrigerate for 12 to 36 hours. Stir the marinade occasionally.

▶ **To make the casserole:**

- Preheat the oven to 400°F. Butter (or grease with goose fat) a 6-quart covered casserole. Earthenware is traditional, but you can also use an enameled cast-iron casserole. (If using earthenware, start the casserole in a cold oven, set the heat at 400°F., and begin timing the baking after the oven has reached that temperature. If using enameled cast-iron, put the casserole into a preheated oven and bake according to the timing instructions.)

- Peel the potatoes and slice them crosswise into large rounds, no thicker than ¼ inch. (With a food processor, use the 4mm slicing blade.) Salt the potato slices lightly and stack them in a large bowl. Mix the onions and leeks together in another bowl.

- Set aside enough potato slices to make a single layer on top of the casserole ingredients. Place half the remaining potatoes in an even layer in the bottom of the casserole. *As you add each layer of new ingredients, sprinkle it lightly with salt, black pepper, and nutmeg.* Spread half the onions and leeks in an even layer on top of the potatoes. Place all the meats in a layer on top of the vegetables.

- Pour in half the meat marinade, including all of its vegetables. Add another layer of the remaining sliced potatoes (except those set aside for the top), followed by the remaining onions and leeks. Pour in the remaining marinade, then arrange a single layer of sliced potatoes on top.

- Pour 1½ cups of Alsatian white wine into the casserole, and dot the top layer of potatoes with butter or goose fat.

- Combine the flour, vegetable oil, and 4 tablespoons of water in a medium bowl, kneading the mixture to form a smooth dough. Add more water, if needed, 1 tablespoon at a time (depending on the absorbency of the flour). Roll the dough by hand into a "rope" long enough to fit completely around the rim of the casserole.

- Moisten the rim of the casserole with water, then press the dough onto it. Carefully place the lid on the casserole, pressing it into the dough to make a tight seal. Some of the dough will ooze out between the lid and the rim of the casserole. Use your fingers to press it against the intersection of the casserole and the lid, to seal the casserole well all the way around.

- Bake at 400°F. on the bottom rack of the oven for 2½ hours. Do NOT open the lid during that time.

- Carry the casserole, with the lid still sealed, to the table or sideboard for serving. Use a wooden mallet to gently break off the bread-dough seal. Serve the *Bäckeoffe* very hot, directly from the casserole, lifting the solid ingredients out with a slotted spoon. Garnish each serving with a liberal sprinkling of snipped chives or chopped parsley.

- Serve as a main dish, on a plate by itself, with no other side dishes, followed by a fresh green salad made of butterhead lettuce (Bibb or Boston-type) dressed with a garlic-and-Dijon-mustard vinaigrette, which helps you digest the casserole.

- Makes 6 to 8 large servings.

▶ **WASTE NOT:** The winey, full-flavored meat broth remaining in the casserole, with its bits of onion and leek, makes an excellent soup stock. Use it within a day after making the *Bäckeoffe*, or freeze it until needed.

# Balkan Rice Casserole

## (Djuveč)

*Pronounced DYOO-vech, this colorful, richly seasoned rice is popular throughout the Balkan region of southeastern Europe. There are many varieties (and spellings) of casseroles called djuveč, including main-dish versions made with cubes of meat. New Mexico chile powder (ground chiles, with no additives) gives this recipe an authentic Balkan flavor, but Hungarian paprika works well, too. Djuveč is a great dish to serve at backyard barbecues, take to potluck dinners, and just eat at home on chilly autumn nights.*

½ cup olive oil
4 medium onions, chopped medium-fine
1 large green bell pepper, seeded and sliced into strips (2 inches long, ¼-inch wide)
1 large red bell pepper, seeded and sliced into strips (2 inches long, ¼-inch wide)
2 to 3 fresh jalapeño peppers, finely chopped
3 large garlic cloves, minced
2 tablespoons New Mexico mild chile powder (or Hungarian mild paprika)
1 teaspoon New Mexico hot chile powder (or ground cayenne pepper, or Hungarian hot paprika)
2 teaspoons salt
1 teaspoon freshly ground black pepper
1 teaspoon dried thyme, crumbled
2½ cups raw medium-grain rice
4 to 6 medium zucchini, halved lengthwise, then sliced crosswise into ¼-inch-thick pieces
1 cup frozen peas, thawed but not cooked
2 cups chicken stock
1 cup white wine
Juice of 1 large lemon
1 bay leaf
3 medium tomatoes, sliced crosswise into ¼-inch-thick rounds (optional)

- Heat the olive oil over medium-high heat, in a 5- or 6-quart Dutch oven or heavy stove-top-and-ovenproof casserole. When the oil is hot, sauté the onions and bell peppers until they are very soft (about 25 minutes).

- Reduce the heat to low and stir in the jalapeños, garlic, chile powders or paprika, salt, pepper, and thyme. Immediately turn off the heat under the casserole, leaving it on the stove. Turn the oven to 350°F.

- Stir the raw rice into the casserole until all the rice is coated with the seasoned oil. Gently stir in the zucchini slices and peas.

- Mix together the chicken stock, wine, and lemon juice, and pour into the casserole. Stick the bay leaf into the mixture. Arrange the tomato slices in an even layer on top of the other ingredients.

- Cover the casserole tightly and bake at preheated 350°F. for 1 hour. Then uncover the casserole and continue to bake for 15 minutes longer. Serve hot, as an accompaniment to grilled meats.

- Makes 12 servings.

▶ **NOTE:** This recipe is flexible, allowing for variations that suit your own tastes. Use whatever ingredients you have on hand. In Russia we usually had to substitute sunflower oil for olive oil and omit the zucchini, but we often added chopped peanuts to the mix. In Texas we like to make *djuveč* with Texas chili powder (a pungent mix of powdered chiles, cumin, and other spices), ground cayenne pepper, 1 cup chopped toasted pecans (instead of the green peas), and 1 cup cubed Longhorn cheese sprinkled over the top when the lid comes off for the last 15 minutes of baking. Other times we use smoked paprika in this casserole and crumble a cup of feta cheese over the top, to melt during the last 15 minutes of cooking.

# Aunt Beulah's Cinnamon Rolls

*Every family has an aunt or cousin or grandmother who's considered the best baker among all the relatives. When I was a child, my father's Aunt Beulah in Oklahoma made the best cinnamon rolls any of us had ever tasted. Hot from the oven, those sweet, gooey rolls, redolent of cinnamon and glazed with buttery white icing, were utterly irresistible. Later I carried her recipe with me to Russia, where I used it for making dinner rolls and sweet breads for many occasions, including big pretzel-shaped* krendel', *a traditional Russian birthday bread.*

▶ **NOTE:** This recipe makes enough dough for 28 cinnamon rolls, 2 large pretzel-shaped breads, or 24 cloverleaf dinner rolls. Or mix and match, making a half portion of one and a half portion of another.

## Dough

**1 package (2¼ teaspoons) active dry yeast**
**½ teaspoon sugar**
**2 cups warm water (divided use)**
**5 to 6 cups all-purpose flour**
**1 large egg**
**½ cup sugar**
**½ teaspoon salt**
**¾ cup solid vegetable shortening, at room temperature**

## Filling (divide between the two halves of dough)

**½ cup (1 stick) unsalted butter, melted and slightly cooled**
**⅛ teaspoon salt**
**1½ cups sugar**
**4 tablespoons ground cinnamon**

## Icing (divide between the two halves of dough)

**2 cups confectioners' sugar, sifted**
**2 tablespoons unsalted butter, melted**
**2 tablespoons milk or cream**
**1 teaspoon vanilla extract**

## Dough:

- Dissolve the yeast and ½ teaspoon sugar in ½ cup lukewarm tap water (100°–105°F.) in a small bowl, and let it sit in a warm place to bubble up.

- Meanwhile, measure your flour by lightly spooning it into a measuring cup, leveling off the top with a knife, and putting the flour into a large bowl.

- Beat the egg well in another large bowl, then stir in the ½ cup sugar and ½ teaspoon salt. Add the vegetable shortening in small bits, mashing until no large lumps remain. Stir in 1½ cups warm tap water, mixing well. (The mixture will look curdled, but that's okay.)

- Stir the bubbly yeast into the egg mixture. Using a large wooden spoon, stir in 5 cups of flour, 1 cup at a time, mixing well after each addition and pressing out the lumps with the back of the spoon, until the dough pulls away from the sides of the bowl. (If the dough is still too sticky, add up to 1 more cup of flour, ¼ cup at a time, mixing by hand if necessary.) Cover the bowl with plastic wrap and let the dough rise in a warm place for 1 to 2 hours or until doubled in size.

- Punch down the dough, turn it out onto a floured surface, and knead lightly. Wipe out the bowl with a paper towel and grease the bowl with vegetable shortening. Form the dough into a ball, place it in the bowl, and turn it over once so all the surface is greased. Cover the bowl loosely with plastic wrap and refrigerate for at least 2 hours, or even overnight. The dough will continue to rise in the refrigerator and must be thoroughly chilled before using. (This dough will keep up to 1 week in the refrigerator, so you can prepare it in advance and use when needed.)

▶ **To Make Cinnamon Rolls:**

- Butter two 9 × 1½-inch (or 9 × 2-inch) round metal cake pans. (Pan size is important.)

- Punch the chilled dough down, turn out onto a floured surface, let it sit for 5 minutes, then knead lightly and divide it in half.

- Working with one-half portion of dough at a time, pat it by hand into a rectangle (like making pizza or focaccia), then roll it out into a rectangle measuring 10 × 14 inches, ¼-inch thick. Stir the salt into the melted butter, and brush ¼ cup of it over the surface of the dough, covering it almost to the edge. Sprinkle ¾ cup of sugar evenly over the butter, then sprinkle 2 tablespoons of cinnamon over the sugar.

- Starting with a long side of the rectangle, *tightly roll up* the dough (like a jelly roll). Pinch the dough together to seal it along the long side, to make a log 14-inches long. Cut the log crosswise into 1-inch-wide pieces. Place the 14 pieces, cut side up, snugly together in one cake pan. Repeat this process with the remaining dough, putting those 14 pieces into the other cake pan. (**TIP:** Aunt Beulah always saved out a bit of extra dough and pressed a little flattened piece of it onto the bottom of each roll, to catch the buttery juices that ooze out during baking.)

- Cover loosely with plastic wrap and let the rolls rise in a warm place for 1 to 2 hours, until doubled in size.

- Preheat the oven to 350°F. Uncover the rolls and bake for 25 to 35 minutes, until medium-brown on top and beginning to pull away from the sides of the pan. Cool in the pan set on a wire rack.

- Meanwhile, stir all the icing ingredients together until the mixture is smooth. While the cinnamon rolls are still very warm, spread this icing over the tops. Serve warm or at room temperature.

- Makes 28 very rich cinnamon rolls.

## ▶ To Make Pretzel-Shaped Bread Loaves (Russian *Krendel'*):

- Make the dough recipe (omitting the filling and icing). After the dough has chilled, punch it down and turn it out onto a large, lightly floured surface. Let it warm up for a few minutes, then knead it to make a smooth, pliable dough. Divide in half (keeping the other half refrigerated). Butter 2 large baking sheets.

- Working with one-half the dough at a time, roll it by hand back and forth, shaping and stretching it into a long (40-inch) rope, slightly thicker in the middle and tapering to thinner toward the ends. Place it on a baking sheet, and twist it into a pretzel shape, tucking the ends underneath the top of the pretzel. Cover loosely with plastic wrap, and let it rise in a warm place for about 1 hour, just until doubled in size. (While the first *krendel'* is rising, form the remaining half of dough into a second pretzel-shaped loaf on the other baking sheet and let it rise until doubled in size.)

- Preheat the oven to 375°F. Working with the first pretzel, uncover the dough and lightly brush the top and sides with an egg wash made from 1 egg well beaten with 1 teaspoon milk. Sprinkle well with granulated sugar. Bake the *krendel'* for about 30 minutes, until medium-brown on top. (Repeat with the other pretzel, baking it after the first comes out of the oven.)

- Remove each *krendel'* from the pan as soon as it comes out of the oven and let it cool on a wire rack. Slice into pieces to serve.

- Makes 2 large pretzel-shaped loaves.

- **NOTE:** You can also knead some raisins, chopped nuts, or chopped candied fruit peel into the dough before rolling and shaping it. Or save a few pieces of the plain dough for making dough decorations on top of the *krendel'*, attached with some of the egg wash before the dough is set aside to rise.

## ▶ To Make Cloverleaf Dinner Rolls:

- Make the dough recipe (omitting the filling and icing). After the dough has chilled, punch it down, turn out onto a lightly on a floured surface, and let it sit for 5 minutes. Then lightly knead, just briefly enough to make a smooth dough, and divide it in half. (Refrigerate the remaining half of dough, for making another batch of 12 rolls whenever you want.) Grease the cups in a standard-size, 12-cup muffin pan (or two 6-cup muffin pans).

- Working with that half-portion of dough, dust your hands with flour, pinch off pieces of dough, and roll them by hand into balls about the size of a large walnut. As you make the balls, place 3 of them together, snugly side by side, in each cup of the muffin pan.

- Brush the tops of the dough with melted butter. Cover loosely with plastic wrap and let the dough rise in a warm place for about 1 hour, or until doubled in size.

- Preheat the oven to 350°F. Uncover the rolls and bake them for 20 to 25 minutes, until golden brown on top. Serve hot.

- One-half portion of dough makes 12 cloverleaf dinner rolls. (Full portion makes 24 rolls.)

## Big Birthday Breads

For friends' birthdays in Irkutsk, I usually baked a Russian *krendel'*, the traditional festive bread for Russian name-day celebrations and Russian Orthodox Christmas. Russian *krendel'* are made with a sweetened yeast dough enriched with eggs, enhanced with spices, and sometimes studded with raisins, almonds, and candied fruit peel. The dough is twisted into a large pretzel shape, brushed with an egg wash, and sprinkled with additional sugar, cinnamon, or chopped nuts. Alla's Granny Polina made her own version with a sweet poppy-seed filling, then slashed the dough with diagonal cuts evenly spaced around the outer side, so the filling would peek through as the *krendel'* baked.

I made my simpler *krendel'* with *testo* (bread dough) from the central food market, or used the sweet dough recipe for my Aunt Beulah's cinnamon rolls, without any spices or other ingredients added. To personalize the gift, I also spelled out the recipient's name in bread-dough letters attached to the top of the giant pretzel. Those *krendel'* were tricky to bake in our Stove-from-Hell, but when they turned out well they were always a much-appreciated contribution to the birthday dinner table.

# Snickerdoodles

*This is my mother's recipe from the 1950s, when these were my favorite kind of cookie as a kid. The first time I tried baking them in Russia, I burned two pans of Snicker-doodles in our Stove-from-Hell before succeeding on the third try. After that, I often made several batches of these cookies for parties in Russia, where they were always devoured by Russians and Americans alike. At our first Christmas party in Vladivostok, some of the Americans even got tears in their eyes when they bit into my Snickerdoodles. For the Russians, those cookies were a new flavor treat, but for the Americans they were a nostalgic taste of home.*

½ pound (2 sticks) unsalted butter, at room temperature
1½ cups sugar
2 large eggs, well beaten
1 teaspoon vanilla extract
2¾ cups all-purpose flour
2 teaspoons cream of tartar
1 teaspoon baking soda
¼ teaspoon salt

## Coating

¼ cup sugar
4 teaspoons ground cinnamon

- Preheat the oven to 400°F. Beat the butter and sugar together in a large bowl until light and fluffy. Stir in the beaten eggs and vanilla until well combined.

- Whisk together the flour, cream of tartar, baking soda, and salt in another bowl. Stir this into the first mixture, stirring well with a wooden spoon to form a smooth dough.

- Mix the ¼ cup sugar and 4 teaspoons of cinnamon together in a small bowl. Pinch off pieces of the dough and roll them by hand into balls about 1 inch in diameter. (If the dough seems too soft and sticky to work with, refrigerate it for 30 minutes—and keep the remaining dough refrigerated while the other cookies are baking.) After you make each ball of dough, roll it gently in the cinnamon-sugar mixture, to coat the entire surface. Place the balls 2 inches apart on an *ungreased* baking sheet.

- Bake at 400°F. for 8 to 10 minutes, or until the cookies just begin to turn golden brown. The cookies will flatten and spread out during baking. Using a spatula, carefully transfer them to a wire rack to cool completely. Store in a tightly covered container.

- Makes approximately 80 cookies.

▶ **NOTE:** Using butter in this recipe produces very flat, thin, crisp cookies. My mother's recipe called for 1 cup of solid vegetable shortening instead, which produces thicker, chewier cookies.

# Sweet Potato Pudding

*In Vladivostok I made this autumnal dessert by adapting a* Joy of Cooking *recipe and adding several touches of my own. In Russia I had to use canned sweet potatoes and white sugar (the only kind we could get), but now I prefer to bake-and-purée fresh sweet potatoes and use brown sugar, for a richer flavor and color. Garnish this dessert with chopped pineapple chunks soaked in spiced rum, or with sweetened whipped cream, or even sour cream mixed with a little sugar (for a Russian twist).*

½ **cup dark raisins**
1 **tablespoon spiced rum**
2 **cups sweet potato purée\***
1 **cup light or dark brown sugar, firmly packed**
¼ **pound (1 stick)) unsalted butter, melted and cooled to room temperature**
6 **large egg yolks, well beaten (set aside 3 of the egg whites to use in this recipe)**
1 **teaspoon finely grated orange peel**
½ **teaspoon finely grated lemon peel**
½ **teaspoon ground cinnamon**
¼ **teaspoon ground nutmeg**
⅛ **teaspoon salt**
1 **cup orange juice**
1 **teaspoon vanilla extract**
1 **rounded teaspoon all-purpose flour**
3 **large egg whites (reserved from above)**
⅓ **cup chopped walnuts**

178

Garnish

**See choices at end of recipe**

**\*Made from two 15-ounce cans of sweet potatoes, drained and puréed before measuring—or 2 pounds fresh sweet potatoes, roasted whole in a 425°F. oven for 45 to 60 minutes, then cooled, peeled, and puréed in a food processor.**

- Mix the raisins and rum together in a small bowl. Cover and let the raisins rehydrate for an hour (or cover and microwave for 30 seconds, then cool before using).

- Butter a 9 x 9-inch square baking pan. Preheat the oven to 350°F.

- Combine the puréed sweet potatoes, brown sugar, melted butter, beaten egg yolks, orange peel, lemon peel, cinnamon, nutmeg, salt, orange juice, and vanilla in a large bowl. Beat or whisk until the ingredients are thoroughly mixed. Dust the raisins with flour to coat them well and stir into the sweet-potato mixture.

- In a separate large bowl, beat 3 egg whites until firm and glossy but not dry, then gently fold into the sweet-potato mixture.

- Pour the batter into the baking pan. Sprinkle the top with chopped walnuts. Bake, uncovered, at 350°F. for 1 hour. Set on a wire rack to cool.

- Serve warm or at room temperature, with your choice of the following garnishes.

- Makes 8 servings. (Refrigerate leftovers.)

▶ **Garnishes:** (Make your choice of garnish while the pudding is baking):

- Combine 1 cup of drained pineapple chunks, chopped into ¼-inch pieces, with ¼ cup spiced rum and ¼ teaspoon ground cinnamon.

- Whip 1 cup of very cold whipping cream until it begins to thicken. Beat 3 tablespoons of confectioners' sugar into the cream, followed by 1 tablespoon rum, beating just until firm peaks form.

- Whisk together 1 cup of sour cream and ¼ cup superfine or confectioners' sugar until well blended.

▶ **WASTE NOT:** Freeze the remaining 3 egg whites to use in other recipes, such as **Pine Nut Meringues** (recipe, page 293).

# Cherry Cobbler

*This old-fashioned, easy-to-make cobbler was a big hit every time I served it for dessert in Russia. I used bottled unsweetened morello cherries imported from Bulgaria, but you can find good bottled cherries in the United States, too. You can tart up the recipe by serving the cobbler in a pool of **Vanilla Custard Sauce** (recipe, page 181)—although this cobbler is simply good enough to eat on its own.*

2½ to 3 cups pitted unsweetened cherries, fresh, frozen, bottled, or canned
   (dark morello cherries are best)*
1 cup sugar (divided use)
1 tablespoon lemon juice
¾ cup all-purpose flour
1½ teaspoons baking powder
¼ teaspoon salt
¾ cup milk
1 teaspoon vanilla extract
3 tablespoons unsalted butter, cut into several chunks
Vanilla Custard Sauce (recipe, page 181)

*If using canned or bottled cherries, drain off the liquid before measuring.
   (Reserve the cherry juice for other uses.) Two 15-ounce cans of cherries
   equal approximately 3 cups of drained cherries.

- Mix the cherries, ½ cup sugar, and lemon juice in a bowl. Let them sit for 30 minutes at room temperature.

- Preheat the oven to 400°F. Whisk the remaining ½ cup sugar together with the flour, baking powder, and salt in a bowl until well combined. Stir the milk and vanilla together in a measuring cup.

- Put the butter into a 9-inch square metal baking pan and place in the hot oven for 3 minutes. While the butter is melting in the oven, gently stir the milk into the dry ingredients, mixing only until no lumps remain. Do not overbeat the batter.

- Carefully remove the hot pan from the oven. Pour the batter evenly over the melted butter in the pan. Spoon the cherries in an even layer over the batter and drizzle on top any cherry juice remaining in the bowl. *Do not stir* the mixture in the pan.

- Bake at 400°F. for 30 to 35 minutes, or until the crust on top is golden-brown and begins to pull away from the sides of the pan. While baking, the fruit will sink to the bottom and the batter will rise to the top. Let the cobbler sit at room temperature for at least 10 to 15 minutes before serving it, for the juices in the center to thicken up as it cools. This cobbler will be very gooey inside, but that's what makes it so good!

- Serve warm, garnished with **Vanilla Custard Sauce**, vanilla ice cream, or whipped cream.

- Makes 6 to 8 servings.

▶ **NOTE:** This cobbler can also be made with other fruits. Use 3 cups of fresh, frozen, bottled, or canned unsweetened fruits, such as blueberries, chopped peaches, or chopped apples. Add ¼ to ½ teaspoon of cinnamon to the fruit mixture when making apple or peach cobbler.

## Waste Not: Fruity Cocktails

When making cherry cobbler with bottled morello cherries, we first drained off the delicious juice, then mixed it with vodka for an instant cocktail to sip while the cobbler was baking. And whenever we opened a can of pineapple chunks to use in dessert recipes, we drained off the sweet pineapple juice and spiked it with spiced rum for a taste of the tropics in Siberia. Nothing ever went to waste in our Russian kitchens.

# Vanilla Custard Sauce

*This rich, sweet, silky-smooth sauce is easy to make, but it requires a bit of patience. You can make it up to two days in advance and refrigerate until needed. Use as a garnish for bread puddings and fruit desserts such as cobblers and compotes.*

**2 cups whole milk or half-and-half**
**1 strip of lemon peel (about 4 inches long and 1 inch wide)**
**4 large egg yolks**
**½ cup sugar**
**1 teaspoon cornstarch**
**⅛ teaspoon salt**
**1 teaspoon vanilla extract**
**1 tablespoon brandy, rum, or sweet sherry (optional)**

- Combine the milk and lemon peel in a medium-size, heavy-bottom saucepan. Bring to a simmer over medium heat. Set aside.

- Beat the egg yolks, sugar, cornstarch, and salt in a medium bowl until the mixture is pale-yellow and very thick (about 3 minutes). Remove the lemon peel from the milk, and very slowly pour the hot milk into the eggs, in a thin steady stream, whisking constantly.

- Pour the mixture back into the saucepan and cook over low heat, stirring constantly with a wooden spoon, for 15 to 20 minutes, or until the foam subsides and the sauce begins to coat the back of the spoon. Don't be tempted to turn up the heat! This sauce doesn't like to be rushed, and if it gets too hot it will curdle.

- Immediately pour the sauce into a glass bowl and stir in the vanilla. Cover with plastic wrap touching the entire surface of the sauce (to keep a "skin" from forming on it) and refrigerate until needed. The sauce will be thin enough to pour, not thick like a pudding, but will thicken up a bit as it cools.

- Just before serving, stir in the (optional) brandy, rum, or sweet sherry. Serve chilled or at room temperature, poured over individual portions of fruit compote, cobbler, or bread pudding in shallow dessert bowls.

- Makes approximately 2 cups (6 to 8 servings).

▶ **TIP:** If a *domovoi* should creep into your kitchen and cause the custard sauce to curdle on the stove (just the sort of mischief that a *domovoi* likes to do), pour the custard directly from the pan into a blender container, and whir on high speed for 30 seconds. The sauce will smooth out again, and the *domovoi* will be thwarted.

▶ **WASTE NOT:** Freeze the leftover egg whites to use for making **Pine Nut Meringues** (recipe, page 293).

# Who's in the Kitchen?

All the Russians we knew in Vladivostok and Irkutsk were initially surprised at Tom's domestic skills—food shopping, cooking, dishwashing, housecleaning—activities that were traditionally a woman's domain in that country. But over time, as our Russian friends came to know more Americans, they gradually began to realize that gender roles were less rigid in the United States—and that American men could pursue their culinary talents and perform household tasks without undermining their masculinity.

# Russian Cure-All

Many Russians believe that by drinking vodka they can kill any germs in the food they eat. A university professor in Vladivostok told me that Russian sailors always carried plenty of vodka with them to Vietnam. "The food is so dirty there," she said. "So our sailors always take bottles of vodka with them when they eat in restaurants, because it kills the germs in the food and keeps them from getting sick."

# Chapter 5
# Winter Feasts

## The Holiday Season

Winter comes early to Russia and leaves late, like a guest who's overstayed his welcome. The days are short and cold, the nights long and cold. It's a season of dormancy for plants and animals, historically a time of scarcity and hunger, yet also, for many people, a respite from the outdoor work they can do only in warmer weather. Winter is also the season of some of Russia's finest festivals: Christmas, for religious believers, and New Year, which is the most important secular holiday on the Russian calendar.

When Tom and I lived in Germany before moving to Russia, our winter holiday season extended from the beginning of Advent, on the fourth Sunday before Christmas (in late November or early December), until Epiphany (Three Kings Day) on January 6. On the Asian side of Russia, our winter holiday season lasted for only three weeks, from late December until the middle of January—but during that time we celebrated two Christmas Eves, two Christmas Days, two New Year's Eves, and two New Year's Days, thanks to historically different ways of calculating the calendar.

"European Christmas," as the Russians in Asia called it, occurs on December 25 on the current calendar, the day on which Christmas is observed only by Catholics and Protestants, not by members of the Russian Orthodox Church. Also known as "Old Christmas" in some parts of the country, December 25 is not a recognized holiday in the Russian Federation.

The official beginning of the winter holidays for Russians is New Year, January 1, the start of a one- to two-week vacation period for many workers and students. But because the Russian Orthodox Church uses a different calendar from secular society, it observes Eastern Orthodox Christmas on January 7—a day that was reinstated as a national holiday in 1992, shortly after the collapse of the Soviet Union. And because of those church and state calendar differences, a week after Orthodox Christmas some people also celebrate "Old New Year," on January 14, the last day of the secular

# Calendar Confusion

There are both historical and calendrical reasons for the dates of winter holidays in Russia.

In 45 BC Julius Caesar introduced to the western world a calendar that closely approximated the time it took for the earth to make one complete revolution around the sun. In 325 AD this "Julian calendar" was adopted by the Christian Church as the basis for calculating the days of the Christian year, replacing older solar-and-lunar-based agrarian calendars that had been used in many societies for centuries. But the Julian calendar's minor deviation from true planetary motion added up over the centuries, causing it to become increasingly less accurate as time went by.

In 1582 a new reformed calendar was introduced to the West by Pope Gregory XIII. That "Gregorian calendar" calculated the time more accurately, dropped 10 days from the old Julian calendar, and changed the ways in which leap years were figured. By the twentieth century, the difference between the older Julian calendar and the newer Gregorian one had become a total of 13 days, as it still is in the twenty-first century.

Until the reign of Peter the Great (Tsar Peter I, who lived from 1682 to 1725), Russians had used an even different calendar, an older agrarian calendar that began each new year on September 1 and calculated the number of each year from the date they thought the world had been created, more than seven thousand years earlier. But in 1699 Peter the Great—who'd recently returned from a journey to Western Europe—decreed that Russia would adopt the Julian calendar, which was still used in many parts of the West at that time. Although most of the countries of Western Europe eventually changed to the more accurate Gregorian calendar by the mid-1700s, Russia continued to use the older Julian calendar for more than two centuries, until shortly after the Bolshevik Revolution.

On February 1, 1918—in a move to bring Russia in line with the rest of the western world—Russia's new Bolshevik government officially changed from the Julian calendar to the newer Gregorian one, with its 13-day difference from the older calendar. But the Russian Orthodox Church continued to adhere to the old Julian calendar. So Christmas Day in Russia (which is still December 25 on the Church's Julian calendar) actually occurs on January 7 (on the newer Gregorian calendar used by secular Russia). And New Year's Day (January 1 on the old Julian calendar) now occurs on January 14 on the modern Gregorian calendar, as the holiday known today as "Old New Year" in Russia.

winter holiday season. But for members of the Russian Orthodox Church, the religious season of Yuletide extends from Christmas Eve, on January 6, until Russian Orthodox Theophany (Epiphany), on January 19.

## "European Christmas" in Vladivostok

In December 1994, Tom and I attended "European Christmas" services at the Lutheran and Catholic churches in Vladivostok, both of which had only recently re-established their congregations in that city after seven decades of Soviet suppression.

St. Paul's Lutheran Church held its Christmas service that year on Saturday morning, December 24, at Vladivostok's municipal House of Culture, with a day-long celebration that was a delightful mixture of Russian and German Yuletide traditions. The cavernous modern hall was decorated with a tall evergreen tree, a Nativity scene, and several large hand-painted posters of German Christmas symbols. The German pastor, Manfred Brockmann, read each line of the liturgy in German, followed by his assistant who translated the words into Russian, and the congregation sang Christmas carols and old Lutheran hymns in both languages.

After the service, we all gathered at one side of the hall for a potluck meal. I had brought platters of homemade German and American Christmas cookies that were soon devoured by the Russian families gathered for that holiday feast. Following lunch, the children staged a pageant re-enacting the Nativity story. Then a folk-dancing group in colorful costumes performed traditional Russian dances, including one from far in their Slavic past featuring a character dressed as a goat, representing the sacrificial scapegoat of ancient pagan times, now appearing as a symbol of the Christ Child's own sacrifice yet to come. And late that afternoon, as the winter sky darkened and flakes of snow began to fall, the Christmas program concluded with an accomplished string quartet, with Pastor Brockmann on violin, performing several pieces by Beethoven and Mozart.

The next morning, December 25, we attended Christmas Mass at Vladivostok's only Catholic church, conducted by Father Myron Effing, an American who was the priest at the Most Holy Mother of God Roman Catholic Parish. The worshippers that day consisted of local Russians, East Asians, and several people from the small American community in Vladivostok. In the sanctuary we all listened to the familiar mass and sang nostalgic Christmas carols in both English and Russian. After joining the congregation for a potluck lunch in an anteroom of the church, Tom and I walked home, hand in hand, through the softly falling snow, knowing that those two Christmas services on the eastern edge of Russia would always hold a special place in our memories and in our hearts.

# Christmas in Vladivostok

On December 23, just before our first Christmas in Vladivostok, a blowing blizzard blanketed the city under a mantle of snow. But the next day my dreams of a Russian white Christmas melted under the winter sun, as the temperature on our balcony reached a balmy 67 degrees Fahrenheit in the afternoon—typical of the changeable weather in seaside Vladivostok.

That evening Tom put together a light Christmas Eve dinner for just the two of us, suitable for the spring-like temperature outside: salmon caviar and smoked salmon on squares of buttered brown bread, cold boiled shrimp, and sautéed scallops garnished with garlic mayonnaise and shredded crab, all accompanied by a dry Colli Verde Spumante from Italy. We dined by candlelight on the glass coffee table in our living room, with German Christmas music playing on a CD in the background. Afterward we nibbled carrot cake left over from Tom's birthday earlier that month and drank cans of Hamm's beer, while making decorations for the evergreen tree we'd acquired the day before, still propped up in one corner of the room.

On Christmas morning, Tom set out to find something we could use for a Christmas tree stand, so we could finally put up our tree and decorate it before "European Christmas" was already over. But Russia was not the kind of country

*Our Christmas tree in Vladivostok, decorated with handmade paper snow-flakes and sea urchin shells scavenged from the nearby shore.*

where you could just drive to the local Walmart and buy a tree stand. Tom had lived long enough in Vladivostok to know that the best source of materials for a makeshift stand would be the piles of garbage outside our apartment building. After foraging in the neighborhood for a fairly long time, he finally returned with an impish look of triumph on his face.

## Trimming the Tree

Our first Christmas season in the Russian Far East, only a few holiday ornaments were for sale in Vladivostok, most of them cheap plastic baubles from China, too gaudy for our tastes. So we made our own simple decorations from whatever materials we could find: paper snowflakes cut from squares of heavy white toilet paper; animal figures cut from a colorful set of children's Cyrillic alphabet cards; sand dollars and sea urchin shells that I scavenged along the shore.

By the next Christmas, we'd collected a few more ornaments for our tree, including small Russian lacquered wooden dolls and tiny terra cotta cats, miniature bottles of Tabasco sauce (brought from the United States), and long, thin, hot red peppers that we'd dried in our kitchen, which we suspended from the Christmas tree branches with red and green yarn. Alla loaned us a string of multi-colored lights shaped like old-fashioned coach lanterns, which also illuminated several translucent red and green glass icicles and glittered off a few small pieces of gold-colored costume jewelry tied to the tree.

But surely the most unusual decorations were eight shiny, silver-plated sprat forks, my birthday gift to Tom that December, each attached to the boughs with a bow of red yarn. Our Russian friends laughed in surprise when they saw that specialized flatware hanging from the evergreen branches, like silver icicles borrowed from a Victorian dining room. And topping the tree was an ornament especially appropriate for maritime Vladivostok: a big orange starfish from the nearby sea, secured with a length of insulated wire that Tom had salvaged from a pile of trash outside our apartment building.

"See what I found in the trash!" he exulted, as he held up a dented, nickel-plated electric samovar that someone had discarded. While I wondered how such a piece of junk could ever be used as a tree stand, Tom disappeared into the kitchen with his Leatherman tool and proceeded to bang away on the samovar for 15 minutes. Once it was disassembled, washed, and polished, he turned it upside down and stuck the base of the tree into a hole in the bottom. But the tree still wobbled too much, so he braced it firmly by ramming five of those empty beer cans into the extra space inside the inverted samovar. *Voilà!* A shiny and elegant, if somewhat unorthodox, stand for our first Christmas tree in the Russian Far East.

Flush with his success at setting up the tree, Tom proceeded to prepare Christmas dinner for us that day, turning out a traditional American holiday meal from ingredients available in the winter markets of Vladivostok: huge roasted turkey legs (the largest I'd ever seen), with fresh garlic and dried hot peppers slipped under the skin; cornbread dressing seasoned with onions, peanuts, and herbs; and our own homemade sauerkraut cooked with white wine, ham, onions, and duck fat. For dessert, I'd already assembled a compote of canned peaches and pineapple, fresh pears, and dark raisins, all the fruits macerated overnight in sweet Azerbaijani wine and spiced with cinnamon, ginger, and vanilla. And we toasted "European Christmas" that day with several glasses of our favorite Russian "table wine"—dry Sovetskoye champagne.

Both of the Christmases we spent in Vladivostok we hosted a big potluck dinner at our apartment to celebrate the season. Guests included our Russian university colleagues and other Russian friends, as well as members of the international community living in Vladivostok, transplanted there from such far-flung places as Germany, Bosnia, Serbia, New Zealand, and the United States. Tom and I knew from our previous parties in Europe that potluck dinners with guests from several countries were a foolproof way to entertain a large number of people while also giving everyone a chance to sample a variety of foods from around the world.

In Vladivostok, our guests arrived to find buffet tables already set with our own favorite potluck fare: Tom's version of Russian potato salad, made with king crab and garlic mayonnaise, shaped into a large dome on a serving platter and decorated with a big "crab" fashioned from red-orange salmon caviar. A large pot of spicy Texas chili and another filled with seasoned sauerkraut. A big bowl of Christmas cole slaw, a melange of white cabbage, green onion tops, and red sun-dried tomatoes. A platter of sliced sausages, cheeses, and pickled cucumbers. Trays with four American carrot cakes and two batches of chocolate brownies. Homemade Russian honey-rye cakes, studded with walnuts and dried apricots. And dozens of my homemade honey-spice cookies, Snickerdoodles, and peanut-butter cookies. We also provided drinks for every taste: Russian champagne, Italian Spumante, Russian vodkas (straight and flavored with hot peppers), Bulgarian white wine, sweet Azerbaijani "Port," Georgian brandy, Russian berry liqueur, carbonated soft drinks, and three kinds of fruit juices, plus hot coffee and tea. It had taken us two weeks of serious shopping and cooking to find and prepare all the foods and drinks for our own part of the buffet.

Nearly 30 people crowded into our small apartment for those potluck parties, bringing a global cornucopia of home-cooked dishes and commercial products that reflected the wide range of shopping ingenuity, culinary skills, disposable incomes, and cultural backgrounds of our friends in Vladivostok: Curried pasta salad with walnuts and sultanas. A colorful fruit salad made with expensive imported ingredients, fresh and canned: bananas, apples, tangerines, and peaches, tossed with tiny local berries that the Russians called "Primorsky cherries." Three-bean salad, German potato salad, Russian cold "borshch salad," and spicy Korean carrot salad. Central Asian rice pilaf with dark raisins and toasted pine nuts. Roasted chicken, Filippino menudo, and whole potatoes stuffed with ground meat. American chocolate bars, candy canes, gum drops, and Tootsie Rolls. Danish butter cookies and Korean fried apple pies. Homemade waffles, spice cakes, and a walnut layer cake. Russian fiddlehead ferns, home-grown fruit preserves, and an exotic dish containing sea slugs, those bottom-feeding marine creatures shaped like knobby cucumbers, a costly seafood delicacy in the Russian Far East.

But Alla's dishes were the star of the show. At our first potluck party, she and Pyotr arrived bearing two big platters of food fit for a tsar. One was a large fish that Alla had skinned and deboned, whole, leaving the head and tail intact. She'd filled the skin with a forcemeat of fish and onions, then formed the fish back into its original shape and baked it in the oven. The other platter held a large, whole, deboned chicken stuffed with a baroque concoction comprising several layers of herbed chicken meat, pork, and veal, accented with prunes and pine nuts. Following an old Russian custom, Alla had also inserted a small silver coin into the stuffing before baking the chicken. According to Alla, the lucky guest who found the coin in his serving would have good fortune throughout the coming year.

At our first party, the Russians initially didn't mingle very much with the foreign guests, each standing apart in their own little groups. But as the afternoon turned into evening, and the food and drink had their effect, the social and cultural barriers dissolved, with the Russians and Americans singing holiday songs in both languages around the Christmas tree and taking sides against each other in a lively game of *Menedzher* (Manager), a sort of Russian version of Monopoly. No one seemed to mind that all of us had to ration the reserve buckets of water that we'd placed in the hall for flushing the toilet because the cold water was cut off all day. The party started at one o'clock in the afternoon and was such a success that it didn't break up until ten o'clock that night, a late hour for social functions in Vladivostok, where most residents tried to avoid the city's mean streets after dark.

## Holiday Shopping Rush

The last week of December was a frenzy of activity in Vladivostok, as shoppers scrambled to purchase foods, gifts, and ornaments for the upcoming New Year's celebration, the most important winter holiday in Russia. Despite the sub-freezing temperatures and streets slick with ice, the stores and open-air markets were packed with last-minute shoppers handing over their hard-earned rubles for fuzzy mohair sweaters, hand-knit shawls, warm flannel nightwear, winter boots, brightly colored woolen scarves, gaudy plastic flowers, new calendars, children's toys, and boxes full of fancily decorated cakes for the special New Year's meal.

During our first winter in Russia, not many holiday decorations were available in Vladivostok, but a year later almost every store, shop, and street stall was stocked with seasonal goods: greeting cards and colored lights, tinsel and tree ornaments, Grandfather Frost and Snow Maiden dolls, and children's masks (much like

*Russian boy enjoying a treat at a winter festival, 1994.*

our Halloween masks) for the Christmas and New Year's mummery that has long been a tradition among Slavic peoples. The season seemed to bring out the best in everyone, from spontaneous laughter to unexpected generosity, even as people bumped and bustled in the crowded markets to buy gloves for grandmother, amber jewelry for a special friend, or a few more bottles of champagne for New Year's Eve.

In 1994, Vladivostok was dressed up like never before in preparation for the winter holiday season. Stores and restaurants were adorned with swags of shiny tinsel, strands of colored lights, and banners proclaiming HAPPY NEW YEAR! in Russian. A big display window in the city's only department store even held a large Nativity scene, with statues of Mary, Joseph, the shepherds, and the Three Kings standing almost two feet tall. (Local television reported that this was the first time such a Christian *crèche* had been displayed publicly since the beginning of the Soviet era seven decades before.) Prominent red and white letters on the window glass spelled out "MERRY CHRISTMAS"— in English. And suspended over the Nativity scene was a beautiful Advent wreath made of evergreen boughs, like those I remembered from Lutheran churches when I was a child in Texas.

The crowds who gathered to gawk at this unusual sight in Vladivostok could also walk a few blocks along the main street to the city's central square, where special market stalls sold spiced wine and gingerbread cookies, amusement-park rides whirled and whistled, and kids swooped down slides made of ice. Towering over all this merriment was the largest New Year's tree (*yolka*) ever put up in Vladivostok, which had been transported to the square and lowered into place by a helicopter.

Russians also thronged to the special open-air *yolka* markets in Vladivostok to buy their own pine, fir, and spruce

*Selecting holiday greenery at a winter festival, 1994.*

# The New Year's Yolka

In Russia, the *yolka* is an evergreen tree that adorns almost every home, office, factory, and school, as well as many public parks and squares, during the winter holiday season. A Yuletide custom originally adopted from Germany in the 1840s, the Russian Christmas *yolka* shifted stance to become a New Year's tree (with a red star on top) under the anti-religious Soviets in the twentieth century, when New Year became the major secular holiday replacing the religious observance of Christmas.

But during part of Stalin's regime, even the New Year's *yolka* was not permitted. Some of my Siberian friends born in the 1940s still remembered when decorated evergreen trees were prohibited because of their possible religious significance, and neighbors informed on people who surreptitiously set up trees inside their own homes. At other times, however, the capricious Stalin allowed the custom to be observed. One Stalin-era propaganda film, shown on television during the New Year's season in Vladivostok in 1993, portrayed a smiling, grandfatherly Josef Stalin welcoming young children to the Kremlin to sing and dance around a tall, ornately decorated *yolka*, glistening under the twinkling chandeliers of the gilded St. George Hall.

In the post-Soviet era, the custom of having a *yolka* at New Year's time was still firmly entrenched. Almost every apartment balcony in Vladivostok sported a freshly cut tree waiting to be taken inside and decorated on New Year's Eve. On the exterior walls of high-rise buildings that didn't have balconies, the trees were suspended upside down from window ledges to keep them cold and fresh, looking like uprooted evergreens blown there by the wind. All of these twentieth-century trees were a modern manifestation from much earlier times, far back in the prehistoric past, when evergreens symbolized the continuance—indeed, the stamina—of life during the harsh dormancy of the long Russian winter.

## An Old Village Custom

In Russian villages some people still observed an old custom of planting an evergreen in the yard when their first child was born, then decorating the outdoor tree with colorful ornaments every New Year. With a wistful look in her eyes, a middle-aged Russian woman in Vladivostok told me that her parents and grandparents had proudly planted an evergreen when she was born. Her ancestors had long since passed away, but that sturdy tree still stood tall in the place of her birth, a reminder of her family who had lived before—and the continuity of life after she herself was gone.

trees, sold off the backs of trucks. The normally overcrowded buses, trolleys, and trams were jammed even tighter with commuters carrying home the prickly trees. Other people trudged along on foot, lugging tall trees shrouded in sheets or burlap bags. Cars raced past with evergreens tied to their roofs. People who wanted to avoid the annual hassle and expense of buying a fresh tree purchased artificial ones—although many Russians considered those to be a poor substitute for a tree that still smelled of the forest.

## Gala Dinners

During the week between "European Christmas" and New Year's Eve, Tom and I attended two formal receptions given by local and foreign dignitaries at Dom Peregovorov, the Negotiations Hall, a modern marble-and-glass cube located several miles outside Vladivostok. The impressive building, which belonged to the provincial administration, served as a site not only for government meetings but also for parties given by the top stratum of local and regional officials. And nestled in the heavily wooded area surrounding Dom Peregovorov were a number of stately dachas previously owned by pre-revolutionary merchants and later Communist elites, now the homes of several local bigwigs, including some reputedly connected with the powerful Vladivostok mafia.

Just inside the glass entrance doors of the Negotiations Hall, the focus of the spacious foyer was a mosaic-encrusted pool with a massive New Year's tree in the center, decorated with hundreds of multicolored lights and glass balls, garlands of silver tinsel, sparkling silver icicles, and wads of cotton "snow." Outdoors, the full moon glistened off the real snow that had sifted over the city that day, while the chauffeurs of the VIP guests huddled patiently inside their cars and vans, smoking cigarettes and eating plates of food sneaked out to them by the catering staff—just like the droshky drivers a century ago, who waited outside in the cold with their horse-drawn carriages while their wealthy masters partied the night away.

Both holiday events we attended at Dom Peregovorov were gala affairs, each with lavish buffets featuring specialties from the Russian Far East. At one party, as we entered the grand foyer, we were greeted by girls in Russian folk costumes, one of them holding a bright silver Star of Bethlehem wrapped in aluminum foil and attached to a long pole. Champagne coupes in hand, the crowd of formally dressed guests enjoyed a live entertainment program in the foyer before the doors to the banquet room opened, revealing the most magnificent buffet of hot and cold *zakuski* I'd ever seen in Russia. Rows of long tables covered with crisp white tablecloths held silver platters filled with the finest foods to be found in Vladivostok that winter: Bright pink prawns and rosy-red Kamchatka crabs. Scallop shells filled with crab-and-pineapple salad. Hard-boiled eggs, cut in half and garnished with glistening salmon caviar. Assorted cold meats (ham, beef, sausages) and cold fish (poached salmon, sprats in oil, herring with onions and vinaigrette sauce). Large whole squid stuffed with seasoned rice. Baked stuffed salmon. Colorful carrot-and-calamari salad. An East Asian shredded cabbage salad dressed with sesame oil and punctuated with chopped green onion tops and pungent fresh ginger. Soy-sauced chicken chunks and tempuraed fish fillets. Squares of buttered bread topped with caviar. And of course the best chilled champagne, ice-cold vodka, and sparkling mineral water to be had in Vladivostok that year.

Before the feast began, two Russians costumed as Ded Moroz (Grandfather Frost)—the Russian equivalent of Saint Nicholas or Santa Claus—and his pretty assistant, Snegurochka (Snow Maiden), entered the banquet hall. After Ded Moroz entertained the assembled guests with a high-spirited Cossack dance, he and Snegurochka passed out small presents to everyone in the crowd, offering the first gift from his bag—a decorated pine cone—to me. And ever since, when I've hung that Russian pine cone on my own Christmas trees back in Texas, I've always remembered that special evening in Vladivostok, when Christmas and New Year, East and West, old and new, past and present, merged into a celebration transcending the barriers of time and place, of people and their politics.

*Papier-mâché Grandfather Frost and Snow Maiden dolls from a holiday market in Vladivostok, 1993.*

# Grandfather Frost and Snow Maiden

Ded Moroz (Grandfather Frost) and Snegurochka (Snow Maiden) are an essential part of the Russian New Year season. The Russian equivalent of Saint Nicholas or Santa Claus, Ded Moroz is a tall, white-haired, white-bearded fellow dressed in a long red, blue, or white robe trimmed with white fur. According to legend, he lives in an ice cave in the far North and travels throughout Russia in a *troika*, a sleigh pulled by three horses yoked in tandem, instead of the nine Nordic reindeer that carry Santa's sleigh in the West.

Bringing gifts to all the children of Russia is such a big job that Ded Moroz has a helper, his granddaughter Snegurochka, a pretty, smiling, young girl decked out in a white fur hat and a long pale blue or white coat trimmed with white fur. She and Ded Moroz make special appearances at children's parties during the holiday season, where they hand out sweets and small gifts to the wide-eyed kids. Families with enough money sometimes even hire a Ded Moroz and Snegurocha to visit their apartments on New Year's Eve, to deliver gifts in person to the children of the house.

Both Ded Moroz and Snegurochka also appear, in slightly different forms, in classic Russian folktales. The pairing of them as characters associated with the New Year seems to date only from the nineteenth century. However, their role as New Year's gift-bringers has become firmly entrenched in contemporary Russian customs. Russians now purchase Ded Moroz and Snegurochka dolls—made of wood, metal, plastic, or *papier mâché*—to decorate their houses during the winter holidays and to give as presents to children. And no *yolka* would be complete without a small effigy of Ded Moroz and Snegurochka placed under it, nestled among the packages under the tree where these two bearers of gifts rightly belong.

# New Year's Eve

The first winter we lived in Vladivostok, our neighbors Alla and Pyotr Brovko invited us to celebrate New Year's Eve at their apartment—"just a small family dinner with us and our sons," said Alla. Knowing that additional food would always be welcome, Tom and I hurried to the nearest open-air market on the morning of December 31, to shop for something we could contribute to the meal. After spending four hours outdoors in weather where the wind chill was well below zero, we were both frozen to the bone by the time we returned home that afternoon. Still bundled up against the cold, I trudged up the five flights of frigid stairs to Alla's apartment to ask what time she wanted us to arrive for dinner that night.

"Come around ten," she said, casually adding that she didn't know when dinner would actually be ready, because the electricity had already gone off three times that day—and it was still off, along with all the hot water and heat.

"Why?" asked I, thinking of all the cakes that were falling in ovens through-out Vladivostok, all the meats not roasting, all the vegetables not boiling.

"God doesn't know," she sighed, pointing heavenward.

"Well, surely the water and electricity will be turned back on sometime this afternoon," I ventured, with typical American optimism. "After all, this is New Year's Eve! We can't lose all of our utilities on *New Year's Eve!*"

Alla just smiled wearily, as if I still had a lot to learn about life in Russia.

When I returned to our apartment, it was so cold that I had to put on a second layer of thermal long underwear beneath my corduroy jeans and heavy wool sweater. There was no way to warm up with even a cup of hot tea, so Tom and I tried to distract ourselves from the cold by reading—first by sunlight through the frosted windows, later by candlelight after dark—all the time expecting that the electricity, heating, and hot water would surely be restored before the big New Year's Eve dinner began in thousands of homes throughout the city. Until the utilities were turned back on, we had no way to bathe, no way to wash our hair, no way to cook all the dishes we'd planned to take to Alla's that night.

At seven o'clock Tom and I began bumping around the dark apartment, flashlights in hand, getting dressed for the party and trying to figure out what kind of cold foods we could prepare for that evening. Looking out the living room window, I saw several kids from our building gathering garbage to start a big bonfire. For once I actually welcomed the sight of trash burning beneath our windows, and for a moment I even entertained the thought of taking potatoes and carrots down to roast in the fire. As the flames flickered against the snow, casting shadows of children in rabbit-fur hats dancing gaily in a circle and throwing firecrackers into the blaze, I understood their primitive desire to defy the darkness, with whatever means at hand, during the depths of that frigid Russian winter.

At 7:30 that evening, the heat began trickling back into the radiators, and a short while later hot water sputtered through the pipes in the kitchen and the bathroom. At 8:30, just as we started putting together our platters of cold food, the return of electricity was greeted with a loud collective cheer from all the apartments in our building. Taking advantage of the situation, we quickly peeled potatoes and zapped them in the microwave. A few minutes later, Tom put a bowl of diced fresh carrots into the microwave, touched the timer, and poof!—the electricity went off again. But we had already cooked enough ingredients to make a potato salad, so—by the light of a solitary candle—we composed our dishes for the party: Tom's signature dish, his Russian potato salad with Kamchatka crab, garlic mayonnaise, and salmon caviar. Smoked salmon garnished with pickled green tomatoes. Canned green peas dressed with homemade wine vinegar and fresh garlic. A platter of sliced pickled red tomatoes and bright green cucumbers. Salmon caviar with butter and bread. Half a leftover carrot cake and a large plate of day-old brownies. Champagne chilled on our balcony, and the remnants of a bottle of Chinese vodka that another Russian neighbor had given us earlier in the day.

Russians customarily dress up in their party best for New Year's Eve, but I dressed for the weather instead: black slacks and a black sweater over my thermal long underwear, with an amber necklace that I hoped would catch the candlelight in the darkened apartment. Food and drink in hand, we arrived at Alla and Pyotr's place at 10:00 p.m., delighted to discover that the electricity in their part of the building had been turned on. But just as we walked through the door, all the lights went off again.

"We have a chicken singing in the oven," trilled Alla, as she cheerfully arranged platters of cold food on the table in her living room, while explaining that the chicken she'd planned to serve for the main course was still uncooked. The table for six had been set with her best faceted crystal wineglasses, cloth napkins, an assortment of porcelain plates of different sizes and patterns, and stainless-steel flatware with handles of ivory-colored plastic. The only light in the room came from three tapers in a baroque-style ceramic candelabrum in the center of the table, assisted by a single candle on the upright piano nearby. Next to the dinner table stood a large New Year's tree festooned with shimmering pink, blue, and silver icicles, garlands of silver tinsel, glass ball ornaments, tufts of cotton "snow," and a string of multicolored lights waiting, like the rest of us, for the electricity to come back on.

Alla placed all the foods on the table together—even the desserts—crowding them onto every inch of available space. In addition to the dishes we'd brought, Alla served her own version of Russian potato salad; a platter of sliced sausages; the most expensive kind of smoked salmon sold in Vladivostok; a plate of canned red peppers from China; a cut-glass bowl of cold beet salad decorated with walnuts on top; a box of chocolates; and a bowl with small wild apples peeled and halved, cooked with blueberries that had turned the dessert a deep magenta hue. Wedged among the plates of food were bottles of Rasputin vodka, mandarin orange liqueur, and Russian champagne. Despite the lack of electricity, hot water, and heat, we all had succeeded in assembling a formidable feast to welcome in the New Year, a candlelit array of colorful foods that seemed symbolic of Russian resilience in the face of adversity.

## The New Year's Pig

Before the 1917 Revolution, roast suckling pig was often served at the tables of affluent Russians as a traditional dish for the New Year's feast. But during the Soviet era, whole piglets were difficult for most people to obtain. A Siberian friend of mine still vividly remembered the freezing night in late December when her father, a truck driver on Sakhalin Island, was stopped by a man on the side of the road who asked if he would take a load of week-old chicks to another village. Her father agreed.

It turned out that the man seeking help was the director of a nearby state farm, who repaid the favor by giving her father a piglet for New Year. At home, she and her grandmother stuffed the pig with seasoned buckwheat kasha and propped its mouth open with a shiny red apple. But they couldn't get the whole piglet into their small oven. So they cut off the head and roasted it in the oven beside the rest of the pig, then sewed the head back on before proudly serving the unexpected treat for dinner on that memorable New Year's Eve.

Many Russians start their New Year's meal only after the clock has struck twelve, the guests have shaken hands (instead of kissing), and everyone has drunk a champagne toast, saying "*S novym godom!*" (the Russian version of "Happy New Year!"). But our meal at the Brovkos' began at 11:00 p.m., with a toast from Pyotr-the-geographer, who happily pointed out that we could celebrate the New Year every hour throughout the night, as midnight crept across Russia's many time zones.

When the magic hour approached in Vladivostok, I was eager to go out on the balcony to watch the Chinese-made fireworks I'd seen people buying at the open-air markets during the weeks leading up to New Year's Eve. But Alla and Pyotr were completely uninterested in my suggestion. "Why do you want to stand out in the cold when the clock strikes twelve?" they asked. Finally, at two minutes after midnight, I persuaded all of the Brovkos to join Tom and me on the freezing balcony.

What a sight we beheld! From top to bottom of every high-rise we could see, people were shooting off red, green, and white Roman candles, while others lighted red fusees that seemed to envelop all the buildings in flames. It was like watching a naval battle among stationary warships, with fireballs continuously being hurled from one gray hulk to another.

Vladivostok was ablaze with fireworks. As we all watched in awe, the battle of tricolored lights was waged in every direction, while high above the city red, white, and green signal flares, fired from ships in the harbor, floated in the sky. Twice we heard salvos from battleships in the bay, the percussive sounds shaking the walls of our 10-story building. But otherwise all we could hear was the constant whoosh-whoosh of Roman candles, as they leapt from balconies into the frigid night air, like anti-aircraft tracer fire over the city.

Alla said she'd never seen anything like it in her life.

"Didn't you always have fireworks on New Year's Eve?" I asked, remembering all the brilliant displays I'd seen in Europe at that time of year.

"No," replied Alla, "Vladivostok was a closed city before, and this is the first year the Chinese have been able to come in and sell fireworks like that."

At 12:30 a.m., just after we stepped indoors, the electricity came on again. "Now we have a chicken singing and dancing in the oven!" laughed Alla, hoping that the power would stay on long enough for the bird to finally roast. I thought the party would soon be winding down, but the fun had just begun. A few minutes before 1:00 a.m. all six of us—bottles of booze and platters of left-over food in hand—headed for the next stairwell in our building, for *another* dinner at the apartment of our neighbors, Sergei and Natasha. Together with them, their two children, Sergei's mother, and Bagheera (their big black dog), we all squeezed around a table set with many of the same kinds of cold foods that Alla had served—not surprisingly, given the ingredients available in Vladivostok and the erratic nature of the electricity that day. In the center of the table, Natasha had also placed a large crystal vase holding a bunch of just-budding pussy willow branches, the first harbinger of spring and a symbol of hope for the coming year.

Gathered around that congenial table, we all nibbled on leftovers, drank champagne, and toasted the New Year with vodka every hour as the calendar changed to 1994 in the next time zones across Russia. Beside the table, Sergei and Natasha's artificial evergreen sparkled with colored lights, while the television next to it blared out a flashy New Year's program from Moscow—a Russian variety review with singers, dancers, and comics, including excellent impersonators of Lenin, Brezhnev, and Yeltsin, like a Russian version of *Saturday Night Live*.

But Natasha, who was both serious and superstitious, thought it was a very bad omen that the electricity had been off earlier that night when the New Year had arrived in Vladivostok. She believed, as many Russians do, that your own state of mind, the circumstances of your immediate environment, and the way you see the New Year in—just at the stroke of midnight—all foreshadow the year to come. I tried to lighten her mood by suggesting that we look at the positive signs of that special evening: Despite the lack of electricity, we were all happy and healthy. We'd watched a fantastic fireworks display. And we'd feasted well in the company of friends.

"What more could we ask for?" I concluded, while silently conceding to myself that I certainly wouldn't relish spending the next year in Vladivostok without electricity, if that was what the darkness at midnight had truly foretold.

## Happy New Year!

After returning home at nearly 6:00 a.m. from those New Year's revelries, we awoke at noon to discover that all the apartments in our stairwell were still without electricity. And it remained cut off for the rest of the day. Alla—who now had electrical power in her part of the building—sent over her younger son to deliver a thermos of hot water so Tom and I could fix tea for breakfast. He also brought an invitation for dinner at their home that night, to eat the (finally) cooked food that Alla had originally planned to serve on New Year's Eve.

We arrived at 7:30 p.m., happy to be back in an apartment that had lights again. Tom began the party by introducing Alla to all-American orange-juice-and-vodka screwdrivers—a "healthy" drink, by Russian standards—which he contended the cook could consume in quantity, without getting drunk, while toiling in the kitchen. Pyotr, in turn, introduced us to Russian Aurora cocktails, a potent combination of vodka and champagne. When I wowed about the strength of that drink, the geographer laughed and suggested another popular Russian cocktail called the Polar Star, made by vigorously stirring half a glass of vodka into another half glass of vodka. By the time Sergei and Natasha showed up, Tom was concocting his own "Vlad Mai Tais," a festive mixture of imported orange and pineapple juices spiked with Russian spiced rum. These boozy *apéritifs* sustained us throughout the early evening, while Alla put the finishing touches on the meal and Pyotr showed color slides of his scientific expeditions to Sakhalin Island, the Kamchatka Peninsula, and the Indian Ocean.

By nine o'clock Alla had laid out a feast fit for starting the new year on a solid culinary footing: Individual portions of beef tongue, decorated with green peas and fancily cut carrots, enrobed in aspic. A platter of pickled cucumber rounds and pickled red, green, and yellow tomatoes all harvested at her dacha. Smoked salmon garnished with sliced onions and pickled red peppers. Shredded carrot-and-cabbage salad. Paprika-seasoned red beans that we'd brought over to cook on her stove earlier in the day. A copious casserole called "The Captain's Meat," rounds of tender beef layered with sliced onions, potatoes, and cheese—a Vlad-ivostok specialty. And Alla's fancy stuffed chicken, with a good-luck coin baked inside, the same fowl that had been singing and dancing in the oven on New Year's Eve while the fickle electricity cut on and off. Natasha had made a rich chocolate-covered walnut torte for dessert. And Alla set out a big pitcher of brine from the pickled cucumbers and tomatoes, the classic Russian hangover cure for the alcoholic excesses of the night before.

Two hours later, when all of us felt so full we couldn't take another bite, Alla announced that it was time to go into the kitchen to make *pel'meni* together! Tom and I thought she was joking, until Alla explained that Siberian *pel'meni* were a traditional Russian food for New Year's Day, and that we had to start making them before January 1 ended at midnight. Alla had prepared the dumpling dough in advance, along with the filling of mixed ground beef, pork, and onions. Working together in her small kitchen, Alla and Natasha and I rolled out the dough, cut it into 2-inch circles with a crystal wine glass, and formed it into bite-size, meat-filled pockets of pasta. Then Alla put a large pot of water on the stove to boil, tossed in some spices, and told us to leave the kitchen so the men could come do their part.

The three of us retired to the living room, where we sat around drinking goblets of white wine and listening to the men singing lustily in the kitchen as they rolled, filled, and formed their own portions of *pel'meni*. After the men had cooked all the dumplings, they served the *pel'meni* with a selection of garnishes: butter, sour cream, Russian hot-spicy mustard, soy sauce, and Russian brown ketchup (which looked and tasted like British bottled brown sauce). While the men knocked back shots of vodka, Alla showed Tom and me the proper way to eat *pel'meni* by popping each one whole into our mouths—pointing out that Russians consider it uncouth to cut their *pel'meni* into pieces.

## Russian Orthodox Christmas

In Russia, January 1 is only the start of the winter holiday season. During the following two-week period, schools are closed, and many factories and offices also shut their doors or work only part time. This is the season for families and friends to visit each other, go to parties, and enjoy outdoor winter activities like sleigh rides, ice-skating, cross-country skiing, and ice fishing. In downtown Vladivostok, dancers, singers, and clowns entertained the crowds on the central square, beneath that massive New Year's tree topped with a huge lighted star. Grandfather Frost and Snow Maiden made daily appearances, the Moscow Circus gave a performance, and a special "New Year's train" wound through the city, carrying kids to amusement parks.

Halfway between the "New" and "Old" New Year (on January 1 and January 14), Orthodox Christmas was celebrated on January 7. After we attended the Christmas service at Vladivostok's St. Nicholas church that snowy day, Tom cooked a special "second Christmas" meal for us at home: Tender beef *pot-au-feu* with turnips, onions, carrots, and cabbage, in a broth seasoned with red wine, garlic, and black peppercorns. He served the broth separately, for the first course, followed by a large platter of the meat surrounded by boiled vegetables and steamed potatoes, with two different sour-cream sauces on the side. For dessert I prepared my "Vladivostok Trifle"—crumbled Russian *pryaniki* (gingerbread cookies), sprinkled with pineapple juice and tossed with raisins macerated in sweet wine, the cookies and fruits then layered with rich vanilla custard and garnished with a light dusting of cinnamon on the top. For that special occasion we pulled the cork on a precious bottle of Robert Mondavi Woodbridge 1991 California Zinfandel, which Tom had purchased locally for $15—a small fortune in a country where the average monthly wage in Vladivostok was less than $100 that year.

# An Orthodox Christmas in Vladivostok

On January 7, 1994, Tom and I attended the Orthodox Christmas service at the onion-domed church of St. Nicholas (the patron saint of seamen), the only functioning Russian Orthodox church in Vladivostok at that time. Constructed in memory of the Russian sailors who died during the Russo-Japanese War of 1904–5, the small church was decorated for the Christmas season with unadorned evergreen trees and boughs, red and white carnations, and a large red candle set in a silver star-shaped sconce. Outside the church, several beggars wrapped in rags shivered in the snow, holding out their hands for alms as worshippers entered and left during the lengthy service.

The congregation comprised several social classes, from mink-coated matrons to poor people in threadbare woolen coats and cheap anoraks, some of the women with string bags full of groceries in hand. But all were united in the warmth of the Yuletide service: the brilliant icons, the flickering candlelight, the aroma of incense, the bowing by believers as they bobbed up and down, making the sign of the cross—all to the accompaniment of the liturgy sung by a nervous young man dressed in black and an off-key amateur choir.

When we left the church that snowy Christmas day, into the biting-cold air and the visual black-white-gray of winter Vladivostok, a sudden movement caught my eye. On a tree limb bent low to the ground sat a large, well-fed, long-haired black-and-white cat, nestled perfectly into the black-and-white surroundings. Suddenly the cat flicked its fluffy tail, bounded down the tree, plowed through the snow, and stopped. Then it quickly turned around and ran up the tree again, looking around for whatever mischief it could get into.

It seemed as if all the energy of wintry Vladivostok was concentrated in the briskness of that run-amok feline, leaving the rest of the city frozen into stillness on that holy day. As we headed home, I glanced back at the church cat. It had leaped to another tree, swept its tail around its plump body, and was now perched on a limb, looking at me with its deep golden eyes, as smugly satisfied as a Cheshire cat in another story, in another century, on another continent far away.

## Watch Where You Step!

An old Russian custom on the night of January 6, Orthodox Christmas Eve, is for a family member to put a piece of bread in one of your house slippers and a piece of coal in the other. Then, without looking, you move the shoes around under your bed, so you don't know which is which. On the next morning, Christmas Day, you slide your right foot into the first slipper you find. If your foot touches bread, you'll have a prosperous new year. If it touches the piece of coal, you'll have a lean, bad year.

## "Old New Year"

"Old New Year" or "Second New Year" on January 14 is traditionally the last occasion (or excuse) for a big party in the middle of the Russian winter, signaling the end of the holiday season. Soon it's back to school for children and back to work for adults—while everyone waits, not always patiently, for the short spring and summer yet to come.

Our final feast of the 1993–94 holiday season in Vladivostok was a dinner for 10 people, children and adults, at the Brovkos' apartment on "Old New Year's Eve," January 13. The temperature was well below zero outside, with strong winds blowing from the north, when Tom and I traipsed over to their apartment carrying bottles of wine and some of our own appetizers to contribute to the meal.

Alla had already laid out several staples of the Russian winter table, including shredded carrot-and-cabbage salad garnished with canned green peas, and her succulent homemade *belyashi*, puffy fried pies made of yeast dough stuffed with seasoned ground pork. We added a big pot of macaroni tossed with a Mediterranean-style tomato, pepper, and eggplant sauce that we'd been hoarding in our freezer ever since we'd cooked it three months before, using up the last fresh vegetables of the season. We also brought a colorful curried-rice salad—made with raisins, peanuts, cubes of chicken, and salt-preserved carrots—which the Russians soon devoured, all of them saying that they'd never tasted such an exotic salad before.

After we'd eaten our fill of those hot and cold *zakuski*, Alla surprised us with her main course: a tray of 10 large fresh herring, each whole fish baked with a stuffing of onions, garlic, and herring roe, with an additional flourish of herring roe on top. The fish were accompanied by baked whole potatoes, still in their skins, split open and slathered with creamy unsalted butter.

Alla explained that it was customary to eat both the herrings and potatoes with only our fingers—a messy procedure that we all agreed to try, even though the foods were steaming hot. As we sucked on our burning, buttery fingers, we complimented her on the rich flavor of the fish while also happily quaffing glasses of an excellent French *vin mousseux* that Pyotr had somehow managed to find at a local kiosk. Thinking I was too full to eat anything else, I changed my mind when Natasha brought out the dessert: a serving plate stacked high with 50 or 60 lacy *blinchiki*—like the best French *crêpes* I'd ever eaten—accompanied by her own homemade strawberry jam and a bottle of Russian champagne.

That evening was traditionally the season's last opportunity for fortune-telling, a New Year's custom that Russians have practiced for centuries. Every group of female friends seemed to include a particular woman known for her ability to predict the future by reading tea leaves, dealing cards, or casting hot candle wax into a plate of cold water to make shapes whose meanings could be interpreted only by the seer. In earlier times, maidens sought to learn whom they would marry in the coming year, but in the 1990s modern Russians seemed to be more interested in how much money they were likely to make during the next 12 months.

After dinner, Alla turned off the lights, lit three candles on the table, and assembled the materials for telling our fortunes with molten wax. In the kitchen, she heated half a teacup of candle wax in a small pan on the stove and filled another small shallow pan with cold tap water. Then she brought both pans out to the youngest person at the table—Sergei and Natasha's eight-year-old daughter, Dasha—who poured the hot wax into the cold water.

Alla asked Dasha to describe what the wax figure in the water looked like. The rest of us were then allowed to add our own comments, as we deciphered this Russian Rorschach test for ourselves. Dasha thought the wax was shaped like a mandarin duck, which Alla interpreted to mean that she would grow up to be as pretty as a mandarin duck—a prediction that greatly pleased the wide-eyed Dasha, who already had the features of an unusual beauty.

The game continued around the table, clockwise, as each of us cast hot wax into the pan of cold water to predict our own future. Whenever Pyotr looked at other people's wax figures, he saw the map of some country or region, not surprisingly for a professional geographer. Tom's wax image did indeed look like a map of Eastern Siberia, the region of Russia to which we were moving only four days later. And everyone agreed that my wax casting looked like a standing bear, which foretold that I would be staying in Russia for another year—an uncannily accurate prediction, even though on that "Old New Year's Eve" in January of 1994, I had no plans to stay in Russia beyond the following June!

On our way home from the party, just before midnight, we had to dodge the discarded New Year's trees blowing around the building like giant green tumbleweeds, their scraggly remnants of tinsel shimmering sadly in the cold moonlight. Just as the clock struck twelve, flares and Roman candles illuminated the neighborhood again—not as many as on the night of official New Year, two weeks earlier, but still a 15-minute display that showed we weren't the only people in Vladivostok celebrating this second New Year's Eve. And the next morning we awoke to snow falling on a blazing bonfire of New Year's trees beneath our window—a fitting end to the winter holiday season in Vladivostok.

# Vladivostok Potato Salad

*This was Tom's signature dish in Vladivostok, where it was always a big hit at our dinner parties. It's his own take on classic Russian potato salad, dressed up with garlicky mayonnaise and the good crabmeat and fresh salmon caviar available in Vladivostok. Everyone who's tasted it—Russians, Americans, others—says it's the best potato salad they've ever eaten.*

▶ **NOTE:** Although the recipe looks long, it's very easy to make. Assemble the salad at least 2 to 4 hours before serving, so all the flavors can meld. Add the crab mayonnaise topping and salmon caviar garnish just before serving.

## Potato Salad

2½ pounds firm boiling potatoes, unpeeled and well scrubbed
Salt
2 medium to large carrots, peeled and diced into ¼-inch cubes
1 cup frozen green peas (for their firm texture and pretty green color)
1 medium onion, finely chopped
2 large hard-boiled eggs, chopped

## Dressing

¾ cup mayonnaise
¾ cup pure sour cream
2 tablespoons olive oil
2 tablespoons lemon juice
3 to 4 large garlic cloves, squeezed through a garlic press
1½ teaspoons salt

## Crab mayonnaise

1 cup mayonnaise
3 large garlic cloves, squeezed through a garlic press
4 to 6 ounces cooked crabmeat

## Garnish

4 ounces salmon caviar
Sprigs of fresh dill
Pickled sweet red pepper strips

- **Vegetables:** Bring a large pot of water to a boil. Add the whole, unpeeled potatoes and 1 teaspoon salt. Cover and cook over medium-high heat until potatoes are tender when pierced with a fork (about 20 to 40 minutes, depending on the size of the potatoes). Drain the cooked potatoes in a colander and let cool completely.

- Meanwhile, bring a small saucepan of water to a boil, add the carrots and ½ teaspoon salt, and cook until just tender (about 3 to 4 minutes). Use a slotted spoon to transfer the carrots to a bowl to cool. Add the frozen peas to the boiling water and cook for 30 seconds. Drain thoroughly and cool.

- **Dressing:** Whisk together the mayonnaise, sour cream, olive oil, lemon juice, garlic, and salt until well combined. (The dressing at this stage will taste too salty. Don't panic! When the dressing is added to the potatoes and other vegetables, the salt will be absorbed and diluted.) Cover and refrigerate until needed.

- **Crab mayonnaise:** Whisk together the mayonnaise and garlic until well combined. Crumble the crabmeat into the mixture and stir gently until the crab is evenly distributed. Cover and refrigerate until time to serve the potato salad.

- **To assemble the potato salad:** Peel the potatoes, cut out the eyes and any dark spots, and slice the potatoes into ½-inch cubes. Gently toss the potatoes, carrots, and onion together in a large bowl. Add the peas and hard-boiled eggs, tossing again gently to keep the peas from being mashed. Pour the dressing over the salad ingredients and mix gently with a wooden spoon. Try not to mash the vegetables together—they should retain their shape. Cover and refrigerate until serving time.

- **To serve:** Mound the potato salad on a serving platter, forming it into the shape of a shallow dome. Use a rubber spatula to spread the crab mayonnaise evenly over the surface of the potato salad, like frosting a cake. Carefully arrange the salmon caviar on top of the crab mayonnaise, to form the shape of a crab. Arrange strips of pickled sweet red peppers and sprigs of fresh dill around the base of the salad.

- Makes 6 to 8 servings.

▶ **TIP:** You can cook all the vegetables and eggs for this salad, and make the dressing and crab mayonnaise, a day in advance. Leave the cooked potatoes whole and unpeeled. Keep all the ingredients chilled, in separate bowls, in the refrigerator. Two to four hours before serving, peel and cube the potatoes, then combine the vegetables, eggs, and dressing, and refrigerate until needed. Cover the potato salad with the crab mayonnaise and garnish with salmon caviar just before serving.

# Persistent Potato Salad

Russian potato salad is one of those simple dishes with a complicated past. Reputedly born in the kitchen of an elite Moscow restaurant around 150 years ago, it spawned an entire family of descendants who eventually migrated from the chandeliered halls of *haute cuisine* to Soviet workers' canteens, student cafeterias, Intourist hotel dining rooms, all-you-can-eat "*biznes lunch*" buffets in modern-day Moscow, and Russian home tables from St. Petersburg to Vladivostok. Along the way, the recipe changed, too, ultimately emigrating beyond the boundaries of the Russian Empire and the Soviet Union to countries across the world. Today, versions of French *salade russe* and Spanish *ensaladilla rusa* are as popular in those countries as in Russia itself.

First known in Russia as *salat Oliv'ye*, this potato salad was supposedly created in the 1860s by Lucien Olivier, a chef of French origin, at his fashionable Ermitage restaurant in Moscow. An aristocratic recipe that included grouse, crayfish, truffles, and olives, this elegant potato salad evolved into more proletarian fare in the twentieth century, from that upscale restaurant appetizer made with costly ingredients to an every-day dish composed of inexpensive, readily available products. Today, this popular potato salad usually includes carrots, onions, cucumbers (fresh or pickled), hard-boiled eggs, and bottled or canned green peas, sometimes also with chunks of leftover cooked meat or fish, all napped with commercial mayonnaise, sour cream, or a blend of the two.

My Russian friends in Vladivostok and Irkutsk called this dish *stolichnyi salat* (capital city salad) or *Moskovskii salat*, both terms supposedly in reference to its Moscow origins. In Siberia we jokingly called it *stolovaya* salad—canteen salad—because it seemed to be a staple dish at every canteen (*stolovaya*) and cafeteria, as well as a standard item on most Russian restaurant menus.

Cold potato salad is such a popular appetizer in Russia that you seldom see a *zakuski* spread without it. (It's a "must" for New Year's Eve dinners and festive family gatherings.) Even if a home cook offers only one *zakuska* to start an everyday meal, it's often some version of this classic potato salad. But cold potato salad is also such an "old favorite" that you'd think the "old" might have trumped the "favorite" by now in Russia, where tradi-tion struggles with modernization and where young, urban, chic Russians often seem to prefer the imported to the homemade. On the other hand, comfort foods well rooted in a person's (and culture's) past provide a sense of stability in a rapidly changing environment, and that might be one explanation for the endurance of this long-loved dish.

# Korean Carrot Salad

*This popular appetizer from Russia's Maritime Territory, on the Pacific coast near China and North Korea, reflects the Korean influence on the cuisine of that region. Korean vendors in the markets of Vladivostok and Ussuriisk sold this spicy salad, ready made, in clear plastic tubes—and many Russians living in proximity to Koreans have incorporated this recipe into their own homemade* zakuski *repertoire.*

1 pound carrots, peeled and grated lengthwise into long thin strips*
1 ½ teaspoons ground cayenne pepper
½ teaspoon salt
3 tablespoons sunflower oil
2 large garlic cloves, squeezed through a garlic press
1 green onion (white and tender green parts), finely chopped

*Russian kitchenware stores sell special graters for making the long, thin, noodle-like carrot strips traditionally used in this salad. A julienne grater works well for this, too, as do the vegetable spiralizers now available in the United States.

- Put the grated carrots into a heatproof medium bowl. Make a well in the center of the carrots, pushing them aside so you see the bottom of the bowl. Put the cayenne pepper and salt into this well.

- Heat the oil in a small skillet until very hot. Pour the hot oil over the spices in the bowl, stirring rapidly to mix them into the oil. Stir the garlic into the oil, then stir the seasoned oil into the grated carrots until all the ingredients are well combined. Add the chopped green onion and toss the ingredients to mix them together well.

- Cover and refrigerate until needed. This salad tastes best if you make it a day in advance, for the flavors to develop fully. Let the chilled carrot salad sit at room temperature for 30 minutes before serving.

- Makes 6 small servings as an appetizer or 4 servings as a side dish to accompany a main course.

# Food on the Move

The recipe for this spicy carrot salad was brought to the Russian Far East by Koreans who migrated there in the nineteenth century. In the 1930s, it traveled to Uzbekistan with the thousands of Koreans whom Stalin deported from the Russian Far East to Soviet Central Asia. Later, the recipe spread to many parts of Siberia and European Russia as well. Korean Carrot Salad can now be found in the United States, too, on the menus of restaurants featuring Uzbek and Russian cuisine in New York City and in other parts of the country. Even in Texas it's a common item in our Russian delicatessens here. There are several variations of this recipe—some more hot-spicy than others—using ingredients such as black pepper, ground coriander seeds, bay leaves, parsley, vinegar, and sugar, as well as foraged foods like wild onions and wild garlic.

# Crab and Pineapple Salad

*At the official Negotiations Hall near Vladivostok, the Russian caterers served this Crab-Pineapple Salad in scallop shells artistically arranged on the lavish buffet tables at elegant holiday dinners there.*

**1 cup mayonnaise**
**1 tablespoon freshly squeezed lemon juice**
**½ teaspoon salt**
**1 pound good-quality lump crabmeat**
**1½ cups canned pineapple chunks, well drained and diced into ¼-inch pieces (measured after draining and dicing)\***
**¾ cup finely chopped green onion tops**
**2 large hard-boiled eggs, finely chopped**

### Garnish

**Lettuce leaves (optional)**
**Ground red pepper (mild or hot)**

**\*Use pineapple canned in water, not in sweet syrup. Reserved the drained juice (see WASTE NOT, below).**

- Whisk the mayonnaise, lemon juice, and salt together in a small bowl.

- Gently toss the crabmeat, pineapple, green onion tops, and chopped eggs together in a large bowl. Add the mayonnaise dressing and toss again to mix well. Cover and refrigerate at least 2 hours.

- Serve cold. For each serving, scoop out ½ cup of the salad and place it on the concave side of a large scallop shell, or on a lettuce leaf on a salad plate. Sprinkle the top lightly with ground red pepper.

- Makes 10 servings as an appetizer.

▶ **WASTE NOT:** Save the pineapple juice for making **Christmas Carrot Cake** glaze (recipe, page 241)—or just mix it with some vodka or rum and enjoy it as an *apéritif* while you prepare the rest of your meal.

## Shell Games

While walking along the beaches near Vladivostok, I liked to collect seashells, as many beachcombers do. But my Russian companions asked why I was so particular about finding eight matching shells of one kind, eight matching shells of another. When I explained that I wanted to serve seafood *zakuski* in the large scallop shells, use the clam shells for individual soy sauce dishes, and scatter sand dollars and sea urchin shells across my dinner table for decorations, they looked at me like I was daft. Only Alla thought that was a good idea—and began picking up useful shells herself. We were just continuing a long tradition: For thousands of years, native peoples living along Russia's seacoasts have used shells as food receptacles, as well as ornaments for clothing, dwellings, and ceremonial objects.

214

# Confetti Cole Slaw

*Tom made this pretty red-and-green-flecked cole slaw for our Christmas potluck parties, using sun-dried tomatoes we'd brought from Texas and Russian green onion tops. (In Texas we always add fresh jalapeños for extra kick.) Our Russian guests—who ate cabbage in myriad ways at home—were surprised at this combination of ingredients, which they'd never tasted before. At one party, they wiped out an entire big bowl of Tom's confetti cole slaw!*

1 green cabbage (2 pounds), cored and finely shredded
1 medium onion, chopped medium-fine
12 green onion tops, thinly sliced crosswise
12 sun-dried tomato halves, rehydrated in hot water, drained, and sliced
 into thin strips*
2 to 3 fresh jalapeño peppers, finely chopped (optional)
⅓ cup sunflower oil
3 tablespoons white or apple cider vinegar
1 tablespoon hot-spicy mustard (Russian brown mustard or French Dijon)
2 large garlic cloves, squeezed through a garlic press
1 teaspoon mustard seeds (yellow or black)
1 teaspoon salt
½ teaspoon freshly ground black pepper

*If your sun-dried tomatoes are packed in oil, just drain off the oil, blot them
 with paper towels, and slice thinly.

- Put the shredded cabbage in a large heatproof bowl. Pour enough boiling water over the cabbage to cover it completely. Let sit for 3 minutes, then drain thoroughly in a colander and let cool.

- Combine the cabbage, onions, sun-dried tomatoes, and jalapeños (optional) in a very large bowl, tossing them together to mix well.

- In a separate bowl, whisk together the oil and vinegar until emulsified (thick and cloudy). Whisk in the mustard, garlic, mustard seeds, salt, and pepper. Let this dressing sit at room temperature for 10 minutes, then whisk again.

- Pour the dressing over the cabbage mixture and toss to mix well. Cover and refrigerate until needed. Toss the salad once more before serving.

- Makes 10 to 12 servings.

▶ **WASTE NOT:** When making cabbage dishes, save the core pieces cut out of the cabbage, brush them with sunflower oil, and roast them in a lightly oiled shallow baking pan, in a preheated 425°F. oven for about 30 minutes (or longer, depending on how thick they are). Sprinkle with coarse salt and black pepper. Makes an unusual garnish for meaty main dishes!

# Seasoned Sauerkraut

*Tom's version of seasoned sauerkraut is based on a classic German-Alsatian way of making it. The first time he cooked this for a German friend, the man exclaimed, "It's just like my grandmother used to make!" Russians, too, always devoured this flavorful sauerkraut whenever we made it for parties in Vladivostok. When they asked Tom for the recipe, he told them, "It's so easy it's like shooting cabbage in a barrel."*

2 tablespoons lard, duck fat, or vegetable oil
½ to ¾ pound thick-sliced smoked bacon, diced into ¼-inch pieces
2 medium onions, finely chopped
2 large garlic cloves, finely chopped
4 pounds sauerkraut (fresh or bottled), rinsed under cold water and drained well
1 apple, peeled and diced
1 cup cooked ham, diced into ¼-inch cubes before measuring (optional)
8 to 12 juniper berries
2 whole cloves
2 teaspoons caraway seeds
1 teaspoon black peppercorns
½ cup dry white wine
½ cup chicken stock
2 bay leaves

- Heat the fat over medium-high heat in a 5-quart stovetop casserole. Add the bacon pieces and sauté until they begin to brown but are not yet crisp (5 to 7 minutes). Remove the bacon with a slotted spoon and set aside. Add the onions and garlic to the pot, and sauté in the hot fat until the onions become translucent.

- Return the bacon to the pot and add the sauerkraut, stirring well to coat it with the fat. Reduce the heat to medium. Stir in the apple, (optional) ham, juniper berries, cloves, caraway seeds, and peppercorns. Add the wine and stock, and stick the bay leaves into the mixture.

- Bring the mixture to a boil over medium-high heat, then reduce the heat to low, cover, and simmer, stirring occasionally, for 45 minutes. Serve hot.

- Makes 8 to 10 servings.

# German Potato Salad

*For our first Christmas party in Vladivostok, one of our Russian guests brought this German Potato Salad—a nostalgic taste of "home" for us, since we'd lived in Germany for 15 years before moving to Russia. It's also a good example of the kinds of recipes brought by European settlers to the Asian side of Russia.*

2½ pounds firm boiling potatoes (preferably small waxy red potatoes), well scrubbed but not peeled
Salt
6 ounces bacon, diced
2 tablespoons vegetable oil
1 medium onion, finely chopped
I large garlic clove, minced
¾ cup beef stock
¼ cup apple cider vinegar
1 teaspoon freshly ground black pepper
½ teaspoon caraway seeds
¼ teaspoon sugar

Garnish

2 to 3 tablespoons chopped fresh chives or green onion tops

- Drop the potatoes into a large pot of boiling water along with 1 tablespoon salt. When the water comes to a boil again, reduce the heat, partially cover, and boil the potatoes gently for about 20 minutes (depending on their size), until they are fully cooked but not mushy. Drain them in a colander.

- Meanwhile, fry the bacon in the vegetable oil in a medium skillet over medium-high heat until crisp. Transfer the bacon to a small bowl, leaving the rendered fat in the skillet. Sauté the onion and garlic in the hot fat until the onion is translucent. Stir in the beef stock, cider vinegar, black pepper, caraway seeds, sugar, and ¼ teaspoon salt. Bring the mixture to a boil over medium heat and boil gently, stirring occasionally, for 3 minutes longer. Cover and turn off the heat.

- When the potatoes are cool enough to handle, but still warm to the touch, peel them and cut them crosswise into round slices about ¼-inch thick. Put the sliced potatoes into a large glass bowl. Stir the cooked bacon into the onion mixture in the skillet, then pour this warm dressing over the potatoes. Use two large wooden spoons to gently toss the ingredients together until the potatoes have absorbed all the dressing.

- Let the potato salad sit at room temperature for 30 minutes, for the flavors to meld. Taste and add a bit more salt and black pepper, if desired. Garnish each serving with a sprinkling of chopped fresh chives or green onion tops.

- Makes 6 servings.

# Texas Chili

*Tom's Texas chili was so popular at our first Christmas party in Vladivostok that he cooked big pots of it for other large gatherings, too, in both Siberia and the Russian Far East. His chili contained whatever meat happened to be available: Russian T-bone whacks cut into small cubes, or imported American ground turkey (sold in big tubes), as in this recipe. (His secret ingredient was unsweetened cocoa powder, which adds depth of flavor.) Our Russian guests loved Tom's chili, saying they'd never eaten such a dish before—and the Americans at those parties devoured it as a true taste of home.*

▶ **NOTE:** Chili tastes even better if you make it in advance and reheat it the next day.

**6 tablespoons vegetable oil (divided use)**
**2 to 3 medium onions, chopped medium-fine**
**1 green bell pepper, chopped medium-fine**
**2 jalapeño peppers, finely chopped (or 3 dried hot red peppers, crumbled, or 2 tablespoons dried red pepper flakes)**
**2 large garlic cloves, minced**
**2 pounds ground turkey\***
**½ cup plus 4 teaspoons Texas chili powder (divided use)**
**1 can (28 ounces) whole or diced tomatoes, liquid included (about 2 cups tomatoes and 1 cup liquid, total)**
**1 to 1½ cups beer (not dark beer)**
**1 tablespoon Tabasco sauce**
**1 teaspoon salt**
**1 rounded tablespoon unsweetened cocoa powder**
**1 teaspoon ground cumin**
**½ to 1 teaspoon ground cayenne pepper (optional, if you like hotter chili)**

Optional

**1½ to 2 cups cooked pinto or red beans, drained before measuring**

**\*Or 2 pounds of beef, coarsely ground or cut into very small cubes**

- Heat 4 tablespoons of oil in a large skillet over medium-high heat. Sauté the onions, green pepper, jalapeños, and garlic together until the onion is translucent. (If using dried hot peppers, add them when you add the chili powder.) Transfer the mixture to a 6-quart stockpot.

- Add the remaining 2 tablespoons of oil to the skillet and sauté the turkey over medium-high heat until lightly browned, breaking it up into small pieces as it cooks. Sprinkle ½ cup chili powder over the beef, reduce the heat to medium, and cook, stirring constantly, for 2 minutes. Transfer the meat to the stockpot.

- Add the tomatoes, with their liquid, to the pot, breaking up any whole tomatoes into smaller chunks. Stir in 1 cup of beer, the Tabasco sauce, and salt. Bring to a boil over medium-high heat, stirring frequently. Reduce the heat and simmer, uncovered, for 1 hour, stirring frequently and adding some beer if the chili seems too dry. (It should be very thick, not too liquid.)

- Stir in the remaining 4 teaspoons of chili powder, plus the cocoa powder and cumin. (If using beans, add them, too.) Simmer the chili, uncovered, for 15 to 30 minutes longer, stirring frequently. Taste and add more salt if needed.

- Serve hot, in bowls, accompanied by plenty of cold beer.

- Make 8 to 12 servings, depending on how hungry you are.

## Chicken, Pork, and Prune Terrine

*Based on Alla's festive stuffed chicken recipe, this tasty terrine combines her ingredients in a loaf pan, instead of wrapped inside a deboned chicken. Although Alla chose to bake her stuffed chicken in the oven, she said the standard technique was to stuff the chicken and sew it up, then wrap the bird in cheesecloth, boil it in spice-seasoned water for three hours, and press it under a heavy weight for two hours while it cooled—in other words, to make a classic French galantine. Alla often baked a small silver coin in the stuffing mixture, too—and whoever found it would supposedly have good luck the rest of the year. But it's best to warn your guests in advance, so someone doesn't break a tooth!*

▶ **ADVANCE PREPARATION:** Make this terrine at least two or three days before you plan to serve it, so the flavors can fully develop.

**¾ to 1 pound bacon (regular-cut, not thick-slice)**
**1½ pounds boneless, skinless chicken breast halves**

**1 pound ground pork or veal (with 20% fat)**
**1 to 2 large garlic cloves, minced**
**½ teaspoon ground allspice**
**Salt**
**Black pepper**
**Brandy**
**1 cup coarsely chopped prunes**
**½ cup toasted pine nuts***
**Garnishes of your choice**

**\*Toast pine nuts in a preheated 325°F. oven for about 8 minutes. Cool before using.**

- Line a 9 × 5 × 3-inch (1½-quart) glass or ceramic loaf pan with slices of bacon (reserving 3 or 4 slices for the top). Start by placing the bacon slices across the width of the pan, slightly overlapping, with the ends hanging over the long sides of the pan. Then cut 4 slices of bacon in half, crosswise, and line the shorter sides of the pan, with the ends of each slice overhanging the pan, too.

- Trim any fat off the chicken and remove the tough membranes. Slice each breast in half horizontally, to make 2 large, thinner pieces. Pound the chicken pieces with a mallet, to a thickness of ¼ inch, then cut each piece lengthwise into ¼-inch-wide strips.

- In a separate bowl, mix together well the pork or veal, garlic, allspice, ½ teaspoon pepper, and ¼ teaspoon salt.

- Arrange strips of chicken side by side, lengthwise, in a single layer in the bottom of the bacon-lined pan, covering the bottom completely. Sprinkle lightly with brandy, salt, and pepper.

- Use your hands to spread the seasoned pork or veal over the chicken in an even layer, pressing down gently to compact the ingredients. Add another single layer of chicken strips, lengthwise, completely covering the pork. Sprinkle with brandy, salt, and pepper.

- Sprinkle ¼ cup of pine nuts evenly over the chicken layer. Arrange the chopped prunes in a layer on top of the nuts. (Don't worry if they mix together a bit.) Sprinkle the prunes with the remaining ¼ cup of pine nuts, and press down gently with your hands.

- Add the remaining chicken strips, side by side, to make a top layer covering the prunes and nuts completely. Sprinkle with brandy, salt, and pepper.

- Fold the overhanging bacon strips over the chicken. Use the remaining bacon strips to finish covering the top, placing them lengthwise, slightly overlapping, in the pan. Press the top down gently with your hands.

- Preheat the oven to 350°F. Bring a big kettle of water to a boil. Tightly cover the loaf pan with a double layer of heavy-duty aluminum foil, shiny side up, to seal the pan well.

- When the oven and water are hot, set the loaf pan in a larger metal pan (such as a roasting pan) and put it into the oven. Carefully pour enough boiling water into the larger pan to come halfway up the sides of the loaf pan.

- Bake for 1 hour and 45 minutes, or until the meat mixture has pulled away from the sides of the pan and the juices are no longer pink when a skewer is inserted into the middle.

- Remove the loaf pan from the hot water and take off the foil. Fold a new double layer of foil into a piece that just fits inside the top edges of the pan. Set three 15-ounce cans of vegetables on their sides on top of the foil, to weight down the terrine. Let it cool at room temperature for 1 hour, then refrigerate for 24 hours with the weights still on top. Finally, remove the weights and refrigerate the terrine, covered, until needed. The flavors are best if the terrine is refrigerated for at least two days after baking.

- To serve, let the terrine sit at room temperature for about 30 minutes, then cut the meat crosswise into 1-inch-thick slices. Use a spatula to carefully transfer them to individual plates. Garnish the plate with your choice of colorful condiments and vegetables: chopped red onions; stalks of fresh green onions; pickled onions, cucumbers, capers, and small mushrooms; hot-spicy mustard; lingonberry or cranberry preserves. Serve at room temperature, as a first course or luncheon dish.

- Makes 8 servings.

## Don't Tell Alla

Let's face it. I doubt that you will actually go to the trouble of boning a whole chicken or skinning a whole fish, all in one piece, before stuffing it. I certainly don't want to! All the other recipes in this book make dishes just like we ate in Russia—but I confess to taking a short cut with Alla's recipes for stuffed chicken and stuffed fish. I use the same ingredients that she did, but bake them in a loaf pan, not inside a whole chicken or fish skin. The result is just as delicious, even if not as dramatic in presentation. My versions are like French terrines, which look very attractive when sliced and served with a colorful garnish. Just don't tell Alla.

# Salmon and White Fish Terrine, Vladivostok Style

*I loved the look and taste of Alla's stuffed fish, but I didn't want to bother with whacking a big fish against the table to loosen its skin, skinning it whole, picking the bones out of the flesh, and then stuffing the seasoned flesh back into the skin. So I turned Alla's recipe into this pretty terrine of Pacific salmon and white fish, garnished with salmon caviar—ingredients readily available in the port city of Vladivostok.*

▶ **NOTE:** Traditionally the fish and onions are both finely ground in a meat grinder, then beaten by hand with the other ingredients to produce the right texture. Modern cooks use food processors and electric mixers instead.

▶ **ADVANCE PREPARATION:** Make this terrine at least a day in advance because it has to chill thoroughly before serving. It's also important to use a glass or ceramic pan of the correct size.

2 tablespoons sunflower oil
4 medium white onions, finely chopped
2 pounds boneless, skinless pike or whitefish fillets (or a combination of the two)*
2 to 3 pieces of country-style white bread (each ½-inch thick), crusts removed
2 large eggs
1½ teaspoons salt
¾ teaspoon finely ground black or white pepper
1 pound boneless, skinless salmon fillet
¼ cup finely chopped green onion tops
2 tablespoons finely chopped fresh dill

Garnish

Salmon caviar
Fresh dill sprigs
Finely chopped chives or green onion tops

*Wild-caught flounder, North Pacific sole, or other similar firm-fleshed white fish can be substituted (but do not use cod, which has the wrong texture).

- Heat the oil in a large skillet over medium heat, and cook the onions, stirring frequently, until soft and translucent but not browned (about 20 minutes). Transfer to a large deep bowl and let cool to room temperature.

- Pat the white fish fillets dry with paper towels, and cut the fish into 2-inch pieces. Pulse them all together in a food processor until finely chopped but not puréed. Transfer to the bowl with the cooled onions.

- Tear the bread into small pieces (about 1 cup or slightly more of fresh white bread crumbs.) Add the bread, onions, eggs, salt, and pepper to the white fish in the bowl. Beat with an electric mixer on low speed to combine the ingredients, then on medium speed for 5 to 7 minutes, scraping down the sides of the bowl occasionally.

- Pat the salmon dry with paper towels and cut it into very small pieces (1/4-inch dice). Add the salmon, green onion tops, and dill to the white fish mixture, stirring well to distribute them evenly throughout.

- Preheat the oven to 350°F. Butter a 9 × 5 × 3-inch (1½-quart) glass or ceramic loaf pan.

- Pack the fish mixture into the loaf pan, smoothing over the top. Place the loaf pan on a small rimmed baking sheet or pizza pan, to catch any liquid that bubbles over during baking.

- Bake for about 1½ hours, until the top has begun to brown and the fish loaf has pulled away from the sides of the pan.

- Remove the terrine from the baking sheet and let it cool on a wire rack for 30 minutes. Carefully run a knife around the edges of the pan, to loosen the fish from it. Invert a platter over the top of the loaf pan and quickly turn them both over together. Remove the loaf pan.

- Let the fish terrine cool to room temperature, then tilt the platter slightly and blot any excess liquid with paper towels. Cover with plastic wrap and refrigerate until well chilled (preferably 12 hours or longer).

- To serve, cut the cold terrine crosswise into slices 1 inch thick. Garnish each slice with a spoonful of salmon caviar, a sprig of fresh dill, and a generous sprinkling of chopped chives or green onion tops. Serve as a first course or a light luncheon dish with a green salad. (Keep leftovers refrigerated.)

- Makes 8 servings.

# Gefilte Fish – East

Alla called her stuffed whole pike "The Fish of the Tsar," a recipe she learned from her Granny Polina. But anyone familiar with the Jewish cooking of Central and Eastern Europe will recognize it also as *gefilte Fisch* (Yiddish for "stuffed fish"), a classic dish in Ashkenazi Jewish kitchens. Although Alla wasn't Jewish, this baked stuffed fish was one of the stars of her culinary repertoire.

According to Alla, in the Russian Far East this dish is made with any of several large, fleshy fish: *shchuka* (pike), *gorbusha* (humpback salmon, pink salmon), *som* (a type of large catfish), *tolstolobik* (silver carp, bighead carp), and *krasnoperka* (another member of the carp family). My 1955 edition of *Kniga o vkusnoi i zdorovoi pishche* (*Book of Tasty and Healthy Food*), Russia's equivalent of our *Joy of Cooking*, says that *ryba farshirovannaya* (stuffed fish) can be made from perch, pike-perch, carp, or bream, in a recipe whose fish stuffing includes beets, carrots, and sugar, like many Jewish recipes do, too.

"The most difficult part is pulling away the skin," said Alla. "Starting at the gills, cut the skin around the throat, then pull off the skin with the head still attached, like a woman taking off her stocking. Don't forget about the fins, or they'll put holes in the skin. Peel the skin down to 2 centimeters before the tail, and cut almost all the way around the skin at the tail, then finish peeling the skin off the fish, with the tail still attached.

"Make the stuffing from the boned fish flesh (adding the meat from another fish if you don't have enough), a piece of white bread soaked in milk, an egg, salt and pepper, and whatever herbs you want—dill, green onion tops, etc. Beat hard with a wooden spoon for 10 to 15 minutes, even beating by throwing the mixture onto the table or against the sides of the bowl. Stuff this back into the fish skin. Oil a baking pan and arrange the fish in the shape you want—straight or curved (if the fish is too big for the pan).

"Prick the skin 10 or 15 times with a needle, and brush with a whole beaten egg to make the skin shiny. Bake no more than 30 minutes in a not-too-hot oven. Maybe add a little water to the pan while cooking. Then let the fish cool. Never cut it hot. Granny sometimes covered the back of the fish with a flour-and-water paste that was removed immediately after taking it out of the oven."

Alla brought her "Fish of the Tsar" to our Christmas party on a large tray, garnished with her home-canned tomatoes and pickled cucumbers—a festive red-and-green contrast to the shiny, silvery skin of the fish. I'd eaten bottled gefilte fish before, in New York—the stuffing just made into fish patties or balls—but that winter in Vladivostok was the first time I'd ever seen the real thing, a whole fish stuffed the old-fashioned way, "just like Granny used to make."

# From the Earth

I like the word "terrine"—it sounds of the earth where all of us, plants and animals, come from, and where we all return to, in the continuous cycle of birth, death, rebirth. In the kitchen a terrine is just a meat, fish, or vegetable loaf cooked in a glazed earthenware pan, round, oval, or rectangular in shape, known in French as a *terrine*. The word originally comes from the Latin *terra*, meaning "earth"—although glass and enameled cast-iron pans are now used for making terrines, too.

The dish cooked in a terrine can be simple or complex—a mixture of ingredients baked in the oven, then usually cooled before being sliced or scooped out to put on your plate. Nothing aristocratic about that, although some of the baroque terrines concocted by royal chefs and imaginative home cooks have surely reached that height. I think of those terrines as really good meatloaves, even if they don't always contain meat. So don't be put off by something called a terrine. It's likely to be very close to the meatloaves your mother or grandmother used to make—maybe just a little better, though, if there's a creative cook in the kitchen.

# The Captain's Meat

*We first ate this Vladivostok specialty at an upscale restaurant (reputedly a mafia hangout) shortly after we arrived in the Russian Far East. Alla made it for us several times, too, with beef or pork, whichever was fresh in the market that day. Sometimes she added a layer of thinly sliced carrots or topped the casserole with sliced tomatoes. Hot from the oven, it was always a welcome main dish on a cold winter night.*

▶ **NOTE:** It's important to use an 11 × 7 × 2-inch metal baking pan.

**2 pounds (approximately) tender boneless beef (such as boneless sirloin tip roast or steak)**
**Salt and freshly ground black pepper**
**½ cup mayonnaise**

1 teaspoon grated horseradish (fresh or bottled)
3 large garlic cloves, minced
1 medium to large onion, thinly sliced crosswise and separated into rings
2 pounds firm boiling potatoes, peeled and thinly cut crosswise into rounds
  (or sliced with the 4mm blade of a food processor)
Butter (unsalted)
2 tablespoons beef stock
1 cup (firmly packed) coarsely shredded hard yellow cheese (such as
  Jarlsberg)

- Preheat the oven to 350°F. Oil an 11 × 7 × 2-inch metal baking pan.

- Trim any fat and membranes off the beef, and cut the meat across the grain into slices ¾-inch thick (the outer measurement of the slices isn't important—just the thickness). Place the beef slices flat in the pan, fitting them together to make a single layer of meat. Sprinkle lightly with salt and pepper. Bake uncovered at 350°F. for 10 minutes.

- Remove the pan from the oven, and increase the heat to 400°F. Mix the mayonnaise and horseradish together in a small bowl, then spread it over the pieces of meat. Sprinkle the garlic evenly over the mayonnaise. Arrange the onion rings in a layer on top.

- Make a layer of slightly overlapping potato slices over the onions (like making scalloped potatoes). Sprinkle with salt and pepper, and dot with 6 to 8 small pieces of butter. Make a second layer of overlapping potato slices the same way. Make a third layer of potatoes, and sprinkle the beef stock, followed by a little more salt and pepper, over the top.

- Cover the casserole tightly with foil. Bake at 400°F. for 50 minutes. Then remove the foil, sprinkle the top evenly with shredded cheese, and bake, uncovered, another 5 minutes.

- Let the casserole sit for a few minutes before serving. Serve hot as a main dish, accompanied by a tomato, onion, and cucumber salad dressed with sunflower oil and white vinegar.

- Makes 6 servings.

▶ **VARIATIONS (take your pick):** Omit the mayonnaise and horseradish, and spread ½ cup of Dijon or Russian hot-spicy mustard over the meat instead. Add a layer of thinly sliced carrots before the first layer of potatoes. Arrange a layer of sliced tomatoes on top of the cheese before the final 5 minutes of baking. Alla sometimes sprinkled thyme, oregano, or parsley over the mayonnaise layer, stuck a bay leaf or a few whole cloves in the casserole, and put a pinch of cinnamon in the beef stock.

# Siberian Beef And Pork Dumplings

## (Pel'meni)

*Since* pel'meni *take a lot of time to make, it's more fun to roll, cut, and fill them by work-ing together with a group of family or friends. You can even make the dough and filling in advance and refrigerate them up to one day before calling in friends to help you construct the* pel'meni. *(Let the dough come to room temperature before rolling it out.) I agree with Sibe-rians who say these little dumplings taste better when they're frozen for at least a day before cooking, so plan ahead when making this recipe.*

### Dough

**3 cups all-purpose flour**
**3 large eggs**
**⅓ cup water**
**1 tablespoon vegetable oil**
**1 teaspoon salt**
**Additional flour for rolling out the dough**

### Pork-Beef Filling

**1 large onion, quartered**
**2 to 4 large garlic cloves, quartered**
**½ pound finely ground pork (with 20% fat)**
**½ pound finely ground beef (not too lean)**
**1 teaspoon salt**
**1 teaspoon freshly ground black pepper**
**¼ teaspoon ground cayenne pepper or hot paprika (optional)**
**¼ cup ice water**

### Spices for Boiling Dumplings

**1 bay leaf**
**1 teaspoon salt**
**10 whole black peppercorns**
**5 whole cloves**
**5 whole allspice berries**

### Garnishes (take your pick)

**1 cup (2 sticks) unsalted butter (for tossing with the *pel'meni* before serving)**
**Additional melted butter for the table**
**Sour cream**

Hot-spicy Russian mustard (or Colman's English mustard)
Mild white vinegar or apple cider vinegar, with coarsely ground black pepper
Chinese black vinegar
Asian chile sauce (Thai or Vietnamese, such as Sriracha)
Soy sauce
Green onion tops, thinly sliced crosswise
Chopped fresh dill

## ▶ Dough:

- Put 1½ cups of the flour into a large bowl with the eggs, water, vegetable oil, and salt. Beat with an electric mixer on low speed for 2 minutes. Gradually add the remaining 1½ cups of flour, stirring with a wooden spoon, then mixing with your hands, until all the flour is incorporated.

- Turn the dough out onto a lightly floured surface and knead until the dough is smooth and elastic (3 to 5 minutes). Form the dough into a flat disk about 1 inch thick, wrap tightly with plastic wrap, and set aside at room temperature for 1 hour.

## ▶ Filling:

- While the dough is resting, put the onions and garlic in a food processor and pulse until they are minced. Add the pork, beef, salt, pepper, and cayenne, and process until all the ingredients are well mixed. Add the water and process to make a fairly smooth mass. (Or put all the ingredients together 2 or 3 times through a meat grinder, mixing in the water last.)

- Cover and refrigerate until you are ready to form the *pel'meni*. (Makes approximately 3 cups of filling.)

## ▶ To form *pel'meni*:

- Divide the dough into 4 equal parts and work with only 1 part at a time. Keep the remaining dough wrapped in plastic so it won't dry out.

- Roll out the dough very thin (about ¹⁄₁₆-inch thick) on a lightly floured surface. (Siberians say you should be able to see your hand through the dough.) Have the filling, a small bowl of water, and 2 lightly floured baking sheets nearby.

- Use a 2½-inch round cookie cutter to cut 1 circle of dough. Roll out the circle a bit more, to form a 3-inch-diameter round.

- Place 1 *level* teaspoon of the meat filling in the center of the dough circle. Dip the tip of your finger in the water and lightly moisten the edge of the dough. Then fold the dough over the filling, bringing the edges of the dough together to form a semi-circle (half-moon shape). Press the edges together *firmly* to seal in the filling.

- Bring the pointed ends of the semi-circle together, overlapping them a bit, and press the ends together *firmly*, moistening them if necessary, to stick together. (The *pel'meni* will look much like little "ears," or like Italian *tortelloni*.)

- As you make the dumplings, place them in a single layer on the baking sheets. Continue this process until all the dough has been used. (Gather up the dough scraps and form them into a ball, then re-roll and cut all the dough scraps, too.)

▶ **NOTE:** If you're working alone, make 1 dumpling at a time. If you have helpers, one person can roll and cut the dough, while the others fill, fold, and seal the edges of the *pel'meni*.

▶ **To freeze pel'meni:** You can cook the *pel'meni* at this point, but they taste even better if frozen first. Freeze the *pel'meni* solid on the baking sheets, then store them in tightly sealed plastic bags in the freezer (up to 3 months).

▶ **To cook *pel'meni*:**

- Fill a large stockpot 2/3 full with cold water. Add the bay leaf, salt, peppercorns, cloves, and allspice. Bring the water to a full boil over high heat, then drop in about 20 *pel'meni* (but don't crowd the pot too much).

- Let the *pel'meni* cook very gently for about 8 minutes after the water comes back to a *low* boil, adjusting the heat to keep the water at a low boil and stirring occasionally as the dumplings rise to the surface. (Cook frozen *pel'meni*, direct from the freezer, not thawed, for about 10 minutes.)

- While the *pel'meni* are cooking, melt 1 cup of butter in a large skillet over low heat. Remove the cooked dumplings with a slotted spoon, drain well, and toss them gently in the melted butter in the skillet. Transfer the *pel'meni* to a large bowl and set aside in a warm place (such as an oven set at 200°F.).

- Repeat this process, cooking the *pel'meni* in batches, until all the dumplings are cooked. Serve immediately, as a main course.

▶ **To serve *pel'meni*:**

● Put the desired number of *pel'meni* (usually about 15 to 20 dumplings per person) into individual shallow soup bowls. Let the diners garnish their *pel'meni* at the table as they wish—with melted butter, sour cream, hot-spicy mustard, vinegar and black pepper, soy sauce, chile sauce, chopped fresh dill, or sliced green onion tops.

● Makes approximately 90 *pel'meni* (4 to 6 servings).

▶ **TIP:** Bite-size *pel'meni* should be eaten whole. Russians consider it uncouth to cut the dumplings into pieces before popping them into your mouth.

# Dumplings in Every Pot

Known as "the national dish of Siberia," *pel'meni* are ear-shaped, bite-size pockets of pasta, which look much like Italian *tortelloni*, filled with minced meat, fish, vegetables, mushrooms, or other ingredients.

Many culinary historians think these boiled pasta dumplings originated in China or Central Asia, then spread into Siberia and eastern parts of European Russia during the Mongol and Tatar occupations of those areas from the thirteenth to the fifteenth centuries. When the Russians regained power over their lost territories west of the Ural Mountains and began pushing their borders southward toward the Caucasus and eastward beyond the Urals, they also adopted some of the foods and cooking techniques of the Asian populations they conquered. Thus in the mid-sixteenth century Russians learned how to make pasta—including *pel'meni*—from their Tatar subjects. On the other hand, some linguists think *pel'meni* originated several centuries before the Mongol invasions, in the lands of the Komi and Udmurt people, Finno-Ugric groups living just west of the Ural Mountains. But no one really knows for certain the origin of these popular little Siberian dumplings.

Although classic *pel'meni* dough is made with wheat flour and always creamy-white in color, modern Siberian cooks sometimes color their dough pale orange (with puréed carrots), pink (with beets), pale green (with spinach or other fresh greens), or even black (with squid ink).

*Pel'meni* are traditionally filled with a mixture of minced meats, such as beef, pork, and mutton, seasoned with onion, salt, black pepper, and sometimes a bit of fresh garlic or even hot red pepper. Deer, elk, moose, bear, horsemeat, and game birds are used in Siberian *pel'meni* fillings, too, as are a variety of fish and shellfish from Siberia's rivers, lakes, and seas. Other versions are stuffed with chopped poultry, cooked potatoes, buckwheat groats, toasted pine nuts, minced mushrooms, or finely chopped greens that grow in Siberia, such as wild garlic, horseradish, dandelion, sorrel, and goosefoot. (One of my Siberian cookbooks has 86 different recipes for *pel'meni*, and another touts 500 recipes for these little dumplings!) Sometimes the cook sneaks into the filling a coin, a button, a ring, a garlic clove, or a whole peppercorn, believed to bring good fortune to the diner who finds it. It's even said that in tsarist times, the royal cooks were instructed to hide precious stones within certain *pel'meni* served to the tsar's special guests.

The *pel'meni* are boiled in water or broth seasoned with herbs and spices, then drained and tossed with butter before serving. Cooked *pel'meni* can also be served swimming in broth. And sometimes raw *pel'meni*, submerged in sour cream, are slow-baked and served in special little covered ceramic pots.

Steaming-hot *pel'meni* served "straight" (without broth) are often garnished with additional butter and globs of rich, nutty-flavored sour cream. But they're just as likely to be eaten with a smearing of hot-spicy Russian mustard or a sprinkling of vinegar (or a mixture of the two)—or even garnished with soy sauce or hot-spicy chile sauce, reflecting the East Asian influence on Russian cooking in that part of the world.

During the winter Siberian cooks make hundreds of *pel'meni* at a time, sharing the labor-intensive work among family and friends. Siberian villagers sometimes still gather for massive, communal *pel'meni*-making bouts where thousands of *pel'meni* are rolled, cut, filled, and formed by hand, the work punctuated by shots of ice-cold vodka every time another 100 dumplings are made. These gatherings often end with *pel'meni*-eating contests, much like hot-dog- or jalapeño-eating contests in America. Then the Siberians hang the remaining uncooked dumplings outdoors, in bags on their houses or balconies, or bury them in the snow, to freeze solid for cooking later, as needed, throughout the long winter.

*Pel'meni* are so popular that some Russian towns have small restaurants called *pel'mennye*, which specialize in serving these Siberian boiled dumplings as a fast-food to be eaten on site or purchased for takeout. In the winter, vendors offer bags of homemade frozen *pel'meni* at street stalls and farmers' markets. And many Russians carry frozen *pel'meni* with them on hunting or fishing trips in the winter, because these dumplings are so easy to cook in a pot of boiling water over an open fire.

No wonder that Siberian *pel'meni* are said to be one of the world's first "frozen convenience foods."

# Lazy Pel'meni

Although handmade *pel'meni* are always considered the best, Russian cooks have found several ways to reduce the time and work involved in preparing them.

- **Bread-machine method (for making the dough):** Have the eggs at room temperature. Put all the dough ingredients into the bread machine pan and follow the instructions for using the "Dough/Pasta" setting on your machine. When the pasta dough is ready, turn it out onto a floured surface and knead by hand for 3 minutes, adding a bit more flour if the dough is too sticky. Form the dough into a flat disk about 1 inch thick, wrap tightly with plastic wrap, and set aside at room temperature for 1 hour, before rolling, cutting, and filling the *pel'meni*.

- *Pel'menitsa* **(for forming *pel'meni*):** A *pel'menitsa* is a Russian cast-aluminum (or hard-plastic) utensil that functions like an Italian ravioli board, producing several *pel'meni* at once (usually 20). But the small hexagonal-shaped *pel'meni* do not look like the traditional ear-shaped dumplings that grandmother always made. You place a thin layer of rolled-out dough on top of the *pel'menitsa*, spoon some of the filling into each of the depressions, cover with another thin layer of dough, and run a rolling pin over the top to seal and cut all the dumplings at once. Then you turn the board over and tap out all the little dumplings together.

- **Chinese dumpling maker (for forming *pel'meni*):** Cut, fill, and seal the rolled-out *pel'meni* dough using an inexpensive plastic Chinese dumpling maker (3 inches in diameter). These produce individual half-moon-shaped dumplings with a fluted edge. Remove the dumpling from the mold, bring the pointed ends of the dough together, overlapping them a bit, and press *firmly* to stick them together, to make ear-shaped *pel'meni*.

- **Pre-made dumpling wrappers:** Save all the steps in making, rolling, and cutting the dough by using commercial Chinese dumpling wrappers. Buy small round wrappers, preferably those made with eggs. Fill, shape, and cook them like handmade *pel'meni*. But the texture of the cooked dumplings won't be the same as that of true Russian *pel'meni*. These are the laziest dumplings of all, and grandmother would not be pleased.

# Siberian Salmon Dumplings

## (Pel'meni)

*Russians living near rivers and the sea like to make* pel'meni *filled with fish. This recipe comes from the Russian Far East where salmon is abundant. The use of ginger and soy sauce reflects China's influence on the cuisine of this region, especially in the south.*

▶ **GENERAL INSTRUCTIONS:** Follow the recipe for making classic Siberian *pel'meni*, using this salmon filling instead of the pork-beef filling.

### Salmon Filling

**1 pound boneless, skinless salmon, cut into ½-inch pieces**
**½ cup (1 stick) unsalted butter cut into ½-inch pieces, at room temperature**
**3 garlic cloves, quartered**
**2 tablespoons grated fresh gingerroot**
**2 teaspoons salt**
**1 teaspoon finely ground black pepper**
**2 cups finely minced green onions, both white and green parts**

- Put the salmon, butter, garlic, ginger, salt, and pepper in a food processor and pulse the ingredients to make a fine paste. Transfer the mixture to a bowl and stir in the minced green onions, mixing well. Cover and refrigerate until you are ready to form the *pel'meni*. (Makes approximately 3½ cups of salmon filling.)

- Make the dough and form the dumplings according to the recipe for classic Siberian *pel'meni*.

- Cook the dumplings for 8 minutes (fresh) or 10 minutes (frozen) in water seasoned with 1 teaspoon salt.

- Serve hot, garnished with melted butter, sour cream, soy sauce, or Asian chile sauce. Sprinkle with fresh dill (for sour cream or butter garnish) or finely chopped green onion tops (for soy or chile sauce garnishes).

- Makes approximately 90 salmon *pel'meni* (4 to 6 servings).

# Siberian Venison-and-Blueberry Dumplings

## (Pel'meni)

*These are often called "taiga pel'meni" because the venison and blueberries come from the great Siberian forest region known as the* taiga. *Wild game has always been a popular filling for* pel'meni, *particularly in the past when Siberian settlers relied on game to provide much of the meat for their tables. In this recipe pork adds the necessary fat to the lean venison, although in earlier times the fat would have come from fattier game such as bear, or even from horses.*

▶ **GENERAL INSTRUCTIONS:** Follow the recipe for making classic Siberian *pel'meni*, using this venison-blueberry filling instead of the pork-beef filling.

### Venison-Blueberry Filling

**½ pound finely ground venison**
**½ pound finely ground pork (with 20% fat)**
**1 large yellow onion, cut into eighths**
**4 large garlic cloves, quartered**
**1 teaspoon salt**
**1 teaspoon finely ground black pepper**
**½ cup finely chopped fresh (or frozen/thawed) blueberries, with their juice**

- Mix the venison and pork together in a large bowl. Put the onion, garlic, salt, and pepper in a food processor and pulse until finely minced. Add the onion mixture and the chopped blueberries (with their juice) to the meat in the bowl, mixing well. Cover and refrigerate until you are ready to form the *pel'meni*. (Makes approximately 3½ cups of venison-blueberry filling.)

- Make the dough and form the dumplings according to the recipe for classic Siberian *pel'meni*.

- Cook the dumplings for 10 minutes (fresh) or 15 minutes (frozen) in water seasoned with a bay leaf, 1 teaspoon salt, 10 black peppercorns, 5 whole cloves, and 5 whole allspice berries.

- Serve hot, garnished with sour cream, melted butter, mild white vinegar or cider vinegar with coarsely ground black pepper, or hot-spicy Russian mustard (or Colman's English mustard).

- Makes approximately 90 venison-blueberry *pel'meni* (4 to 6 servings).

# Siberian Venison-and-Cranberry Dumplings

## (Pel'meni)

*Another version of "taiga pel'meni" is made with dried cranberries instead of fresh blueberries. I've found that sweetened dried cranberries (like those sold in most American supermarkets) make an especially tasty filling.*

▶ **GENERAL INSTRUCTIONS:** Follow the recipe for making classic Siberian *pel'meni*, using this venison-cranberry filling instead of the pork-beef filling.

### Venison-Cranberry Filling

**½ pound finely ground venison**
**½ pound finely ground pork (with 20% fat)**
**1 large yellow onion, cut into eighths**
**4 large garlic cloves, quartered**
**1 teaspoon salt**
**1 teaspoon finely ground black pepper**
**½ cup finely chopped dried cranberries**
**¼ cup ice water**

- Mix the venison and pork together in a large bowl. Put the onion, garlic, salt, and pepper in a food processor and pulse until finely minced. Add the onion mixture and chopped dried cranberries to the meat in the bowl, mixing well. Add the ice water and beat with a wooden spoon until the meat mixture is smooth. Cover and refrigerate until you are ready to form the *pel'meni*. (Makes approximately 3½ cups of venison-cranberry filling.)

- Make the dough and form the dumplings according to the recipe for classic Siberian *pel'meni*.

- Cook the dumplings for 10 minutes (fresh) or 15 minutes (frozen) in water seasoned with a bay leaf, 1 teaspoon salt, 10 black peppercorns, 5 whole cloves, and 5 whole allspice berries.

- Serve hot, garnished with sour cream, melted butter, mild white vinegar or cider vinegar with coarsely ground black pepper, or hot-spicy Russian mustard (or Colman's English mustard).

- Makes approximately 90 venison-cranberry *pel'meni* (4 to 6 servings).

# Russian Crêpes

## (Blinchiki)

*These light, delicate crêpes were a favorite party dish of our Russian neighbor, Natasha. If you've never made crêpes before, the first couple out of your pan will probably be a mess. But just keep trying—you'll get the hang of it. And these light, lacy pancakes are well worth the effort!*

▶ **ADVANCE PREPARATION:** Since it takes a while to cook all of these crêpes, start early or make them in advance (see **NOTE** at end of recipe).

▶ **NOTE:** Pan size is very important to produce the right width and thinness of these crêpes. Use a heavy skillet (preferably cast iron or non-stick) measuring at least 8 inches *across the bottom*. You'll also need a ¼-cup ladle (or measuring cup) for scooping the batter and a heatproof basting brush for buttering the skillet. (Many Russian cooks grease their skillets with a goose feather or half a raw potato dipped in oil or melted butter, or they rub the hot skillet with a cube of pork fat skewered on a fork.)

**2 large eggs, separated**
**2½ cups milk**
**¼ teaspoon salt**
**2 cups all-purpose flour**
**2 tablespoons unsalted butter, melted and slightly cooled (for batter)**
**4 tablespoons unsalted butter, melted (for frying)**
**Garnishes or fillings of your choice**

● Beat the egg yolks well in a medium bowl, then whisk in the milk and salt. Gradually sift in the flour, whisking to make a smooth batter. Stir in 2 tablespoons of melted butter. Cover and let sit at room temperature for 1 hour.

● Just before cooking the crêpes, beat the egg whites until stiff but not dry, and fold them into the batter.

● Brush the skillet with a thin film of melted butter. Place the pan over medium-high heat and when hot, ladle ¼ cup of batter into it, quickly tilting and rotating the pan so the bottom is covered completely and evenly with a thin layer of batter. Cook over medium-high heat for 2 minutes, occasionally lifting the edge of the crêpe with a spatula to keep it from sticking.

● Turn the crêpe over, and cook for about 1 minute longer. Take the pan off the heat, and transfer the crêpe to a plate, with the second (spotty) side up.

● Repeat with the remaining batter, each time brushing the hot pan lightly with melted butter and swirling the batter over the bottom before you put it back on the heat. (If the batter becomes too thick to spread easily, thin it with a little milk.) Stack the crêpes on top of each other with the second (spotty) side up, covered loosely with aluminum foil to keep warm.

- Makes 18 to 20 crêpes (6 servings of 3 crêpes each), which can be topped with, or wrapped around, a variety of garnishes and fillings.

▶ **Garnishes:** Spread warm *blinchiki* with melted butter, fruit or berry preserves, warmed honey, or even sweetened condensed milk (a particularly Russian indulgence), then fold into quarters or roll up into tubes for eating. Rolled or folded *blinchiki* can also be garnished with chocolate sauce and a dusting of confectioners' sugar, or a drizzle of thinned sour cream and a sprinkling of granulated sugar.

▶ **Fillings:** Ground or finely chopped pre-cooked meats or vegetables napped with a thick béchamel sauce; fresh white curd cheese mixed with sour cream, horseradish, and chopped chives; diced fresh or dried fruits cooked with sugar, fruit juice, and cinnamon; fresh white curd cheese beaten with sugar, egg, sour cream, vanilla, and lemon zest, with a few brandy-soaked raisins stirred in. Put 2 heaping tablespoons of filling on the center of each crêpe and roll it up, tucking in the open ends, to make a little packet. Heat, covered, in a 350°F. oven for about 15 minutes, or pan-fry lightly in butter until golden brown on all sides. Serve hot.

▶ **NOTE:** These crêpes can be made in advance, cooled to room temperature, and the whole stack wrapped tightly with plastic. Keep in the refrigerator for 3 days (or wrap tightly in aluminum foil and freeze up to 3 months). Thawed *blinchiki* can be reheated in foil in a 300°F. oven for few minutes, or in waxed paper in a microwave for a few seconds (depending on how many you're reheating in one stack).

## Your Fill of Crêpes

In Russia, the large, lacy-thin crêpes known as *blinchiki* are often spread with butter, jam, or honey, as a tea-time treat; rolled up around meaty mixtures for a main dish; wrapped around a sweet fruit or creamy cheese filling for dessert; and even stacked with layers of filling in between, then baked and cut into wedges for serving. In Siberia, you might find *blinchiki* wrapped around pieces of smoked duck and garnished with sea-buckthorn preserves; in the Russian Far East, stuffed with salmon, shrimp, or Kamchatka crab meat, and topped with glistening beads of bright-orange salmon caviar.

# Walnut Torte with Chocolate Icing

*Walnuts were an expensive ingredient when we lived in Vladivostok, so Russian cooks used them mainly for special occasions. Guests were always happy when our neighbor, Natasha, baked her luscious chocolate-covered, two-layer walnut torte for dinner parties in our apartment building. Usually she decorated the top with walnut halves—but for one of our holiday parties she surprised us by writing "Merry Christmas," in English, with light buttercream piped on top of the dark chocolate icing.*

▶ **NOTE:** It's important to use the correct size of cake pans (8-inch round) for this recipe.

## Walnut Torte

**2 cups coarsely chopped walnuts (plus 10 walnut halves for decoration)**
**8 large eggs, separated, at room temperature**
**1¼ cups sugar (divided use)**
**⅓ cup unseasoned dry bread crumbs**

## Filling

**½ cup apricot jam**
**2 teaspoons dark rum**

## Chocolate Icing

**One (14-ounce) can sweetened condensed milk**
**4 ounces bittersweet baking chocolate, chopped into small chunks**
**⅛ teaspoon salt**
**1 tablespoon dark rum**

- Preheat the oven to 350°F. Toast all the walnuts in a single layer on a baking sheet for 8 minutes, then let them cool to room temperature on the pan.

- Separate the eggs, putting the whites and yolks into separate very large bowls. Set aside.

- Grind the nuts by hand with a nut grinder or grater (which takes a while). The easier way is to carefully grind them in a food processor. Process only ½ cup at a time with ½ teaspoon of the sugar added to each ½ cup of nuts, pulsing the nuts in several very short bursts—only 1 or 2 seconds at a time—so they don't turn into oily nut butter. After grinding each ½ cup of nuts, transfer them to a medium bowl.

- Butter *only* the bottoms (*not* the sides) of two 8-inch round cake pans and line the bottom with baking parchment. Butter the parchment paper and dust with flour. Set aside ¼ cup of the sugar (to beat with the egg whites). Heat the oven to 350°F.

- Stir the remaining sugar (scant 1 cup) into the egg yolks, then beat with an electric mixer on high speed until the mixture is very thick and pale colored (3 to 4 minutes).

- In another large bowl, using clean beaters, beat the egg whites on medium speed until soft peaks form. Then beat on high speed while gradually adding the reserved ¼ cup of sugar, until the egg whites form stiff peaks, still glossy but not dry.

- Working quickly, toss the chopped walnuts and bread crumbs together well, then fold them into the egg-yolk mixture.

- Gently stir ¼ of the beaten egg whites into the egg-yolk mixture (to lighten it), then carefully fold in the remaining egg whites, just until no white lumps remain. Do not let the batter deflate.

- Divide the batter evenly between the 2 cake pans and gently smooth over the tops. Bake at 350°F. for about 30 to 35 minutes, until the cake begins to pull away from the sides of the pans and a toothpick inserted in the center comes out clean.

- Let the cake layers cool in the pans, set on wire racks, for 20 minutes. Then carefully run a knife around the edge to loosen the cake from the pans. Try not to snag the cake with the knife. Put a wire rack over each pan, and invert the cake layer onto it. (The bottom of the layer will now be on top.) Peel off the baking parchment. Let the layers cool completely.

- Combine the sweetened condensed milk with the chocolate in a small heavy-bottom pan. Cook over low heat, stirring constantly, until the chocolate is melted and the mixture is hot (about 10 minutes). Remove from heat and stir in the salt. Using a wooden spoon or electric mixer, beat in 1 tablespoon of rum, drop by drop. Keep beating until the mixture is cool and thick enough to spread without running (about 10 minutes). If it is still not thick enough, refrigerate for 30 minutes.

- Stir the apricot jam together with 2 teaspoons rum until well combined.

- Place one layer of the walnut torte on a serving platter, with the bottom of the layer facing up. Spread the apricot jam over it, and wait 5 minutes for it to soak in. Place the other cake layer on top, with the top side facing up. (If the sides of the cake are uneven, trim with a knife and eat the trimmings for a treat while you work.) Spread the chocolate icing over the sides and top of the cake. Arrange 10 walnut halves evenly in a circle around the top edge of the cake.

- Cover with a cake cover or very large bowl (not touching the icing) and refrigerate for 2 hours for the icing to set. Let the cake sit, uncovered, at room temperature for 15 minutes before serving. Keep leftover cake refrigerated, covered with plastic wrap.

- Makes 10 servings.

# Torte Law

Classic European tortes are not difficult to make, but they can be tricky for the novice baker. If you've never made one before, take this short course in Torte Law before you begin baking—so your cake will stand up in the court of good taste.

▶ Follow the recipe instructions exactly, to the letter of the law.

▶ Do not substitute ingredients (unless the recipe allows it).

▶ Always use the correct size of pan—and butter only the bottom, not the sides.

▶ Use a spotlessly clean bowl and beaters for beating the egg whites.

▶ If you don't know how to fold beaten egg whites into the heavier part of the cake batter, ask an experienced home baker to show you how—or watch a demo on YouTube.

▶ Accept the fact that the center of your torte will probably fall while the cake is cooling—no matter how faithfully you've followed the law.

▶ Remember that although the Russian legal system is different from those in the western world, Torte Law is the same in kitchens around the globe.

# Christmas Carrot Cake

*This has been Tom's birthday cake and our traditional Christmas cake since our first winter together in 1970. Before moving to Russia, I had baked this cake every December—in Germany, in Texas, and elsewhere—so of course I continued the tradition in Vladivostok. The only changes I had to make in Russia were to substitute roasted peanuts for walnuts or pecans, omit the orange liqueur (unavailable), bake the cake in our two round "Teflon tank" pans instead of the one big Bundt pan I'd always used before—and figure out how to keep the Stove-from-Hell from burning the whole thing to a crisp. I always made several of these carrot cakes for our Christmas parties in Russia, because they were so popular with guests from all over the world.*

## Cake

3 cups all-purpose flour
2 teaspoons baking powder
2 teaspoons ground cinnamon
1 teaspoon baking soda
½ teaspoon salt
2½ cups sugar
1½ cups vegetable oil
2½ cups finely shredded raw carrots (about 1 pound)*
1 cup well-drained, crushed sweetened pineapple, measured after draining
    (one 15-ounce can—reserve the juice for making the glaze)
3 large eggs
2 teaspoons vanilla extract
1 cup chopped walnuts or pecans

* Shred the carrots finely with a conventional box grater or in a food processor fitted with the smallest shredding blade. (A Microplane grater makes the carrots too fluffy and wet.)

## Glaze

½ cup orange or pineapple juice
½ cup confectioners' sugar
1 tablespoon orange liqueur*
1 tablespoon brandy or rum*
1 tablespoon unsalted butter

*Or 2 teaspoons vanilla extract (instead of the liquor)

- **Cake:** Preheat the oven to 350°F. Butter and flour a large (12-cup) fluted tube pan (Bundt pan or Springform tube pan).

- Whisk the flour, baking powder, cinnamon, baking soda, and salt together in a large bowl. Whisk in the sugar. Add the vegetable oil, shredded carrots, crushed pineapple, eggs, and vanilla. Stir until all the dry ingredients are completely moistened, then beat with an electric mixer on medium speed for 3 minutes, until the batter is well mixed. Stir in the chopped nuts.

- Pour the batter into the prepared baking pan. Bake at 350°F. for 1 hour, or until a skewer inserted in the thickest part of the cake comes out clean. Let the cake cool completely in the pan, set on a wire rack.

- **Glaze:** Combine the orange or pineapple juice with the confectioners' sugar in a small saucepan. Bring the mixture to a boil and let it boil gently, stirring frequently, for 10 minutes. Cool slightly and stir in the orange liqueur and brandy (or the vanilla). Then beat in the butter with a wooden spoon, until the glaze is smooth.

- When the cake has cooled completely, invert it onto a serving platter. Use a toothpick to poke small holes all over the top of the cake (so the glaze can soak in more easily). Slowly brush the warm glaze over the entire top of the cake, letting some of the glaze dribble down the sides. Use all of the glaze.

- Makes 1 large cake (10 to 12 servings).

▶ **VARIATION: Pumpkin-Spice Cake:** Substitute 2½ cups peeled, shredded raw pumpkin for the carrots. Add 1 teaspoon freshly grated nutmeg and ⅛ to ¼ teaspoon ground cloves (in addition to the cinnamon in the recipe).

# Honey-Spice Cookies

*These were our Russian version of gingersnaps, adapted from* Joy of Cooking *and made with locally available ingredients. We baked dozens of them for Christmas parties at home and for the potluck meal at Vladivostok's Lutheran church on Christmas Eve, where they were quickly devoured by the Russians. Warning: Crunchy, spicy, and not too sweet, these cookies are addictive!*

▶ **NOTE:** If you really want to kick up the taste, add ½ to 1 teaspoon of ground cayenne pepper to the spice mixture.

**¾ cup unsalted butter, cut into small pieces**
**2 cups sugar**
**2 large eggs, well beaten**
**½ cup dark honey**
**2 teaspoons white vinegar**
**1 teaspoon vanilla extract**
**3¾ cups all-purpose flour**
**1½ teaspoons baking soda**
**1 tablespoon powdered ginger**
**2 teaspoons ground cinnamon**
**½ teaspoon ground nutmeg**
**¼ teaspoon ground cloves**

- Preheat the oven to 350°F. Butter a large baking sheet.

- Beat the butter and sugar together in a large bowl until the mixture is light and fluffy. Stir in the beaten eggs, honey, vinegar, and vanilla, until all the ingredients are well combined.

- Whisk the flour, soda, ginger, cinnamon, nutmeg, and cloves together in another large bowl. Add to the butter-sugar mixture, stirring with a wooden spoon to form a smooth dough. Cover and refrigerate for 30 minutes.

- Pinch off pieces of the dough and roll them by hand into small balls, about ¾-inch in diameter. Place on the buttered baking sheet, 1½ inches apart. Bake on the middle rack of the oven, 1 baking sheet at a time, at 350°F. for about 15 minutes. The cookies will puff up at first, then flatten out as they bake. Use a spatula to transfer the cookies to a wire rack to cool completely.

- Roll the remaining dough into balls and bake, 1 sheet at a time. Store the cookies up to 1 month in a tightly covered container.

- Makes approximately 150 spicy cookies.

244

# Peanut Butter Cookies

*We were delighted when jars of peanut butter suddenly showed up in one store shortly before we left Russia in late 1994. That unexpected find inspired me to bake old-fashioned American peanut-butter cookies for our last Christmas party in Vladivostok. Our Russian guests instantly fell in love with this new taste treat—and were surprised how easy these cookies are to make.*

**½ cup (1 stick) unsalted butter, slightly softened at room temperature**
**1 cup sugar**
**1 cup chunky peanut butter**
**1 large egg, beaten**
**1 teaspoon vanilla extract**
**1½ cups all-purpose flour**
**½ teaspoon baking soda**
**½ teaspoon salt**

- Preheat the oven to 375°F. Lightly butter a baking sheet.

- Beat the butter and sugar together in a large bowl until light and fluffy. Add the peanut butter, beaten egg, and vanilla, stirring until well combined.

- Whisk the flour, soda, and salt together in another bowl. Add to the peanut butter mixture, stirring with a wooden spoon to make a stiff dough.

- Pinch off pieces of the dough, and roll them by hand into balls about 1-inch in diameter. Place the balls on a baking sheet, 1½ inches apart, and press each one almost flat with the tines of a fork, then press again from another angle to make a cross-hatch design on top.

- Bake at 375°F. for about 12 minutes. Don't let the cookies brown on the bottom, or they'll turn out tough instead of tender. Use a spatula to transfer them to a wire rack to cool completely. Store in a tightly covered container.

- Makes approximately 70 yummy cookies.

# Chapter 6
# Siberian Spring

## Welcoming Springtime

Spring comes late to Siberia. Even in the southern part where we lived, not far from the border with Mongolia, the first serious snows began in October and the temperature stayed well below freezing until the following March. That part of Siberia could still be pelted with snow flurries well into May, and in some years snow had fallen as late as June and as early as August. Russians joke that in Siberia winter lasts for 12 months and the rest is summer.

In Irkutsk, prudent local gardeners, fearing a late frost, always waited until mid-June to plant their hothouse seedlings outdoors. And Siberian mothers told their children in springtime, "Don't put up your boots yet, or it will snow again." Eventually, though, the onset of warmer weather slowly brought a regeneration of the landscape, with leafing trees, blooming flowers, and soft green grasses.

During March and April, however, the Siberian winter in Irkutsk melted into the mucky "mud season," the time of transition when the city slowly emerged from its mantle of snow like a sepia-toned photograph developing in a tray of chemicals. The roads turned to rivers of mud, which froze overnight, then thawed during the day into clogged arteries of squelching mire. The only signs of spring were the first few silvery catkins on the branches of pussy willows, the budding white birches, and the street cleaners, usually old women, hunched over their brushwood brooms like worn-out witches sweeping away the wiles of winter.

In the midst of this muddy season with its frequent snowfalls, Russians could feel in their bones the coming of spring, the certain knowledge that the days were getting longer even if the temperature outdoors still often dropped below freezing at night. Yet it wasn't until mid-May that spring suddenly burst forth from the liberated landscape, as wildflowers, wild garlic, and

*Sharon and Tom Hudgins in front of their university department in Irkutsk, early March 1994.*

fiddlehead ferns emerged from the earth, rivers ran free of ice, and cuckoos called from the bird cherry trees.

Siberians seemed to seize every opportunity to celebrate during that transitional time between winter and summer. At work our students and colleagues observed spring holidays such as Defenders of the Fatherland Day, a national military holiday on February 23, and International Women's Day on March 8, when they dressed up in their finest clothes and exchanged gifts of chocolates and flowers at school. And at home, we grabbed any excuse to party with our friends, cooking multi-course meals for each other as if to defy the lingering winter that still sometimes frosted our windows with ferns of ice.

In March, near the date of the spring equinox, we hosted an Italian-inspired "Welcome to Springtime" dinner for American colleagues living in our high-rise village. To celebrate the official changing of the seasons, we began with an *aperitvo* of Russian champagne, accompanied by an *aperitivo* of salmon caviar on triangles of buttered toast. Then we sat down to a first course of Italian *risotto al fungi*, made with dried, earthy-scented mushrooms that we'd carried all the way from Vladivostok, 2,500 miles by Trans-Siberian train. The main course was roasted 2-inch thick "T-bone whacks" and chunks of roasted, herbed potatoes, served with a ruby-red Bulgarian wine. Next came a green salad made with part of a precious head of Romaine lettuce (the first lettuce we'd seen since arriving in Russia seven months before), dressed with equally scarce Turkish olive oil and our own homemade wine vinegar. For dessert I whisked up bowls of boozy *zabaglione*, the frothy eggs spiked with potent Georgian brandy. And we ended that dinner with glasses of Hungarian sweet red wine, our only substitute for a good Port. I don't know which made us more giddy—the realization that the long Russian winter was finally fading or the eight bottles of wine the five of us polished off that festive evening.

## "Butter Week" Festival in Irkutsk

March was also the month of Maslenitsa, the seven-day "Butter Week" festival that immediately precedes the seven-week fasting period leading up to Easter. Maslenitsa itself is a secular festival, equivalent to Shrovetide in Britain, Fasching (Fasnacht, Fasnet) in Germanic lands, and Carnival or Mardi Gras in many Latin countries. All of these festivals date from the earlier pre-Christian era when people gathered together near the time of the vernal equinox to chase away the evil spirits of winter by lighting bonfires, making loud noises, burning sacrifices, and presenting offerings to the sun, to welcome the return of spring and celebrate the regeneration of life.

In the Christian era, Russian Maslenitsa evolved into a period of last-minute merrymaking before Lent began, a culinary orgy during which people devoured huge quantities of circular *bliny*—yeast-raised pancakes, golden rounds symbolizing the sun—drenched in melted butter or smothered with sour cream. The name of the festival comes from *maslo*, the Russian word for butter (and oil), referring to the richest food consumed during the week before the beginning of the Great Fast of Lent and Holy Week, when many Orthodox Christians abstain from eating meat, fish, eggs, animal fats, and dairy products for seven long, lean weeks.

In 1994, Maslenitsa occurred during the week ending on March 13, the last Sunday before Lent that year. Tom and I went downtown that day to see how the Siberians celebrated this spring festival, which had only recently been revived in Irkutsk after the collapse of communism in Russia. Despite the freezing weather, outdoor activities had been organized at several sites around the city. Municipal parks were decorated with images of the sun, shining

*Ice cream vendor at the Maslenitsa ("Butter Week") Festival in Irkutsk, mid-March 1994.*

from atop tall poles. Brightly painted plywood murals depicted sun symbols, birds and flowers, Carnival characters, and even religious themes. Handsome horses, with rows of brass bells on their harnesses, provided pony rides for the kids and pulled sleighs full of revelers. And in the winter playgrounds, children in puffy parkas and snow boots shrieked in delight as they whooshed down slides made of ice, while their parents watched from the sidelines, licking ice cream cones in the frigid air.

Throngs filled the public square in front of the sports stadium downtown, where the major events of Maslenitsa were being held. Hundreds of people in fur coats and fur hats milled around in front of an outdoor stage, their breath forming clouds of condensation in the frosty air. Folk dancers in colorful costumes from different parts of Eastern Siberia performed to live music, while jesters and clowns worked the crowd. And towering over the multitude was a giant effigy of Maslenitsa—the Old Witch of Winter—constructed of paper, cloth, and wood, her grotesque form covered with long red ribbons and straw streamers that rustled like whispered warnings in the chilly wind.

Opposite the stage was a long row of gaily decorated food stalls laden with treats. Children and adults wandered from one stall to the next, dividing their attention between the wares being hawked and the entertainment on stage, their ears tuned to the sounds of celebration, their noses turned toward the aroma of freshly cooked foods.

*Shashlyk (shish-kabob) vendor at the Maslenitsa ("Butter Week") Festival in Irkutsk, mid-March 1994.*

## Buttering Up the Sun

The iconic food of Maslenitsa is the sun-symbol *blin*, a round pancake with a somewhat spongy texture that's perfect for soaking up melted butter. Traditionally made of buckwheat flour leavened with yeast, *bliny* can also be made with wheat or rye flour, or even finely ground barley, oats, millet, or cornmeal, or a combination of flours. Many Russians believe the best are pure-buckwheat *bliny* whose batter has been allowed to rise three times before cooking. Although *bliny* appear to be a simple food, making perfectly shaped pancakes is a skill. A Russian proverb says, "The first *blin* is always a lump"—another way of saying "Practice makes perfect," or "If at first you don't succeed, try again."

At one stall a hefty woman in a karakul-lamb coat cooked *bliny* on a tiny, four-burner, gas stove that looked like it belonged in a museum of early twentieth-century kitchen appliances. Fresh from the skillet, the hot *bliny* were slathered with butter, sour cream, or jam, then handed to the customers on squares of hand-cut paper, while the vendor totaled up the bills on a wooden abacus. Nearby, aluminum trays full of extra *bliny*, folded into quarters, awaited reheating on the stove. Other trays held *bliny* rolled into cones and filled with sweetened pastry cream.

Women in bright red smocks and floral-printed shawls sold the most extensive array of baked goods I'd ever seen in Irkutsk: sweet and savory pastries, muffins and meringues, small rolls and giant cookies, chocolate layer cakes and a variety of yeast breads, all displayed on folding tables set up in the snow. At one stand a big nickel-plated samovar was decorated with *sushki*, crunchy little bread rings, threaded onto two heavy strings and draped over the samovar's shiny surface.

Other food stalls offered meat products traditionally prohibited by Russian Orthodox fasting guidelines even during Maslenitsa week: *shashlyki*, skewers of meat grilled over hot coals; small meatballs and large meat patties; savory buns with bits of fried bacon on top; cylinders of bread dough with a forcemeat filling. One vendor sold fancy boxes of commercially made candies. Another stood stoically beside crates of unwrapped ice cream cones, frozen solid in the frigid air. From the back of a truck, a woman handed out hot pizzas baked in a portable oven. And all this festive fare was washed down with cans of Coca-Cola for the kids, cups of hot tea for the women, and shots of vodka for the men.

At one side of the square a high pole had been erected, made from the slender trunk of a tall tree stripped of its branches and bark, sanded smooth, and slicked with grease. As the aromas of buttery *bliny* and grilled meat wafted through the air, we watched a succession of shirtless men and boys try to climb the pole and grab the prizes attached to the top: an electric samovar, a fringed paisley shawl, a mystery prize hidden inside a plastic bag. One of my Russian friends recalled seeing the same game at a Siberian village festival many years before, in which a live cock was tied to the top of the greased pole. The first climber who succeeded in grabbing the squawking fowl and carrying it back down was declared the winner.

At 2:30 in the afternoon on that snowy square, a big bonfire was set ablaze at the foot of the Maslenitsa witch, and five minutes later all that remained of the frightening figure was a pile of harmless ashes. All day the sky had been gray and cloudy, the weather cold and windy. But just after the effigy burned to the ground, the clouds suddenly broke, the sun came out, and the snow began to melt, as if right on celestial cue. That Maslenitsa Sunday, March 13, was the first day the temperature rose above freezing in Irkutsk that year. Maybe there really is some truth to those ancient Siberian superstitions.

## The Season of Lent

That spring my birthday in early April happened to be on the same Sunday that Easter was observed by Roman Catholic and Protestant churches around the world. But in 1994, the Russian Orthodox Church did not celebrate Easter until almost a month later, on May 1, because of the different ways these

*Traditional wooden house in Ulan-Ude, Eastern Siberia, decorated with the fancy fretwork called "wooden lace."*

# Easter: A Moveable Feast

When we lived in Siberia in 1994, Easter occurred on two different Sundays almost a month apart. That year, the date of Easter for Catholic and Protestant churches was April 3. But the Russian Orthodox Church, the dominant church in Russia, observed Easter on May 1. Why?

Unlike Christmas and New Year in most of the western world, Easter does not always occur on the same date every year. Moreover, different branches of the Christian faith use different calendars and different ways of determining the date of this important religious celebration. In some years they all celebrate Easter on the same Sunday, but in other years they observe Easter as much as five weeks apart, between late March and early May.

In all Christian churches, the date of Easter is initially determined as the first Sunday following the first full moon occurring on, or after, the spring equinox. So Easter always depends on the phases of the moon, the dates of which vary from month to month and from year to year. Hence, the date of Easter always varies, too.

Catholic and Protestant churches calculate the date of Easter on the Gregorian calendar, which is also the calendar used by most of the secular world. But many Eastern Orthodox churches use the older Julian calendar, which is 13 days behind the Gregorian calendar. In addition, many Eastern Orthodox churches have another criterion for figuring the date of Easter. When the initial calculated date for Easter Sunday on the Julian calendar also falls on the first Sunday during the Jewish spring festival of Passover, those Eastern Orthodox churches do not observe Easter until the following Sunday.

Since the Jewish calendar, the Julian calendar, and the Gregorian calendar all differ in the ways they are calculated, in some years Passover might occur at the same time as Easter, but in other years on a different date. Because of all these variables, someone looking at the Gregorian calendar in 2016 would see that Easter was celebrated by Catholics and Protestants on March 27 and by Russian Orthodox on May 1.

branches of the Christian religion determine the date of Easter, which varies from year to year on their church calendars. So, from one perspective, my birthday was on Easter; from another, it occurred during Lent.

Ignoring the Russian superstition that you shouldn't tempt Fate by celebrating someone's birthday ahead of time, two of our American colleagues gave a party for me on the evening before I officially turned a year older. Dessert that night was rich chocolate pound cake that our host had baked from a recipe e-mailed to him that day from his sister in Massachusetts. (The globe-shrinking instantaneity of e-mail was still a great novelty to us back then.) My only birthday candle was a single utility candle stuck into the cake—the same kind we used for light when the electricity was cut off. And the simple gifts seemed to recall an earlier era, before mass-produced consumer goods flooded the market: a bunch of budding pussy willow branches from our hosts; a jar of homemade wild raspberry jam and a bottle of rose-hips extract from two of our Russian students; an amber necklace and amber earrings from Tom.

I woke that Easter morning to a landscape covered with a thick layer of freshly fallen snow—an appropriate Siberian backdrop for the birthday dinner-for-two that Tom cooked for us that evening: champagne for an *apéritif*, followed by an assortment of cold *zakuski* with white wine; Caucasian-style stuffed cabbage rolls, flavored with walnuts, raisins, and dried apricots; roasted potato chunks tossed with Turkish olive oil, dried rosemary, and thyme; a small green salad made from the last few remaining leaves of our single head of lettuce; and a sinfully sweet dark chocolate cake shaped like a hedgehog and decorated with spiky "quills" of rich chocolate frosting, which Tom had bought at the best bakery in Irkutsk. (He called it my "KGB Hedgehog Cake" because the bakery was located next to the offices of the notorious state security organization there.) To top off the celebration, we opened a gift that Tom had purchased especially for the occasion: a bottle of Chateau La Fleur Fourcadet 1991 Bordeaux Superieur—a French wine as rare as lettuce in the middle of Siberia.

During that spring in Irkutsk, we took advantage of the widely differing dates of "Western" Easter and Orthodox Easter to stretch out our own Easter-season activities over the months of March and April and even into early May. On that side of the world I missed the little cakes shaped like lambs that I'd always baked during Lent in Germany, but none of the stores in Irkutsk sold the special three-dimensional cake molds needed for making them. I also fondly remembered all the "egg trees" we'd decorated

254

## Fasting Before Easter

In the Russian Orthodox Church, the Great Fast of Lent and Holy Week is the longest and strictest of the year, covering a period of seven weeks from the Monday after Maslenitsa through Holy Saturday, the day before Easter. During that time, devout believers abstain from eating meat and meat products (such as lard), eggs, dairy products, fish, some kinds of vegetable oil, and alcoholic beverages—although shellfish are still permitted, as are wine and oil on most weekends, and fish on certain feast days, too, as a fore-taste of the Resurrection.

Fasting is voluntary, a matter of individual choice. In combination with meditation and prayer, fasting is undertaken by the believer as a way to become spiritually closer to God. In pre-Christian times, however, fasting was probably a practical necessity, a way to ration the dwindling food supply over the last cold weeks of winter before the return of spring, with its warmer weather and its promise of abundant plants and animals once again.

each year in Europe—bunches of pussy willow branches arrayed in a tall crystal vase and hung with dozens of colorful hand-painted eggs, each one an intricate work of folk art. Later, on a return visit to Irkutsk in 2008, I saw one of these egg trees in a recently re-opened historic Orthodox church there. But the only seasonal items in Irkutsk in 1994 were a few Russian Easter breads in some of the bakeries; several Easter postcards that were reproductions of earlier, pre-Soviet paintings; and some plastic shopping bags (rarities themselves!) printed with a picture of three Easter eggs in a shallow basket, surrounded by pussy willow branches and delicate flowers, with the Cyrillic letters "XB" (for "*Khristos voskrese*"—"Christ is risen") at the bottom of the scene.

One Saturday I spent the day dyeing Easter eggs to decorate our apartment and give to friends. As usual in Siberia, I had to improvise with whatever materials I could find. I tied onion skins onto some of the eggs and wrapped strands of jute, colored cotton yarn, and American dental floss around the others. Then I immersed the eggs in separate dye baths made of chopped beets, red cabbage, and walnut shells boiled in water with vinegar and salt added as mordants, and a touch of vodka thrown in for good measure. By the end of the day, I had bowls full of beautiful eggs, in colors ranging from shades of brown to rose pink to bright red, with abstract designs imprinted on them from the onion skins and yarn.

I gave some of those Easter eggs to our Russian and American colleagues, and took others to our Russian neighbor next door. The little boy who answered the door was delighted at the unexpected gift, smiling broadly and saying over and over, "*Spasibo! Spasibo!*" ("Thank you! Thank you!") A few minutes later, his grandmother knocked on our door and handed me two large duck eggs dyed a subtle beige color, with designs like rice grains speckling the entire surface of the shells. I still haven't figured out how she got her Easter eggs to look like that.

During Lent in Irkutsk that spring, we attended an Orthodox Palm Sunday service at the Znamensky Convent church, one of the surviving treasures of eighteenth-century ecclesiastical architecture in Eastern Siberia. Hidden behind the church's exterior of whitewashed stone was an ornate interior decorated by master woodcarvers, icon painters, and fresco artists. And in the small tree-shaded churchyard enclosed within the convent's stone walls lay the graves of several Russian historical figures, including a number of "Decembrists," aristocrats from European Russia who were sentenced to prison and exile in Siberia after leading an uprising against the tsar in December of 1825—and who later died in that faraway land.

Before the church service began, a group of women holding pussy willow branches gathered in a side chapel where a priest blessed the branches, sprinkling them with holy water. As one of the earliest plants to bud in the Siberian spring, the pussy willow is a symbol of the Easter season in many northern countries, supplanting the palm fronds of warmer climes, traditionally taken to church to be blessed on Palm Sunday. On one wall of the Znamensky church, lighted candles beneath an icon illuminated a few jam jars filled with raw rice, the grains symbolizing death and resurrection, the deceased rising again like planted seeds. After the service was over, snowflakes fluttered around us as we walked through the quiet churchyard, where small offerings had been left on the tombstones of three Decembrist children: a cracker, a slice of cake, some pieces of wrapped candy, an apple, a few flowers, a small plastic toy.

# A Spanish Meal in Siberia

On the night before that Orthodox Palm Sunday, we hosted a large dinner party at our apartment for 11 Russian and American colleagues from the university in Irkutsk. Wanting to serve a meal that none of our guests was likely to have eaten before, we decided on a menu featuring a variety of regional dishes from Spain. And for dessert I planned to make *paskha*, a Russian Easter specialty, in honor of the season.

As the guests arrived that evening, I presented each of them with two Easter postcards, reproductions of old paintings of traditional Russian Easter foods. On the back of one postcard I'd written the dinner menu in Spanish. On the back of the other was the recipe for the special holiday dessert.

We welcomed our guests with glasses of our old stand-by *apéritif*, Russian dry champagne. Then we gathered at the table for a first course of hot and cold Spanish *tapas*, made with ingredients we'd been able to find after many days of shopping in Irkutsk: slices of Spanish chorizo sausage and Russian aged cheese; mushrooms sautéed with ham in olive oil; Galician-style squid

## Paskha or Paska? A Confusion of Names

In Russian, *paskha* is the word for Easter; in Ukrainian, the word is spelled *paska*. For Russians, *paskha* is also the name of a special cheese dessert made only for Easter, always accompanied by the Russian Easter bread *kulich*, a tall, cylindrical, yeast-raised, sweet bread decorated with white icing. For Ukrainians, however, *paska* is the name of their own Easter bread, a wide, round, yeast-raised loaf, somewhat like an Italian *panettone*, decorated on top with religious and seasonal symbols made of bread dough. To muddle matters further, some Ukrainians also make an "Easter cheese *paska*" similar to the Russian *paskha*, as well as a tall, cylindrical Easter bread like Russian *kulich*, which the Ukrainians call "Easter *babka*." That's why there is sometimes confusion about these culinary terms among ethnic Russians, ethnic Ukrainians, and their descendants, wherever they live in the world.

seasoned with paprika, onions, and sweet red peppers; poached white fish with lemon and cilantro; a pseudo-*Romesco* sauce richly flavored with *chipotle* peppers we'd brought from Texas; and garlicky *ensaladilla rusa*, the Spanish version of Russian potato salad—all accompanied by Bulgarian dry white wine and plenty of yeasty flatbread, much like the flatbreads made in eastern Spain.

After we'd eaten our fill of these *tapas*, I ladled out bowls of cold Andalusian *gazpacho*, showing our guests how to sprinkle the top of their soup with fried croutons and finely chopped bell peppers, cucumbers, and onions. Although Russian cuisine includes a number of cold soups made from fruits and vegetables, that tomato-based Spanish *gazpacho* was a revelation to all the Russians at the table. They liked it so much that several of them even asked, rather sheepishly, for a second helping—and for the recipe, too.

Our main course was Catalan-style *pollo con vino tinto*—chicken leg quarters braised in red wine with onions, garlic, mushrooms, and slivers of ham—accompanied by Valencian-style rice studded with raisins, walnuts, and dried apricots. With this course we served red-wine sangria, redolent of oranges and lemons steeped in brandy. That sangria turned out to be a special treat for the Siberians, who all said they'd never tasted anything like it before. Despite my warning that this Spanish drink packed an unexpected alcoholic punch belied by its fruity taste, the Russians continued drinking glass after glass with seemingly little effect. Compared to the large quantities of vodka that many Russians routinely consume, my potent Spanish sangria must have seemed like nothing stronger than a cool fruit juice drink that grandmother would serve to the kids.

Dessert was the biggest surprise of all. The day before, I'd made a Russian Easter *paskha*, a kind of uncooked cheesecake chock full of ingredients forbidden during Lent: *tvorog* (fresh white cheese), butter, eggs, and sour cream, the rich mixture traditionally shaped in a special carved wooden *paskha* mold or just in a flower pot. (Lacking both, I had to use a plastic bucket with holes punched in the bottom.) On the night of the party, I'd carefully unmolded the chilled *paskha* and decorated it with dark raisins, golden sultanas, and toasted almonds, forming flowers on one side and the Cyrillic letters "XB" on the other.

To a chorus of delighted exclamations from all the guests, I placed the *paskha* in the center of the table for everyone to see before I cut it into servings. But it was my turn to be surprised. None of the Russians knew what it was.

# Russian Easter Kulich

The tall, cylindrical, Russian Easter *kulich*, with its puffy round top spread with white icing that drizzles down the sides, is unmistakably phallic-looking. Some people say that the shape of a *kulich* represents the domes of a Russian Orthodox church, or the hat of a Russian Orthodox priest, or the mushrooms that Russians so love to eat. But the form is actually a not-too-subtle visual reference to the regeneration of life every spring. (Certain Easter breads in France and Italy have this same suggestive shape, too.)

In earlier times, large quantities of Easter *kulichi* were baked at home in tall round pans reserved only for that use once a year. Women competed with their friends and relatives to make the biggest, tallest, lightest, and puffiest *kulichi* (surely a hint about the manliness of their husbands, too). Today, many Russians just buy an Easter *kulich* at their local bakery.

*Kulichi* traditionally contain plenty of eggs, another symbol of the regeneration of life. Since eggs were among the foods proscribed during the seven-week fasting period before Easter, their generous use in this cake-like bread is a way of celebrating the end of that fast. One domestic recipe published in 1924 calls for 10 pounds of flour and 100 egg yolks, with the dough kneaded by hand for one and a half hours.

In the past, several superstitions surrounded the making of these *kulichi*: The dough was often mixed and kneaded on Good Friday, and girls in the family stayed up all night with it, singing hymns while it was rising. The dough had to rise three times—not only to produce a light, tender texture, but also as a symbolic reference to the Holy Trinity. It was considered bad luck if the dough did not rise properly or if the loaves fell during baking. So the women said a prayer and crossed themselves before putting the *kulichi* into the oven, and forbade any loud noises or disturbances in the house that might cause the *kulichi* to collapse. When the *kulichi* came out of the oven and then out of their pans, some cooks gently placed the breads on their sides, atop a down pillow covered with a kitchen cloth, and rotated the *kulichi* occasionally while they cooled, to keep them from deflating.

When I explained that *paskha* was a traditional Russian Easter dessert, dating back centuries into Russian history, they all looked at me with blank faces. I went on to say that *paskha* is normally served with *kulich*—a tall, cylindrical, saffron-scented yeast bread studded with raisins, nuts, and candied fruit peel, with white icing drizzled over its domelike top. But only three of the Russians were even vaguely aware of what a *kulich* was, although several bakeries in Irkutsk were selling *kulichi* that spring.

Sizing up the situation, I decided that it would be impolite to mention that I'd been making *paskha* and *kulich* at Easter for many years, in the United States and Europe. But as I explained to our guests the significance of these traditional Easter desserts, I couldn't help noting to myself the irony of an American from Texas introducing these sophisticated, highly educated Russians to the Easter foods that had once been well known to their Christian ancestors. It would be like a Russian living in America 100 years from now, explaining Thanksgiving turkey or Christmas fruitcake to her American dinner guests.

I spooned the creamy *paskha* into individual dessert bowls and, continuing the Iberian theme, surrounded each portion with a pool of Spanish orange custard sauce, which paired well with the sweetened white cheese, despite that very un-Russian combination. And three hours after sitting down to that Spanish dinner, we concluded the meal with glasses of Osborne Veterano Spanish brandy—a taste that suddenly brought back my own memories of balmy spring nights in southern Spain, perfumed with the scent of jasmine and serenaded by the sweet song of nightingales.

## Easter Blessings

*Paskha*, *kulich*, and dyed eggs are such an important part of the Easter feast that many people take them to the church to be blessed by the priest on Holy Saturday. Many of the eggs are dyed red, to symbolize Christ's blood. Sometimes other foods are brought for blessing, too—bread, salt, horseradish, sausages, hams—all carried to the church in a basket, covered with a special cloth ornately hand-embroidered with Easter symbols.

# A Siberian Easter Feast

For Orthodox Easter Sunday our Russian colleagues Gennadi and Nataliya invited us and three other American professors to an Easter dinner at their apartment in Irkutsk. The night before, we had attended the magnificent Divine Liturgy at the Znamensky Convent church, a service lasting several hours, culminating at midnight with the joyous announcement of Christ's resurrection. Afterward, at the homes of millions of believers throughout Russia, no expense was spared for the special Easter meal that broke the long Lenten fast—actually or only symbolically—a religious holiday feast rivaled only by the secular New Year's dinner celebrated by Russians of all beliefs.

We arrived at Gennadi and Nataliya's apartment at one o'clock in the afternoon, bearing gifts of vodka and home-dyed Easter eggs. Although they lived in a typical gray, pre-fab concrete, Soviet-era high-rise building, the interior of their apartment was so strikingly stylish that that it looked more like an apartment in Scandinavia than anything I'd ever seen in Siberia. Boldly colored modern paintings hung on the white walls, some of them painted by Gennadi himself. The tiny living room, with its picture window overlooking the partially frozen Angara River, was almost filled by a divan and matching chair covered in a black-and-white zebra-striped fabric. A black, upright, Jugendstil-era Beckstein piano occupied one end of the room. And the remaining space was taken up by two tables pushed together to accommodate the eight of us gathered for the Easter feast.

Never had I seen a Russian dinner table set so beautifully. Atop dainty white cloths draped over the tables were pretty pink-and-silver Japanese porcelain plates, silver-plated flatware, pastel paper napkins, handmade place cards, and more stemmed wine glasses than I'd ever seen in a Russian home: heavy cut-crystal sherry glasses from Eastern Europe, modern balloon-shaped red-wine glasses, and black-stemmed champagne flutes from France. (Nataliya was the only Russian I knew who served champagne in flutes.) A crystal vase of silk daffodils graced the center of the table—the first time I'd seen any flowers, real or silk, on a dinner table in a Russian home. And a basket of five hand-painted, lacquered wooden eggs—a gift for each guest—completed the artistic ensemble.

Competing for space on that elegant Easter table were bottles of Russian champagne, imported white wine, and varieties of vodka, along with the

# An Orthodox Easter in Irkutsk

The most important festival on the Christian religious calendar, Easter is celebrated at Orthodox churches all over Russia with a magnificent Divine Liturgy lasting several hours, beginning on Holy Saturday evening and culminating at midnight with the annual revelation of Christ's resurrection.

In 1994 we attended our first Russian Easter service at the Znamensky Convent Church in Irkutsk. As midnight approached, a feeling of expectancy rippled through the church's crowded nave and among the overflow mass of people assembled outside in the churchyard. At the stroke of twelve, in a re-enactment of the Gospel story, the Metropolitan of Irkutsk approached the coffin that had been placed on a bier in front of the iconostasis. Raising the shroud on the bier, he saw that Christ was no longer in the tomb. Holding a large white candle in his hand, the high priest lighted his own candle from one burning on the altar, then passed the flame to the worshipers standing nearest him, each also holding a single white taper. They, in turn, passed the flame to others with unlit candles, and so on, throughout the church and into the crowd gathered in the dark outside.

As hundreds of candles flickered to life, the Metropolitan began the Procession of the Cross, the most dramatic part of the Easter service. Holding an ornate golden cross in front of him, the high priest was followed by several other priests, deacons, and acolytes, carrying candles, crosses, and beautiful banners richly embroidered with silver and gold. The priestly procession, followed by the crowd of believers, set off to circle the church in a symbolic search for the vanished body of Christ. After finding no trace of Jesus, the Metropolitan mounted the steps of the church and proclaimed to the multitude, *"Khristos voskrese!"* ("Christ is risen!")— to which the faithful responded, *"Voistinu voskrese!"* ("Truly, He is risen!") Bells pealed from the steeple as people in the crowd turned to those standing next to them and repeated the jubilant greeting and response, then kissed each other three times on the cheeks, the triple kiss of the Holy Trinity. The priests continued to chant and swing their censers, sending clouds of incense floating over the crowd, as church bells chimed throughout the city.

A sea of tiny candle flames flickered in the light breeze, as we followed the procession of priests back into the church. Joyful singing filled the air. Later, as we carried our own lighted candles out of the church and across the yard, they stayed lit until we passed through the arched gate in the convent walls—a good omen! Then we blew out the flames and headed home in the dark.

# The Russian Easter Table

Paintings from pre-Soviet Russia depict the traditional Russian Easter feast as a lavish buffet set on a table covered with a white cloth: bottles of vodka, wine, and brandy; an extensive array of *zakuski* (caviar, pickled mushrooms, spicy sausages, smoked fish, and much more); three kinds of roasted meats, symbolizing the Holy Trinity (ham in rye-bread crust, suckling pig, spring lamb, or sometimes a turkey or duck); and a variety of breads and confections, including the essential *paskha* and *kulich*. The table is decorated with flowers and brightly colored eggs, and in the center is a little lamb molded out of butter, holding a piece of fresh greenery in its mouth.

The feast at home begins soon after the Easter midnight church service, and in some households continues until Sunday evening or as long as there is still food on the table. Before the anti-religious Soviet era, the Russian Easter buffet table remained set for at least three days, even up to a week, constantly being replenished as guests arrived to taste Aunt Natasha's *kulich* or cousin Tamara's *paskha*. Today, the feasting traditions are more in tune with modern times—less extensive and long-lasting, but still a special way to celebrate the coming of spring, as well as Christ's resurrection.

first-course *zakuski*. Gennadi began the festive midday meal with a formal champagne toast, after which we slowly drank the bubbly brew on empty stomachs as we savored the sunshine streaming through the picture window, warming our skin while the wine worked its wonders within. Next came sherry glasses topped up with local Baikalskaya vodka, the smoothest vodka I'd ever drunk. Already giddy from those two potent *apéritifs*, none of us refused a glass of imported lemon-flavored vodka, which we all proclaimed to be the best fruit-flavored vodka we'd ever tasted.

By that time, Nataliya was insisting that we eat some of the *zakuski* set out on the table: a large salmon, baked whole and served cold, swimming on a red sea of Balkan *lecho* (similar to French *ratatouille*); Baltic "Herring in a Coat," its pinkish color especially appropriate for springtime; and a platter piled with *lobiani*, small rounds of flatbread topped with a mixture of mushrooms, red kidney beans, and thick walnut sauce—Gennadi's version of this Georgian specialty and one of the most delectable *zakuski* I ate during my entire time in Irkutsk.

Soon after we began nibbling on those *hors d'oeuvres*, Gennadi and Nataliya suggested that we all drink a round of Bloody Marys, "Russian-style." Gennadi filled each balloon glass halfway with tomato juice, sprinkled in some salt and pepper, then placed a dinner knife at a 45-degree angle into the glass and slowly poured vodka down the knife blade until the clear liquor floated in a half-inch layer on top of the tomato juice. We all sipped this concoction as if it were another of the cold foods among the *zakuski* spread, as we complimented our hosts on their culinary accomplishments.

Perhaps we were too effusive in our praise, though, because when we finished those potent cocktails, Gennadi insisted that—purely for purposes of comparison—we drink another round of Bloody Marys, this time "Maryland-style." None of the five Americans at the table knew what he was talking about. But who were we to refuse balloon glasses half filled with a mixture of vodka and tomato juice, with chopped fresh cilantro on top? (*Cilantro?* The style in *Maryland?*) By that point, none of us was sober enough to dispute Gennadi's assertion that these gargantuan cocktails had to be drunk in one draw, Russian-style. Once again Russian reality had outpaced my expectations. Never had I envisioned starting an Easter dinner chug-a-lugging cilantro-flavored Bloody Marys in Siberia.

Tom and I knew that all those delicious dishes on the table were merely a prelude to the main course. But our American colleagues—who'd never been invited to a Russian home for such a feast—ate and drank their fill of all the *zakuski*, with no notion of what was to come next. So they were completely surprised when Nataliya brought out the main course: German-style stuffed-beef rolls (*Rinderrouladen*), accompanied somewhat incongruously by commercial shrimp chips from Vietnam and crunchy potato sticks, like crinkle-cut French fries, from Korea. As that multi-course meal progressed, I reflected that it might well prefigure the urban Siberian cuisine of the future: a fusion of East and West, Asia and Europe, the old and the new, as forgotten recipes were resurrected, as new foods were imported into Russia, and as more Russians became acquainted with the cooking of other countries through travel, cookbooks, culinary magazines, and television shows. (And indeed my prediction was correct, as I learned on several trips to Siberia more than a decade later.)

For the dessert course, Nataliya completely changed the table setting, once again demonstrating her flair for design. Modern black, white, and gold porcelain chargers supported dessert plates dished up with molded pink gelatin topped with banana slices and slabs of rich vanilla ice cream. (For a moment I felt as if I'd been transported back to the America of my childhood, when such brightly colored gelatin desserts were standard fare at school cafeterias and church socials.) On a little serving cart in the corner, a traditional Ukrainian Easter bread sat on a cake plate lined with bright green paper "grass" and surrounded by dyed Easter eggs. Three small candles stuck into the bread symbolized the Holy Trinity, and one large candle in the center signified the Resurrection. As if all this bounty were not sufficient for the celebration of Easter, Nataliya also passed around three desserts baked by Gennadi's mother: a traditional Russian Easter *kulich*, crowned with raspberries; light, fluffy meringue cookies, made with the many egg whites left over from her *kulich* recipe; and a large, rectangular, richly flavored blackberry pie with lattice-work pastry on top.

Gennadi offered us snifters of precious Remy Martin cognac to complete the meal. But none of us was willing to waste such a treasure on our over-loaded palates. So, six hours after we'd arrived for that midday repast, we all sat around the table and finished off the remaining champagne and white wine, as the sky darkened outside. And, as a fitting finale to that Russian Easter feast, Nataliya lighted the candles in the brass sconces on the piano, and Yuliya, their teenage daughter, entertained us by playing selections from Borodin and Bach, ending with a rousing rendition of a Scott Joplin rag.

# Spanish Sangria

*In Europe we always spiked our* sangria *with Spanish sherry brandy and French Cointreau (orange liqueur). Sometimes we also "lightened" it with sparkling water, for sipping in the heat of summer. But since we didn't have any orange liqueur or sparkling water in Siberia, we just perked it up with bottled orange juice instead. You can make* sangria *with whatever wine you have on hand, red or white—just an ordinary table wine, nothing fancy. This recipe gives you several options.*

**2 large oranges, unpeeled, thinly sliced crosswise, and seeds removed**
**1 large lemon, unpeeled, thinly sliced crosswise, and seeds removed**
**½ cup brandy**
**½ cup orange liqueur ***
**2 bottles (.75 liter each) red or white wine**
**½ to 1 cup sugar**
**1 quart sparkling water, chilled (optional)**

***Or 4 cups orange juice**

- Stir together the orange and lemon slices, brandy, and orange liqueur in a 4-quart jar. Cover and refrigerate at least 4 hours, preferably 12 hours.

- Two or three hours before serving, add the wine (and orange juice, if you didn't use orange liqueur) to the jar. Add ½ to 1 cup of sugar (depending on how sweet you want it), stirring until the sugar is completely dissolved. Cover and refrigerate until serving time.

- Just before serving, add the sparkling water if you want a lighter sangria. Serve the sangria over ice cubes in large tumblers or big wine glasses.

- Makes 10 to 16 servings, depending whether you used orange juice, and/or sparkling water.

# Spanish Squid with Red Peppers

*This is our own twist on a popular Spanish* tapa *from the region of Galicia, where it's made with sliced octopus. In Siberia we used commercially canned calamari and Bulgarian bottled red peppers. In the Russian Far East we bought fresh whole squid from a local fisherman, who kept them cool by submerging them in a primitive water-well dug in the ground. In Texas we've found that frozen squid works just fine in this recipe—and you don't have to clean them yourself.*

**2 tablespoons olive oil**
**1 medium-large onion, quartered lengthwise and thinly sliced lengthwise**
**3 large garlic cloves, thinly sliced**
**2 teaspoons Spanish smoked mild paprika**
**½ teaspoon hot paprika (optional)**
**1 pound frozen squid or calamari rings (not breaded), thawed and cut on a
    slight diagonal into 2-inch-long strips**
**16-ounce jar of roasted red bell peppers, drained and sliced into ¼-inch-
    wide strips (about 2 cups, after slicing)**
**1 tablespoon fresh lemon juice**

**Garnish**

**Coarse salt**

**\*If using whole squid, slice them crosswise into rings about ⅓-inch wide,
then cut the rings into 2-inch-long strips.**

- Heat the oil in a large (12-inch) skillet and sauté the onion over medium-high heat until it begins to soften. Add the garlic and continue sautéing until the onion is translucent.

- Reduce the heat to medium. Sprinkle the mild (and optional hot) paprika over the onion, and cook, stirring constantly, for 30 seconds. Immediately stir in the squid, pepper strips, and lemon juice. Mix well, cover, and cook for 10 minutes, stirring once or twice during that time.

- Refrigerate until needed, but serve at room temperature, garnished with coarse salt and accompanied by plenty of good country-style white bread to soak up the delicious juice.

- Makes 4 to 6 servings as an appetizer.

# Spanish Mushrooms with Ham

*This is a popular dish in Spain, where larger portions are served as an appetizer in restaurants and smaller ones as a* tapa *at many bars throughout the country. We often included it among the array of appetizers at our Spanish meals in Russia because mushrooms were so plentiful there.*

1½ **pounds fresh mushrooms (champignons, cremini, or porcini), washed and sliced lengthwise ¼-inch thick**
4 **large garlic cloves, thinly sliced**
¼ **cup olive oil**
2 **teaspoons freshly ground black pepper**
1 **teaspoon salt**
½ **cup cooked ham, measured after slicing into thin strips 2 inches long (julienned)**
2 **tablespoons brandy (Spanish is best)**

▶ **TIP:** Use an egg slicer to cut the mushrooms quickly.

- Combine the mushrooms, garlic, olive oil, pepper, and salt in a large (12-inch) skillet. Cook over medium heat, stirring frequently, until the mushrooms begin to soften (about 10 minutes). Stir in the ham and brandy, and cook 5 minutes longer.

- Use a slotted spoon to transfer the mushroom mixture to a bowl. (Save the pan juices—see **WASTE NOT**, below.) Cover the bowl and let the mushrooms sit at room temperature for 30 minutes, for the flavors to develop. Serve then, or refrigerate until needed, but serve warm or at room temperature.

- Makes 6 servings as a small appetizer or 4 servings as a side dish.

▶ **WASTE NOT:** Use the flavorful pan juices for cooking rice or in making soups or stews.

# Spanish Gazpacho

*Gazpacho was originally a simple peasant dish, consisting only of bread, garlic, salt, vinegar, oil, and water, made by Spanish farm workers for their midday meal in the fields. After Spanish explorers brought tomatoes and peppers from Central and South America to Spain 500 years ago, those ingredients gradually came to be used in Spanish cooking, including this red gazpacho (one of many kinds and colors of gazpachos made in Spain). This is my own favorite recipe for classic tomato-based gazpacho, which I've eaten many times in Spain— and made in Russia, too.*

6 medium-size ripe red tomatoes, coarsely chopped*
1 large onion, coarsely chopped
2 medium cucumbers, peeled, seeded, and chopped
1 green bell pepper, seeded and coarsely chopped
1 red bell pepper, seeded and coarsely chopped
3 large garlic cloves, squeezed through a garlic press
1 cup coarsely crumbled bread (country-style white bread, crust removed)
2 tablespoons tomato paste
3 cups tomato juice
6 tablespoons olive oil
¼ cup red wine vinegar
1 tablespoon Spanish sweet (mild) paprika
1 to 2 teaspoons salt
⅛ teaspoon ground cumin

## Garnishes

See below

*If fresh tomatoes aren't available, use best-quality canned tomatoes, draining off the juice to use later in the recipe.

- Combine the tomatoes, onion, cucumbers, peppers, garlic, and crumbled bread in a very large bowl, tossing them all together to mix. Purée these ingredients, 3 cups at a time, in a blender. After each batch is thoroughly puréed, pour it into another large bowl.

- In a separate bowl, whisk the tomato paste into the tomato juice until the paste is completely dissolved. Whisk in the olive oil, wine vinegar, paprika, 1 teaspoon salt, and cumin. Add this to the puréed vegetables, whisking well until all the ingredients are thoroughly combined. Cover and refrigerate for several hours, or overnight, before serving. Taste and add more salt if needed.

• Serve the chilled gazpacho in individual soup bowls. Pass around small bowls of various garnishes (see below) for each diner to sprinkle on top of the gazpacho. Offer a selection of at least 4 garnishes.

• Makes 8 servings.

▶ **Gazpacho Garnishes:** Separate bowls of ½ cup (or more) of *each* of these vegetables, diced into ¼-inch pieces: onion (or spring onions sliced into thin rings), green bell pepper, red bell pepper, yellow bell pepper, peeled cucumber; ¼ cup chopped parsley; ¼ cup chopped chives; fried croutons (recipe follows).

▶ **Fried Croutons:** Trim the crusts off 4 or 5 slices of country-style, chewy-textured white bread, and cut the bread into small cubes (about 2 cups of cubes). Heat ¼ cup olive oil in a small skillet, and fry the bread cubes until they are crisp but not brown. Drain on paper towels before serving.

# Mushroom Risotto

*In Irkutsk we made this classic Italian rice dish with dried mushrooms that we'd brought with us on the train from Vladivostok, and garnished it with local Siberian pine nuts. In Italy* risotti *are served before the main (meat) course of a meal. But the meaty mushrooms in this richly flavored* risotto *make it an excellent main course, too, especially when accompanied by a green salad and a good white wine. Leftovers (if there are any!) can be made into rice croquettes or added to omelets.*

▶ **NOTE:** The Italians flavor this *risotto* with grated Parmesan cheese, but in Russia we had to use whatever hard cheese we could find. Shredded Jarlsberg or Gruyère cheese works well in this recipe, too.

1 ounce dried porcini mushrooms (sliced or whole)
2 cups chicken stock
3 tablespoons olive oil
4 tablespoons unsalted butter (divided use)
1 medium onion, finely chopped
2 large garlic cloves, minced
2 cups raw medium-grain rice (such as Italian Arborio)
½ cup white wine
¼ cup grated firm yellow cheese
Salt
Freshly ground black pepper

Garnish

½ cup (or more) grated yellow cheese
⅓ cup toasted pine nuts*

*Toast the pine nuts in advance, in a preheated 325°F. oven for about 8 minutes.

- Soak the dried mushrooms in 3 cups of room-temperature water in a large bowl for 30 minutes (for sliced mushrooms) to 1 hour (for whole mushrooms). Use a smaller bowl placed on top to keep the mushrooms submerged. Drain the rehydrated mushrooms, straining the water through a sieve lined with a clean kitchen towel or a coffee filter into another bowl. Reserve the mushroom liquid, and coarsely chop the mushrooms.

- Measure the volume of mushroom liquid. Combine with 2 cups of chicken stock plus enough water to make a total of 6 cups of liquid. Pour this into small saucepan, bring to a simmer over medium heat, and keep it simmering while you cook the rice.

- Heat the oil and 2 tablespoons of butter together in a heavy 3-quart pan over medium-high heat. Sauté the onion and garlic until the onion is golden. Add the rice and stir constantly for 2 to 3 minutes, until all the rice grains are well coated with cooking fat. Pour in the white wine and stir constantly until all the liquid has been absorbed.

- Ladle ½ cup of the simmering liquid into the rice. Stir gently and constantly with a large wooden spoon until all the liquid has been absorbed (about 2 to 3 minutes). Keep repeating this process—adding ½ cup of hot stock and cooking until all of it is absorbed. After the rice has been cooking like this for about 15 minutes, add the mushrooms and ¾ teaspoon salt. Then continue stirring in the rest of the liquid, ½ cup at a time. Total cooking time for the rice: about 25 to 35 minutes after you began ladling in the liquid. (The cooked rice should be thick and creamy, like a rice pudding.)

- Turn off the heat and stir in ¼ cup shredded cheese and the remaining 2 tablespoons butter. Taste and add more salt, if desired. Grind a good amount of black pepper over the risotto and stir gently.

- Serve hot in shallow soup bowls. Garnish each serving with shredded cheese and a sprinkling of toasted pine nuts.

- Makes 4 large (main course) or 6 smaller (first-course) servings.

# Valencian-Style Rice

*This recipe was inspired by the* arroces *(rice dishes) of Valencia, a region of eastern Spain whose cuisine was greatly influenced by the Muslims of Arab and Berber descent who lived there for centuries. It's a sweet-savory side dish that pairs well with braised, roasted, or grilled meats. You can use it as a stuffing for many kinds of vegetables, too, including cabbages, peppers, and zucchini. In Russia we liked to serve this fruity, nutty rice as an accompaniment to* **Spanish Chicken in Red Wine** *(recipe, page 273).*

½ cup coarsely chopped toasted walnuts*
½ cup chopped dried apricots (cut into pieces the size of raisins)
½ cup dark or golden raisins (or a combination of both)
3 tablespoons olive oil
1 large onion, finely chopped
2 large garlic cloves, minced
1½ cups raw medium-grain rice
2 teaspoons salt
1 teaspoon Spanish smoked mild paprika
3 cups chicken stock**
3 tablespoons lemon juice

*Toasted in a preheated 350°F. oven for 8 to 10 minutes.
**For a sweeter version, use 2 cups chicken stock and 1 cup orange juice.

- Toss the walnuts, apricots, and raisins together in a bowl.

- Heat the oil in a 2-quart heavy-bottom pan over medium-high heat, and sauté the onion until golden. Stir in the garlic and sauté for 1 minute. Reduce the heat to medium, add the rice, and stir until all the rice grains are well coated with oil. Add the salt and paprika, and cook for 1 minute more, stirring constantly to mix well.

- Combine the chicken stock with the lemon juice, pour it into the pan, stir well, and bring to a boil over high heat. Tightly cover the pan, reduce the heat to low, and cook for 20 minutes.

- Fluff the rice with a fork. Add the walnut-apricot-raisin mixture, and fluff the rice again with a fork to combine all the ingredients well. Cover tightly and continue to cook over low heat for 10 minutes longer. Fluff the rice once more. Serve hot.

- Makes 6 cups (8 to 10 servings).

# Spanish Chicken in Red Wine

*Called "pollo con vino tinto" in Spain, this braised chicken dish is an Iberian version of French* coq au vin rouge. *Our globalized version in Russia was made with whatever ingredients we could find in the market—American chicken leg quarters, Turkish olive oil, Russian mushrooms, Siberian pine nuts, Bulgarian red wine—but it still tasted much like the dish we first ate in Spain many years before.*

▶ **NOTE:** Start prepping and cooking this dish about 3 hours before you plan to serve it. If it finishes cooking a bit sooner, just turn off the heat and leave the lid on the pot until serving time (reheat if necessary).

2½ to 3 ounces dried whole porcini or cremini mushrooms
6 ounces bacon, diced
4 tablespoons olive oil (divided use)
2 large onions, coarsely chopped
4 large garlic cloves, thinly sliced
2 tablespoons Spanish mild paprika
8 large chicken thighs (about 3½ pounds), skin removed
1 cup cooked ham, sliced into thin slivers (optional)
1 bottle (3 cups) red wine
1 teaspoon dried thyme
1 teaspoon salt
1 teaspoon freshly ground black pepper
2 bay leaves

Garnish

½ cup toasted pine nuts*

* Toast the pine nuts in a preheated 325°F. oven for about 8 minutes.

- Rinse the dried mushrooms in a colander to remove any grit, then soak them in 6 cups of room-temperature water in a large bowl for 1 hour. Squeeze some of the moisture out of the rehydrated mushrooms and cut them lengthwise into quarters. Strain the soaking liquid into another bowl, through a sieve lined with a clean dish towel or a coffee filter, and reserve the liquid.

- Heat the bacon and 3 tablespoons of olive oil in a large enameled pot or stovetop casserole over medium heat. Cook the bacon until it just begins to brown, then transfer it with a slotted spoon to a bowl, leaving the rendered fat in the pot. Sauté the onions in the fat over medium-high heat until translucent. Add the garlic and continue sautéing until the onions are lightly browned. Reduce the heat to medium, sprinkle in the paprika and cook, stirring constantly, for 1 minute more. Use a slotted spoon to transfer the onions to the bowl with the bacon.

- Add the remaining 1 tablespoon of oil to the pot, and brown the chicken on both sides in the hot fat. Stir in the ham (optional). Pour the wine into the pot and stir in the mushrooms, bacon, onions, thyme, salt, pepper, and bay leaves. If needed, add enough of the reserved mushroom liquid to bring the level of liquid almost to the top of the solid ingredients without drowning them.

- Bring the mixture to a boil over high heat, reduce the heat to very low, cover the pot tightly, and simmer for 1 hour.

- To serve, put 1 chicken thigh on each plate. Use a slotted spoon to scoop out some of the mushrooms, bacon, ham, and onions as a garnish on top of each serving, then sprinkle each with 1 tablespoon of toasted pine nuts.

- Makes 8 servings.

▶ **VARIATION:** Another delicious Spanish version of this braised chicken uses white wine instead of red, omits the ham, and stirs dark raisins, chopped dried apricots, and toasted pine nuts into the pot when you add the wine.

▶ **WASTE NOT:** Refrigerate any remaining mushroom liquid to use as a vegetable stock for other recipes. Refrigerate the winey cooking liquid with any solids left in the chicken braising pot, then skim off the fat and freeze the liquid to use later as the base for a boozy soup.

# Stuffed Cabbage Rolls

## (*Golubtsy*)

*Popular throughout Russia, these stuffed cabbage rolls are called* golubtsy, *"little pigeons" or "little doves," because their shape resembles the plump birds sitting with their wings tucked in. Although the filling is often a forcemeat made mostly of seasoned ground beef or pork, we prefer a lighter stuffing based on rice and ground turkey. For my birthday in Irkutsk, Tom splurged on expensive walnuts and dried apricots for his own version of* golubtsy, *which combines sweet and savory flavors characteristic of dishes from Turkey and the Caucasus region of Russia.*

▶ **ADVANCE PREPARATION:** Make the **Valencian-Style Rice** beforehand. Since the rice recipe makes 6 cups and the cabbage rolls need only 2 cups, save the leftover seasoned rice for a side dish for other meals. It takes most of an afternoon to cook the cabbage leaves, prepare the stuffing, and bake the cabbage rolls, so start early! But once you taste these fat "little doves," you'll know it was worth the work.

2 cups pre-cooked Valencian-Style Rice (recipe, page 272)
1 large (3½- to 4-pound) green cabbage
Salt
4 tablespoons sunflower oil (divided use)
1 medium-large onion, finely chopped
3 large garlic cloves, minced
½ cup finely chopped green onion tops
½ pound ground turkey (or beef)
1 teaspoon dried thyme
1 teaspoon dried oregano
¾ teaspoon black pepper
½ to 1 teaspoon dried hot red pepper flakes
½ teaspoon allspice
¾ cup tomato sauce (one 8-ounce-weight can)
1 tablespoon tomato paste
¾ cup pure sour cream
¼ cup cream (or half-and-half)

Garnish

Chopped fresh cilantro

- Cut the core out of the cabbage, but leave the cabbage whole. Pull off any ratty-looking outer leaves.

- Place the cabbage, cored side down, on a steamer rack in a large pot with cold water reaching just up to the bottom of the rack. Cover the pot tightly, turn the heat to high, and steam the cabbage for about 45 minutes (more or less, depending on its size), until the cabbage leaves are pliable but not falling apart. Add more water during steaming, if needed, to keep the pot from boiling dry.

- Remove the cabbage and let it sit upright on a wire rack until it's just cool enough to handle. Carefully peel off the leaves, trying to keep each leaf whole, and place them in a single layer on paper towels or clean kitchen towels to dry. (You'll need 12 good, large leaves for this recipe.)

- Heat 3 tablespoons of oil in a large skillet, and sauté the onion over medium-high heat until translucent and golden. Add the green onion tops and garlic and sauté for 2 minutes more. Combine the onion mixture with the pre-cooked rice in a large bowl.

- Heat 1 tablespoon of oil in the same skillet and sauté the meat over medium-high heat until it is no longer pink, breaking it up into small pieces as it cooks. Stir in the thyme, oregano, red pepper flakes, black pepper, allspice, and 1 teaspoon salt, and cook until all the liquid in has evaporated. Add the meat to the rice, stirring to mix well.

- Lightly oil an 11 × 7-inch shallow glass or ceramic baking dish. Preheat the oven to 350°F.

- Cut the tough part of the rib out of the bottom end of 1 cabbage leaf. Put ¼ cup (firmly packed) of the meat-and-rice stuffing on the middle of the leaf, and press the stuffing together with your fingers to make a compact ball. Fold the bottom of the leaf over it, tucking in the sides as you roll up the cabbage toward the top end of the leaf, to make a little fat, cylindrical cabbage packet. Place the cabbage roll, seam side down, in the baking dish. Repeat with the remaining leaves and filling. The 12 cabbage rolls should fit snugly in the pan.

- Whisk together the tomato sauce and tomato paste, and pour this evenly over the cabbage rolls. Cover the pan tightly with aluminum foil. Bake at 350°F. for 30 minutes, then uncover the pan and bake 10 minutes longer.

- Remove from the oven and let the cabbage rolls rest in the pan for 10 minutes. Meanwhile, whisk together the sour cream and cream (or half-and-half).

- Serve hot, with 2 cabbage rolls on each plate. Drizzle some of the sour cream over the top and garnish with a generous sprinkling of chopped cilantro.

- Makes 6 servings (2 cabbage rolls each).

## Decorating the Doves

Alla's Granny Polina insisted that "Without *smetana* [sour cream], *golubtsy* are not *golubtsy*." And indeed, in Russia these stuffed cabbage rolls (often called "little doves") are almost always garnished with a liberal amount of sour cream. A canteen in Vladivostok went even further, dressing up their garlicky *golubtsy* with plenty of fresh cilantro sprinkled over the *smetana* on top. But in the Caucasus region of the former Soviet Union, where these stuffed cabbage rolls are also very popular, they're often served simply on their own or topped with a richly flavored tomato sauce. Tom likes to mix these regional traditions, using a Turkish- or Caucasus-style rice-and-dried-fruit stuffing and decorating his "little doves" with tomato sauce, sour cream, *and* cilantro—proving that sometimes gilding the *golubsty* is a good way to go.

# Stuffed Beef Rolls

## (*Rinderrouladen*)

*These stuffed-and-braised beef rolls are a popular dish in Germany (where they're called* Rinderrouladen*), as well as in many parts of Eastern Europe, too. This is a good example of the recipes brought to Siberia by Europeans who settled there during the past 300 years. Although* Rinderrouladen *take time to make, the result is well worth the effort.*

5 tablespoons vegetable oil (divided use)
4 thick or 6 regular bacon slices, diced
3 large onions, finely chopped (divided use)*
3 large garlic cloves, minced
¼ cup minced fresh parsley
1 teaspoon salt
1 teaspoon black pepper
2 pounds boneless round steak, sliced into 12 pieces (each about 5 × 5 × ¼ inches)
2 to 3 tablespoons hot-spicy mustard (Russian brown mustard, French Dijon, or German Düsseldorfer)
1 large sour dill pickle, cut into 12 thin sticks (each 3 × 3 × ¼ inch)
1 large carrot, cut into 12 thin sticks (each 3 × 3 × ¼ inch)
⅓ cup all-purpose flour
2 tablespoons unsalted butter
½ to 1 cup beef stock
1 bay leaf
1 tablespoon tomato paste
¼ cup pure sour cream, at room temperature

## Garnish

Snipped fresh chives

**\*Use 2 onions for the stuffing and 1 onion for the braising liquid.**

- Heat 1 tablespoon of oil in a large skillet, and sauté the bacon, 2 chopped onions, and the garlic together over medium-high heat until the onion is soft and golden. Turn off the heat and stir in the parsley, salt, and pepper. Set aside to cool.

- Use a heavy kitchen mallet to pound the meat slices very thin (⅛ inch).

- Smear one side of a meat slice with ½ teaspoon mustard, and put 2 level tablespoons of the onion mixture in the center, spreading it out a bit (but not all the way to the edges). Place 1 piece of pickle and 1 piece of carrot near one edge of the meat. Roll up the meat slice tightly, and tie it securely near both ends and in the middle with kitchen twine. Repeat with all the other meat slices, making a total of 12 stuffed beef rolls. Dredge each of them in flour.

- Heat the butter and remaining 4 tablespoons of oil in a large (8-quart), heavy covered casserole over medium-high heat. When the fat begins to bubble, brown the beef rolls on all sides, in 2 or 3 batches, and transfer them temporarily to the skillet that cooked the onions.

- Sauté the remaining 1 chopped onion in the hot fat in the casserole, until it begins to brown.

- Place all the beef rolls in a single layer on top of the onions in the casserole. Add ½ cup beef stock and the bay leaf. Bring to a boil over high heat, then reduce the heat to medium-low, cover the casserole tightly, and simmer the beef rolls 1 to 1½ hours or until tender. Add a little more stock, if necessary, to keep about 1 inch of liquid in the pot at all times.

- Transfer the cooked beef rolls to a baking pan, leaving the liquid in the casserole. Cover the beef tightly with aluminum foil and keep warm in a 200°F. oven.

- Remove the bay leaf from the braising liquid. Pour all the contents of the casserole into a blender, and purée until smooth. Return the purée to the casserole. Dissolve the tomato paste in the hot liquid, over medium-high heat, then reduce the heat to low and whisk in the sour cream. Heat gently, stirring constantly, to make a nice sauce. (Don't let it boil.) Add a little more beef stock if the sauce is too thick.

- Cut the strings off the beef rolls. Serve the *Rinderrouladen* hot, with the sauce spooned over the top. Garnish with snipped fresh chives. Classic accompaniments are **Braised Red Cabbage** (recipe, page 121) and **Mashed Red Potatoes** (recipe, page 75).

- Makes 6 servings (2 beef rolls each).

▶ **TIP:** These beef rolls are easier to make if you ask your butcher to slice the meat ¼-inch thick.

▶ **WASTE NOT:** Save the scraps from trimming the beef, to toss into soups.

# Russian Buckwheat Pancakes

## (Bliny)

*My Russian friends considered* bliny *made solely with buckwheat flour to be the "original, traditional, classic" version—although they conceded that pancakes with a combination of wheat and buckwheat flours were "more refined," lighter in texture, and easier to make. This recipe is for old-fashioned, pure buckwheat, farmhouse-style Russian* bliny, *with their darker color, spongier texture, and nuttier taste. (For lighter Russian* crêpes, *see the recipe for* **Blinchiki**, *page 236.)*

▶ **RUSSIAN COOKS' ADVICE:** Although a Russian proverb says the first pancake is always a flop, in my experience the first three or four out of the pan are usually a mess. (All the more reason for the cook to hide the evidence by devouring them immediately.) Don't give up: you'll soon get the hang of frying perfectly round *bliny*.

▶ **ADVANCE PREPARATION:** Start early to make *bliny*, because it takes a while for the batter to rise and nearly two more hours to cook a big batch, as in this recipe. It's a good idea to make them in advance and reheat them later for serving (see **NOTE** at end of recipe).

▶ **NOTE:** Pan size is important for making the right width and thickness of *bliny*. Use a heavy skillet (preferably cast iron or non-stick) measuring about 5 to 6 inches across the bottom. You'll also need a very large bowl for the batter, a ¼-cup ladle or measuring cup for scooping up the batter, and a heatproof basting brush for buttering the skillet.

**4 cups whole milk, at room temperature (divided use)**
**1 tablespoon active dry yeast**
**3 teaspoons sugar (divided use)**
**4 cups buckwheat flour (divided use)**
**3 large eggs, separated**
**½ cup pure sour cream**
**1 teaspoon salt**
**2 tablespoons unsalted butter, melted and slightly cooled (for batter)**
**6 tablespoons unsalted butter, melted (for frying)**
**Toppings of your choice (see end of recipe)**

● Heat 1 cup of milk to lukewarm (105°F.–115°F.). In a medium bowl, whisk the yeast and 1 teaspoon sugar into the warm milk until dissolved. Stir in 1 cup of buckwheat flour, mixing to a smooth batter. Cover and set aside in a warm place until foamy (about 30 minutes).

- In a very large bowl, whisk the egg yolks well, then whisk in the sour cream, salt, and 2 tablespoons melted butter, along with the remaining 2 teaspoons of sugar and 3 cups of milk, until all the ingredients are well combined. Stir in the foamy yeast mixture.

- Add the remaining 3 cups of buckwheat flour, ½ cup at a time, stirring with a wooden spoon to make a smooth batter. Cover with plastic wrap and a kitchen towel, and set aside in a warm place for the batter to rise (about 1½ hours). It will bubble up considerably, then fall a bit, but that's okay.

- In a separate bowl, beat the egg whites until stiff but not dry. Gently fold the whites into the buckwheat batter. Cover and set aside for a few minutes.

- Brush the skillet with a thin film of melted butter. Place the pan over medium-high heat and when very hot, lift it up and pour ¼ cup of batter into it, quickly tilting and rotating the pan to cover most of the bottom with an even layer of batter. Cook over medium-high heat for 1½ minutes, or until lightly browned, then turn the pancake over, and cook for 1 minute longer.

- Immediately take the pan off the heat, and transfer the pancake to a plate, with the first (browner) side up.

- Repeat with the remaining batter, each time brushing the hot pan lightly with melted butter and tilting the pan in all directions to spread the batter over the bottom, before you put it back on the heat. (Halfway through, if the batter becomes too thick to spread easily, thin it with 1 or 2 tablespoons of milk, but don't make it too thin.) Stack the *bliny* on top of each other with the first side up, covered loosely with aluminum foil to keep warm (or set them, covered with foil, in a warm oven).

- Makes approximately 25 to 30 *bliny* (each 5 inches in diameter). Serve with a selection of toppings and plenty of ice cold vodka. Russians say that *bliny* should always be eaten with your fingers, not with a knife and fork.

▶ **Toppings:** Traditional toppings for *bliny* include plenty of melted butter (for drizzling on the *bliny* or dipping them into), sour cream, smoked fish, pickled herring, red and black caviar, chopped hard-boiled eggs, creamed or marinated mushrooms, fresh farmer's cheese (*tvorog*), chopped wild garlic leaves, and finely chopped onions (spring onions, green and white parts, are less assertive than older onions). Although *bliny* are eaten mainly with savory toppings, they're sometimes served for tea or dessert, spread with jam or sweetened condensed milk, or dipped into honey or rich dark birch syrup.

▶ **NOTE:** *Bliny* are best when fresh and hot, but they can also be made in advance, cooled to room temperature, and the whole stack wrapped tightly with plastic. Keep in the refrigerator for 3 days (or wrap tightly in aluminum foil and freeze up to 3 months). Thawed *bliny* can be reheated in foil in a 300°F. oven for few minutes or reheated (uncovered) in a microwave for several seconds (depending on how many you're reheating in one stack). Some cooks prefer to reheat them individually in a dry skillet or on a griddle, over medium heat, with no butter or oil added. Warm each *blin* for about 1 minute on each side.

## Size Matters

Don't let a Russian hear you refer to *bliny* as "*crêpes*." Bliny are one of three types of pancakes made by Russian cooks, and *bliny* differ from the other two. *Olad'i* are the smallest and thickest, about 3 to 4 inches wide, often leavened with *kefir* and baking soda. *Blinchiki*, the Russian version of *crêpes*, are the largest and thinnest, about 7 to 8 inches in diameter, their batter sometimes lightened with beaten egg whites. *Bliny* are yeast raised, spongy in texture, and mid-range in size. Although modern restaurant chefs like to make miniature *bliny* for cocktail canapés, classic Russian *bliny* measure about 5 to 6 inches across and are neither as thick as *olad'i* nor as thin as *blinchiki*. Like Goldilocks said, they're "just right." And Russians know it takes a good cook to make those perfect *bliny*.

## Pan Perfect

Some Russian cooks still treasure their grandmother's special *bliny* pan—four or more shallow cast-iron skillets, molded together side by side, with one long handle attached, for frying several *bliny* simultaneously on top of the stove, or baking multiple *bliny* in a traditional Russian wood-burning oven, as in earlier times. And many Russian cooks still grease their *bliny* pans with a goose feather or half a raw potato dipped in oil or melted butter, or rub the hot skillet with a cube of pork fat skewered on a fork.

# Russian Easter Cheese Dessert

## (Paskha)

*I've made* paskha *at Eastertime all over the world—in Texas, in Europe, in Russia—using whatever white curd cheeses were available, from American farmer's cheese to Italian ricotta, German* Quark, *and Russian* tvorog. *A Siberian-Buryat friend even gave me her homemade* tvorog *for my* paskha *in Irkutsk, which was richer and creamier than any store-bought kind. In Texas I can now get several kinds of* tvorog *at my local Russian delis. But if you can't find real Russian* tvorog, *a good substitute is American farmer's cheese or a combination of ricotta and cream cheese, as in this recipe. Although the recipe looks long,* paskha *is actually easy to make—and our guests always love this special Russian Easter treat.*

▶ **SPECIAL EQUIPMENT:** For molding the *paskha* (if you don't have a classic Russian mold) you will need two 1-quart (4-cup) terra cotta flower pots (6 inches in diameter at the top and 6 inches tall)—or one 2-quart (8-cup) flower pot (7 inches in diameter at the top and 7 inches tall)—and cheesecloth for lining the pots. The flowerpots should be new and clean, not previously used for anything else. If this is the first time you are using the terra cotta pots for making *paskha*, soak them for several hours in cold water, then let them dry thoroughly, to remove the aroma of clay.

*Russian Easter paskha (sweetened cheese dessert) decorated with the letters "XB," for "Christ Is Risen."*

▶ **NOTE:** This version of *paskha*, made with ricotta and cream cheese, releases little (if any) moisture as it chills overnight. If you don't want to shape it in a special Russian *paskha* mold or a flower pot, simply chill it in the mixing bowl, then mound it in a pretty cut-glass bowl for serving.

▶ **INGREDIENTS:** It is very important to use *unsalted* butter and pure, full-fat sour cream containing no stabilizers or other additives. If you prefer not to eat uncooked eggs, use eggs that have been pasteurized in their shells.

½ cup golden raisins
¼ cup finely chopped candied citron*
¼ cup finely chopped candied orange peel*
¼ cup brandy
1 pound (2 cups) whole-milk ricotta cheese, at room temperature**
1 pound full-fat cream cheese, at room temperature**
1 cup (2 sticks) unsalted butter, at room temperature
2 cups confectioners' sugar, sifted after measuring
4 large egg yolks
2 teaspoons vanilla extract
1 cup pure sour cream
½ cup finely chopped toasted blanched almonds***
1 tablespoon fresh lemon juice
Finely grated peel of 1 lemon

## Decorations

Dark raisins, whole unblanched almonds, dried or candied fruit pieces, whole fresh strawberries, fresh edible flowers

*If unavailable, use other candied or dried fruits, preferably without additives. Avoid artificially colored fruits, which are often sold in America for fruitcake baking.
**Or a total of 2 pounds full-fat Russian *tvorog* cheese or American farmer's cheese
***Toast almonds in a preheated 350°F. for 8 to 10 minutes. Cool before using.

▶ **ADVANCE PREPARATION:** Combine the raisins, candied citron, candied orange peel, and brandy in a shallow bowl and let them soak for 6 to 8 hours, stirring occasionally. (Or just cover them tightly and microwave for 1 minute, then cool before using.)

● Just before assembling the *paskha*, line the terra cotta flower pots with a double layer of cheesecloth—dampened first in cold water and wrung out—leaving enough cheesecloth to hang over the edge about 4 inches all around.

▶ **To make paskha:** Process the ricotta cheese and cream cheese together in a food processor until smooth. Add the butter and continue processing until smooth. Combine the egg yolks and confectioners' sugar in a large bowl and beat with an electric

285

mixer on high speed until the mixture is light and fluffy (about 4 minutes). Beat in the butter-and-cheese mixture, 1 cup at a time, along with the vanilla, beating with the electric mixer on high speed until the mixture is very smooth.

- Stir in the sour cream. Add the soaked raisins and candied fruit (along with any brandy remaining in the bowl), chopped toasted almonds, lemon juice, and grated lemon peel. Stir until all the ingredients are well mixed.

- Spoon the cheese mixture into the prepared flowerpots, pressing it firmly into the pots. Fold the excess cheesecloth over the top of the mixture. Place a small saucer (smaller than the diameter of the pot) on top of the cheesecloth and put a heavy weight (such as a large can of vegetables) on the saucer. Set the flowerpots on a small rack with a saucer underneath to catch any drips. Refrigerate the *paskha* for at least 24 hours before serving.

- To unmold the *paskha*, remove the weight and saucer, then unfold the cheesecloth on top. Place an inverted serving platter over the top of the flowerpot. Holding the flowerpot and serving platter firmly together, quickly invert them so the *paskha* is sitting on the platter. Carefully remove the flowerpot and peel the cheesecloth off the *paskha*.

- Decorate the *paskha* with dark raisins, whole unblanched almonds, and/or pieces of candied fruits. It is traditional to form the letters "XB"—the Cyrillic initial letters for "*Khristos voskrese!*" ("Christ is risen!")—on the side of the *paskha*, using the nuts or fruits. You can also make designs such as a cross, flowers, borders, etc., or put a row of fresh strawberries around the bottom and a few large strawberries on top. (Some Russians decorate the base with non-toxic greenery and place a fresh lily or rose on top.)

- Serve *paskha* as an accompaniment to *kulich* (Russian Easter bread). The *paskha* can be spread on slices of *kulich* or served in a small mound next to a slice of *kulich* on a dessert plate.

- Makes 8 cups (32 servings of ¼ cup each—*paskha* is very rich!). Leftover *paskha* can be kept in the refrigerator, tightly wrapped in plastic, for up to 1 week.

***Traditional carved wooden pasochnitsa used for molding Russian Easter paskha desserts.***

# Russian Easter Paskha

*Paskha* is a cheesecake-like pudding made with many ingredients proscribed during the long Lenten fast: *tvorog* (fresh white curd cheese), butter, eggs, and sour cream or sweet cream. There are many versions of this traditional Russian Easter dessert, some of them uncooked, others cooked. The rich, creamy mixture can be sweetened with sugar, or with fruit or berry syrups, purées, or preserves that also add a pastel color to the *paskha*. Other flavorings include vanilla, grated lemon or orange zest, chopped candied fruits or fruit peel, raisins or currants soaked in brandy, and sometimes even powdered cocoa, cardamom, or mace. Many Russians have their own special recipe for *paskha*, often a treasured family secret.

The *paskha* is customarily formed in a *pasochnitsa*, a wooden, ceramic, or plastic mold shaped like a truncated four-sided pyramid. The flat top at the narrower end has drainage holes in it, and the wider bottom, at the lower end, is open so the inverted mold can be filled with the *paskha* mixture. Often there are also carved or molded motifs on the interior sides, in the form of a Russian Orthodox cross and the Cyrillic letters "XB" (for "Christ is risen"), which make raised designs on the unmolded *paskha*. (Cooks lacking this special mold just use a flower pot or even a colander.) The mold is set upside down on its narrower end, lined with damp cheesecloth, and the *paskha* mixture is packed into it, with a heavy weight set on top of it to compress the cheesy mass. Then the mold is put in a cool place—on the verandas of Siberian village houses, the balconies of urban apartments, the inside of modern refrigerators—to chill for 24 hours and let any excess moisture drain out of the holes.

The *paskha* mold is finally inverted onto a serving plate, and the mold and cheesecloth carefully removed. The *paskha* is then decorated with candied fruit peel, raisins, nuts, colored sugar, or even home-dyed seeds and grains, whatever the cook has on hand. Traditional motifs include an Orthodox cross, the letters "XB," and spring flowers. Often the *paskha* is also surrounded by colored Easter eggs, and some cooks put a fresh flower on top for a final flourish.

*Paskha* is always served with *kulich*. First, the dome of the *kulich* is sliced off horizontally and set aside. Then half-inch-thick rounds are sliced off the *kulich* horizontally, starting at the top of the bread, and the dome is placed back on top of any remaining *kulich* to keep it fresh. Some of the *paskha* is either spread on a slice of *kulich* or served separately on the same dessert plate as the piece of *kulich*.

# Granny Polina's Easter Desserts

When Alla's Siberian grandmother Polina made *paskha*, she always wore clean clothes and covered her head with a clean kerchief. (She also warned that a woman should never make *paskha* during her menstrual period, or the *paskha* would spoil.)

Polina shaped her *paskha* in a metal or ceramic mold and set it in a cool place to chill and drain overnight. Then she unmolded it onto a plate and decorated it with grains of millet that she'd dyed various colors with beet, berry, and carrot juice, using them to form the sign of the Cross and the Cyrillic letters "XB" for "Christ is risen."

Polina's *kulich* contained pine nuts, a local Siberian "gift of the forest." In addition to the large *kulich* she baked for the whole family, she also made smaller, individual *kulichi* for Alla and her brothers, each little bread decorated with their own name on it. And when her light, delicate *kulichi* came out of the oven, she always put them on a pillow to cool.

# Russian Easter Bread

## (*Kulich*)

*Traditionally, these Russian Easter breads took a lot of kneading by hand, and they also had to rise three times in a warm place. Today, modern Russian cooks use their bread machines for the initial mixing and rising of the dough. This recipe, which uses bread flour in a bread machine, is a bit denser in texture than a good Russian grandmother's* kulich, *but it's also easier to make.*

▶ **SPECIAL EQUIPMENT:** For baking the *kulichi* you need two (13-ounce net weight) or three (10-ounce net weight) metal coffee cans (paper labels removed), washed and thoroughly dried, plus enough parchment paper to line the bottoms and sides of the cans.

### For the bread machine dough

½ **cup warm milk (100°F.)**
3 **large eggs, at room temperature**
4 **tablespoons unsalted butter, at room temperature, cut into pieces**
1 **teaspoon vanilla extract**
3½ **cups bread flour**
½ **cup sugar**
2½ **teaspoons active dry yeast**
1 **teaspoon ground carda-mom**
1 **teaspoon freshly grated nutmeg**
½ **teaspoon salt**
⅛ **teaspoon finely crushed saffron threads, dissolved in 1 teaspoon brandy**
**Grated peel of 1 lemon**

### Additions to prepared dough

¼ **cup dark raisins**
¼ **cup golden raisins**
¼ **cup diced candied orange peel***
¼ **cup diced candied citron***

*Several kulichi (Russian Easter breads) made for an Easter feast in the 1990s.*

**2 tablespoons brandy**
**2 tablespoons bread flour**
**½ cup chopped toasted almonds\*\***

**\*If unavailable, use other candied or dried fruits, preferably without addi-**
   **tives. Avoid artificially colored fruits, which are often sold in America for**
   **fruitcake baking.**
**\*\*Toast almonds in a preheated 350°F. oven for 8 to 10 minutes. Cool before**
   **using.**

*Kulich* **Icing (recipe follows)**

**Decorations (optional): Colored sugar, chocolate sprinkles, candied almonds,**
   **1 small candle for each** *kulich*

▶ **To make the dough:**

- Put the milk, eggs, butter, vanilla, bread flour, sugar, yeast, cardamom, nutmeg, salt, saffron, and lemon peel into a bread machine container in the order specified in your own bread machine's instructions. Process the ingredients using the "Dough" setting on the bread machine.

- While the dough is processing, combine the raisins, candied fruit peel, and brandy in a shallow bowl. Stir occasionally.

- Butter the insides of the 2 or 3 coffee cans, and line the bottom and sides of the cans with baking parchment.

- When the bread machine's dough cycle is completed, transfer the dough to a lightly floured surface. Punch the dough down, cover it loosely with plastic wrap, and let it rest for 10 minutes. Meanwhile, sprinkle 2 tablespoons of flour over the brandy-soaked fruits, mix well, then chop the fruits finely. Add the chopped almonds and mix well.

- Sprinkle the fruit-nut mixture over the dough, 1 handful at a time, kneading and folding the dough until the fruits and nuts are evenly distributed throughout. Form the dough into 2 or 3 equal-size balls, and put 1 ball into each of the coffee cans. Cover with plastic wrap and let the dough rise in a warm place until it reaches the top edge of the cans (30 to 60 minutes). Preheat the oven to 400°F.

▶ **To bake the** *kulichi*:

- Remove the plastic wrap and set the coffee cans upright *on the lowest rack* in the oven. Bake at 400°F. for 10 minutes. Reduce the oven temperature to 350°F. and continue baking for 30 minutes. After the first 10 minutes of baking at 350°F., cover the tops of the dough loosely with aluminum foil to keep them browning too much.

- Let the *kulichi* cool in the cans for 10 minutes, set on a wire rack. Make **Kulich Icing** (recipe follows). Remove the *kulichi* from the cans, peel off the baking parchment, and let them cool for 10 minutes more.

- Spread the icing on the *kulichi* while they are still warm, covering the domed tops completely and letting some of the icing dribble down the sides. Decorate the icing with colored sugar, chocolate sprinkles, or candied almonds, if desired, or stick a small candle in the top of each *kulich* and light it for a festive presentation.

▶ **To serve:** Slice off the dome top, horizontally, then slice the *kulich* horizontally into $\frac{1}{2}$-inch thick rounds, replacing the top on any leftover *kulich* still standing. Spread the slices with *paskha*, butter, or cream cheese, if desired. Cut the remaining top into 4 wedges for a final serving.

- Makes 2 or 3 Russian Easter breads.

▶ **NOTE:** *Kulichi* can be made in advance and frozen up to 2 months. After removing the *kulichi* from the pans, let them cool to room temperature, but do not spread the icing on them. Wrap the *kulichi* tightly in plastic wrap, then enclose them in a plastic bag. Freeze until needed. Let the *kulichi* thaw completely at room temperature before spreading the icing on them.

## *Kulich* Icing

**2½ cups confectioners' sugar**
**2 to 3 tablespoons cream, milk, or orange liqueur**
**2 teaspoons fresh lemon juice**
**1 teaspoon vanilla extract**

- Sift the confectioners' sugar into a bowl. Add the remaining ingredients and beat with a wooden spoon until the mixture is smooth. Use for glazing the tops of warm *kulichi*.

# Butter Lamb

## (Easter Table Decoration)

*Butter lambs are a traditional Easter table decoration in Russia and much of Eastern Europe. They represent Christ as the sacrificial lamb—but on Easter Sunday these cute lamb effigies are sacrificed to the hunger of diners finally breaking the long Lenten fast, when butter was a forbidden food. The same molds for making butter lambs are also used for baking sweet little lamb cakes for an Easter dessert in many Central European countries.*

▶ **SPECIAL EQUIPMENT:** A 2-cup or 4-cup three-dimensional metal or ceramic lamb mold with two sides that clamp together.

▶ **Butter:** ¾ pound (3 sticks) butter for a 2-cup mold, or 1½ pounds (6 sticks) butter for a 4-cup mold.

- Let the butter come to room temperature in a bowl, then beat it with a wooden spoon until completely smooth.

- Take the lamb mold apart and oil both parts of the interior thoroughly with a light-tasting oil (such as canola). Clamp the mold back together again. Pack the softened butter into the mold, filling it completely. Chill in the refrigerator for several hours or overnight, until the butter is very firm.

- To unmold, let the butter-filled mold sit at room temperature for about 30 minutes, then place it on a serving plate with the mold sitting upright. Carefully remove the clamps and separate the two halves of the mold. Use your fingers to smooth out any ridges or rough spots along the line where the two sides of the mold were clamped together. Stick two whole cloves into the butter for the lamb's eyes.

- Cover the butter lamb loosely with plastic wrap and refrigerate until serving time. Just before serving, arrange sprigs of fresh herbs around the base. (In Russia and Eastern Europe, it is also customary for the butter lamb to hold a sprig of rosemary in its mouth, since rosemary is the herb of love and remembrance.)

- Butter lambs can be used solely as table decorations (with the butter later used as an ingredient in other dishes). Or serve the butter for spreading on bread and on Easter *kulich*, slicing off the butter from the tail end of the lamb and eventually ending with the head itself.

# Zabaglione

*Italians make this classic foamy dessert with sweet Marsala wine, but in Russia we used Georgian Aragvi brandy, considerably stronger in alcohol. The Russians have a similar eggy concoction called* gogol-mogol, *usually made with milk (and far less alcohol) and often uncooked. It's considered a healthy, fortifying treat for children and a soothing remedy for sore throats. But my boozy Italian zabaglione is definitely a dessert for adults.*

**6 large egg yolks**
**6 tablespoons sugar**
**¾ cup sweet Marsala wine (or cream sherry), at room temperature***

***For a less alcoholic version, substitute white wine. For a stronger one, use brandy or rum. Your choice of liquid will determine the final taste.**

- Put about 2 inches of water in a medium-size saucepan or the bottom of a double boiler. Place a medium-large heatproof bowl, or the top of the double boiler, on top of the pan containing the water, and check that the water does *not* touch the bottom of the top pan.

- Separate the top and bottom pans, putting the pan with water on the stove over medium heat to bring the water to a simmer. Put the egg yolks and sugar in the other pan. Beat vigorously with a wire whisk until the mixture is pale and very creamy and forms a "ribbon" that folds back on itself when you lift the whisk out of the mixture.

- Set this pan over the pan containing the *simmering* (not boiling) water on the stove. The hot water must not touch the pan containing the egg mixture. Adjust the heat, if necessary, to keep the water just at the simmer point. Slowly add the Marsala while whisking constantly. Then continue whisking constantly, in one direction only, for about 4 to 6 minutes, or until the mixture doubles in volume and forms soft mounds on a spoon. *Do not let the zabaglione boil or it will curdle.*

- Quickly spoon the *zabaglione* into small stemmed glasses and serve immediately.

- Makes 4 very rich servings.

▶ **NOTE:** You can also flavor the *zabaglione* with ⅛ teaspoon ground cinnamon, 1 teaspoon vanilla extract, or 1 tablespoon finely grated lemon peel or orange peel. Whisk the flavoring into the *zabaglione* as soon as you take it off the heat, just before you spoon it into the serving glasses.

# Pine Nut Meringues

*Meringue cookies are a good way to use up leftover egg whites from* **Russian Easter Cheese Dessert (Paskha,** *recipe, page 283) or* **Vanilla Custard Sauce** *(recipe, page 181). Toasted pine nuts give these seductive cookies a distinctive Siberian flavor.*

▶ **NOTE:** It's best to make these on a dry (not humid) day.

½ **cup toasted pine nuts, coarsely chopped\***
1 **cup sugar**
2 **teaspoons cornstarch**
4 **large egg whites, at room temperature**
1 **teaspoon vanilla extract**
⅛ **teaspoon salt**

**\*Toast the pine nuts in advance for about 8 minutes in a preheated 325°F. oven. Cool before chopping.**

- Preheat the oven to 225°F. Line 2 baking sheets with parchment paper. (You'll need 2 baking sheets that can sit together on the middle rack of your oven.)

- Whisk the sugar and cornstarch together in a small bowl.

- With an electric mixer on high speed, beat the egg whites, vanilla, and salt together in a large bowl until soft peaks form. Decrease the mixer speed to medium, and very slowly add the sugar, beating constantly. Scrape down the sides occasionally with a rubber spatula. Then increase the mixer speed to high and beat until the egg whites are glossy and stiff peaks form. Fold in the chopped pine nuts.

- Drop the mixture by well-rounded teaspoonfuls onto the baking sheets, placing the meringues about ½-inch apart.

- Bake at preheated 225°F. for 1 hour, then turn off the oven and leave the meringues inside for 2 more hours. Be patient: *Do not open the oven door!* Store the meringues in a tightly covered container.

- Makes 48 irresistible, crunchy meringue cookies.

*Russian Orthodox Cathedral of the Theophany, Irkutsk, Siberia, 2007.*

# Chapter 7
# Dinner On (and Off) the Diner

## Trans-Siberian Commuter Train

Train travel, outings with Russian and Buryat friends, and jobs on several expedition trips have taken me to more parts of Siberia than I ever thought I'd see—from the fuming volcanoes of Kamchatka's "land of fire and ice" to the dense forests of the Maritime Territory where Siberian tigers roam, from the grassy steppes of the Buryat lands to the rocky shores of fabled Lake Baikal, the world's oldest, largest by volume, and deepest lake.

It all started on the train. I've been hooked on train travel ever since I was a kid in Texas where my father was a fireman on the Missouri-Kansas-Texas (Katy) Railroad, shoveling coal on the last steam engines running on that line. Even back then in a small Texas town, I dreamed of someday riding the Trans-Siberian Railroad across the vast expanse of Russia, a country that, to my young mind, seemed to radiate mystery, romance, and intrigue.

That dream finally came true in 1994, when Tom and I boarded a Trans-Siberian train in Vladivostok on a snowy night in January. We were headed to our next teaching assignment in Irkutsk, almost 2,500 miles into the heartland of Siberia, near the halfway point on that legendary railway line. Riding through winter landscapes that looked like scenes from *Doctor Zhivago*, we thought our three-day trip on the Trans-Siberian Railroad would be a once-in-a-lifetime journey that we'd later remember as the high point of our travels in Russia. But 10 days later we were on the train again, rolling down the tracks to attend a conference in the city of Ulan-Ude, the capital of Russia's Buryat Republic. And during the rest of that year in Russia, we rode the rails so many times that I came to think of the Trans-Siberian as our "commuter line."

Dining on Russian trains in the mid-1990s was an adventure itself. Most Russians avoided the dining cars, which had a reputation for high prices and

*Platform vendor selling homemade food from a baby carriage, along the Trans-Siberian tracks, 1994.*

poor food. So we traveled like the Russians did, carrying food with us from home: cheese, boiled eggs, smoked sausages, canned fish, and packages of ramen noodles that we rehydrated with hot water from the big coal-fired boiler at the end of each sleeping car, which we also tapped for brewing tea.

At various stops along the way, we also bought food from the freelance vendors on the station platforms—usually grandmotherly looking women who cooked the food at home, then brought it to the station on sleds in winter and in baby carriages in summer. As the train pulled into the station, those *babushki* quickly spread blankets on the ground, unpacked their wares, and laid out a bounteous buffet of pickled cucumbers and tomatoes, marinated mushrooms, and sauerkraut salads; smoked or salted fish and old glass canning jars brimming with beads of salmon caviar; fresh white farmer's cheese and thick sour cream; roasted potato chunks and chicken drumsticks; thick pancakes and hot *pirozhki*, those little savory pies filled with meat, potatoes, cabbage, or onions; fruit preserves and fresh berries; salted sunflower seeds and Siberian pine nuts; gingerbread cookies, sweet pastries, and plump yeast buns. They wrapped our selections in old newspapers or handed them to us in paper cones made from pages torn out of books and magazines. Buying from these local vendors was a good way to sample Russian regional specialties all along the route, and regular travelers on the trains knew which private vendors at each station always had the best foods for sale.

## Street Eats

Food stalls around Trans-Siberian railway stations and vendors on the train platforms often sell popular street foods that originated with ethnic groups from the Black Sea to East Asia. *Chebureki* are large, half-moon-shaped, deep-fried turnovers made from pastry dough filled with ground lamb or beef and minced onions, seasoned with salt and pepper, and sometimes also cilantro, parsley, green onion tops, or dill. Said to have been invented by Tatars living in Crimea, *chebureki* are much like the Mongolian meat-filled fried pastries called *khuushuur*, peddled by vendors along the railroad tracks in the Buryat-Mongolian region of southern Siberia. Buryat vendors also sell round, meat-filled steamed dumplings known as *buuza*, made from pasta dough wrapped around a ground-meat filling, with a small hole in the top to let the steam escape. (Their shape is said to symbolize the felt *gers* [yurts] that the nomadic Buryats lived in for centuries.) Big yeast-raised steamed buns called *pyan-se* are the latest street-food fad in the Russian Far East. Stuffed with a mixture of shredded cabbage and chopped pork or beef seasoned with soy sauce, these buns were supposedly introduced into the local cuisine by ethnic Koreans living on Sakhalin Island off the coast of eastern Russia. Some versions even have a filling of salmon or Korean *kimchi*. *Pyan-se* are recognizable by their large round size, white color, and distinctive fern-leaf or herringbone pattern across the top, where the dough was pinched together to enclose the filling.

# From Caviar to Mystery Meat

Constructed between 1891 and 1916, the Trans-Siberian Railroad was—and still is—the longest continuous passenger line in the world. Running nearly 6,000 miles between Moscow and Vladivostok, it links two continents, Europe and Asia. Early on, railroad station buffets were built along the route, and around 1900 first-class dining cars on some of the long-distance trains began catering to well-heeled travelers. But most ordinary passengers brought their own less expensive provisions from home, or bought foods from freelance vendors on the station platforms, as they still do today.

In the early twentieth century, dining cars on a few luxury trains served such delicacies as wild game, fresh sturgeon, filet mignon, smoked fish from Lake Baikal, caviar from the Caspian Sea, and champagne from France. But during the seven decades of the Soviet period, from the 1920s to the 1990s, eating on Russian trains was a proletarian experience at best. Served on soiled tablecloths by surly waiters, food in the sparsely stocked dining cars was often no better than at a factory workers' canteen. Foreign travelers described the dining-car meals as monotonous mystery-meat-and-mashed-potatoes, all smothered under greasy brown gravy. Savvy rail riders knew that the best eats could be found on the station platforms—home-grown, home-cooked foods usually hawked by little old *babushki* bundled up in shawls.

Railroad culinary fare has improved on the Trans-Siberian route in this century, with dining cars now run by private concessionaires instead of the Russian government. Many of these rolling restaurants feature a spruced up décor, better food, and faster service. New restaurants and buffets have opened at several of the larger stations, along with specialty shops selling freshly baked breads and pastries, hamburgers and rotisserie chickens, imported sausages and cheeses, fresh fruits and fancy boxes of chocolates. Even at the smaller stations there's usually a kiosk or two where travelers can buy beer, vodka, cigarettes, and packaged snack foods. But many passengers still bring their own food, homemade or store-bought, for the long journey. And at some stops on the line, locals still sell home-cooked foods pulled to the station on sleds, wheeled from home in baby buggies, or driven there by car and kept warm on the running engines of their parked automobiles.

# Luxury Line

Fast-forward to 2006, when I discovered what it was like to travel almost like a tsar. That summer National Geographic Expeditions hired me to be a lecturer on their Trans-Siberian Railroad tour from Vladivostok to Moscow, with a side trip down to Mongolia. At last a chance to return to my old stomping grounds in Siberia, to ride the railroad route I knew so well, and finally to complete the full Trans-Siberian journey beyond Irkutsk all the way to Moscow by train.

Over the next two years I traveled across Russia five times with National Geographic Expeditions on private chartered trains run by Golden Eagle Luxury Trains Limited, a British company that specializes in high-end railway travel. After the collapse of the Soviet Union in 1991, a few foreign companies had begun operating private trains in Russia, reviving the luxury (and nostalgia) of early railway travel before the Bolshevik Revolution in 1917 put an end to such "bourgeois" indulgences. By the twenty-first century, four charter-train companies were offering 12- to 15-day tours on the Trans-Siberian tracks. Think *Orient Express*—Russian-style.

Initially the carriages on Golden Eagle's trains, including the dining cars, were old Soviet/Russian VIP railroad cars (some even dating back to 1914), which were leased from the Russian government and refurbished to modern standards. Travelers on those luxury trains probably didn't realize they were sipping champagne and nibbling on caviar in the same railway carriages formerly used by some of the most notorious political figures in twentieth-century Russia.

In 2007 the British company inaugurated a completely new, $25 million train named the *Golden Eagle Trans-Siberian Express*—the only privately owned train in Russia where every sleeping cabin had its own toilet and shower. This luxury-level train also included two elegantly appointed dining cars, a separate modern galley (kitchen car), and a comfortable lounge car where passengers quaffed cocktails to the sounds of live classical music played on the piano or strummed on a guitar by Russian musicians.

Very good multi-course meals were prepared every day by Russian chefs who cooked all the dishes from scratch, including fresh breads and pastries baked overnight while the passengers slept in their cozy cabins, rocked to sleep by the rhythm of the rails. Except at breakfast, no two dishes were ever served twice during those 12 days on the train, and the imported wines poured freely at every lunch and dinner made the journey through two continents seem even more leisurely.

# Foreign Flavors

During one of my cross-country trips on the *Golden Eagle Trans-Siberian Express*, I became friends with Rupak Mitra, who at that time was executive chef for the Indian company that owns the luxury Taj hotels and resorts. Mitra was working with the *Golden Eagle* chefs to develop new vegetarian main dishes and more elaborate desserts for the Russian dining-car menu. He was also interested in learning more about Russian cuisine. So when the train stopped for a few hours in Irkutsk, I went downtown and bought several Russian cooking magazines for him. As the train rolled along the tracks toward Moscow, he looked at the magazines' food photos and selected several recipes that interested him, which I translated into English since Mitra couldn't read Russian.

Later, when I was back home in Texas and Mitra had returned to Mumbai, I e-mailed him the recipes for 16 Russian dishes that Tom and I had learned to make in Siberia and the Russian Far East (many of which are in this cookbook). But when he sent a reply to thank me for the recipes, I was surprised to learn why he had such an interest in Russian cooking. It turned out that many wealthy Russian tourists staying at the Taj hotels didn't want to eat Indian food. Like some travelers I've met in other countries, they were wary of sampling the local cuisine when abroad, preferring instead the familiar foods of home. So Mitra and his staff used my recipes to prepare Russian meals to please their well-heeled Russian guests at those upscale hotels in South Asia.

As the train gently swayed back and forth over rough stretches of track, waiters wearing white shirts and black bow ties adroitly balanced platters of cold sturgeon, smoked salmon, and boiled shrimp, which they served onto china plates emblazoned with the train's *Golden Eagle* logo. Other waiters filled cut-crystal glasses with chilled vodka and dry champagne. One enticing course followed another, while outside the dining-car windows Siberia slowly slipped by like a passing dream.

*Elegantly decorated dining car on the Golden Eagle Trans-Siberian Express, 2008. (Courtesy of Golden Eagle Luxury Trains)*

The menus often featured foods from the different regions we crossed: fresh seafood in the Russian Far East, *pel'meni* dumplings as we rolled through Eastern Siberia, an outdoor picnic of smoky grilled meats on the shore of Lake Baikal; ethnic Tatar dishes in Tatarstan on the European side of Russia. Other meals included classic dishes popular across the entire country: beety *borshch*, creamy mushroom soup, beef Stroganov, chopped meat cutlets, stuffed peppers, and little savory *pirozhki* pastries. And on every trip, all the travelers fell in love with the colorful first-course *zakuski* served on board the train: buckwheat *bliny* with red and black caviar; shrimp and crab salads with mayonnaise, apples, and green peas; mushrooms and tomatoes stuffed with garlicky cheese; beet salad with walnuts and prunes; julienned chicken and vegetables suspended in aspic; colorful carrot salad with walnuts and red currants; cold salmon with pickled onions and green olives; chicken salad with cucumbers and peas; crunchy green apples and green onions mixed with sweet peppers, pine nuts, and salty sheep's cheese; grilled eggplant slices topped with sliced tomatoes and pretty rosettes of cream cheese.

During those trips I got to know one of the *Golden Eagle*'s master chefs, Ilkhomudin Kamolov, who gave me the recipes for some of my favorite dishes on the train. Originally from Soviet Tajikistan, he'd been cooking on trains for 30 years. And he was proud that the *Golden Eagle* chefs didn't just open packages of pre-cooked food and reheat them, as cooks on many Western European trains did. "That's not really cooking," he told me. "On this train everything is fresh. Here we do everything ourselves, from peeling the potatoes to plating the food."

Since my first trip on the Trans-Siberian tracks in 1994, I've logged more than 40,000 miles on that line, traveling on all classes of Russian trains from cheap "hard class" to pricey luxury level. I've also eaten more than 250 meals in dining cars, in sleeping cabins (with food bought from platform vendors), and at railroad station restaurants. I love dining on—and off—the diner. And I can hardly wait to ride those Russian rails again.

## Dacha Days

On a cold Friday evening in October 1994, Tom and I joined our Russian friend, Larisa, on a grungy "hard class" railway carriage for the 12-hour trip by train, two buses, and on foot to her dacha 200 miles north of Vladivostok. We arrived at sunrise the next morning, surrounded by the gold and orange foliage of the autumnal forest, with deep purple mountains on the near horizon, feathery wisps of fog lingering in the valleys, and the border of China not far away.

Dachas are the country cottages that for many Russians are the escape valve on the pressure cooker of urban life, a place to go on weekends, holidays, and in the summer to retreat from the stresses of living in crowded cities and to enjoy nature unencumbered by concrete and steel. In the 1990s, dachas ranged from large, romantic-looking, two-story wooden houses trimmed with the fancy fretwork known as "wooden lace," to small A-frame cabins that were little more than tool sheds. Most of them didn't have electricity, running water, or indoor plumbing—but almost all had a garden where their owners grew fruits, vegetables, and flowers. Dachas and their gardens have a long history in Russia, and in the Soviet era they were especially important sources of the fresh foods that were often scarce in the state-run stores. By the end of the 1990s, Russian statistics claimed that nearly three-quarters of the population still grew some or all of their own food, and slightly more than half the people grew at least half of the food they ate.

Although dachas are normally located on small plots of land out in the country-side, the one belonging to Larisa and her husband, Nikolai, was on a street in a rural village. Their two-bedroom clapboard house had a small kitchen with a traditional wood-burning, brick-and-plaster Russian stove built into one wall, and a glass-enclosed verandah where Larisa also cooked on

*Large dacha near Lake Baikal, 2008.*

a three-burner stove fueled by gas from a large portable canister. That village dacha did have the luxury of electricity, but all the water had to be hauled in large metal milk cans from a public spigot two blocks away. And the only traffic we saw on the village streets that weekend were a couple of cows and a gaggle of geese. "The longer I'm out here, the more I feel like when I was a kid visiting my relatives in the Deep South," said Tom.

Behind Larisa's house were a root cellar, two wooden outdoor toilets, a woodpile, and assorted buckets, barrels, and tools. But pride of place went to the garden, a large plot of land where she grew the biggest variety of vege-tables I'd ever seen at a dacha: carrots, onions, garlic, potatoes, tomatoes, and cucumbers; cauliflower, sorrel, and huge white radishes; watermelons, pumpkins, and three kinds of smaller squash; red and green cabbages; sweet and hot peppers; parsley, melissa (lemon balm), and dill. Like many Russians, Larisa believed that only home-grown foods were truly safe to eat. And when she noticed Tom wiping some dirt off a kitchen counter, she laughed and told him, "You don't have to do that. That's *country* dirt. I'm only afraid of *city* dirt. Country dirt won't hurt you."

Tom and I spent the weekend helping Larisa harvest the last produce from the garden, shredding cabbage for sauerkraut, processing seeds for next year's planting, preparing meals with ingredients fresh from the earth, and drinking cup after cup of hot tea sweetened with preserves made from berries that grew near the house. But I was surprised that such a knowledgeable gardener thought her bushy basil, grown from seeds someone had sent from America,

# Wild Things

Autumn is the start of hunting season in Russia. In addition to foraging for wild fruits, berries, mushrooms, nuts, and other edible plants, the people of Siberia—from indigenous groups to contemporary Russians—have always hunted mammals, fish, and birds for food. Native Siberians not only killed animals to eat, but also used the rest of the animal for making clothes, tools, and shelter from the skins, bones, feathers, and other parts. And they performed simple or elaborate rituals to honor those animals, too, thanking them for their sacrifice to the people who needed the animals' bodies to sustain human life.

Europeans who began expanding into northeast Asia in the 1500s hunted for food by necessity. But much of that territorial expansion was driven by the commercial value of animal pelts—the search for the so-called "soft gold" of Siberia. Over the next three centuries, hunting for profit nearly decimated the Siberian populations of sea otters, sables, squirrels, martens, and minks.

As European settlement took hold in Siberia, so did hunting for sport, especially by the nineteenth century and continuing even to the present. Sport-hunting and profit-hunting have overlapped, too, with Western hunters paying huge sums of money to trophy-hunt Siberian bears, wolves, and other large game, and with poachers illegally killing endangered Siberian tigers and Amur leopards to sell their skins and organs to wealthy Chinese and other East Asians willing to pay high prices for them on the black market.

was only an ornamental plant, not an edible herb. Larisa was delighted when I explained how to make Italian *pesto* using her fresh basil and the pine nuts foraged from the forest nearby.

Before we left on Sunday evening for the overnight trip back to Vladivostok, Larisa loaded up our rucksacks and tote bags with potatoes, beets, cauliflower, cabbages, and melissa, which we lugged by bus, train, and tram back to our apartment in the city. And for the next two months we silently thanked Larisa every time we made a soup or salad from those delicious vegetables so lovingly grown in her dacha garden.

## Creation Story

Vladivostok is the capital of Primorskii Krai, the Maritime Territory located on the southernmost edge of Russia's Far East. It's a region known for an unusual variety of flora and fauna, unlike that of any other place in Russia. Almost 2,000 different plants grow within the borders of Primorskii Krai, including 250 species of trees and shrubs. Local legend says that when God was creating the Earth, he was so busy that he forgot about this remote area near the Great Ocean. When he realized the oversight, he shook out the remnants in his bag, showering that small corner of the planet with the unique combination of plants and animals found there today.

Twelve years later we spent a sultry summer day at another dacha in a remote region two hours' drive from Vladivostok over difficult roads. That country retreat was little more than an unkempt two-room shed, so small and dusty that we were glad we weren't staying overnight. The nearest water supply was a communal spigot 200 yards away on a dirt road, and the toilet was a colorfully painted wooden outhouse downhill from the dacha. But on that warm and sunny July day, we all enjoyed making cold *okroshka* soup for the start of our mid-afternoon lunch, cooking *shashlyki* (shish-kebabs) and new potatoes on a primitive outdoor grill, and sipping beer from plastic cups as we sat around a rickety old table graced with a jam jar full of wildflowers.

After that long, lazy lunch disturbed only by swarms of mosquitoes, Tom and I walked down a narrow path into the lush, jungle-like forest behind the dacha. The fertile forests in that southernmost part of the Russian Far East boast an unusual variety of plants, unlike in any other part of Russia. Subtropical vines curl around conifers, rowan trees grow next to lotuses and lianas, cork trees tower over hot-pink orchids. Summer and early autumn are the seasons for many of the wild foods that locals are so adept at foraging: cherries, grapes, cranberries, and cloudberries; apples, apricots, plums, and pears; mushrooms, horseradish, and sorrel; Manchurian walnuts and Siberian filberts; and the precious "root of life," wild ginseng.

While I was stooping to look at some pretty red mushrooms near the path, Tom suddenly tensed up and whispered, "I feel like we're being watched. Let's head back to the dacha." I knew what he meant. I'd felt the same sense of unease. That was Siberian tiger territory, and it wasn't wise to venture too far, alone and unprotected, into the land that belongs to those magnificent felines.

## The Russian Summer Kitchen

In old Russian *izby* (wooden cottages) the traditional stove was a large, handmade, floor-to-ceiling construction of clay or stone (later bricks) plastered on the outside and sometimes decorated with glazed tiles or painted folk art. Built into one corner or one wall of the cottage's main room, this wood-fired stove provided a steady source of heat, day and night. It was used not only for cooking, but also for heating the house and drying mushrooms, berries, fruits, herbs, and wet clothing. Constructed with ledges on different levels, the stove was also a cozy place where children, elders, and cats slept to keep warm.

But a big heated stove can be uncomfortable in summer (yes, summer can be warm, even hot, in many parts of Russia). So the big estates in the past, and even some of the village cottages, had a separate "summer kitchen" outside the main house, where meals were cooked and where summer's bounty of fruits, berries, and vegetables was preserved for eating throughout the year. I've seen these summer kitchens still being used in the Russian Far East—from Reineke Island in the south, in the Sea of Japan, to the rugged coast of the Sea of Okhotsk and the interior of the Kamchatka Peninsula in the north. They look much like the summer kitchens I saw as a child in the American Deep South, half a century before. Most of the Russian outdoor kitchens were just slapped-together wooden sheds, completely open to the elements on one or even more sides, with a wood-burning iron or masonry stove, a few crude wooden shelves, and a jumble of glass jars, aluminum pots, and rusty utensils. In those very basic summer kitchens, Russians cooked the fresh foods of summer and preserved the rest to sustain them through the hard winter, until the next cycle of harvest and home-canning began.

# Back of Beyond

Although I've eaten many memorable meals along the main Trans-Siberian line, that Russian ribbon of steel has also taken me into the Buryat-Mongolian lands of southern Siberia, where the Trans-Mongolian railway branch carried me even farther into Mongolia itself. And in both Buryatia and Mongolia, I encountered foods I'd never tasted before. Other travels have taken me to remote regions of Siberia and the Russian Far East, some of them accessible only on foot or from the ocean, by making "wet landings" from Zodiacs (small rubber dinghies) onto wild seashores where brown bears hunt for berries, seals and sea lions snooze on the rocks, and Steller's sea eagles soar overhead. Thanks to Russian and Buryat friends, university colleagues, several expedition companies, and my willingness to taste anything set before me, I've had the good fortune to learn much more about a part of the world that many people would consider "the back of beyond."

Shortly after Tom and I moved to Vladivostok, Russian colleagues took us on a hike to a nature reserve outside the city. Stopping at a ramshackle research station, we lunched on a potluck jumble of foods we'd all carried from home in our backpacks or foraged along the way. That decrepit wooden building deep in the forest looked like a hermit's lair from a century before, with a rusty old shotgun and a World War II gas mask hanging from nails in the wall. Surrounded by rickety shelves lined with dusty jars of desiccated plants, we knocked back shots of wheat vodka between bites of Russian and American picnic fare—meat and fish pâtés spread on thick slices of bread, boiled eggs, *pirozhki* with fillings of fish, cabbage, or potatoes—as a

## Surprising Siberian Feast

"We had come to Kamchatka with minds and mouths heroically made up for an unvarying diet of blubber, tallow candles, and train-oil; but imagine our surprise and delight at being treated instead to such Sybaritic luxuries as purple blueberries, cream, and preserved rose leaves!" —George Kennan, *Tent Life in Siberia* (1870)

308

*Siberian rural houses with their potato patches in back, 2006.*

Janis Joplin tape played in the background. I'd brought sticky buns as our contribution to the meal, baked from an old family recipe and sweetened with my own sea-buckthorn jam made from golden-orange berries bought at the Vladivostok farmers' market. But my favorite dish among all those crowded onto the rough wooden table was Russian *tvorozhniki*, little patties of fresh white curd cheese fried in butter, drizzled with sour cream, and sprinkled with sugar. Those rich, cheesy pancakes were so seductive I could have devoured the entire platter by myself.

A few months later and two thousand miles away, a Russian military intelligence officer, who was interested in Siberian religions, took us to visit the Ivolginski Datsan, a colorful Buddhist lamasery situated on the windswept steppes of Buryatia, about 20 miles from the city of Ulan-Ude. The ground was covered with snow, the ruts in the roads frozen solid, and the temperature 10 degrees below zero, Fahrenheit. So imagine our surprise when he parked the car in a field outside the monastery walls and began laying out food on

*Siberian village house near Lake Baikal, 2007.*

the hood: whole wheat bread, pickled cucumbers, slices of sausage, a box of chocolates, a bottle of vodka, and a thermos of homemade coffee liqueur, a Russian version of Kahlua. As we stood around outside the car, stamping our feet to keep warm and eating fast before the food froze, I tried to photograph that Siberian winter picnic to record it for posterity. But it was so cold my fingers stuck to the metal on my camera and the shutter refused to budge.

When the weather finally warmed in May and June, we hiked with Siberian friends into the *taiga*—the great expanse of dense forest that extends over thousands of miles of subarctic Russia—where the Russians fished for trout in a cold mountain river and cooked *ukha* (fish soup) in a big iron pot suspended from an iron tripod over an open fire. And after Lake Baikal began to thaw in late spring, we picnicked on its shores several times with Russian and American colleagues, laying out spreads of buttered bread with caviar, chunks of sausage and cheese, smoked chicken, and boiled eggs, while our bottles of beer and champagne chilled in the still-frigid waters of the lake. For dessert I often

# Gift of the Forest

Pine nuts are among the many "gifts of the forest" that have nourished the people of northeast Asia for thousands of years, ever since early hunter-gatherers in the Siberian *taiga*—the great forest of coniferous trees that extends across much of subarctic Eurasia—found a satisfying food source in the plump, oily, pine-tree seeds nestled within the brown cones of the Siberian pine (*Pinus sibirica*), Siberian dwarf pine (*Pinus pumila*), and Korean pine (*Pinus koraiensis*), which grow from western Siberia to the Russian Far East.

Long valued for their healthful properties as well as their taste, Siberian pine nuts are a good source of protein, unsaturated fats, vitamins, amino acids, and minerals. Before the Soviet era, pine nut oil was both a valued export product from Russia and an important cooking ingredient during the fasting periods of the Russian Orthodox Church, when the consumption of animal fats was forbidden. Alla told me that before the Bolshevik Revolution, Empress Alexandra, wife of Tsar Nicholas II, even had pine nut oil specially sent to her from Siberia, as a beauty product to keep her skin soft and supple.

Today's Siberians consume pine nuts in many forms: raw, straight from the cones and shelled; toasted and sometimes salted; pressed (preferably cold pressed) into pine nut oil; processed into pine nut butter; ground into pine nut meal; and rolled into pine nut flakes— all of which are used as ingredients in cooking, from appetizers and main dishes to confections and desserts. I've also found pine nut vodka and sweet pine nut liqueur on supermarket shelves in Vladivostok—two drinks whose flavors always remind me of the dense Siberian forests.

brought along my "Baikal brownies," American chewy chocolate brownies studded with pine nuts from the Siberian forest. Brownies were a new taste treat for the Russians, and they all wanted the recipe.

In mid-May, Vladimir, one of our students, invited Tom and me on a picnic with his family—his mother, his wife, and their two small children. It was an

---

## Salt-Preserved Greens

Russians preserve wild garlic in late spring and wild sorrel in early autumn for a treasured taste of greens throughout the winter. Sorrel leaves are air-dried overnight, sprinkled with salt, and stacked in layers in a container with a weight on top to press the leaves down into the brine that forms inside. Siberians near Lake Baikal showed me how they preserved wild garlic leaves by stacking them in 3-liter jars, in alternate layers with garlic, salt, and small round river stones polished smooth by the moving water. Chopped salt-preserved greens were often used for seasoning soups, and wild garlic leaves were combined with sour cream to make a cold winter salad whose flavor stirred up memories of a warmer spring.

---

opportunity to enjoy the long-awaited springtime weather while also gathering *cheremsha*, the wild garlic that grows in abundance in that part of Siberia. Russians especially value the flat broad leaves as one of the first fresh greens to emerge from the earth after the long winter—just like the Siberian bears do, who also feast on *cheremsha* when they wake up from hibernating in the forest. No wonder the Latin name for this plant, which is rich in vitamin C and minerals, is *Allium ursinum*, bear's garlic.

I was surprised at the spot Vladimir chose for the picnic—the site of a former gulag (prison camp) several miles from Irkutsk. In the forest clearing where we foraged for the green shoots of garlic, we soon turned up traces of the painful past: rotted fence posts, rusty barbed wire, and the remnants of a railroad track running to nowhere. But these grim reminders of Soviet Russia were tempered by the warm Siberian sunshine, the wildflowers in full bloom, and the trilling of songbirds in the trees.

Surrounded by these sights and sounds of eternal Russia, we grilled *shashlyki* over an open fire, munched on spring onions and pickled green tomatoes, drank homemade berry juice, and finished the meal with a Siberian specialty baked by Vladimir's mother: a dense, moist, richly flavored cake made with finely ground bird cherry flour and sour cream. But as we enjoyed that picnic in the "new" Russia of the 1990s, I couldn't help wondering if our presence in that particular place was somehow an affront to whatever sad spirits of the past still lingered there.

# Bird Cherry Torte

Known as *cheremukha* in Russian, bird cherry (*Prunus padus*) is a species of native cherry that grows in northern Asia. Sweet-smelling white blossoms on the bushy trees scent the springtime air, and the astringent-tasting small black fruits are beloved by birds. Russians pick the fruit in late summer or early autumn, let it dry until shriveled, then grind it into a dark-colored flour whose flavor hints of almond, cherry, and chocolate. Siberians make cakes and *pryaniki* (gingerbreads) with it. The Mongolic Buryats, who have lived in this region for centuries before the Russians arrived, also make several dishes from dried-and-ground bird cherries.

Vladimir's mother gave me her recipe for Bird Cherry Torte, a traditional Siberian sweet made for special occasions: Mix together 1 cup of bird cherry flour, ¾ cup of white flour, 1 cup of milk or *kefir*, 1 teaspoon of baking soda, and 3 well-beaten eggs. Bake in a 12 × 12-inch square metal pan in a slow oven (325°F.) until done. While the cake is still hot, mix 2 cups of sour cream with 1 cup of sugar in a blender, then spread it over the hot cake and let it soak in. Let the cake sit for 12 to 24 hours before serving. Just before serving spread the top with a layer of unsweetened sour cream. Since this flat, single-layer cake is so moist and dense, serve it directly from the pan it was baked in.

(Note: Her recipe is based on 250-milliliter cups. Bird cherry flour is hard to find in the West, but can be ordered online from companies in Russia.)

Many Siberians are good at foraging for wild foods, hunting for game, and fishing the country's rivers and streams, even though those skills are no longer as necessary for survival as they were in earlier times. From late spring through early autumn, millions of Russians also go "silent hunting" for the mushrooms that spring up in the forests and fields. And I know modern urban Russians who still enjoy scouring the countryside for wild fruits, berries, nuts, fiddlehead ferns, sorrel, horseradish, and garlic, to supplement the foods grown at their dachas and bought in the stores.

Although more wild edibles grow in the temperate parts of southern Siberia, there's plenty to eat in the northerly reaches, too, as the native Siberians have always known. On hikes with botanists and field biologists in the higher latitudes of the Russian Far East, I've picked wild raspberries, lingonberries, salmonberries, crowberries, cranberries, and cloudberries, the best I've ever tasted, on the mossy tundra of the north. I've dug up and chewed on the roots of *sarana* flowers, several lily-like plants with bulbous white roots that look somewhat like garlic pods. In the past, Siberians dried these starchy roots and ground them into flour, for making a nutritious porridge and a dried paste that early European explorers described as the Siberian substitute for bread. One native Siberian told me that during World War II thick porridge made from dried *sarana* roots kept his family alive at times when other foods were scarce.

Twice we sailed with a group of Russian colleagues on a rusty little research boat to Reineke Island in the Gulf of Peter the Great, south of Vladivostok. Although we all brought home-cooked foods to contribute to the midday meal, the star of the show was Amir's *ukha*, Russian fish soup, cooked on the sandy shore of the island. After building a driftwood fire, Amir filled a big metal bucket with water, set it over the fire, and plopped into it his "flying fish," a large whole chicken. When the chicken had boiled thoroughly, he removed it from the pot

## Kamchatka Peninsula, 1865

"… previous to the settlement of the country by the Russians, the only native substitute for bread was a sort of baked paste, consisting chiefly of the grated tubers of the purple Kamtchatkan lily. The only fruits in the country are berries and a species of wild cherry. Of the berries, however, there are fifteen or twenty different kinds, of which the most important are blueberries, 'maróshkas,' or yellow cloud-berries, and dwarf cranberries. These the natives pick late in the fall, and freeze for winter consumption. Cows are kept in nearly all the Kamtchadal settlements, and milk is always plenty. A curious native dish of sour milk, baked curds, and sweet cream covered with powdered sugar and cinnamon, is worthy of being placed upon a civilized table." —George Kennan, *Tent Life in Siberia* (1870) and tossed in chunks of peeled potatoes and a couple of sliced onions. When the potatoes were cooked, Amir finally added the fish, large pieces of flounder and salmon, and a handful of herbs. "Ukha should be stirred only with a lacquered spoon," insisted Amir, who'd brought one with him that day. And a few minutes later, just before serving the soup, he poured a good amount of vodka into the pot. "That's what makes a *real* Russian ukha!" he exclaimed, knocking back a shot of vodka himself. Maybe the sea air had made me especially hungry, but that fish soup on Reineke Island was the best *ukha* I'd ever eaten.

## Fish Tales

Siberia's rivers and lakes, as well as the seas off the coast of the Russian Far East, teem with fish. Lake Baikal is famous for its *omul'*, a tasty fish endemic to Baikal's clear waters. The Amur River on the border between Russia and China is home to dozens of species, including huge taimen and Kaluga sturgeon. Fishermen cast their lines for trout, char, carp, catfish, grayling, pike, and perch. All six species of Pacific salmon live in the Russian Far East: king (Chinook), red (sockeye), silver (coho), pink (humpback), chum (dog salmon), and masu (cherry salmon). Ships off Russia's eastern shore harvest herring, halibut, flounder, squid, and huge Kamchatka crabs. And divers scour the ocean floor for spiky sea urchins, fan-shaped scallops, and leathery sea cucumbers, delicacies that bring high prices in today's markets.

Some Siberians also hunt sea birds (or their eggs) and sea mammals—whales, seals, sea lions, walruses—which they eat raw, cooked, or preserved. Native Siberians preserve fish and mammal flesh by drying, smoking, salt-curing, fermenting, or freezing, as well as cooking the meat submerged in the animals' own fat (like French *confits* of goose or duck). Northern Siberians even make a kind of flour from dried fish that has been finely ground and pressed through a sieve.

For thousands of years, native Siberians have used other parts of those animals, too—sea mammal skins, bones, and organs for clothing, tools, building materials, and containers, as well as fish skins and bird feathers for clothing and ceremonial objects.

# Ukha through the Ages

A classic Russian fish soup today, *ukha* in earlier times was also made with other meats, as well as grains and mushrooms. But from who-knows-when, it has been known primarily as a kind of basic fish stew cooked by outdoorsmen over an open fire, on the beaches of oceans and banks of rivers where the fish had been freshly caught. This simple stew was hungrily devoured by the fishermen who dipped their cups or spoons into the communal soup pot, usually just a metal bucket or iron pot filled with water, fish, a few potatoes, and some herbs.

Over time, and with the influence of French cooking in Russia, *ukha* evolved from a rustic, chunky fish stew into a lighter, but still richly flavored, clear fish soup, strained through a fine sieve and sometimes further clarified with egg whites. Served in soup bowls at the table, this refined type of *ukha* is usually accompanied by small savory pastries such as *pirozhki* or *rasstegaï* (often with fish in their filling, too). Sometimes the boiled fish strained out of the broth is even served as a separate course, garnished with grated fresh horseradish.

Different "colors" of *ukha* are produced by using certain kinds of fish and other ingredients that impart their particular hues to the soup: pike, whitefish, perch, and onions for "white" *ukha*; carp, rosefish, cinnamon, cloves, and pepper for "black" *ukha*; sterlet, salmon, and saffron for "red" or "amber" *ukha*. Regional variations include *ukha* made with milk in northern parts of European Russia and *ukha* containing tomatoes in southern parts of the country. Regardless of its other ingredients, *ukha* should be made with at least two different kinds of fresh fish, preferably more.

## Raw Liver and More

Surely the most surprising foods we ate in Siberia were served to us by the local Buryats, a Mongolic people whose ancestors have lived around Lake Baikal for a millennium. Today the Buryats are the largest indigenous ethnic group in Siberia. Historically nomadic herders of cattle, horses, sheep, and goats, they eventually traded their portable felt *gers* (yurts) for a more settled life in the rural villages and larger cities of southern Siberia. But Buryats are really horsemen at heart. They're Siberia's cowboys, in fur hats instead of Stetsons.

During our sojourn in Siberia, we met several Buryats who introduced us to their traditional native cuisine, which differed in many ways from that of their Russian neighbors. When they learned of our genuine interest in Buryat foods, some of them invited us to a village on the steppes north of Irkutsk for a day of feasting with Buryat families there. It was a place where strong winds blew across an arid landscape reminiscent of West Texas, where cattle and horses wandered down the unpaved streets of the small town and clouds of dust filled the air.

The morning began with a big breakfast at a cavernous civic hall, which included traditional Buryat tea, milky and salty; flat, round *shan'gi* buns topped with sour cream; raw fish from Lake Baikal; and wake-up shots of cold vodka. An hour later, that unorthodox breakfast was followed by coffee, cognac, and chocolate candies at a local official's office. And that was just the warm-up for a copious champagne-fueled lunch at a children's camp in the forest several miles from town. (The kids drank fruit juice, but the adults certainly didn't.) A recent rain had made the dirt track to the camp so deep with mud that we had to walk part of the way when our local transportation, a Russian four-wheel-drive vehicle, bogged down in the mire. On the way both to and from that lunch our hosts also stopped at a "sacred spot" near the roadside, for all of us to make an offering to the Buryats' spirit-gods by dipping the third finger of our right hand into our glasses of vodka and flicking some of the alcohol into the air—before we finished off the rest of the vodka ourselves.

Barely able to stay awake after all that morning and midday booze, we returned to the village later that afternoon where a Buryat family was preparing the next meal for us. The Tabikhanovs welcomed us to their home in the traditional manner by handing each of us a bowl of *tarag*, a cool, refreshing, thankfully non-alcoholic, cultured-milk drink similar to thin yogurt. Although we appreciated that gesture of hospitality, fermented milk was not the best thing to add to our stomachs already brimming with vodka, cognac, and champagne.

Eight members of three generations of Tabikhanovs lived together in single-story wooden house that had electricity but no running water or indoor plumbing. It reminded me of farmhouses I knew as a child in Texas, except for the graceful Central Asian-looking peaked archway that led into the Tabikhanov kitchen. To my surprise, the house had three cookstoves: in the entry hall, a gas stove hooked up to a large orange gas canister; a modern Russian electric range in the kitchen; and a traditional Russian brick-and-plaster, wood-burning stove built into one wall of the kitchen, used for both cooking food and heating the house.

As soon as we finished drinking the *tarag*, we all went outside to watch Rodion, the head of the household, ritually slaughter a sheep in our honor for the meal. After flipping the sheep on its back, he quickly used a long knife to make an incision in its breast, then reached into the chest to squeeze the aorta and stop the heart from beating—the way that Buryats and their Mongolian cousins have killed their livestock for centuries, a method of slaughter which ensures that little blood is lost and none of it touches the earth (for religious reasons). It was all over in a few seconds. Then Rodion and two neighbors butchered the sheep in the backyard, while the women processed the innards on wooden tables nearby. When the sheep's liver was removed, fresh and steaming, from the carcass, it was immediately cut into chunks, sprinkled with coarse salt, and passed around to all of us as a special treat. Dreading the thought of eating my portion of that bloody liver, I was saved by my camera. Just at the moment I started to photograph the event, I ran out of film. By the time I'd changed rolls of film, Tom and the Buryats had devoured all of the liver, washing it down with *tarasun*, potent moonshine distilled from soured milk, which the Buryats quaffed by the mugful as if it were nothing more than water.

## Native Treats

Every culture has certain foods that are considered special treats. The native Evenk people who live in several regions of Siberia eat frozen strips of raw reindeer liver dipped in salt—a dark-brown delicacy sometimes called (by foreigners) "Evenk chocolate." The Buryats favor raw horse liver—thinly sliced, topped with a layer of the best yellow-white horse fat, rolled up, and frozen solid, then cut crosswise into thin rounds that look much like our chocolate-vanilla pinwheel cookies in the West. The Buryats dip these icy rounds into chopped raw onions and garlic before devouring them with delight.

As we watched on the sidelines, Rodion removed the sheep's heart, lungs, and trachea in one piece and hung them from a nail on the barn. The stomach and intestines were taken out and washed in cold water, while the muscle meat and the bones were thrown into a big iron cauldron of boiling water, set on a blazing wood fire in the yard. Soon the sheep's head—unskinned, with wool and eyeballs still intact—was placed on the ground next to the fire, to singe the wool a bit before the head with thrown into the pot, too. Occasionally Grandmother Tabikhanova and a couple of the men also tossed a small piece of raw meat into the fire as an offering to their gods.

When the meat was cooked, we all went indoors and crowded around a large table in the living room. Rodion offered the first toast, welcoming us to his house and saying how honored his family was to prepare this feast for us. Then his wife passed around platters of appetizers to start the meal: pieces of sausage and raw fish, sliced tomatoes and cucumbers from her garden, and thick pieces of dense, chewy white bread, all accompanied by plenty of vodka, Russian champagne, and Bulgarian wine. The next course was mutton broth from the boiling cauldron outside, which we drank from bowls while Grandmother Tabikhanova went outside to throw a small portion of broth as an offering into the fire.

Then Tom and I, as the guests of honor, were served the most important part of the feast. The entire sheep's head, wet wool and sightless eyeballs still attached, was placed in front of Tom. Rodion said it was traditional for the male guest to sing a *töölei*, a special song about the sheep's head. But since Tom didn't know any Buryat sheep's head songs, we moved on to the next ritual. Rodion handed Tom a hunting knife and told him to cut off the sheep's left ear, cut a cross on the top of its head, and slice out a piece of the right cheek. Rodion then took the ear and cheek outside to throw into the fire as another offering to the Buryat gods.

My turn was next. Placed in front of me was the sheep's stomach, filled with a mixture of fresh cow's milk, fresh sheep's blood, garlic, and spring onions, tied up with the sheep's intestines, and boiled in the big pot along with the rest of the meat. I knew that somehow I had to eat that repulsive blob without throwing up: I couldn't insult a group of people who'd been so kind and generous to us. All the Buryats around the table waited expectantly for me to take the first bite. But I didn't know how or where to begin. Finally Rodion's wife leaned over with a large knife and sliced off the top of the stomach. The contents had not been fully cooked, and blood oozed out onto my plate. Then she took a soup spoon, scooped out some of the semi-coagulated mass, and handed the spoonful to me. Trying to focus my mind on something else—anything else—far away, I swallowed the junket-like lump and forced a smile.

The other guests waited expectantly for me to make the next move. Suddenly it occurred to me: pass the dish around. That's exactly what the Buryats wanted. Happily and hungrily, they scooped out and devoured large portions of that blood pudding until none of it was left (to my great relief), while Tom and I concentrated on the big platter of boiled mutton in the middle of the table. More vodka. More toasts. Declarations of friendship. More vodka. More wine. More champagne. And five hours after arriving at the Tabikhanovs' house, we concluded that memorable meal with large bowls of *salamat*—rich sour cream porridge, swimming in melted butter—which we were not allowed to eat until Grandmother Tabikhanova had put an offering of *salamat* into the fire.

We could barely get up from the table, much less walk in a straight line. But by that point, nobody noticed. At nine o'clock that evening, we climbed into a car with a local driver and bounced down the rutted, muddy streets of the village for the *next* meal, at the house of a respected Buryat elder who was well known for her good cooking.

The fourth and final feast of that long day remains only a pleasant blur in my memory. I recall a beautifully set table in a cheerful kitchen, with white painted cabinets, fresh flowers in a vase on the windowsill, and a view of the garden outside, luminous in the lingering Siberian summer twilight. I remember cups of hot tea sweetened with homemade berry preserves, rich mounds of Buryat clotted cream, tales of Buryat ancestors, a family photo album with pictures of a man in military uniform and a beautiful Buryat woman adorned with silver-and-coral jewelry—those fleeting images accompanied by a bottle of sweet raspberry liqueur that proved to be an excellent *digestif* after the excesses of that long and eventful day.

All those culinary experiences on the Asian side of Russia—from cities to trains to the outback, from the early 1990s until recently—have led me to conclude that Siberians are actually a lot like Texans: Bigger is better, food is friendship, and no guest ever leaves the table hungry.

# Russian Mimosa Salad

Just as "mimosa" is the name for two very different kinds of trees, Mimosa Salad can also be different in various parts of the world. In Russia this pretty salad is made with layers of grated or finely chopped ingredients often stacked in a large straight-sided glass mold so their colors show through, or shaped in small round molds, like deep-sided ramekins, then unmolded before garnishing. Classic recipes call for individual layers of chopped cooked salmon, finely chopped blanched white onions, boiled and grated carrots and potatoes, the chopped whites of hard-boiled eggs, sometimes cooked corn kernels or minced fresh green onion tops, too, and mayonnaise (always mayonnaise!). Before serving, the chilled salad is garnished with a yellow layer of grated hard-boiled egg yolks.

This salad's name comes from the garnish, which resembles the bright yellow flowers of a species of acacia tree, also known as mimosa. Like Russian potato salad, Mimosa Salad is a must on the New Year's table and at other family feasts. It's also served in the dining cars of some Trans-Siberian trains and sold as a take-out food at train-station delis. You can even serve it as a brunch dish at home, accompanied by that other kind of "mimosa"— the popular cocktail made from equal parts of chilled sparkling white wine and fruit juice (orange, pineapple, or grapefruit, for the matching yellow hue).

# Garlic Cheese

*This spicy, garlicky cheese is a popular appetizer in many parts of Russia. Chefs on the Golden Eagle Trans-Siberian Express stuff ripe red tomatoes with it. At a home-cooked dinner in a remote Siberian village, I was served this cheese atop thick slices of tomato. And restaurants in Vladivostok often include it as one of several zakuski at the start of a meal. Russians make it by putting all the ingredients through a meat grinder—but you can also grate the cheese by hand or even use a food processor.*

½ pound medium-sharp white cheddar cheese, finely shredded*
½ pound Emmentaler or Jarlsberg cheese, finely shredded*
¼ cup pure sour cream
¼ cup mayonnaise
8 to 10 large garlic cloves, squeezed through a garlic press
½ teaspoon ground cayenne pepper or hot paprika (optional)
¼ teaspoon salt

* Use a box grater, not a Microplane grater, which makes the cheese too soft.

- Toss the shredded cheeses together by hand in a large bowl. Whisk together the sour cream, mayonnaise, pressed garlic, hot pepper (optional), and salt in a small bowl, then add to the cheese, stirring to mix well.

- Cover and refrigerate at least 4 hours (preferably overnight) for the flavors to develop. Let the cheese mixture come to room temperature before serving. Use as a stuffing for small firm ripe tomatoes or cherry tomatoes, a topping for baked potatoes, or a spread for dark bread.

- Makes approximately 3 cups.

▶ **Tomatoes Stuffed with Garlic Cheese:** Use small, firm, ripe round tomatoes or large cherry tomatoes. Slice off enough of each tomato's top to remove the stem but retain as much of the whole tomato as possible. Carefully slice each tomato ⅔ of the way down from the top toward the bottom, without cutting all the way through to the bottom. Rotate the tomato a quarter of a turn and slice downward again in the same way. Gently open up the tomato, scoop out and discard the seeds, and fill the tomato with some of the garlic cheese (at room temperature), mounding the cheese into a small dome on the top. Garnish with chopped chives for color. Refrigerate any leftover cheese.

# Stuffed Mushrooms

*From late spring through fall, Russians flock to the forests and fields to pick mushrooms, an important ingredient in many dishes. Russians use mushrooms fresh and also preserve them by drying or pickling to have available during the long winter. These easy-to-make stuffed fresh mushrooms are equally delicious as an appetizer or as a side dish to accompany broiled or grilled meats.*

**16 large fresh *Boletus edulis* mushrooms (or 16 large champignons, about 1 pound)**
**6 tablespoons unsalted butter, melted (divided use)**
**1 shallot, finely chopped**
**1 large garlic clove, finely chopped**
**1 tablespoon finely chopped parsley or wild garlic**
**1 teaspoon mild or medium-hot paprika**
**½ cup dry bread crumbs**
**½ cup finely crumbled blue cheese, sheep's cheese (such as feta), or finely grated yellow cheese (such as Cheddar)**

- Preheat the oven to 350°F. Brush any dirt off the mushrooms, or wash them lightly and pat dry with paper towels. Carefully twist the stem off each mushroom, leaving the cap whole. Trim any tough fibrous ends off the mushroom stems, then finely chop the remaining stems.

- Heat 3 tablespoons of butter in a medium skillet. Sauté the minced mushroom stems, shallot, and garlic over medium-high heat for about 5 minutes. Remove the pan from the heat and stir in the parsley, paprika, and bread crumbs. Add the cheese and mix well.

- Lightly brush the outside of each mushroom cap with the remaining 3 tablespoons of melted butter. Stuff the interior of each mushroom cap with a heaping tablespoon of the filling, shaping the filling by hand into a small dome. Use all the filling in the 16 mushroom caps.

- Arrange the mushrooms, filling side up, in a single layer in a lightly oiled glass baking dish. Bake at 350°F. for 15 to 20 minutes. Serve hot, as a first course or as an accompaniment to broiled steaks or grilled meats. For a spicy version, top each mushroom with a small dot of ***Adzhiga*** (recipe, page 114) just before serving.

- Makes 4 servings as an appetizer, or 6 to 8 servings as an accompaniment to other dishes.

# Trans-Siberian Chicken Salad

*This recipe was given to me by a chef on the* Golden Eagle Trans-Siberian Express *train, where his chicken-salad appetizer was always popular with guests in the dining car.*

**2 pounds boneless, skinless chicken breasts**
**Chicken stock or water**
**¾ cup white onions chopped medium-fine**
**¾ cup frozen green peas**
**¾ cup peeled-and-seeded cucumber diced into ¼-inch pieces**
**½ cup coarsely chopped walnuts**
**1⅓ cups mayonnaise**
**1 tablespoon lemon juice**
**Salt**

## Garnish

**Whole lettuce leaves**
**Toasted walnut halves**

- Place the chicken breasts in a single layer in a large (12-inch) skillet. Add enough chicken stock or water to cover them to a depth of 1 inch above the chicken. Slowly bring the liquid to a simmer, uncovered, over medium-low heat. Then cover the skillet, leaving the lid slightly ajar, and reduce the heat to low. Poach the chicken for 8 to 10 minutes, depending on its thickness. Remove from the liquid, let cool completely, and dice into ¼-inch cubes. (Makes 4 cups of diced cooked chicken.)

- Pour boiling water over the chopped onions in a bowl and let them blanch for 3 minutes. Drain thoroughly in a colander, then use your hands to squeeze out as much liquid as possible.

- Pour boiling water over the frozen peas in a bowl, let them sit for 3 minutes, then drain thoroughly. Toast the chopped walnuts and walnut halves (for garnish) for 8 minutes on a baking sheet in a preheated 350°F. oven. Whisk together the mayonnaise and lemon juice.

- Combine the chicken, onions, peas, cucumbers, and chopped walnuts in a large bowl, tossing the ingredients together to mix thoroughly. Add the mayonnaise mixture and stir gently until well combined. Taste and add salt as needed.

- Serve on whole lettuce leaves and garnish with toasted walnut halves.

- Makes: 6 cups (twelve ½-cup servings).

# "Green Bean Casserole" Salad

*When this salad was served as an appetizer on the* Golden Eagle *train, all the Americans in the dining car burst out laughing. The Russian chefs surely had no idea they'd created a cold version of classic American green bean casserole. But this Russian twist on an American Thanksgiving favorite turned out to be very good indeed. Surprise your guests with it at your next holiday dinner.*

**2 pounds fresh or frozen French-cut green beans**
**1 cup bottled or canned mushrooms (champignons or chanterelles, the** *least* **pickled or vinegary kind you can find)**
**½ cup pure sour cream**
**2 teaspoons Dijon mustard**
**1½ teaspoons salt**

## Garnish

**Crisp-fried onions (the packaged kind is okay—use the brownest, crispest onions you can find)**

- Boil or steam the green beans until they are just tender but still a bit crisp. Plunge them into a large bowl of cold water to stop the cooking, then drain thoroughly. Refrigerate the green beans for at least 1 hour.

- Drain the bottled mushrooms and rinse thoroughly under cold running water. Drain well again and pat with paper towels to absorb more of the moisture. Slice the mushrooms lengthwise into ¼-inch-wide strips.

- Whisk together the sour cream, Dijon mustard, and salt in a small bowl.

- Toss the green beans and mushroom slices together in a large bowl. Add the sour-cream dressing and toss until all the green beans are coated with it. Cover and refrigerate until serving time. (Recipe can be made 1 day in advance.)

- Garnish each serving with a sprinkling of crisp-fried onions on top.

- Makes 6 to 8 servings.

# Beet Salad with Walnuts and Prunes

*This richly flavored, pretty pink appetizer is often served as one of several* zakuski *at the start of a Russian meal, including dinners on the* Golden Eagle *train. Even people who say they don't like beets are usually seduced by this salad. (Watch them sneak back for second helpings.)*

**2½ pounds fresh beetroots (weight without stalks and leaves), unpeeled**
**Vegetable oil**
**½ to ¾ cups coarsely chopped walnuts**
**16 pitted prunes**
**4 large garlic cloves, minced**
**1 teaspoon salt**
**1 teaspoon freshly ground black pepper**
**¾ cup pure sour cream**

- Preheat the oven to 400°F. Wash and dry the unpeeled beets and rub them lightly with vegetable oil. Bake them on a baking sheet lined with aluminum foil, for 1 hour (or longer, depending on their size), until the beets are tender when pierced with a fork. Let them cool completely.

- While the beets are cooling, reduce the oven temperature to 350°F. and toast the walnuts in a single layer on a baking sheet for 8 minutes. Slice the prunes in half lengthwise, then slice each half lengthwise into thin strips (julienne).

- Peel the cooled beets, cut off the tough ends, and shred the beets coarsely (about 4 to 5 cups of shredded beets). Combine the beets, walnuts, prunes, garlic, salt, and pepper, tossing to mix well. Gently stir in the sour cream, mixing well. Cover and refrigerate for several hours before serving. (This salad is even better when made a day in advance.) Let it warm up a bit at room temperature before serving.

- Makes 8 to 10 servings.

# Russian Cole Slaw

*This crunchy cabbage salad often accompanies grilled* shashlyki *(shish-kabobs) at Russian picnics. Chefs on the* Golden Eagle *train prepare it for picnics on the shore of Lake Baikal, where pork, beef, chicken, and fresh fish from the lake are charcoal-grilled in the open air. Sunflower oil is essential for a real Russian flavor.*

**One 2½- to 3-pound green cabbage, cored and shredded**
**2 large carrots, peeled and coarsely shredded**
**1 white onion, chopped medium-fine**
**½ cup sunflower oil**
**¼ cup white vinegar**
**2 large garlic cloves, minced**
**1½ teaspoons salt**
**1½ teaspoons whole coriander seeds**
**1 teaspoon coarsely ground black pepper**

- Put the shredded cabbage into a large bowl and pour a kettle full of boiling water over it. Let the cabbage blanch in the hot water for 3 minutes, then drain in a colander, rinse with cold water, and drain thoroughly.

- Toss the cabbage, carrots, and onion together in a large bowl. Whisk together the oil, vinegar, garlic, salt, coriander seeds, and black pepper in a small bowl until the mixture is emulsified (thick and cloudy). Pour this dressing over the vegetables and toss to mix well.

- Cover and refrigerate for 12 to 24 hours. Before serving, toss the salad again, taste, and add more salt and pepper if desired.

- Makes 8 servings.

# Mongolian Spicy Beef Salad

*I first tasted this spicy beef salad at a nomad camp in the Gorkhi-Terelj National Park in Mongolia. It's also typical of the cold meat salads eaten by ethnic Mongolians who live in southern Siberia. The recipe shows the influence of northern Chinese and Russian ingredients (pickled vegetables) on traditional Mongolian cuisine, which emphasizes meat and milk dishes, not vegetables.*

2½ to 3 pounds boneless chuck roast (choice grade), roasted until well done, then cooled*

1 cup bottled pickled mushrooms (12-ounce net weight bottle), rinsed, drained, and dried

1 large sour dill pickle

½ large onion

½ large fresh red bell pepper

10 to 12 large fresh spinach leaves, washed and dried

¼ cup sunflower oil

¼ cup white vinegar

1½ to 2 teaspoons ground cayenne pepper

1 teaspoon salt

## Garnish

½ cup fresh green onion tops, thinly sliced crosswise into rounds (measured after slicing)

*Or any other cut of boneless beef suitable for roasting

- Trim the fat and any heavily charred areas off the roasted beef. Cut the beef across the grain into thin pieces, lay each piece flat, and slice the pieces lengthwise across the grain into thin strips (about 3 to 4 cups of beef strips).

- Julienne (slice into matchstick-size pieces) the mushrooms, dill pickle, onion, bell pepper, and spinach leaves. Put all of these into a large bowl with the beef strips and toss to mix well.

- In another bowl, whisk together the sunflower oil and vinegar until the mixture becomes cloudy and a bit thick. Whisk in the cayenne and salt. Pour over the beef and vegetables, tossing them together until all the pieces are well coated with this dressing. Cover and refrigerate for several hours, for the flavors to meld.

- Before serving, let the salad sit at room temperature for about 15 minutes, then toss the ingredients together once more. Garnish each serving generously with sliced green onion tops.

- Makes 6 large servings or 8 to 12 side-dish servings.

## You Are What You Eat

Meat and milk have traditionally been the mainstays of the nomadic Mongolian herders' diet, supplemented by wild foods foraged from the land: berries, fruits, pine nuts, onions, garlic. Over many centuries, contact with the Chinese, and later the Russians, eventually brought cultivated root vegetables, cabbages, cucumbers, capsicum peppers, grains (wheat, rice, barley, millet), and a few spices (black pepper, red pepper) to the Mongolians' table. But the Mongolians are really meat eaters. They have an old saying that "meat is for man and grass is for animals."

# Mushroom Cream Soup

*Hot soups are often a transitional course between the appetizers and the main dish of a Russian meal. Creamy mushroom soups are especially welcome on cool autumn days. I've enjoyed this soup at several places in Russia, including on the dining cars of luxury trains. Wild mushrooms are the Russians' preference, but cultivated ones make a very good soup, too.*

**6 cups unsalted or low-salt chicken stock**
**¼ cup dried mushroom powder ("Mushroom Dust," recipe, page 129)**
**2 pounds fresh mushrooms, cleaned**
**10 tablespoons unsalted butter (divided use)**
**4 shallots (or 1 small onion), finely chopped**
**½ cup brandy**
**1 tablespoon Worcestershire Sauce**
**1 teaspoon salt (or more, to taste)**
**1 teaspoon freshly ground black pepper (or more, to taste)**
**2 cups half-and-half (or 1 cup milk and 1 cup cream)**
**2 tablespoons all-purpose flour**

● Stir together the chicken stock and mushroom powder. Trim any tough fibrous stems off the fresh mushrooms. Finely chop half the mushrooms; chop the other half a bit more coarsely.

- Melt 8 tablespoons (1 stick) of butter in a large stockpot over medium-high heat. Add the chopped shallots or onion and sauté until golden. Add the fresh mushrooms, stir well, then pour in the brandy and stir again. Add the chicken stock, Worcestershire sauce, salt, and pepper.

- Bring the mixture to a boil over high heat. Cover the pan, reduce the heat to medium, and cook for about 20 minutes, or until the mushrooms are tender.

- Remove the lid and reduce the heat to low. Slowly pour in the half-and-half, stirring constantly. Leave the soup on the stove, over low heat, while you mash together the flour and remaining 2 tablespoons of butter in a small bowl until well combined. Stir this into the soup. Increase the heat to medium and cook for a few minutes longer, stirring constantly with a wooden spoon, until the soup begins to thicken and coats the spoon. *Do not let it boil.* Taste and add more salt and pepper if desired.

- Serve hot, each serving accompanied by one or more *pirozhki* on the side (**Pirozhki** recipe, page 30).

- Makes 6 large servings or 10 smaller servings.

▶ **MAKE-AHEAD TIP:** Prepare the soup up to the point just before you add the half-and-half. Let the mushroom mixture cool to room temperature, then freeze until needed. Defrost it in a stockpot over very low heat, stirring frequently, then add the half-and-half and follow the rest of the recipe.

# Russian Fish Stew

## (*Ukha*)

*Although I've eaten this simple fish stew in Russian restaurants and on Trans-Siberian trains, the best I ever tasted was on the sandy shore of an island off the coast of the Russian Far East. The man who cooked it over a driftwood fire said the soup should be stirred only with a lacquered wooden spoon and a good amount of vodka poured into the pot just before serving.*

**12 cups (3 quarts) richly flavored fish stock***
**3 bay leaves**
**10 whole peppercorns**
**10 whole coriander seeds**
**¾ cup vodka (divided use)**
**1 to 2 teaspoons salt (depending on whether fish stock is salted)**
**1½ pounds firm boiling potatoes, peeled and cut into 1-inch cubes**
**1 medium to large onion, quartered and thinly sliced**
**1½ pounds salmon fillets, cut into 2-inch-square pieces****
**1½ pounds flounder fillets, cut into 2-inch-square pieces****

### Garnish

**Green onion tops (thinly sliced crosswise into rings)**
**Chopped fresh parsley**
**Chopped fresh dill**

\* **Make your own fish stock in advance, or use a good-quality commercial fish stock.**

\*\***Or 1 pound each of 3 different kinds of fish.**

*Russian friend cooking ukha (fish soup) on an island off the coast of the Russian Far East, summer 1994.*

- Combine the fish stock, bay leaves, peppercorns, and coriander seeds in a large stockpot. Bring to a boil over high heat. Reduce the heat to medium and add ¼ cup of vodka and 1 to 2 teaspoons salt (depending on saltiness of the stock).

- Add the potatoes and onions. Bring to a boil, reduce the heat, partially cover, and simmer for 20 minutes. Add the fish pieces and bring the soup back to a simmer over medium heat. Partially cover the pot and let the soup simmer gently for about 5 minutes (or a bit longer, depending on the thickness of the fish)—just until the fish is cooked but not falling apart. Stir in the remaining ½ cup of vodka. Taste and add more salt if needed.

- Ladle the soup into individual bowls, dividing the fish and potatoes evenly among them. Garnish each serving with a sprinkling of sliced green onion tops, chopped parsley, and chopped dill. Serve hot.

- Makes: 10 servings (2 cups each).

# Russian Piquant Meat Stew

## (Solyanka)

*A traditional stew in Russia for centuries,* solyanka *today is usually made from leftover meats or fish, perked up with pickles, olives, capers, and lemon. A popular dish in restaurants and canteens during the Soviet era, it remains on many Russian menus today. You'll often find versions of* solyanka *served on the dining cars of Trans-Siberian trains and at train station buffets.*

¼ pound bacon, diced
2 tablespoons vegetable oil
2 medium onions, finely chopped
2 large garlic cloves, minced
1 tablespoon sweet (mild) paprika
¼ cup tomato paste
¾ pound cooked sausages, cut crosswise into ¼-inch rounds*
¼ pound cooked ham, cut into thin strips (julienned)*
4 small or 2 medium sour dill pickles, seeded and cut into thin strips, 2 inches long
7 cups beef stock
1 bay leaf
1 teaspoon freshly ground black pepper
½ teaspoon salt
½ cup pitted whole black or green olives
1 tablespoon pickled capers

**Garnish**

**Fresh lemon slices**
**Sour cream**

**\*Or a total of 1 pound of any leftover cooked meats, chopped or thinly sliced**

- Heat the bacon and oil together in a large soup pot over medium heat to melt some of the bacon fat. Increase the heat to medium-high, add the onions, and sauté until golden. Reduce the heat to low, stir in the garlic and paprika, and cook, stirring constantly for 1 minute. Quickly stir in the tomato paste.

- Add the meats, pickles, beef stock, bay leaf, pepper, and salt. Bring to a boil over high heat, then reduce the heat and simmer, partially covered, for 10 minutes. Add the olives and capers and simmer 5 minutes more.

- Serve hot, each bowl garnished with 2 thin slices of lemon and a large dollop of sour cream.

- Makes 6 large servings.

# Shish-Kabobs

## (Shashlyki)

*The smoky smell of* shashlyki *makes every Russian's mouth water. Yours will, too, when you inhale the aroma of marinated meat cooking over an open fire. Cubes of skewered, grilled meat—slightly charred on the outside and still juicy inside—are a favorite food for picnics and weekend outings at dachas, the country cottages where many urban Russians escape the stresses of daily life. And even in the depths of the Russian winter, you'll find street stands serving up skewers of hot pork, beef, or lamb grilled over charcoal. On its journey across Russia, the* Golden Eagle Trans-Siberian Express *stops by the shore of Lake Baikal, where the chefs offload grills and prepare a picnic lunch of* shashlyk *accompanied by grilled vegetables and a variety of salads.*

**2½ to 3 pounds boneless pork or beef**
**1 cup white wine**
**½ cup sunflower oil**
**¼ cup white vinegar (or 2 tablespoons white vinegar and 2 tablespoons sour dill pickle brine)**

**1 large onion, sliced crosswise into thin rings**
**4 large garlic cloves, minced**
**6 whole cloves or whole juniper berries, crushed**
**2 bay leaves, crumbled**
**1 teaspoon crushed red pepper flakes**
**1 teaspoon salt**
**1 teaspoon black pepper**

- Trim most of the fat off the meat, and cut the meat into 1½- to 2-inch cubes. Make 2 or 3 small cuts in each cube of meat, so the meat doesn't "seize up" while grilling.

- Combine the meat with all the other ingredients in a large bowl. Stir to mix well. Cover and refrigerate for 24 hours, turning the meat 2 or 3 times while it marinates.

- Before grilling, let the meat-and-marinade sit, uncovered, for about 30 minutes or until the meat comes to room temperature. Heat your charcoal until a fine gray-white ash appears on top of the charcoal.

- Remove the meat from the marinade, but do not pat it dry. Thread the meat cubes on metal skewers, leaving a small space between each piece of meat. (Or alternate the cubes of meat with squares of meat fat on the skewer, which keeps the meat moist as it grills.) Discard the marinade.

- Grill the meat about 4 inches above the hot coals for approximately 15 minutes, turning the meat 2 or 3 times as it cooks, until it is no longer pink in the middle.

- Serve hot, accompanied by chilled vodka or a hearty red wine. Traditional side dishes include onion quarters, chunks of bell peppers, whole fresh red tomatoes, and pickled green tomatoes, all skewered-and-grilled over the charcoal fire. A Russian summer favorite is new potatoes—whole, small, firm potatoes, boiled, and peeled—then skewered and reheated over the fire to give them a smoky flavor.

- Makes 4 servings.

# Stuffed Bell Peppers

*Old-fashioned comfort foods like stuffed peppers are popular in the dining cars of Russian trains, even luxury trains like the* Golden Eagle Trans-Siberian Express. *These easy-to-make stuffed peppers are filled with a pre-cooked rice, meat, and herb mixture, then braised in the oven and served in a pool of creamy tomato sauce.*

▶ **NOTE:** Make the rice in advance, so it's ready to be combined with the other ingredients.

## Stuffed Peppers

1 cup raw medium-grain rice, cooked in 2 cups beef or chicken stock until just tender (3½ cups total of cooked rice)
6 tablespoons sunflower oil (divided use)
1 large onion, chopped medium-fine
4 large garlic cloves, minced
½ cup finely chopped green onion tops
1 pound ground beef, pork, or turkey
1 to 2 teaspoons lightly crushed brown or yellow mustard seeds
1½ teaspoons dried thyme
1½ teaspoons dried marjoram
1½ teaspoons rubbed sage
1½ teaspoons black pepper
1 teaspoon salt
6 large bell peppers
1 cup beef or chicken stock
1 cup white wine
⅓ cup finely shredded hard yellow cheese (such as Cheddar)

## Sauce

1 cup cooking liquid (from the casserole)
2 cups canned tomato purée
2 teaspoons dried marjoram
¼ cup flour dissolved in 2 tablespoons cold water
1 cup pure sour cream, at room temperature

● Heat 2 tablespoons of oil in a large skillet and sauté the onion until translucent. Stir in the garlic and green onion tops, and sauté for 2 minutes more. Combine these with the 3½ cups of cooked rice in a large mixing bowl.

- Heat 2 tablespoons of oil in the same skillet and sauté the meat over medium-high heat until it is no longer pink, breaking up the meat into small pieces as it cooks. Reduce the heat to medium-low and stir in the mustard seeds, thyme, marjoram, sage, pepper, and salt. Cook 2 minutes longer. Combine the meat with the rice mixture.

- Preheat the oven to 375°F.

- Slice off the top of each pepper. Remove the seeds from inside the peppers, rinse out the interiors, and shake out the water. Fill each pepper to the brim with the rice mixture, packing them firmly with the stuffing, then replace the tops on the peppers.

- Spread 2 tablespoons of oil around the inside of a large, deep ovenproof casserole. Place the peppers upright in the pan. Pour in the stock and wine. Cover tightly and bake in the oven at 375°F. for 50 minutes.

- Remove the pepper tops and set aside. Sprinkle the shredded cheese on top of the stuffing in each pepper. Cover the casserole and return to the oven for 10 minutes more. Then carefully transfer the cooked peppers to a shallow baking dish and keep them warm in the oven while you make the tomato sauce.

- Pour out 1 cup of the liquid from the casserole into a saucepan. Stir in the tomato purée and marjoram. Bring to a boil over medium heat, stirring frequently. Whisk the flour into the cold water until smooth, then slowly add it to the tomato sauce. Cook, stirring constantly, until the mixture thickens. Whisk in the sour cream. Cook over medium-low heat just until the sauce is warm. Do not let it boil.

- Serve the stuffed peppers hot, surrounded by a pool of the sauce, with the pepper tops placed beside them.

- Makes 6 servings.

# Buryat Sour Cream Porridge

## (Salamat)

*The first time I ate this Buryat-Mongolian specialty in Siberia, I realized that it was the same as* rømmegrøt *(don't try to pronounce it), an old traditional dish in Norway. In Siberia, Mongolia, and Norway it's made with a kind of naturally soured cream containing at least 40% fat, which is not available in the United States. But you can make this same creamy-rich porridge with heavy whipping cream soured with lemon juice. Both the Buryats and the Norwegians serve this dish for special occasions, but the Norwegians dress it up with sugar and cinnamon, which is my preference, too.*

**4 cups (1 quart) pure heavy whipping cream (36% – 40% fat), containing no additives**
**¼ cup freshly squeezed lemon juice (strained before measuring)**
**2 cups whole milk**
**1 cup all-purpose flour (divided use)***
**½ to ¾ teaspoons salt**

**Garnish**

**⅓ cup sugar mixed with 1½ teaspoons ground cinnamon**

***The Mongolians often use rye flour in this dish, but the Norwegians use wheat flour.**

- Stir the cream and lemon juice together in a large heavy saucepan until well blended. Leave the mixture uncovered, at room temperature, for 30 minutes to sour. Just before cooking the cream, start heating the milk in a separate small saucepan so it will be hot when you need it.

- Bring the soured cream to a boil over medium heat, stirring constantly with a wooden spoon. Boil gently for 6 to 7 minutes, stirring constantly to prevent sticking.

- Reduce the heat to low and sift ½ cup flour over the cream, stirring vigorously to mix well. The mixture will look curdled and will begin to separate into melted butter and small white globs of the cream-flour mix. Don't panic—that's exactly what it's supposed to do.

- Continue cooking the mixture over low heat, stirring rapidly (almost beating it) with the wooden spoon. As the melted butter separates out and rises to the top, skim it off and put it in a small saucepan. Keep stirring the cream and skimming off the melted butter until no more butter separates and rises to the top (about 10 minutes). Remove the pan from the heat and let it sit for 1 minute. Skim off any additional butter that rises to the top. Keep the butter warm over low heat on the stove.

- Put the pan with the soured cream back on the stove, over low heat. Sift the remaining ½ cup of flour over the cream and stir until it begins to blend in. Add the hot milk, a small amount at a time, stirring vigorously after each addition. Continue stirring, over low heat, until the mixture is smooth. Add ½ teaspoon salt, stir well, and taste. Add another ¼ teaspoon salt if you want.

- Serve hot, in soup bowls, for a special treat on cold winter days. Spoon a small amount of the warm melted butter over the porridge and sprinkle cinnamon-sugar over the top. (The Norwegians always serve a glass of chilled cranberry or black currant juice with this rich sour cream porridge.)

- Makes 4 to 6 servings.

▶ **WASTE NOT:** Save the leftover clarified butter to use for flavoring cooked vegetables.

## Sacred White Foods

Over thousands of years Mongolic people have developed a large number and variety of dairy products from the milk of their herd animals: horses, cattle (including yaks), sheep, goats, Bactrian camels, and reindeer. Milk is boiled, curdled, fermented, dried, distilled—to make many forms of cream and butter (both sweet and soured), lacy-thin "milk skins," buttermilk, cheese, yogurt, sour cream porridge, *kumis* and other alcoholic beverages, to name only a few.

Mongolians also consider dairy products to be a special category of comestibles called "white foods." Fresh milk and other liquid milk products hold such an important place in Mongolian life that they are used in many sacred rituals rooted deep in the past. Today, nomadic herders and urban dwellers alike toss, sprinkle, or splash milk into the air, onto the ground, or onto an object as a way to venerate the spirits, bless an animal or special possession, or pray for protection on a journey or from the precariousness of Nature around them.

# Curd Cheese Pancakes

## (*Syrniki* or *Tvorozhniki*)

*Russians call these rich little patties* syrniki, *from* syr, *the Russian word for cheese—or* tvorozhniki, *from* tvorog, *the type of fresh white curd cheese they're made from. Fried in butter, garnished with sour cream, and sprinkled with sugar, they're a beloved breakfast food on many Russian tables and a morning treat on the* Golden Eagle *train. Russians also carry them on picnics, eat them for breakfast or lunch in students' and workers' canteens, and sometimes serve them as a light meal in the evening. Leftovers (if you have any!) can also be used as a sandwich filling between two slices of dark rye bread.*

**1 pound (2 cups) *tvorog* (farmer's cheese)***
**2 large egg yolks**
**2 tablespoons sugar**
**⅛ teaspoon salt**
**2 tablespoons pure sour cream**
**¼ teaspoon baking soda**
**½ cup all-purpose flour**
**5 tablespoons unsalted butter (divided use, for frying)**
**Flour (for dusting)**

**\*If there is any liquid in the cheese container, drain the cheese in a colander before using.**

- In a medium bowl, break up the cheese into small pieces with a fork, and mash it further to make it as smooth as you can. (Russians press it through a sieve.)

- Add the egg yolks, sugar, and salt, stirring to mix well. Mix the sour cream and baking soda together in a small bowl, then stir into the cheese mixture. Sift in the flour, and beat with a wooden spoon to make a smooth, soft dough.

- Dust a large piece of aluminum foil with flour. Scoop out heaping tablespoons of the dough, plopping them onto the foil to make 12 equal-size portions. To make each pancake, dust your hands with flour, form the dough into a ball, and press it into a round, flat patty, about 3 inches wide and ¼-inch thick. Dust both sides with flour, shaking off the excess.

- Melt 3 tablespoons of butter over medium heat in a large (12-inch) non-stick skillet. When the butter begins to bubble and pop, fry 6 patties in the pan for about 5 minutes on each side, until lightly browned. Transfer them to a plate, cover loosely with foil, and keep warm in a 150°F. oven. Melt the remaining 2 tablespoons of butter in the skillet, and fry the other 6 patties.

- Serve warm or at room temperature, with the garnish of your choice. Leftovers can be refrigerated, then reheated for about 30 seconds in a microwave oven.

- Makes 12 small pancakes (4 servings).

▶ **Garnishes (take your pick):** Sour cream, granulated sugar, ground cinnamon, vanilla sauce, fruit sauce (especially applesauce), jam, honey, birch syrup, even thin slices of lemon sprinkled with sugar and served on the side.

▶ **VARIATIONS:** Some cooks boost the flavor by adding other ingredients such as raisins plumped in brandy, ½ teaspoon vanilla extract, a little lemon juice or grated lemon peel, or a bit of grated nutmeg. You can also make a "lazy" version by forming the dough into small balls about the size of a walnut, and cooking them in boiling water to make little dumplings (serve with a garnish of sour cream or melted butter).

# A Taste for Tvorog

The most popular cheese in Russia is *tvorog*, a soft, white, fresh curd cheese with a slightly tangy taste, which is eaten on its own and also used as an ingredient in many recipes, both sweet and savory. Its flavor is sharper and its texture much drier and firmer than American cottage cheese (curd cheese), with a fat content ranging from no-fat to almost as high-fat as cream cheese. In Russia, *tvorog* is so important that some cookbooks include a separate chapter about dishes made with it, and there are even entire cookbooks of *tvorog* recipes.

*Tvorog* has been made in Slavic households for at least a thousand years, usually from naturally soured cows' milk, but sometimes from sheep's or goats' milk. Most of it is now produced commercially from cows' milk to which a souring agent, such as *kefir* or sour cream, is added. The milk is heated to lukewarm, then kept in a warm place for several hours until the soft curds separate from the liquid whey, which is drained off for other uses. The *tvorog* can be eaten right away or pressed into bricks, dried, and aged up to two months.

Although commercially produced *tvorog* is sold in most grocery stores in Russia, many Russians still say the best-tasting *tvorog* is made at home or bought at the farmers' markets. (Some of the cookbooks listed in the Bibliography have recipes for making your own *tvorog* at home.) In Texas, I buy it at our local Russian delis, which sell 10 kinds of *tvorog*, full fat and low fat, salted and unsalted, as well as two sweetened versions with apricots or raisins added. An acceptable American equivalent is farmer's cheese, a slightly different soft, white, bland-tasting, fresh curd cheese, but you need to add a little sour cream to it for that real Russian tang. Another good substitute is equal weights of farmer's cheese and ricotta, for savory dishes, and equal weights of farmer's cheese (or ricotta) and cream cheese, for sweet dishes.

# Baikal Brownies

## (Chocolate Brownies with Pine Nuts)

*Making these brownies in Russia was a labor of love. I had to sift the impurities out of the flour and cocoa, whisk the big grains of Russian "sandy sugar" with the eggs for 30 minutes to dissolve the sugar, and then keep an eye on the batter as it baked in the Stove-from-Hell. But it was worth all that effort. The Russians loved this new treat (even more when I included local pine nuts harvested from the forests around Lake Baikal). And our American friends in Russia eagerly devoured these brownies as a beloved taste of home.*

▶ **NOTE:** It's important to use a 13 × 9 × 2-inch metal baking pan for these dense, chewy-textured brownies.

**½ cup pine nuts**
**¾ cup unsweetened cocoa powder (not Dutch-process type)**
**1 cup all-purpose flour (plus 1 tablespoon flour for the pine nuts)**
**4 large eggs, at room temperature**
**¼ teaspoon salt**
**2 cups sugar**
**1 teaspoon vanilla extract**
**12 tablespoons (1½ sticks) melted unsalted butter, at room temperature**

- Preheat the oven to 325°F. Toast the pine nuts in a single layer on a baking sheet for about 8 minutes. Let the nuts cool, then chop them coarsely.

- Meanwhile, increase the oven heat to 350°F. Butter and flour a 13 × 9 × 2-inch metal baking pan.

- Whisk the cocoa powder and 1 cup of flour together in a medium bowl until well combined. Toss the pine nuts together with 1 tablespoon of flour in a small bowl.

- Beat the eggs and salt together in a large bowl with an electric mixer on low speed until the mixture is light and foamy. With the beater running on medium speed, add the sugar gradually, 1 tablespoon at a time, beating well after each addition. Continue beating until the mixture is pale ivory in color, thick and creamy in texture. Stir in the vanilla, then gently fold in the melted butter until no streaks remain.

- Using a light touch, fold half the flour-cocoa mixture gently into the egg mixture, only until the ingredients are completely combined. Then fold in the remaining half, followed by the flour-dusted pine nuts.

- Spread the batter evenly in the baking pan. Bake on the middle rack of the oven at 350°F. for 20 to 25 minutes, or just until a toothpick inserted in the center comes out clean. Don't overbake. Cool in the pan, set on a wire rack, then cut into approximately 2-inch squares.

- Makes 24 fudgy chocolate brownies.

▶ **VARIATION:** For **Texas Brownies**, replace the pine nuts with ½ cup chopped toasted pecans.

# Baked Siberia

*My Siberian version of this classic flambéed dessert features vodka-soaked cranberries and blueberries nestled in the layer of vanilla ice cream, representing the white-blue-red colors of the Russian flag. Making this dramatic dessert is a real production, but it's worth the effort for special occasions.*

▶ **ADVANCE PREPARATION:** Make the cake and prepare the ice cream at least a day before you plan to serve it. The meringue must be spread on the frozen ice cream and cake, then baked just before serving.

▶ **NOTE:** It is very important to use the correct pan sizes for this recipe.

## Ice cream

½ **cup dried cranberries**
½ **cup dried blueberries**
¼ **cup lemon-flavored vodka (or ¼ cup unflavored vodka and ¼ teaspoon fresh lemon juice)**
1½ **quarts (6 cups) best-quality vanilla ice cream**

## Cake

1 **cup plus 2 tablespoons all-purpose flour**
¾ **cup sugar**
1½ **teaspoons baking powder**
½ **teaspoon salt**
4 **tablespoons unsalted butter, at room temperature**
½ **cup milk (divided use), at room temperature**
1 **teaspoon vanilla extract**
1 **large egg, at room temperature**
**Finely grated peel of ½ lemon**

## Meringue

**4 large egg whites, at room temperature**
**¼ teaspoon cream of tartar**
**1 cup sugar**
**⅓ cup water**
**1 teaspoon vanilla extract**

## Flambé (optional)

**¼ cup 80-proof vodka**

### ▶ Ice cream:

- Combine the dried berries with the vodka in a small bowl, cover tightly with plastic wrap, and microwave for 1 minute. Keep the bowl covered until the berries have cooled completely and absorbed all the vodka. Stir occasionally while the berries are soaking.

- Line with plastic wrap a 1½-quart (6-cup) glass soufflé dish or freezer-proof bowl that measures 7 to 8 inches across the top. Let several inches of the plastic lining hang over the sides.

- Let the ice cream soften slightly in its package, in the refrigerator. Working quickly, spoon the ice cream into a medium bowl, stir the berries into it, and pack the ice cream into the freezer bowl, smoothing over the top. Fold the excess plastic wrap over the top and freeze the ice cream solid.

### ▶ Cake:

- Butter and flour an 8-inch round cake pan. Preheat the oven to 350°F. Have all ingredients at room temperature.

- Whisk together the flour, sugar, baking powder, and salt in a large bowl. Add the butter (cut into large chunks), 6 tablespoons of milk, and the vanilla. Beat with an electric mixer on medium speed until well blended (about 2 minutes). Add the egg, remaining 2 tablespoons of milk, and lemon peel. Beat on medium speed for 2 more minutes, scraping down the sides of the bowl as you beat.

- Spread the batter evenly in the cake pan and level the top with a rubber spatula. Bake at 350°F. for about 35 minutes, or until a toothpick inserted in the center comes out clean.

- Let the cake cool in the pan on a wire rack for 15 minutes, then remove it from the pan and cool completely on the rack. Wrap tightly in plastic wrap and refrigerate until needed.

► **Assembly (Step 1):** Unwrap the cake and slice off the rounded top, to make a flat layer of cake. Remove the bowl of ice cream from the freezer and unwrap the plastic across the top. Place the cake (top side down) on top of the ice cream, trimming off any overhanging edges of cake. Cover again with plastic wrap and put back in the freezer while you make the meringue.

► **Meringue:** Put the egg whites and cream of tartar into the bowl of a stand mixer fitted with the whisk attachment. Combine the sugar and water in a small, heavy-bottom saucepan.

● Bring the sugar mixture to a boil over medium-high heat, stirring occasionally to dissolve the sugar. When the mixture boils, cover the pan and cook for 3 minutes, then uncover and continue cooking, *without stirring*, until it reaches 240°F. on a candy thermometer.

● Meanwhile, beat the egg whites on medium-high speed until soft peaks form (about 2 to 3 minutes). When the sugar syrup has reached the correct temperature, pour it into the egg whites in a thin, steady stream with the mixer running on medium speed. Add the vanilla, increase mixer speed to medium-high, and beat until the egg whites are cool and very fluffy (about 10 minutes).

● While the eggs are beating, set your oven rack on the first level below the center and preheat the oven to 500°F. For the flambé (optional) put ¼ cup of vodka in a small saucepan over medium-low heat on the stove.

► **Assembly (Step 2):** Have ready a 12-inch round heatproof serving platter (with a rim, if you plan to flambé the dessert). Working quickly, remove the ice cream-cake combination from the freezer and set the bottom half of the bowl in a pan of warm tap water for about 10 seconds to loosen the edges of the ice cream. Dry off the bowl, unwrap the plastic across the cake, and invert the platter over the cake. Turn the plate and bowl over together and remove the bowl, so the cake is on the bottom and the ice cream on top. Peel off all the plastic. Working quickly, cover the ice cream cake completely with all the meringue, to seal it with meringue right down to the platter. Use a rubber spatula to make pretty swirls in the meringue.

► **Baking:** Bake for about 2 to 3 minutes in the preheated 500°F. oven to brown the meringue. Watch carefully to keep it from burning. Remove from the oven and serve immediately. (If you want to flambé the Baked Siberia, bring the saucepan of warm vodka to the table, light the vodka with a long match, and carefully pour the flaming vodka over the top, or around the bottom, of the Baked Siberia. Let the flames go out before you slice the dessert.)

● Makes 8 very rich servings.

344

- Use your own favorite recipe for one 8-inch round, single-layer cake. The cake must be dense enough to support the ice cream on top.

- Use dried berries that are not super firm, or they'll be too hard when frozen.

- Brown the meringue with a kitchen blowtorch instead of in the oven.

- Make the entire Baked Siberia in advance, then freeze it up to 2 days before serving. Let it stand at room temperature for 5 minutes, then slice and serve immediately.

# Land of Fire and Ice

When I lived in Irkutsk, the capital of Eastern Siberia, in 1994, there were very few good places to eat in the city. So imagine my surprise when I returned to Irkutsk in 2006 and dined at an upscale restaurant in a lovely setting on the Angara River that flows through the town. "Oh, Baked Alaska!" I exclaimed when the waitress brought the surprise dessert at the end of our four-course meal. "*Nyet, nyet*," she said, flashing a pretty smile as she torched the meringue with flaming vodka. "In Russia we call it Baked Siberia!"

That creamy-cold, fluffy-white, fiery dessert contained all the elements of Siberia, truly a "land of fire and ice." The Kamchatka Peninsula, in Russia's Far East, boasts one of the largest concentrations of active volcanoes in the world, mountains of lava and ash that are snow-capped even in summer. And two towns in Asian Russia, Oimyakon and Verkhoyansk, claim the title of the coldest permanently inhabited place on the planet, with temperatures sometimes plunging to minus-90°F. in winter, then soaring to plus-90°F. in summer. Winter or summer, though, Siberians love their ice cream. You'll see them licking ice cream bars on the beaches in July and buying ice cream cones from bundled-up street vendors in January.

# Bibliography

## Selected Bibliography in English

Badmaev, A. A. "Everyday Diet of the Buryats in the Late 19th and Early 20th Centuries." *Archeology, Ethnology and Anthropology of Eurasia* 37, no. 1 (March 2009): 101–109.

Balzer, Marjorie Mandelstam, ed. *Russian Traditional Culture: Religion, Gender, and Customary Law*. Armonk, NY: M. E. Sharpe, Inc., 1992.

von Bremzen, Anya. *Mastering the Art of Soviet Cooking: A Memoir of Food and Longing*. New York: Workman, 2013.

von Bremzen, Anya, and John Welchman. *Please to the Table: The Russian Cookbook*. New York: Workman, 1990.

Burlakoff, Nikolai. *The World of Russian Borsch: Explorations of Memory, People, History, Cookbooks & Recipes*. Ossining, NY: AElitaPress.org, 2013.

Caldwell, Melissa, ed. *Food and Everyday Life in the Postsocialist World*. Bloomington: Indiana University Press, 2009.

Chamberlain, Lesley. *The Food and Cooking of Russia*. London: Allen Lane, 1982.

Gagarine, Princess Alexandre, translator and compiler. *The Russian Cook Book*. London: William Heinemann, 1924.

Glants, Musya, and Joyce Toomre, eds. *Food in Russian History and Culture*. Bloomington: Indiana University Press, 1997.

Goldstein, Darra. *A La Russe: A Cookbook of Russian Hospitality*. New York: Random House, 1983.

———. "The Eastern Influence on Russian Cuisine." In *Proceedings of a Conference on "Current Research in Culinary History: Sources, Topics, and Methods,"* 20–26. Boston: Schlesinger Library and Culinary Historians of Boston, 1986.

*Guide to the Great Siberian Railway*, edited by A. I Dmitriev-Mamonov and A. F. Zdsiarski, English translation by L. Kukol-Yasnopolsky, revised by John Marshall. St. Petersburg, Russia: Ministry of Ways of Communication, 1900.

Hudgins, Sharon. "Buttering Up the Sun: Russian Maslenitsa from Pagan Practice to Contemporary Celebration." In *Celebration: Proceedings of the Oxford Symposium on Food and Cookery 2011*, edited by Mark McWilliams, 141–150. Totnes, Devon, UK: Prospect Books, 2012.

———. "From Kaluga to Chak-Chak: Eating Locally along the Trans-Siberian Tracks." In *Food and Landscape: Proceedings of the Oxford Symposium on Food and Cookery 2017*, edited by Mark McWilliams. Totnes, Devon, UK: Prospect Books, 2018 (forthcoming).

———. *The Other Side of Russia: A Slice of Life in Siberia and the Russian Far East*. College Station: Texas A & M University Press, 2003.

———. "Raw Liver and More: Feasting with the Buriats of Southern Siberia." In *Food on the Move: Proceedings of the Oxford Symposium on Food and Cookery 1996*, edited by Harlan Walker, 136–156. Totnes, Devon, UK: Prospect Books, 1997.

———. "Siberian Stuffed: A Profusion of Pel'meni." In *Wrapped and Stuffed Foods: Proceedings of the Oxford Symposium on Food and Cookery 2012*, edited by Mark McWilliams, 212–221. Totnes, Devon, UK: Prospect Books, 2013.

Ivanits, Linda J. *Russian Folk Belief*. Armonk, NY: M. E. Sharpe, 1989.

Jones, Catherine Cheremeteff. *A Year of Russian Feasts*. Bethesda, MD: Jellyroll Press, 2002.

Kennan, George. *Tent Life in Siberia and Adventures among the Koraks and Other Tribes in Kamchatka and Northern Asia*. New York: G. P. Putnam's Sons, 1870.

Kropotkin, Alexandra. *The Best of Russian Cooking*. New York: Charles Scribner's Sons, 1964.

Liakovskaya, Lydia. *Russian Cuisine*. Translated by Valery Fatayev. St. Petersburg: Ivan Fedorov Holding Company, 2000.

Mack, Glenn R., and Asele Surina. *Food Culture in Russia and Central Asia*. Westport, CT: Greenwood Press, 2005.

Papashvily, Helen, and George Papashvily. *Russian Cooking*. Time-Life Foods of the World. New York: Time-Life Books, 1969.

Petrova, Nina. *The Best of Russian Cooking*. New York: Crown, 1979.

Pouncy, Carolyn Johnston, translator and editor. *The Domostroi: Rules for Russian Households in the time of Ivan the Terrible*. Ithaca, NY: Cornell University Press, 1995.

Sacharow, Alla. *Classic Russian Cuisine*. Translated by Ursula Zilinsky and Courtenay Searls-Ridge. New York: Arcade Publishing, 1993.

*Secrets of Russian Cooking* (in English and Russian). Translated by O. Chorakaev. Moscow: Raduga, 2001.

Smith, Alison K. *Recipes for Russia: Food and Nationhood under the Tsars*. DeKalb, IL: Northern Illinois University Press, 2008.

Smith, R. E. F., and David Christian. *Bread and Salt: A Social and Economic History of Food and Drink in Russia*. Cambridge, UK: Cambridge University Press, 1984.

Soper, Musia. *Cooking the Russian Way*. London: Spring Books, 1961.

Toomre, Joyce. *Classic Russian Cooking: Elena Molokhovets' "A Gift to Young Housewives."* Translated and with an introduction by Joyce Toomre. Bloomington: Indiana University Press, 1992.

Trutter, Marion, ed. *Culinaria Russia – Ukraine – Georgia – Armenia – Azerbaijan*. Translated by Nichola Coates, Katherine Taylor, and Rae Walter. Potsdam, Germany: Tandem Verlag, 2007.

Visson, Lynn. *The Russian Heritage Cookbook*. Dana Point, CA: Casa Dana Books, 1998.

Volokh, Anne, with Mavis Manus. *The Art of Russian Cuisine*. New York: Macmillan, 1983.

# Selected Bibliography in Russian

Arutiunov, S. A., and T. A. Voronina, eds. *Traditsionnaia pishcha kak vyrazhenie etnicheskogo samosoznaniia* [Traditional food as an expression of ethnic identity]. Moscow: Nauka, 2001.

Begunov, V. L. *Kniga o syre* [Book of cheese]. Moscow: Pishchevaia Promyshlennost', 1974.

Cherepnin, V. L. *Pishchevye rasteniia Sibiri* [Edible plants of Siberia]. Novosibirsk: Nauka, Sibirskoe Otdelenie, 1987.

Goncharov, Iu. M. *Semeinyi byt gorozhan Sibiri vtoroi poloviny* XIX – *nachala* XX *v.* [Family life of the townspeople of Siberia of the second half of the 19th – beginning of the 20th century]. Barnaul: Altaiskii Gosudarstvennyi Universitet, 2004.

Gosteva, Galina. *Chto edali na Rusi* [How they ate in Russia]. Moscow: Lepta Kniga, 2006.

Ioffe, L. V., compiler. *Zimniaia kladovaia* [The winter pantry]. Irkutsk: Vostochno Sibirskoe Knizhnoe Izdatel'stvo, 1993.

Kengis, R. P. *Domashnee prigotovlenie tortov, pirozhnykh, pechen'ia, prianikov, pirogov* [Homemade cakes, small pies, cookies, gingerbreads, large pies], 3rd. ed. Moscow: Agropromizdat, 1985.

*Kniga o vkusnoi i zdorovoi pishche* [Book of tasty and healthy food]. Moscow: Pishchepromizdat, 1955.

*Kniga o vkusnoi i zdorovoi pishche* [Book of tasty and healthy food], 8th ed. Moscow: Legkaia i Pishchevaia Promyshlennost', 1984.

*Kniga o vkusnoi i zdorovoi pishche* [Book of tasty and healthy food], 10th ed. Moscow: Agropromizdat, 1990.

Kovalev, N. I. *Rasskazy o russkoi kukhne* [Stories of Russian cuisine.]. Moscow: Ekonomika, 1994.

Kovalev, V. M., and N. P. Mogil'nyi. *500 retseptov slavianskoi trapezy* [500 recipes for Slavic meals]. Moscow: MP MIK, 1992.

*Kulinariia* [Cookery]. Moscow: Ekonomika, 1966.

Kuzenkov, O. A., and G. V. Kuzenkova, compilers. *Entsiklopediia pravoslavnoi kukhni* [Encyclopedia of Orthodox cuisine]. Nizhnii Novgorod: Khristianskaia Biblioteka, 2006.

Lavrent'eva, Liudmila. *Kalendar' Russkoi traditsionnoi edy: na kazhdyi den' i dlia kazhdoi sem'i* [Calendar of Russian traditional eating: on every day and for all families]. St. Petersburg: AZBUKA, 2013.

Liakhovskaia, L. P., *Kulinarnye sekrety* [Culinary secrets]. Leningrad: Lenizdat, 1984.

Liakhovskaia, L. *Sekrety domashnego konditera* [Secrets of the home pastry cook]. Moscow: Ekonomika, 1993.

Maslov, N. N., compiler. *Konditer: Prakticheskoe rukovodstvo k prigotovleniiu vsevozmoshnykh konditerskikh izdelii* [Pastry cook: Practical guide to preparing all kinds of pastry] (facsimile reprint of 4th edition, Petrograd: Izdanie V. I. Gubinskago, 1915). St. Petersburg: Gippokrat, 1992.

Oborotova, E. A. *Ot pechki* [From the stove]. Novosibirsk: Nauka-Tsentr, 2003.

Osipov, N. P. *Starinnaia russkaia khoziaika, kliuchnitsa i striapukha* [The old Russian housewife, housekeeper and cook] (facsimile reprint of edition published in St. Petersburg, 1794). Moscow: Gosudarstvennaia Publichnaia Istoricheskaia Biblioteka Rossii, 2014.

Pokhlebkin, V. V. *Bol'shaia entsiklopediia kulinarnogo iskusstva: vse retsepty V. V.Pokhlebkina* [Great encyclopedia of culinary arts: all the recipes of V. V. Pokhlebkin]. Moscow: Tsentropoligraf, 2006.

Shovgurova, A. S., and V. A. Viatkina. *Kalmykskaia kukhnia: traditsionnye i sovremennye bliuda* [Kalmyk cuisine: traditional and modern dishes]. Elista, Kalmyka, Russia: Kalmykskoe Knizhnoe Izdatel'stvo, 1982.

Simonenko, P. F., compiler. *Obraztsovaia kukhnia i prakticheskaia shkola domashniago khoziaistva* [The exemplary kitchen and practical school of homemaking] (facsimile reprint of 1892 edition, Moscow). Moscow: Golos, 1991.

*Starinnaia kukhnia* [Old-fashioned cuisine]. Nizhnii Novgorod: Kur'er, 1993.

Starostina, L. A., and M. N. Vechtomova. *Bliuda iz tvoroga* [Dishes made from fresh cheese]. Moscow: Ekonomika, 1986.

Tikhonovich, Anatoly. *Starinnaia sibirskaia kukhnia* [Old Siberian cuisine]. Tomsk: Tom'lad, 1992.

Tsyndynzhapov, G., and E. Badueva. *Buriatskaia kukhnia* [Buriat cuisine]. Ulan-Ude: Buriatskoe Knizhnoe Izdatel'stvo, 1991.

Usacheva, E. V. *Sibirskaia kukhnia* [Siberian cuisine]. Rostov-on-the Don: Feniks, 2000.

Usov, V. V., *Russkaia kukhnia* [Russian cuisine]. Moscow: Planeta, 1992.

# Recipe Index

## A

*Adzhiga* (Russian Red Salsa), 114

Alsatian Meat-and-Potato Casserole (*Bäckeoffe*), 167

Appetizers (*Zakuski*), cold

    Beet Salad with Walnuts and Prunes, 325

    Beet, Potato, and Sauerkraut Salad, Russian (*Vinegret*), 24 (see also *color photo gallery*)

    Carrot, Apple, and Raisin Salad, 153

    Chicken, Pork, and Prune Terrine, 218

    Crab-and-Pineapple Salad, 212

    Garbanzo Salad, 158

    Garlic Cheese, 321

    "Green Bean Casserole" Salad, 324

    Green Pea and Red Pepper Salad, 63

    "Herring under a Fur Coat," 155

    Korean Carrot Salad, 211

    Mimosa Salad, Russian, 320

    Mongolian Spicy Beef Salad, 327 (see also *color photo gallery*)

    Red Cabbage Salad, 154

    Salmon and White Fish Terrine, Vladivostok Style, 221

    Salmon Salad, 61

    Sandwiches, Assorted Open-Face (*Buterbrody*), 23

    Sauerkraut-and-Bacon Salad, 25

    Spicy Butternut Squash Salad, 26

    Squid with Red Peppers, Spanish, 266

    Trans-Siberian Chicken Salad, 323

    Vladivostok Potato Salad, 208

    White Radish Salad, 27

Appetizers (*Zakuski*), hot

    Fiddlehead Ferns with Pork and Paprika, 28

    Mushrooms with Ham, Spanish, 267

    Stuffed Mushrooms, 322

    Stuffed Squid, 36

Apple-Horseradish Sauce, 80

Aunt Beulah's Cinnamon Rolls, 172

# B

*Bäckeoffe* (Alsatian Meat-and-Potato Casserole), 167
Baikal Brownies (Chocolate Brownies with Pine Nuts), 340
Baked Siberia (Russian Baked Alaska), 341
Balkan Rice Casserole (*Djuveč*), 170
Beans
    "Green Bean Casserole" Salad, 324
    Spicy Tex-Mex Beans, 162
Beef
    Beef-and-Pork Dumplings, Siberian (*Pel'meni*), 226 (see also *color photo gallery*)
    Bell Peppers, Stuffed 334
    Captain's Meat, 224
    Cold Summer Soup, Russian (*Okroshka*), 64 (see also *color photo gallery*)
    Goulash Stew with Mushrooms, 71
    Meat-and-Potato Casserole, Alsatian (*Bäckeoffe*), 167
    *Pirozhki* Fillings (Meat, Sauerkraut, Potato-Bacon), 33
    Shish-Kabobs (*Shashlyki*), 332 (see also *color photo gallery*)
    Spicy Beef Borshch, 68
    Spicy Beef Salad, Mongolian, 327 (see also *color photo gallery*)
    Stuffed Beef Rolls, (*Rinderrouladen*), 278
    Stuffed Cabbage Rolls (*Golubtsy*), 275
    T-Bone "Whacks," Roasted, 123
    Texas Chili, 217
Beef-and-Pork Dumplings, Siberian (*Pel'meni*), 226 (see also *color photo gallery*)
Beef Borshch, Spicy, 68
Beef Rolls, Stuffed (*Rinderrouladen*), 278
Beef Salad, Mongolian Spicy, 327 (see also *color photo gallery*)
Beet, Potato, and Sauerkraut Salad (*Vinegret*), 24 (see also *color photo gallery*)
Beets
    Beet, Potato, and Sauerkraut Salad (*Vinegret*), 24 (see also *color photo gallery*)
    Beet Salad with Walnuts and Prunes, 325
    "Herring under a Fur Coat," 155
    Spicy Beef Borshch, 68
Beet Salad with Walnuts and Prunes, 325
Berries
    Frozen Cranberry Cream, Siberian, 45 (see also *color photo gallery*)
    Venison-and-Blueberry Dumplings, Siberian (*Pel'meni*), 234
    Venison-and-Cranberry Dumplings, Siberian (*Pel'meni*), 235
    Whipped Raspberry Pudding, 83
Beverages
    Fruity Cocktails, 180

Spanish Sangria, 265
Bird Cherry Torte, 312
*Blinchiki* (Russian Crêpes), 236
*Bliny* (Russian Buckwheat Pancakes), 280
Borshch, Chicken-and-Vegetable, 35
Borshch, Spicy Beef, 68
Breads
    Bread Loaves, Pretzel-Shaped, Russian (*Krendel'*), 174
    Cinnamon Rolls, Aunt Beulah's, 172
    Crêpes, Russian (*Blinchiki*), 236
    Croutons, Garlic-Rye, 68
    Dinner Rolls, Cloverleaf, 174
    Easter Bread, Russian (*Kulich*), 288
    Gingerbread Squares, 81
    Onion Tart, German (*Zwiebelkuchen*), 130
    Pancakes, Russian Buckwheat (*Bliny*), 280
Brownies, Baikal (Chocolate Brownies with Pine Nuts), 340
Buckwheat
    Buckwheat Pancakes, Russian (*Bliny*), 280
    Fluffy Buckwheat Kasha, 79
    Garlic-Lovers' Kasha, 78
    Savory Buckwheat Kasha, 77
Buckwheat Kasha, Fluffy, 79
Buckwheat Kasha, Savory, 77
Buckwheat Pancakes, Russian (*Bliny*), 280
*Buterbrody* (Assorted Open-Face Sandwiches), 23
Butter Lamb (Easter Table Decoration), 291
Butternut Squash Salad, Spicy, 26

# C

Cabbage (*see also* Sauerkraut)
    Braised Green Cabbage with Carrot and Caraway, 73
    Braised Red Cabbage, 121
    Confetti Cole Slaw, 214
    Red Cabbage Salad, 154
    Russian Cole Slaw, 326
    Stuffed Cabbage Rolls (*Golubtsy*), 275
Cabbage Rolls, Stuffed (*Golubtsy*), 275
Cabbage, Green, Braised with Carrot and Caraway, 73
Cabbage, Red, Braised, 212
Cakes

Bird Cherry Torte, 312
Christmas Carrot Cake, 241
Gingerbread Squares, 81
Pumpkin Spice Cake, 242
Walnut Torte with Chocolate Icing, 238
Captain's Chicken, 39
Captain's Meat, 224
Carrot Cake, Christmas, 241
Carrot Salad, Korean, 211
Carrot, Apple, and Raisin Salad, 153
Casseroles
Alsatian Meat-and-Potato Casserole (*Bäckeoffe*), 167
Balkan Rice Casserole (*Djuveč*), 170
Captain's Chicken, 39
Captain's Meat, 224
Scalloped Potatoes, 76
Cheese
Curd Cheese Pancakes (*Syrniki*, *Tvorozhniki*), 338
Easter Cheese Dessert, Russian (*Paskha*), 283
Garlic Cheese, 321
Cherry Cobbler, 179
Chicken
Captain's Chicken, 39
Chicken-and-Vegetable Borshch, 35
Chicken in Red Wine, Spanish, 273
Chicken, Pork, and Prune Terrine, 218
Trans-Siberian Chicken Salad, 323
Chicken-and-Vegetable Borshch, 35
Chicken in Red Wine, Spanish, 273
Chicken Salad, Trans-Siberian, 323
Chicken, Pork, and Prune Terrine, 218
Chili, Texas, 217
Chocolate Brownies with Pine Nuts (Baikal Brownies), 340
Christmas (*see* Holidays)
Cinnamon Rolls, Aunt Beulah's, 172
Cold Summer Soup, Russian (*Okroshka*), 64 (see also *color photo gallery*)
Cole Slaw, Confetti, 214
Cole Slaw, Russian, 326
Cookies
Baikal Brownies (Chocolate Brownies with Pine Nuts), 340
Honey-Almond Bars, 132
Honey-Spice Cookies, 243
Peanut Butter Cookies, 244
Pine Nut Meringues, 293

Snickerdoodles, 176
Crab-and-Pineapple Salad, 212
Crêpes, Russian (*Blinchiki*), 236
Croutons, Garlic-Rye, 68
Curd Cheese Pancakes (*Syrniki, Tvorozhniki*), 338
Curry, Clean-Out-the-Fridge, 62
Custard Sauce, Vanilla, 181

# D

Desserts
    Baikal Brownies (Chocolate Brownies with Pine Nuts), 340
    Baked Siberia (Russian Baked Alaska), 341
    Bird Cherry Torte, 312
    Buckwheat Pancakes, Russian (*Bliny*), 280
    Cherry Cobbler, 179
    Christmas Carrot Cake, 241
    Cinnamon Rolls, Aunt Beulah's, 172
    Crêpes, Russian (*Blinchiki*), 236
    Easter Bread, Russian (*Kulich*), 288
    Easter Cheese Dessert, Russian (*Paskha*), 283
    Frozen Cranberry Cream, Siberian, 45 (see also *color photo gallery*)
    Gingerbread Squares, 81
    Honey-Almond Bars, 132
    Honey-Spice Cookies, 243
    Peanut Butter Cookies, 244
    Pine Nut Meringues, 293
    Pretzel-Shaped Bread, Russian (*Krendel'*), 174
    Pumpkin Spice Cake, 242
    Snickerdoodles, 176
    Sour Cream Porridge, Buryat (*Salamat*), 336
    Sweet Potato Pudding, 177
    Vanilla Custard Sauce, 181
    Walnut Torte with Chocolate Icing, 238
    Whipped Raspberry Pudding, 83
    Zabaglione, 292
*Djuveč* (Balkan Rice Casserole), 170
Drinks (*see* Beverages)
Duck, Roasted with Apples and Raisins, 125
Dumplings (*Pel'meni*) (see also *color photo gallery*)
    Siberian Beef-and-Pork Dumplings (*Pel'meni*), 226
    Siberian Salmon Dumplings (*Pel'meni*), 233
    Siberian Venison-and-Blueberry Dumplings (*Pel'meni*), 234
    Siberian Venison-and-Cranberry Dumplings (*Pel'meni*), 235

# E

Easter (*see* Holidays)
Easter Bread, Russian (*Kulich*), 288
Easter Cheese Dessert, Russian (*Paskha*), 283
Easter Table Decoration (Butter Lamb), 291
Enchiladas, Turkey Mole, 163

# F

Fiddlehead Ferns with Pork and Paprika, 28
Fish (*see also* Seafood)
    Fish Stew with Garlic-Rye Croutons, 67
    Fish Stew, Russian (*Ukha*), 330
    "Herring under a Fur Coat," 155
    Salmon and White Fish Terrine, Vladivostok Style, 221
    Salmon Dumplings, Siberian (*Pel'meni*), 233
    "Salmon in a Coat," 38
    Salmon Pie, Russian (*Kulebyaka*), 41 (see also *color photo gallery*)
    Salmon Salad, 61
    Salmon-Trout Soup, Macedonian, 66
    Spaghetti with Salmon and Sour Cream, 72
Fish Stew with Garlic-Rye Croutons, 67
Fish Stew, Russian (*Ukha*), 330
French "Stomped Vegetable Soup," 117
Frozen Cranberry Cream, Siberian, 45 (see also *color photo gallery*)
Frozen Desserts
    Baked Siberia (Russian Baked Alaska), 341
    Frozen Cranberry Cream, Siberian, 45 (see also *color photo gallery*)

# G

Garbanzo Salad, 158
Garlic Cheese, 321
Garlic Mayonnaise, 115
Garlicky Green Peas, 124
Garlic-Lovers' Kasha, 78
Garlic-Rye Croutons, 68
Gazpacho, Spanish, 268
Gingerbread Squares, 81
*Golubtsy* (Stuffed Cabbage Rolls), 275
Goulash Stew with Mushrooms, 71
"Green Bean Casserole" Salad, 324
Green Pea and Red Pepper Salad, 63
Green Peas, Garlicky, 124

# H

"Herring under a Fur Coat," 155
Holidays
    Christmas Carrot Cake, 241
    Easter Bread, Russian (*Kulich*), 288
    Easter Butter Lamb (Table Decoration), 291
    Easter Cheese Dessert, Russian (*Paskha*), 283
Honey-Almond Bars, 132
Honey-Spice Cookies, 243
Horseradish
    Apple-Horseradish Sauce, 80
    Horseradish: Do It Yourself, 116
    Hot Tips, 116
    Mashed Red Potatoes with Horseradish and Sour Cream, 75

# K

Kasha
    Fluffy Buckwheat Kasha, 79
    Garlic-Lovers' Kasha, 78
    Savory Buckwheat Kasha, 77
Korean Carrot Salad, 211
*Krendl'* (Russian Pretzel-Shaped Bread Loaves), 174
*Kulebyaka* (Russian Salmon Pie), 41 (see also *color photo gallery*)
*Kulich* (Russian Easter Bread), 288

# M

Main Dishes (Meat)
    Alsatian Meat-and-Potato Casserole (*Bäckeoffe*), 167
    Balkan Pork-and-Pepper Stew (*Mučkalica*), 127
    Captain's Meat, 224
    Fiddlehead Ferns with Pork and Paprika, 28
    Goulash Stew with Mushrooms, 71
    Roasted T-Bone "Whacks," 123
    Shish-Kabobs (*Shashlyki*), 332 (see also *color photo gallery*)
    Siberian Beef-and-Pork Dumplings (*Pel'meni*), 226 (see also *color photo gallery*)
    Siberian Venison-and-Blueberry Dumplings (*Pel'meni*), 234
    Siberian Venison-and-Cranberry Dumplings (*Pel'meni*), 235
    Stuffed Beef Rolls (*Rinderrouladen*), 278
    Stuffed Bell Peppers, 334
    Stuffed Cabbage Rolls (*Golubtsy*), 275
    Texas Chili, 217

Main Dishes (Poultry)
    Captain's Chicken, 39
    Chicken in Red Wine, Spanish, 273
    Roasted Duck with Apples and Raisins, 125
    Stuffed Bell Peppers, 334
    Stuffed Cabbage Rolls (*Golubtsy*), 275
    Texas Chili, 217
    Turkey Mole Enchiladas, 163
Main Dishes (Seafood, *see also* Fish)
    "Salmon in a Coat," 38
    Salmon Pie, Russian (*Kulebyaka*), 41 (see also *color photo gallery*)
    Siberian Salmon Dumplings (*Pel'meni*), 233
    Spaghetti with Salmon and Sour Cream, 72
    Stuffed Squid, 36
Mayonnaise, Blender, 115
Mayonnaise, Garlic, 115
Meat Stew, Russian Piquant (*Solyanka*), 331
Mimosa Salad, Russian, 320
Mongolian Spicy Beef Salad, 327 (see also *color photo gallery*)
*Mučkalica* (Balkan Pork-and-Pepper Stew), 127
Mushroom Cream Soup, 328
Mushroom Dust, 129
Mushroom Risotto, 270
Mushrooms
    Goulash Stew with Mushrooms, 71
    Mushroom Cream Soup, 328
    Mushroom Dust, 129
    Mushroom Risotto, 270
    Mushrooms with Ham, Spanish, 267
    Mushroom-Sour Cream Sauce, 128
    Sauerkraut with Mushrooms, 119
    Stuffed Mushrooms, 322
Mushrooms with Ham, Spanish, 267
Mushrooms, Stuffed, 322
Mushroom-Sour Cream Sauce, 128

# N

Nuts
    Beet Salad with Walnuts and Prunes, 325
    Chocolate Brownies with Pine Nuts (Baikal Brownies), 340
    Pine Nut Meringues, 293
    Walnut Torte with Chocolate Icing, 238

# O

*Okroshka* (Russian Cold Summer Soup), 64 (see also *color photo gallery*)
Onion Tart, German (*Zwiebelkuchen*), 130

# P

Pancakes
    Buckwheat Pancakes, Russian (*Bliny*), 280
    Crêpes, Russian (*Blinchiki*), 236
    Curd Cheese Pancakes, Russian (*Syrniki, Tvorozhniki*), 338
*Paskha* (Russian Easter Cheese Dessert), 283
Pasta
    Beef-and-Pork Dumplings, Siberian (*Pel'meni*), 226 (see also *color photo gallery*)
    Salmon Dumplings, Siberian (*Pel'meni*), 233
    Spaghetti with Salmon and Sour Cream, 72
    Venison-and-Blueberry Dumplings, Siberian (*Pel'meni*), 234
    Venison-and-Cranberry Dumplings, Siberian (*Pel'meni*), 235
Peanut Butter Cookies, 244
*Pel'meni* (*see* Dumplings)
Peppers, Stuffed Bell, 334
Pickled-Green-Tomato Sauce, 166
Pies
    *Pirozhki* Fillings (Meat, Sauerkraut, Potato-Bacon), 33
    Salmon Pie, Russian (*Kulebyaka*), 41 (see also *color photo gallery*)
    Small Savory Pies, Russian (*Pirozhki*), 30
Pine Nut Meringues, 293
*Pirozhki* (*see* Pies)
*Pirozhki* Fillings (Meat, Sauerkraut, Potato-Bacon), 33
Pork
    Alsatian Meat-and-Potato Casserole (*Bäckeoffe*), 167
    Balkan Pork-and-Pepper Stew (*Mučkalica*), 127
    Beef-and-Pork Dumplings, Siberian (*Pel'meni*), 226 (see also *color photo gallery*)
    Chicken, Pork, and Prune Terrine, 218
    Fiddlehead Ferns with Pork and Paprika, 28
    Goulash Stew with Mushrooms, 71
    Shish-Kabobs (*Shashlyki*), 332 (see also *color photo gallery*)
Pork-and-Pepper Stew, Balkan (*Mučkalica*), 127
Porridge, Buryat Sour Cream (*Salamat*), 336
Potatoes
    Beet, Potato, and Sauerkraut Salad, Russian (*Vinegret*), 24 (see also *color photo gallery*)
    Mashed Red Potatoes with Horseradish and Sour Cream, 75
    Meat-and-Potato Casserole, Alsatian (*Bäckeoffe*), 167

*Pirozhki* Fillings (Meat, Sauerkraut, Potato-Bacon), 33
Potato Salad, German, 216
Potato Salad, Vladivostok, 208
Scalloped Potatoes, 76
Potato Salad, German, 216
Potato Salad, Vladivostok, 208
Potatoes, Red, Mashed with Horseradish and Sour Cream, 75
Potatoes, Scalloped, 76
Puddings
Buryat Sour Cream Porridge (*Salamat*), 336
Cherry Cobbler, 179
Sweet Potato Pudding, 177
Whipped Raspberry Pudding, 83
Zabaglione, 292
Pudding, Sweet Potato, 177
Pudding, Whipped Raspberry, 83
Pumpkin Spice Cake, 242

# R

Red Cabbage, Braised, 212
Red Cabbage Salad, 154
Rice
Balkan Rice Casserole (*Djuveč*), 170
Mushroom Risotto, 270
Salmon Pie, Russian (*Kulebyaka*), 41 (see also *color photo gallery*)
Stuffed Bell Peppers, 334
Stuffed Cabbage Rolls (*Golubtsy*), 275
Stuffed Squid, 36
Tex-Mex Rice, 160
Valencian-Style Rice, 272
Rice Casserole, Balkan (*Djuveč*), 170
Rice, Tex-Mex, 160
Rice, Valencian-Style
*Rinderrouladen* (Stuffed Beef Rolls), 278
Risotto, Mushroom, 270
Rolls, Cinnamon, 172
Rolls, Cloverleaf Dinner, 174

# S

Salads
Beet Salad with Walnuts and Prunes, 325
Carrot, Apple, and Raisin Salad, 153

Confetti Cole Slaw, 214
Crab-and-Pineapple Salad, 212
Garbanzo Salad, 158
German Potato Salad, 216
"Green Bean Casserole" Salad, 324
Green Pea and Red Pepper Salad, 63
"Herring under a Fur Coat," 155
Korean Carrot Salad, 211
Mongolian Spicy Beef Salad, 327 (see also *color photo gallery*)
Red Cabbage Salad, 154
Russian Beet, Potato, and Sauerkraut Salad (*Vinegret*), 24 (see also *color photo gallery*)
Russian Cole Slaw, 326
Russian Mimosa Salad, 320
Salmon Salad, 61
Sauerkraut-and-Bacon Salad, 25
Spicy Butternut Squash Salad, 26
Trans-Siberian Chicken Salad, 323
White Radish Salad, 27
Vladivostok Potato Salad, 208
*Salamat* (Buryat Sour Cream Porridge), 336
Salmon and White Fish Terrine, Vladivostok Style, 221
Salmon Dumplings, Siberian (*Pel'meni*), 233
"Salmon in a Coat," 38
Salmon Pie, Russian (*Kulebyaka*), 41 (see also *color photo gallery*)
Salmon Salad, 61
Salmon-Trout Soup, Macedonian, 66
Salsa, Russian Red (*Adzhiga*), 114
Salsa, Tex-Mex, 159
Sandwiches, Assorted Open-Face (*Buterbrody*), 23
Sangria, Spanish, 265
Sauces
    Apple-Horseradish Sauce, 80
    Apple-Raisin Sauce, 126
    Blender Mayonnaise, 115
    Garlic Mayonnaise, 115
    Mushroom-Sour Cream Sauce, 128
    Pickled-Green-Tomato Sauce, 166
    Russian Red Salsa (*Adzhiga*),114
    Tex-Mex Salsa, 159
    Vanilla Custard Sauce, 181
Sauerkraut
    Beet, Potato, and Sauerkraut Salad, Russian (*Vinegret*), 24 (see also *color photo gallery*)
    *Pirozhki* Fillings (Meat, Sauerkraut, Potato-Bacon), 33

Sauerkraut-and-Bacon Salad, 25
Sauerkraut, Seasoned, 215
Sauerkraut with Mushrooms, 119
Sauerkraut-and-Bacon Salad, 25
Sauerkraut, Seasoned, 215
Sauerkraut with Mushrooms, 119
Scalloped Potatoes, 76
Seafood (*see also* Fish)
Crab-and-Pineapple Salad, 212
Stuffed Squid, 36
Squid with Red Peppers, Spanish, 266
Vladivostok Potato Salad, 208
*Shashlyki* (Shish-Kabobs), 332 (see also *color photo gallery*)
Shish-Kabobs (*Shashlyki*), 332 (see also *color photo gallery*)
Side Dishes (*see also* Salads)
Braised Green Cabbage with Carrot and Caraway, 73
Braised Red Cabbage, 121
Fluffy Buckwheat Kasha, 79
Garlicky Green Peas, 124
Garlic-Lovers' Kasha, 78
German Potato Salad, 216
Mashed Red Potatoes with Horseradish and Sour Cream, 75
Sauerkraut with Mushrooms, 119
Savory Buckwheat Kasha, 77
Scalloped Potatoes, 76
Seasoned Sauerkraut, 215
Spicy Tex-Mex Beans, 162
Stuffed Mushrooms, 322
Tex-Mex Rice, 160
Valencian-Style Rice
Snickerdoodles, 176
*Solyanka* (Russian Piquant Meat Stew), 331
Soups (*see also* Stews)
Chicken-and-Vegetable Borshch, 35
French "Stomped Vegetable Soup", 117
Macedonian Salmon-Trout Soup, 66
Mushroom Cream Soup, 328
Russian Cold Summer Soup (*Okroshka*), 64 (see also *color photo gallery*)
Spanish Gazpacho, 268
Spicy Beef Borshch, 68
Spaghetti with Salmon and Sour Cream, 72
Squid with Red Peppers, Spanish, 266
Squid, Stuffed, 36

Stews
    Balkan Pork-and-Pepper Stew (*Mučkalica*), 127
    Clean-Out-the-Fridge Curry, 62
    Fish Stew with Garlic-Rye Croutons, 67
    Goulash Stew with Mushrooms, 71
    Russian Fish Stew (*Ukha*), 330
    Russian Piquant Meat Stew (*Solyanka*), 331
    Texas Chili, 217
Sweet Potato Pudding, 177
*Syrniki* (Russian Curd Cheese Pancakes), 338

## T

T-Bone "Whacks," Roasted, 123
Terrine, Chicken, Pork, and Prune, 218
Terrine, Salmon and White Fish, Vladivostok Style, 221
Texas Chili, 217
    Tex-Mex
    Garbanzo Salad, 158
    Nichevo Nachos, 150
    Spicy Tex-Mex Beans, 162
    Tex-Mex Rice, 160
    Tex-Mex Salsa, 159
    Turkey Mole Enchiladas, 163
Torte, Bird Cherry, 312
Torte, Walnut with Chocolate Icing, 238
Turkey
    Stuffed Bell Peppers, 334
    Stuffed Cabbage Rolls (*Golubtsy*), 275
    Texas Chili, 217
    Turkey Mole Enchilidas, 163
Turkey Mole Enchiladas, 163
*Tvorozhniki* (Russian Curd Cheese Pancakes), 338

## U

*Ukha* (Russian Fish Stew), 330

## V

Vanilla Custard Sauce, 181
*Vinegret* (Russian Beet, Potato, and Sauerkraut Salad), 24 (see also *color photo gallery*)
Venison-and-Blueberry Dumplings, Siberian (*Pel'meni*), 234
Venison-and-Cranberry Dumplings, Siberian (*Pel'meni*), 235

# W

Walnut Torte with Chocolate Icing, 238
White Radish Salad, 27

# Z

Zabaglione, 292
*Zakuski* (*see* Appetizers, cold, and Appetizers, hot)
*Zwiebelkuchen* (German Onion Tart), 130

# Subject Index

Page numbers in *italics* refer to illustrations. For specific recipes, see separate Recipe Index.

## A

Advent, 183
apartments, 1, 47–60, 140, 260
appetizers (*zakuski*), 13, 15, 17–19, 22, 23, 54, 139, *144*, 155, 194, 205, 210, 211, 256–57, 262–63, 301, 318, 321, 325. See also *color photo gallery*
Asian Russia, xi–xviii, xxi, 183, 344. *See also* Siberia

## B

*babushki* (Russian grandmothers), 105, 296–97, 298
Baikal, Lake, 8, 94, 148, 295, 301, 309–10, 314, 315
bears. *See* foods, wild
beef, 39, 87, 92–93, 138, 161, 202, 203, 263, 297, 327, 332
beer. *See* beverages, alcoholic
beets, 70, 157. *See also* food markets; food stores; *color photo gallery*
berries, 3, 9, 10, 13, 46, 60, 65, 84, 101, 103–5, 142–43, 189, 303–6, 307, 312–13, 328. *See also* specific names of berries (blueberries, cranberries, etc.). See also *color photo gallery*
beverages, alcoholic
    beer, 113, 149, 186, 298
    brandy, 1, 133, 140, 146, 189, 259, 262
    champagne (*shampanskoye*), 20, 113, 138, 146,188, 189, 260, 298, 299
    cocktails (mixed drinks), 180, 202, 257, 263, 320
    cognac, 264
    *kefir*, 97, 103, 111, 282, 339
    *kumis*, 337
    *kvas*, 65, 70, 103
    liqueur, 133, 140, 145, 147, 189, 199, 309, 310, 319
    *tarasun*, 317
    wine, 19, 53, 54, 58, 103, 111, 133, 138, 139, 146, 188, 189, 206, 247, 253
    *See also* vodka
beverages, non-alcoholic
    berry drinks (*sok, kompot*), 9, 84
    buttermilk, 97, 131, 337
    coffee, xix, 14, 88, 111, 133
    fruit juice, 1, 84, 140, 189

milk, 86, 91, 96–97, 131, 313, 328, 337, 337, 339
  *tarag*, 316
  water, 55–56
  *See also* tea
bilberries, 104, 105
birch, 97, 107, 142–43
bird cherry, 312
birthdays, 3, 140–41, 144–45, 146, 175, 251, 253
blackberries, 13, 104, 264
*blinchiki* (Russian crêpes). *See* pancakes
*bliny* (Russian buckwheat pancakes). *See* pancakes
blueberries, 60, 104, 147, 199, 234, 307, 313
*borshch*, 70
brandy. *See beverages*, alcoholic
breads, 18–19, 23, 86, 109–10, 137, 175, 205, 259, 262, 298, 299, 313
  "black bread," 110
  *bubliki*, 109
  cornbread, 133
  flatbreads, (*lavash, naan*), 110
  *kalachi*, 109
  *krendel'*, 175
  *kulich*, (Russian Easter bread), 256, 258, 259, 262, 286, 287
  *paska* (Ukrainian Easter bread), 256, 264
  rye, 65, 110, 262
  sourdough, 110
  *sushki*, 109, 250
  *testo* (yeast dough), 109
  whole wheat, 109
  *See also* buns; gingerbread; tortillas
breakfast, 55, 56, 60, 78, 95, 98, 316
Brovko family, 1–4, 13, 15, 197–200, 205
  Alla, viii, 1–4, 6–15, 16, 40, 94–95, 97, 107, 138, 149–52, 189, 201–3, 205–6, 220, 223, 287
  Polina (Granny), 4–7, 9, 40, 174, 223, 277, 287
buckwheat, xvii, 77, 78, 107, 199, 230–31, 249, 280
buns, 250, 296, 297
  *bulochki*, 109
  cinnamon rolls, 175
  dinner rolls, 175
  *pyan-se*, 297
  *shan'gi*, 316
Buryats, 297, 312, 315–19. See also *color photo gallery*
Butter. *See* dairy products
"Butter Week" Festival. *See* Maslenitsa

# C

cabbage, 10, *11*, *73*, 74, 122. *See also* dachas, 303–4; food markets; food stores; sauerkraut

cakes, 82, 111, 113, 188, 189, 190, 238, 240, 241, 253, 312

calendars, 3, 183–85, 252. See also Gregorian calendar; Julian calendar

carp. *See* fish

casseroles, 39, 40, 76, 138, 139, 170, 202, 324

Catherine II (Empress of Russia), 99

Catholic Church. *See* churches

caviar, xxiv–xxv, 95, 208, 237, 298, 299. *See also* appetizers (*zakuski*); *color photo gallery*

Central Asia, xvii, xviii, 10, 87, 102, 104, 110, 132, 212, 230

champagne (*shampanskoye*). *See* beverages, alcoholic

chebureki. *See* pastries, savory

cheese, xxiii–xxiv, 18–19, 98, 118, 133, 256, 283, 286, 321, 337, 338–39

chefs, xviii, 299, 300, 302. See also *color photo gallery*

chicken, 20, 40, 93, 94, 189, 218, 220, 273

chile powder (New Mexico), 90, 161

chiles (peppers). *See* peppers, capsicum

chili (dish), 95, 161, 217

chili powder (Texas), 90, 161

China, xvii, 12, 22, 36, 75, 91, 230–31, 233

Chinese products, 21, 74, 87, 103, 198, 200, 232, 328

Christmas
    dates of, 183–85
    "European," 185–88
    parties, 188–90
    Russian Orthodox, 184, 203–5

churches
    Catholic, 183, 185, 251, 252
    Lutheran, 185, 191
    Protestant, 183, 251, 252
    Russian Orthodox, 183–85, 204, 251, 252, 254, 255, 261, *294*

cloudberries, 305, 313

cocktails. *See* beverages, alcoholic

cognac. *See* beverages, alcoholic

condiments, 32

cookbooks, xiii–xiv, xvi, xix–xx, 15, 22, 44, 50, 230–31, 339

cooking magazines. *See* food magazines

cookware. *See* kitchen equipment

corn. *See* grains

cornmeal. *See* flour

crab. *See* seafood

cranberries, 10, 44, 84, 105, 142–43, 235, 305, 313

crayfish. *See* fish
crêpes. *See* pancakes (*blinchiki*)
crowberries, 313
cultural differences, culinary, 139–40, 149–52, 262–64, 324
currants, 105, 142–43, 286, 301

## D

dachas, 13, 14, 57, 101, 140, 141, 302–6
dairy products, *xxv*, *96*
    butter, xxiii, 97, 108, 247, 262, 291, 337
    buttermilk, 97, 131, 337
    ice cream, 98, *248*, 344
    *kefir*, 97, 103, 111, 282, 339
    milk, 86, 91, 96–97, 131, 313, 328, 337, 337, 339
    sour cream, xxiii, 97, 131, 337, 339
    *tarag*, 316
    *tarasun*, 317
    *tvorog*, xxiii–xxiv, *xxv*, 98, 283, 286, 338, 339
    yoghurt, 337
    *See also* cheese; *color photo gallery*
Ded Moroz. *See* Grandfather Frost
delicatessens (delis). *See* food stores
DeWitt, Dave, ix
dining cars. *See* Trans-Siberian Railroad
*domovoi*, 49
Donskoy, Vladimir, ix
drinking rituals. *See* rituals, drinking
drinks. *See* beverages, alcoholic; beverages, non-alcoholic
duck. *See* foods, wild
dumplings, Siberian. See *pel'meni*

## E

Easter
    dates of, 251–53
    feasts, 260, 262–64
    Russian Orthodox, 252, 254, 261
    "Western," 252
    *See also* Easter foods; Holy Week; Palm Sunday
Easter foods, Russian
    baskets, 259
    bread (*kulich*), 256, 258, 259, 262, 286, 287, *288*
    butter lamb, 262, 291
    eggs, 253–55, 259, 262

lamb cakes, 253
   cheese dessert (*paskha*), 256, 257, 259, 262, *283*, 286, 287
eggs, 89, 101–2, 247, 254–55, 258, 259, 260, 262, 286, 314
Epiphany (Three King's Day), 183, 185
etiquette, 136–37, 146, 147
"European Christmas," 185–88
European Russia, xiii, xvii–xviii, 10, 61, 108, 155, 212, 230–31

# F

farmers' markets. *See* food markets
fasting, religious, 247, 250, 254, 258, 310
fats, cooking, xxiii, 107, 108, 310
fermented foods. *See* foods, fermented
festivals. *See* Maslenitsa; New Year
fiddlehead ferns, *27*, 29, 103, 245, 312. See also *color photo gallery*
fish, 8, *17*, 91, 94–95, 223, 314. *See also* appetizers; caviar; herring; salmon; seafood; *color photo gallery*
flour, xxiv, 87, 88, 106–7, 249, 280
   bird cherry (*cheremukha*), 313
   buckwheat, 249, 280
   cornmeal, 106, 133
   fish, 314
   rye, 82
   *sarana* lily, 313
food magazines, xvi, xx, 16, 300
food markets (farmers', moveable, open-air), xv, xix, 85–88, 92–97, 99, 101–7, 110, *112*, 111–13, 120, 190. *See also* food stores; *color photo gallery*
food shopping, 87, 88–89. *See also* food markets; food stores
food shortages, 85, 89–92, 108, 133
food stores, xv, xix, 21, 85–86, 88–89, 95, 97, 103, 107, 113, 125
foods, fermented, xvii, 10, 103, 337. See also beverages; dairy products; *kimchi*; sauerkraut
foods, foraged. *See* foods, wild
foods, imported, xvii–xviii, 12, 94, 99, 165, 189. *See also* Chinese products; food markets; food stores
foods, wild, 125, 230–31, 305, 312, 328
   birds, 125, 304, 314
   honey, 107
   land animals, 108, 234, 304, 307, 317
   marine mammals, 108, 304, 314
   plants, 22, 142–43, 311, 312, 313
   *See also* berries; fiddlehead ferns; fish; garlic, wild; mushrooms; pine nuts; seafood; *color photo gallery*
fruits, 13, 14, 65, 84, 91, 101, 104, 141, 142–43, 180, 305

# G

game, wild. *See* foods, wild
garlic, wild (*cheremsha*), 9, 245, 312. See also *color photo gallery*
*gastronom, gastronomy*. *See* food stores
gefilte fish, 223
*Gift to Young Housewives, A* (Molokhovets), xiv, 15
gingerbread (*pryanik*), 81, 82, 110, 312
*Golden Eagle Trans-Siberian Express*, ix, xx, 299–302. See also *color photo gallery*
Goldstein, Darra, ix, xiv, 82
gooseberries, 13, 101, 104
grains (barley, corn, millet, rice, rye, wheat), 78, 106, 107, 249, 328. *See also* buckwheat
Grandfather Frost (Ded Moroz), 190, 194, *195*, 196, 203
Granny Polina. *See* Brovko family
Great Patriotic War (World War II), 8–9, 313
Gregorian calendar, 184, 252
grocery stores. *See* food stores

# H

Hagman, Larry, 90
haskap berries, 60
herring, 141, 155, 157, 206. *See also* appetizers
"high-rise villages", 47–58
holidays, 147–48, 246. *See also* Christmas; Easter; Maslenitsa; New Year
Holy Trinity (symbolism), 258, 261, 262, 264
Holy Week, 247, 254
honey. See foods, wild
hors d'oeuvres. *See* appetizers
horseradish, 32, 65, 101, 102, 105, 106, 116, 259
horses, 108, 234, 316, 337
hospitality, 3, 12, 18–19, 21, 22, 137, 316. *See also* etiquette
hunting (animals), 304; "silent hunting" (mushrooms), 120
hypermarkets. *See* food stores

# I

ice cream. *See* dairy products
inflation (prices), 88–89
Irkutsk, *5, 246, 294*
    markets, food stores, 85–88, 92–94, 96–98, *99*, 101–7, 109, *112*, 113. See also *color photo gallery*
    restaurants, xvi, 135–36, 344
    "White House Cook," 5–6

*See also* apartments; birthdays; Easter; Maslenitsa
Ivaschenko, Yelena, viii, 20–21. See also *color photo gallery*

# J

jam. *See* preserves
Jones, Catherine Cheremeteff, ix
Julian calendar, 184, 252
juniper berries, 142

# K

Kamchatka crabs. *See* seafood
Kamchatka Peninsula, 295, 306, 307, 313, 344
Kamolov, Ilkhomudin, ix, 302
kasha, 78. *See also* buckwheat
Katayeva, Svetlana, 20–21
Kazakov, Nikolai, 140, 149, 152
Kazakova, Larisa, viii, 140–41, 149, 302–4
*kefir*. See beverages, alcoholic; dairy products
Kennan, George, 307, 313
*kimchi* (Korean), 10, 105, 297
kiosks. *See* food stores
kitchen equipment, xiii, xxv, 48, 50–52, *58*, 232, 282, *285*, 286
kitchen stoves, 49–50, 57, 133, 303, 306, 317
kitchens, apartment, *39*, 48–52, 58, *59*, 60, *134*. See also *color photo gallery*
kitchens, summer, 306
kitchens, village, 50, 303, 306, 316–17, 319
*Kniga o vkusnoi i zdorovoi pishche* (*Book of Tasty and Healthy Food*), 43, 223
Konstantinov, Gennadi, viii, 260–64
Koreans, xvii, 87, 105, 135, 212, 297. See also *color photo gallery*
Korotkina, Galina, viii, 16–20, *39*. See also *color photo gallery*
*krendel'*. *See* breads
*kulebyaka* (*coulibiac*). *See* pies
*kulich* (Russian Easter bread). *See* Easter foods
*kulinarii*. See food stores
*kumis*. *See* dairy products
*kvas*. *See* beverages, alcoholic

# L

Lake Baikal. *See* Baikal, Lake
Lent, period of, 251–55
Lent, fasting. *See* fasting, religous
*limonnik* (berries), 101

lingonberries, 9, 10, 313
liqueur. *See* beverages, alcoholic
Littler, Tim, ix
Lutheran Church. *See* churches

# M

Mack, Glenn, ix
Maritime Territory (Russian Far East), 107, 295, 305
market economy, 85, 88, 89, 103, 111–13, 125
markets. *See* food markets
Maslenitsa ("Butter Week" Festival), 247–51, 254
meals (non-Russian)
    Alsatian, 137–40
    Buryat, 315–19
    Christmas parties (potluck), 188–90
    Italian, 246–47
    Mardi Gras, 148–49
    Spanish, 256–59
    Tex-Mex, 149–52
    Thanksgiving, 165
meat. *See* beef; chicken; foods, wild; pork; turkey
Mikhalkovskaya, Nataliya, viii, 260–64
milk, milk products. *See* dairy products
Mitra, Rupak, 300
Molokhovets, Elena, xiv, 15
Mongolians, 297, 307, 327, 328, 336, 337. *See* also Buryats; *color photo gallery*
Moscow, viii, xix, 44, 56, 90, 210, 298, 299
mushrooms, 22, *99*, 101, 120, 136, 304, 312, 322. See also *color photo gallery*
mustard, xxiv, 32, 105–6

# N

New Year
    dates of, 183–85
    "Old New Year," 205–7
    parties, 193–95, 197–203, 205–7
    traditions, 190–93, 194–96, 199, 203, 206–7
    tree (*yolka*), 191–93, 194, 196, 198–99
nuts. *See* foods, wild; pine nuts

# O

oil, cooking. *See* fats, cooking
*okroshka* (cold soup), 60, 64, 305. See also *color photo gallery*

"Old New Year." *See* New Year
olive oil. *See* fats, cooking
Oseland, James, 16
*Other Side of Russia, The* (Hudgins), xv
ovens. *See* kitchen stoves

# P

Palm Sunday, 255
pancakes
 *blinchiki*, 14, 206, 237, 282
 *bliny*, 247, 249–50, 282
 *olad'i*, 282
 *syrniki, tvorozhniki*, 308, 338
*paska* (Ukrainian), 256
*paskha* (Russian). *See* Easter foods
*pasochnitsa* (*paskha* mold), *285*, *286*
pasta, xvii, 106. See also *pel'meni*
pastries. *See* pies
*pel'meni* (Siberian stuffed dumplings), 15, 103, 202–3, 230–31, 232. See also *color photo gallery*
*pel'menitsa* (*pel'meni* mold), 232
pepper, black. *See* spices
peppers, capsicum, xiii, xvii, 101, 103, 105, 142–43, 150, 161, 328. See also *color photo gallery*
Peter I (Tsar Peter the Great), xviii, 18, 99, 184
picnics, 301, 305, 307–14. See also *color photo gallery*
pies, 3, 13, 32, 44, 109, 205, 296, 297. See also *color photo gallery*
pine nuts, 107, 108, 287, 310, 328. See also *color photo gallery*
*pirog, pirogi*. See pies
*pirozhok, pirozhki. See* pies
pork, 87, 92, 93, 107, 199, 259, 262
porridge, 78, 313, 319, 336, 337
potatoes, xvii, 76, 91, 99, 157, 210, *308. See also* food markets; food shopping; food stores; *color photo gallery*
potato salad, 188, 210, 216
preserves, 9, 14, 29, 100, 103–05, 120, 307, 311. *See also* sauerkraut
*pryaniki* (gingerbread cookies). *See* gingerbreads
public utilities (electricity, heating, water), 53–58, 197–201

# R

Rachlin, Rachel, 13
railroads. *See* Trans-Siberian Railroad
raspberries, 104, 142–43, 313
Rasputin, Valentin, 8

recipes. *See* separate Recipe Index

religious offerings, 255. *See also* rituals, Mongolic

restaurants, xvi, xix, 135–36

rituals, drinking, 20, 142–43, 146, 263

rituals, Mongolic, 316, 317–19, 337

Russia, Asian. *See* Asian Russia

Russia, European. *See* European Russia

*Russian Cooking* (Papashvily), 22

Russian Far East
   culinary influences on, xvii–xx, 10, 12, 20–21, 74, 212, 297. *See also* foods, imported
   definition of, xxii
   foods of, xxiv, 13, 17, 22, 26, 27, 29, 40, 94–95, 99, 101, 105–6, 194, 223, 303, 305, 307, 313–14

Russian Federation, xi, xxi, 85, 91,

Russian Orthodox Church. *See* churches

# S

salads, 8, 21, 61, 102, 139, 155, 157, 189, 194, 205, 212, 246–47, 301, 320. *See also* appetizers; potato salad; *color photo gallery*

*salamat* (Buryat sour cream porridge), 319, 336

salmon, 8, 10, 44, 61, 72, 314. *See also* appetizers; caviar

salmonberries, 313

salsa, 114, 158

samovar, 12, *58*

sandwiches, open-face (*buterbrody*), 18, 23

*sarana* (lily), 313

sauerkraut, xvii, 9–11, 14, 74, 303. *See also* appetizers

sea cabbage. *See* foods, wild

sea cucumbers. *See* seafood

sea-buckthorn (berries), 103, 236, 308

seafood, 17, 21, 22, 94–95, 314. *See also* appetizers; *color photo gallery*

sea slugs. *See* seafood

seaweed. See foods, wild; seafood

shish-kabobs (*shashlyki*), *249*, 305, 332. See also *color photo gallery*

shopping, 50–52, 190–91.*See also* food shopping

shrimp. *See* seafood

Siberia
   culinary influences on, xvii–xx, 10, 12, 297. *See also* foods, imported
   definition of, xxi
   Eastern, xxi, 5, 255
   foods of, 8, 29, 108, 230–31, 234, 310–12, 314, 328, 337
   Western, xxi, 108, 310

Siberians, native, xvii, xviii, 213, 304, 313–19, 328. See also *color photo gallery*

*Siberia, Siberia* (Rasputin), 8
*Sixteen Years in Siberia* (Rachlin), 13
Snegurochka. *See* Snow Maiden
Snow Maiden (Snegurochka), 190, 194, *195*, 196, 203
sour cream (*smetana*). *See* dairy products
Soviet Union, xi–xii, xvi–xviii, 14, 50, 141, 183, 299
spices, xvii, 32, 82, 90, 91, 111, 113, 142–43, 161
squid. *See* seafood
stoves. *See* kitchen stoves
strawberries, 13, 104, 142–43
*stroganina* (frozen raw meat dish), 8, 317
sugar, 89–90, 91, 104, 106–7
summer kitchens. *See* kitchens, summer
supermarkets. *See* food stores
superstitions, 7, 137, 189, 201, 206–7, 230–31, 248, 250–51, 258, 287
Surina, Asclc, ix

**T**

Tabikhanov family, 316–19. See also *color photo gallery*
tableware, 1, 48, 53, 138, 144, 198, 213, 230–31
Tarasov, Mikhail, 21
Tarasova, Galina, viii, 16, 20–21, 22
Tatar, 10, 230–31, 297
T-bone whacks. *See* beef
tea, xvii, 11–12, 48, *58*, 316, 319
*Tent Life in Siberia* (Kennan), 307, 313
terrine, 220, 224
*testo* (yeast dough). *See* breads
Texas chili powder. *See* chili powder (Texas)
Tex-Mex, 149–52, 159–63, 217
Thanksgiving. *See* holidays
toasts, toasting. *See* rituals, drinking
tomatoes, xvii, 100. *See also* dachas; food markets; food stores; preserves; *color photo gallery*
    tortes. *See* cakes
tortillas, 150–51
Trans-Siberian Railroad, 295–302
turkey, 93, 150–51, 165, 188
*tvorog* (fresh white curd cheese). *See* dairy products

**U**

*ukha* (fish soup), 309, 313–15, *330*
Ukraine, Ukrainian, 70, 256

Ural Mountains, xxi, 230–31
Ussuriisk, 92, *95*, *96*, 97, 211. See also *color photo gallery*
Ust'-Ordynskii (Buryatiya). See *color photo gallery*
utilities. *See* public utilities

# V

vegetables. *See* dachas, 303–4; food markets; food stores; *color photo gallery*
vendors
    festivals, 190–91, *248*, *249*, 250
    markets, 86–88, 92–93, 95–97, 101, 103, 105–6, 110, 111, 113
    street, xix, *17*, 32, 190–91
    train station platforms, 296–98
    See also *color photo gallery*
*vinegret* (salad), 21. See also *color photo gallery*
venison. *See* foods, wild
vinegar, 32, 105, 108–9, 122
Vladivostok, 2, *17*
    markets, food stores, 85–113. See also *color photo gallery*
    restaurants, xvi, 135–36
    *See also* apartments; Christmas; kitchens, apartment; New Year
vodka, 18–18, 20, 141, 142–43, 146, 180, 182, 202, 262, 263, 310, 314, 316, 344

# W

weddings, 3, 18–19, 145–47
"White House" (Bely Dom, Irkutsk), 5–6
"White House Cook," 4–6
whortleberries, 104
wild foods. *See* foods, wild
wild game. *See* foods, wild
wild garlic (*cheremsha*). *See* foods, wild
wine. *See* beverages, alcoholic
World War II. *See* Great Patriotic War

# Y

*yolka* (New Year's tree). *See* New Year

# Z

*Zakuski*. See appetizers